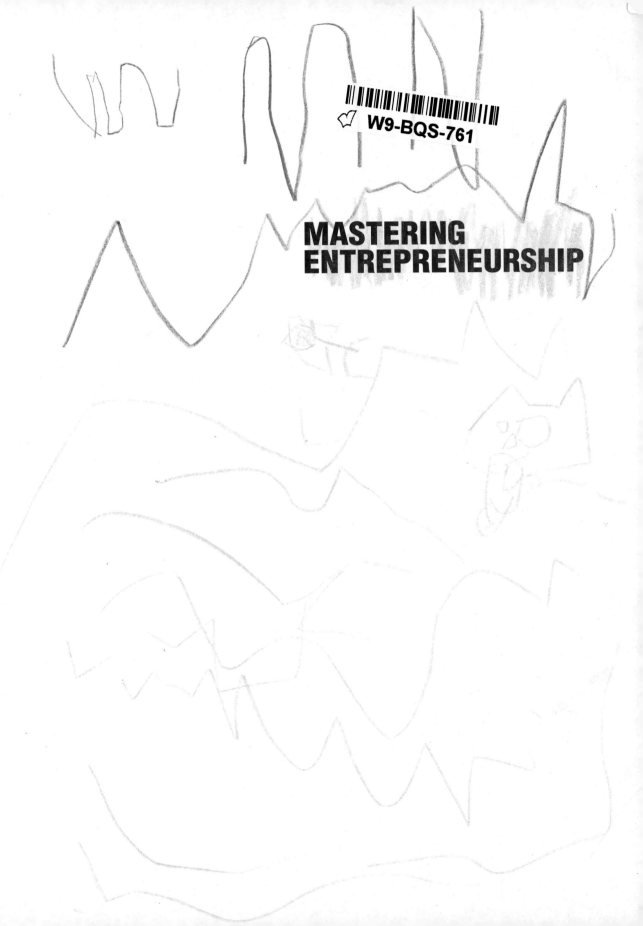

MASTERING
ENTREPRENEURSHIP

FINANCIAL TIMES

MASTERING
ENTREPRENEURSHIP

Sue Birley   Daniel F. Muzyka

FINANCIAL TIMES
Prentice Hall

An imprint of Pearson Education

London · New York · San Francisco · Toronto · Sydney · Tokyo · Singapore
Hong Kong · Cape Town · Madrid · Paris · Milan · Munich · Amsterdam

PEARSON EDUCATION LIMITED

Head Office:
Edinburgh Gate
Harlow CM20 2JE
Tel: +44 (0)1279 623623
Fax: +44 (0)1279 431059

London Office:
128 Long Acre
London WC2E 9AN
Tel: +44 (0)20 7447 2000
Fax: +44 (0)20 7240 5771
Website: www.business-minds.com

First published in Great Britain in 1997
under the title *Mastering Enterprise*
This edition 2000

© Compilation: Pearson Education Limited 2000

Note: Licences have been granted by individual authors/organizations
for articles throughout this publication. Please refer to the respective
articles for copyright notice.

ISBN 0 273 64928 0

British Library Cataloguing in Publication Data
A CIP catalogue record for this book can be obtained from the British Library.

10 9 8 7 6 5 4 3 2 1

Typeset by Land and Unwin (Data Sciences) Limited, Bugbrooke
Printed and bound in Great Britain by Redwood Books, Trowbridge, Wiltshire

The Publishers' policy is to use paper manufactured from sustainable forests.

Contents

Preface

When *Mastering Enterprise* was first published in spring 1997 the world of entrepreneurship was just beginning to invade public consciousness. Though entrepreneurs and the financiers and investors – venture capitalists, business angels and the like – who back them had long existed, they had only then started to impact on business, business academics and the world at large. Entrepreneurs such as Richard Branson, Bill Gates and their peers were public heroes. They had shown that not only could starting your own business be fun, it could also make you seriously rich.

The interest flowed into newspaper articles, books and, more particularly, business schools. Courses in entrepreneurship were becoming among the most popular selected by MBA students – not just by those who wanted to start their own businesses but also by students interested in becoming venture capitalists, management consultants or bankers.

Mastering Enterprise was on the leading edge of this wave. The first spin-off from the original FT Mastering Management series, it built on the same formula of academic theory and practical advice to provide one of the most comprehensive guides to entrepreneurship available.

And what of this second, revised, updated and expanded edition now retitled *Mastering Entrepreneurship*?

It is fortunate in retaining the same respected specialists in entrepreneurship as academic editors – Sue Birley of Imperial College Management School in London and Dan Muzyka, formerly at INSEAD, near Paris, and now Dean of the Faculty of Commerce and Administration at the University of British Columbia in Canada. Leaders in their field, they have again brought together their network of top entrepreneurship "gurus" – Howard Stevenson, Bill Bygrave, Neil Churchill and many others – as contributors.

Mastering Entrepreneurship appears at a time of unprecedented technological advance and amid an upsurge of entrepreneurial activity around the globe. The two come together in the world of the dot-com start-up.

Never, it seems, have more people been starting their own companies, particularly to exploit the World Wide Web, and never have so many been prepared to back them and support them – sending the valuations of these companies to staggering heights, at least at the time of their initial public offerings.

Mastering Entrepreneurship fully captures that mood, explaining and detailing what has, is and will happen, in a new section devoted to e-business start-ups. Other new areas covered include women entrepreneurs – 35 per cent of MBA students taking entrepreneurship courses are women – and the growing globalization of entrepreneurial start-ups. Many new cases studies have been added and existing ones updated.

Just as the first *Mastering Enterprise* captured the growing interest in the subject, so *Mastering Entrepreneurship* provides a means of understanding and perhaps even joining the new world of global high-tech enterprise.

George Bickerstaffe
Former Editorial Director, *FT Mastering Series*

About the academic editors

 Sue Birley

Sue Birley is Professor of Entrepreneurship and Director of the Science Enterprise Centre at the Management School, Imperial College of Science, Technology and Medicine, London, and a Director of Process Systems Enterprise Ltd and IC Innovations Ltd. She has published numerous books and articles and sits on the editorial boards of a number of leading journals in the entrepreneurial and management fields. She is a Fellow of the British Academy of Management. She has also won and lost money in entrepreneurial ventures.

 Daniel F. Muzyka

Daniel F. Muzyka is Dean of the Faculty of Commerce and Business Administration and Professor of Management at the University of British Columbia, Canada, and is currently Visiting Professor at INSEAD, Fontainebleau, France. He was formerly the IAF Professor of Entrepreneurship and Associate Dean, MBA at INSEAD. His research interests include entrepreneurship, venture capital and corporate strategy, especially applied to growing businesses. He has experience in finance and corporate strategy with the General Electric Company and as a strategy consultant, principally with Braxton Associates. He has also been involved in starting up an entrepreneurial business.

Introduction

Today there is a great deal of interest from many quarters in the topic of entrepreneurship. In this world of downsizing, restructuring and technological change, notions of traditional careers and ways of creating value have all been challenged and individuals are increasingly wondering whether they should strike out on their own, whether their fortune would be better realized through the pursuit of opportunities *they* believe and *they* have decided to pursue. In effect, people are depending more upon their own initiative to realize success than upon "the system" to deliver.

At the same time that individuals are wondering whether their best opportunities should not be realized through their own initiative, investors, corporate executives and government officials are all wondering how to maximize economic value creation. Investors are wondering whether a better risk–return balance can be realized by backing these individuals. Corporate executives in search of ways to improve company growth, renewal and performance are pressing for more internal entrepreneurial activity. Government officials concerned with overall economic performance are asking themselves: "Where is the next Bill Gates in my region and how do I help him emerge?" In short, entrepreneurship has many interested parties who need to understand it, to realize it, and to promote it.

This is a book dedicated to the subjects of entrepreneurship and entrepreneurs, no matter where they undertake their activities. Through the knowledge contained in the book, we hope that those with entrepreneurial ambitions will be better able to achieve those ambitions. In addition, we hope that those wishing to promote entrepreneurial activity can improve their performance through a better understanding of entrepreneurial behavior and opportunity.

Entrepreneurship

What exactly is entrepreneurship? Clearly, it describes the process and activities undertaken by entrepreneurs. These are individuals who organize, operate and assume the risks associated with a business venture they establish in pursuit of an opportunity they and others have identified. The entrepreneurial process is directed at capturing the value associated with business opportunities.

A major question that continues to exercise academics is the exact definition of "entrepreneurship" and how far it extends. At one end of the spectrum are the "Silicon Valley" or "Route 128 (Boston)" group who see entrepreneurship as something related to founding and growing high-technology businesses. These people see entrepreneurship as the creation of significant new wealth through the implementation of new concepts. At the other end of the spectrum are those who see any novel activity which creates organizational change and economic value as entrepreneurship.

The one thing entrepreneurship researchers generally agree upon, however, is that "entrepreneurship" is different from "small business." Most small businesses have limited growth potential and are primarily focussed on creating a fair return for the efforts of the small numbers of those who work in the enterprise.

What is excluded from discussion in some narrower definitions of entrepreneurship? The answer is that some academics see topics such as entrepreneurial activity in the public sector or in larger organizations as not a central part of entrepreneurship. Groups of "new venture only" enthusiasts will not see anything short of independent, high-growth entrepreneurial activity as "real entrepreneurship." A broader audience accepts that there are a number of variations on entrepreneurial activity. Most will agree that the limited pursuit of opportunities, that is, capturing some of the value available, still constitutes entrepreneurship. Lifestyle ventures, venture opportunities pursued by entrepreneurs in search of a different style of working, are commonly recognized as still being part of entrepreneurship. Some academics will accept that purchasing businesses for the purpose of adding new value is also a form of entrepreneurial activity, while others feel that such management buy-outs of existing businesses are not fully entrepreneurial in nature.

In this book we have accepted a broader definition and scope for entrepreneurial activity. We believe that the entrepreneurial process of identifying opportunity and realizing value is alive in both the public and private sector and in larger organizations. We take this broader perspective for several reasons. For example, in the case of the public versus private sector, the distinction between the two is increasingly unclear. Take, for example, the notorious PSA (Property Services Agency) in the UK which was responsible for the management of the fabric of all government buildings. It was bought by its management in 1994 and sold for many times the purchase price two years later. Value creation and privatization activities in eastern Europe have also blurred the line between the public and private sectors.

In the case of larger organizations, it is clear that corporations are increasingly interested in promoting entrepreneurial activity. Furthermore, some "entrepreneurial businesses" such as Microsoft and Richard Branson's empire maintain their high levels of entrepreneurial activity despite their scale.

No matter what the definition of entrepreneurship we use, it is clear that the primary engines of the activity are the entrepreneurs themselves. Whether you are a corporate executive searching for more entrepreneurial activity, or a government minister attempting to deal with structural unemployment through the emergence of more entrepreneurial activity, you are attempting to mobilize more entrepreneurs.

Entrepreneurs

So who are these entrepreneurs? How can we recognize them? Is there a limited supply? Are they "born or made?" Unfortunately the answers are not simple. We used to believe that they were drawn from those in society who were "socially marginal" – the uneducated, the immigrant, or the poor – and who had an overwhelming need to prove themselves, had a strong "need for achievement." Consequently, early studies in the field describe the characteristics of those who started businesses in terms of both demographics and

motivations in an attempt to arrive at an "Identikit entrepreneur." Often-cited examples of successful entrepreneurs in the US only reinforce this model. Examples of immigrants who have "made it big" are abundant, especially on the East Coast and around New York and in California's rich entrepreneurial climate.

We have come to realize that these early attempts at classifying entrepreneurs and their motivations were, at best, incomplete. These did not work because the environment changed and their characteristics changed. Indeed, recent studies have shown the successful entrepreneur is just as likely to be highly educated, and have worked in a large corporation in a senior management position before becoming an owner-manager, than to have left school and started a business at the age of 16. In other words, the supply of entrepreneurs is marvellously diverse and variable over time. It is influenced in part by genetic powers, by family background and early business experiences, and by the economic environment. To put it another way, the population can be viewed as having a range of inclinations towards enterprise, with those in the middle most susceptible to change from employee to owner.

We know that the socio-economic climate (in the case of "external" entrepreneurs) and the corporate environment (in the case of 'internal entrepreneurs") can significantly influence the emergence of entrepreneurs and entrepreneurial activity. Economic and tax policy, the provision of low-cost resources, appropriate training, and high-profile role models are all mechanisms which have been shown to move the goal posts. Indeed, that is exactly what most governments throughout the world are attempting to do. Organizations are similarly looking at their "macro environment" in terms of whether it supports or suppresses entrepreneurship.

The book

We have four wishes with regard to the book's value to entrepreneurs. First, we hope we can encourage those with entrepreneurial ambitions that it is never too late nor entirely inappropriate for anyone to think of themselves as a potential entrepreneur. Second, we also hope that they will realize that there are many paths to entrepreneurship, from new ventures to buy-outs, to realizing opportunities within larger firms. Third, we hope they will recognize that there is no such thing as a perfect opportunity. Whether an opportunity is successful depends more on how it is implemented than on its pure economic characteristics. Finally, but most importantly, we hope that entrepreneurs will realize that pursuing an opportunity should bear a health warning: it will not be easy. There are always problems to deal with and challenges to overcome.

The series of topics covered in this book explore the process of founding a venture and highlight some of the issues faced by those creating or remolding an organization, the commercial problems they confront, the family dilemmas that emerge as the business grows, and the decisions they make. As such, the book is concerned with exploring the creation and management of those new ventures that result in significant wealth for the owners. In other words, the focus is upon the development of new or reformed significant businesses rather than the development of new products or services. Clearly, this includes entirely new businesses developed by high-profile entrepreneurs such as the Tata family in India, Richard Branson and his Virgin Group, or Ted Turner of CNN, and by others less well known but equally successful.

Entrepreneurial process

Creating a new opportunity does not usually happen overnight. Whatever the eventual form of organization that emerges, whatever the route to market, the study of entrepreneurship is the study of the *process* through:

- identifying and developing an opportunity in the form of a vision
- validating and conceptualizing a business concept and strategy that help attain the vision (for example, start-up, buy-out, franchise, etc.)
- marshaling the required resources to implement the concept
- implementing the business concept or venture
- capturing the full opportunity through the growth of the enterprise
- extending the growth of the enterprise through sustained entrepreneurial activity
- capturing the value through a business exit.

All of these activities take time and there are no rules as to how long each stage may take. In addition, it is often the case that entrepreneurs have to "loop back" as they engage in the process. For instance, they find their business concept needs refining in light of what the potential resource suppliers want. An idea can be in gestation, perhaps through the process of invention, for many years or it may emerge in an instant. A manager may have a growing awareness of the possibilities of a buy-out through press coverage but may be unsure how his or her employers would react – until they suddenly announce that the business is for sale! The embryo entrepreneur may always have carried a latent desire – until the right opportunity came along.

A certain set of behaviors must accompany the identification and pursuit of the opportunity. Entrepreneurs normally do not have the resources, power or "authority" in hand that is required to just go and implement a venture. They must engage others in their ideas. They must leverage resources they do not control – or use "other people's money" in the popular language. They must focus on growing rather than being particularly efficient. All of this suggests that there is a very clear reality driving the behavior we see in entrepreneurs.

Given the powerful underlying logic of entre-preneurial activity, the sequence and contents of the book are modeled on the entrepreneurial process. The book begins by considering entrepreneurship and entrepreneurial behavior but immediately moves to the entrepreneurial process. The early parts of the book deal with identifying the opportunity, while the final stages deal with the entrepreneurial exit.

The topics

The entrepreneurial territory that is covered in the book includes a wide variety of activities, beyond the classic entrepreneurial new venture. The following are addressed both directly and indirectly within the book:

- **Leveraged buy-out** or **management buyout (MBO):** the process by which the incumbent management team buys the business which they are managing, often a subsidiary, from the owners. In the process, it may have changed size, have new systems, or new arrangements with customers. It will certainly have new "owner-managers" and it will probably have new investors in the form of venture capitalists.

■ **Leveraged** or **management buy-in (MBI):** the process by which a management team from outside the company purchases the company or the subsidiary from the owners. Often, they will involve the incumbent management in the acquisition, a process sometimes called a "buy-out/management buy-in."

■ **Franchising – the franchisee:** in Europe this has traditionally been seen as a "small business activity" whereby individuals purchase a single franchise outlet. This is certainly not the case in the US where "franchise entrepreneurs" have built their business through the acquisition of multiple outlets, territories, and franchises. So, for example, in a single town they may own both Pizza Hut and Burger King as well as non-food Jiffy Lube. As a result of a recent EU Directive, which required the possibility of the ownership of multiple units in all member states, this is a phenomenon which is emerging in Europe and is certainly present in Asia.

■ **Franchising – the franchisor:** The franchisee opportunity is not the only reason we include franchising in the series. Clearly, it is also one of the mechanisms available to entrepreneurs to build wealth based upon a business or product concept. Indeed, one third of retail businesses in the US are franchises. Franchising is a way that many entrepreneurs can rapidly grow their businesses. This is particularly true of service businesses where the service is delivered locally. Franchising the business concept permits the growing entrepreneur to involve further entrepreneurial energy, in the form of franchisees, in pursuing the opportunity, and permits the lead entrepreneur to leverage off the resources of franchisees in promoting and extending the business concept.

■ **Corporate venturing:** an activity which some large organizations have used as a way of injecting enterprise and so revitalizing the business portfolio. The aim is to find new "windows of opportunity," evaluate their potential, and invest in them for the long term. The latter may be through investing in existing early-stage businesses needing development

capital, joint ventures, or new subsidiaries within a "venturing division." For the large, mature organizations this means grappling with the questions of motivating and rewarding those directly involved, the "corporate entrepreneurs." However, this is just the tip of the iceberg.

■ **Entrepreneurial corporation:** a form of larger organization which provides an extension beyond those companies involved in promoting increased entrepreneurial activity through corporate venturing. More interestingly, the series will touch on the ways in which a number of companies trying to create new managerial systems in a rapidly changing environment are attempting to become "entrepreneurial organizations."

■ **Family businesses:** here we are interested in those businesses owned and managed by a family through more than one generation, and the stresses and strains that this places upon both the family and the business relationship, particularly during the succession times. Clearly, the ways in which the business is managed and the extent of involvement of both children and extended family will vary according to the particular family culture. In parts of the world, the family business and network are a primary mode of building and extending entrepreneurship. Indeed, in Thailand, more than 80 percent of the top 100 companies are owned and managed by their Thai-Chinese founders and of these, 97 percent by the second generation.

The book seeks to address entrepreneurship in its many forms with the recognition that the primary vehicles for entrepreneurship do vary around the globe. In the US, the classic start-up is the much-vaunted vehicle for "real" entrepreneurs. In Europe, many entrepreneurs prefer buying a business as a basic vehicle for their ambitions.

Interest

Who might be interested in this book? In short, it contains something for almost everyone, for all those interested in pursuing their entrepreneurial ambitions as well as those who are interested in promoting and supporting entrepreneurs. The book and the chosen content were designed and selected from the outset to appeal to multiple audiences, including:

- **Potential entrepreneurs:** wish to consider "taking the plunge" and become an entrepreneur? Think you have identified a business opportunity that others are not pursuing? Considering buying out the business you are managing within that holding company? For individuals in these circumstances, you will discover a wide spectrum of information, ranging from how to test your opportunity, to opportunities for exiting the business. Many of the articles will build your knowledge and experience in the field, leading to a more successful entrepreneurial experience. You will also find some insight into "what it takes" to be successful. This book should help you answer the question: "Do I have the right stuff?"
- **Existing entrepreneurs:** managing the growth of the business is always a challenging opportunity. Owner-managers of existing businesses will find some insights into common challenges in growing the business. Additional insight will come from observations about how to preserve entrepreneurship as you grow and how to make money on exit. For the owner-manager, this book becomes a helpful compendium of information about the collective experiences of other owner-managers.
- **Investors:** private investors, bankers, and others directly involved in financing, evaluating and supporting entrepreneurs, including venture capitalists, can benefit in two ways. For those with limited experience with entrepreneurs and entrepreneurial business, the book provides a well-rounded briefing on entrepreneurial behavior, business and challenges. For those with extensive experience, the book can help frame and share existing experiences and will help raise additional questions for investigation.
- **Advisers:** consultants, accountants and bankers who are interested in supporting entrepreneurs will find some helpful insight into the challenges faced by entrepreneurs. Furthermore, they should find some ideas on how to frame and present common entrepreneurial opportunities and problems.
- **Business partners:** those who are suppliers,

customers or alliance partners of entrepreneurial businesses will benefit significantly from this book. Further understanding about their behavior, patterns and needs can aid in building a better business and personal relationship. Insight can help in negotiation, leading to a "win–win" for all parties.
- **Policy-makers:** policy-makers can benefit from this book by understanding the objectives, motivations and needs of an entrepreneur and entrepreneurial business. This can lead to more appropriate public and tax policy. Government officials may also benefit through ideas on how to support entrepreneurs and entrepreneurial initiative in their organizations.

Finally, the book can also appeal to the simply curious who will benefit through understanding their friends, neighbors and associates as well as an important sector of the economy.

The authors
The people who have contributed to the series of articles in this book were chosen from among the world leaders in their fields. The group includes both academics and practitioners from entrepreneurship and related fields. They come from institutions and organizations from around the world, from Wharton and Harvard in the US to Imperial College and INSEAD in Europe. We also draw on the experience and insight of an international cast of consultants, investors and entrepreneurs.

While the study of entrepreneurship is a relatively new field of endeavor for academia, the individuals who have contributed their knowledge to this series often have ten or more years of experience and insight which they have brought to bear in preparing their contributions. We all hope you will find our insights to be helpful and will use the book as an on-going resource; a place you can regularly return to for clarification and support.

Book structure
As mentioned earlier, the book was organized to consider entrepreneurial topics from formation to exit: from framing the original business concept, to assembling the team and resources, to planning and capturing the value. Part 1 begins with a consideration of the nature of entrepreneurship and entrepreneurs.

Particular emphasis is placed in the beginning on the nature of entrepreneurial behavior, a key element in the successful pursuit of entrepreneurial opportunity.

Parts 2, 3, and 4 are all focussed on the early stages of an entrepreneurial pursuit. Part 2 deals primarily with the nature of opportunity. Section 1 covers the main issues associated with assessing an opportunity and section 2 deals with the emerging phenomenon of e-commerce. This is followed very naturally by Part 3 which deals with the sources and structuring of financial resources.

Part 4 contains a series of articles focussed on issues of getting started: managing the beginning of your venture.

Parts 5 and 7 contain knowledge and insights on topics related to the successful pursuit of the venture opportunity. Part 5 addresses the important topic of teams and people in entrepreneurial initiatives. Successful entrepreneurs are rarely found without a profoundly dedicated and powerful team aiding their pursuit of the opportunity. Part 7 aids our understanding of growth by pointing out the stages of growth and the challenges associated with growth.

Part 6 discusses several topics related to the nature of entrepreneurship around the world. Entrepreneurial challenges and practices, as well as the environment for entrepreneurs, are somewhat different in the various parts of the world. We hope you will find this section insightful in identifying the underlying regional differences in entrepreneurial perspectives and ambitions.

Parts 8 and 9 deal with issues of entrepreneurship and larger organizations. Part 8 is focussed on the theme of management buy-ins and buy-outs. Many entrepreneurs find a foundation for their entrepreneurial ambitions in existing businesses that are part of larger firms. They may choose to purchase an existing business as an outsider (buy-in) or purchase part of a firm from the firms they work for (buy-out). These activities can create value by aiding existing companies or pieces of companies in achieving their full potential by pursuing existing or new opportunities to their fullest.

Part 9 deals with the full spectrum of topics surrounding entrepreneurial activity in larger organizations: how to build and preserve a high level of such activity, as well as alternative modes of pursuing opportunities outside of the existing organizational processes (for example, corporate venturing).

Part 10 focusses on the topic of entrepreneurial exit. What are the options for entrepreneurial exit? How can you capture the most value? This, we believe, is the fitting end for any work dedicated to entrepreneurship: capturing the value.

We hope you will find this book useful both as something that is worth reading from cover to cover and as an overview of the field of entrepreneurship. In style, we have attempted to balance the work between something that is completely journalistic in nature and an academic work, full of content but less easy to wade through. In content, we have tried to commission and select pieces that answer a broad variety of questions and sometimes take very different perspectives but that deal with some of the common problems and opportunities facing entrepreneurs. We also hope it will serve as a reference source. The ability to move from distinct article to distinct article as well as to navigate among the chapters we hope will provide for a strong framework to index the work. Finally, we hope that it will inspire you as a "would-be" entrepreneur to act. The challenge, fun and reward in entrepreneurship are found less in reading about it and more in doing it. As the saying goes: just do it!

Sue Birley
Daniel Muzyka

INTRODUCING
ENTERPRISE

1

Contributors

 Manfred F. R. Kets de Vries is the Raoul de Vitry d'Avaucourt Professor of Human Resource Management and Clinical Professor of Management and Leadership at INSEAD, Fontainebleau, France. He is also a clinical psychoanalyst. His research interests include leadership, entrepreneurship, family business, succession planning, cross-cultural management and the dynamics of corporate transformation and change.

 Candida G. Brush is Associate Professor in Management Policy and Research Director of the Entrepreneurial Management Institute at Boston University, USA, and associate member of faculty at Jonkoping International Business School.

 Howard H. Stevenson is Sarofim-Rock Professor of Business Administration and Senior Associate Dean and Director of External Relations at Harvard Graduate School of Business, Harvard University, USA. The Sarofim-Rock Chair was established at Harvard Business School in 1982 to provide a continuing base for research and teaching in the field of entrepreneurship.

 Juan Roure is Professor at IESE, the business school of the University of Navarra in Barcelona and Madrid, Spain, a Visiting Professor at INSEAD, France, and Academic Co-ordinator of EFER and Europe's 500 Association.

Contents

Introduction

Part 1 is about those fascinating people, the entrepreneurs. We begin by posing the commonly asked questions – who are they, where do they come from, how do they behave, do they take risks, and can we pick them? Reassuringly, we are left with the conclusion that there is no simple answer and, more important, that there is no such thing as an "Identikit" entrepreneur. Those who take the path of enterprise are marvelously heterogeneous.

Creative rebels with a cause

Manfred Kets de Vries details the unique – and sometimes aberrant – behavior traits that make up an entrepreneur.

What are entrepreneurs like? What distinguishes them from other business people? What makes them so special? Although as a group they are not easy to get a handle on, some characteristics seem to be common to all of them.

Entrepreneurs seem to be achievement oriented, like to take responsibility for decisions, and dislike repetitive, routine work. Creative entrepreneurs possess high levels of energy and great degrees of perseverance and imagination, which combined with a willingness to take moderate, calculated risks enables them to transform what often began as a very simple, ill-defined idea into something concrete.

Entrepreneurs can instill highly contagious enthusiasm in an organization. They convey a sense of purpose and determination. By doing so, they convince others that they are where the action is. Whatever it is – seductiveness, gamesmanship or charisma – entrepreneurs somehow know how to lead an organization and give it momentum. Most importantly, entrepreneurs are the driving force of any country's economy; they represent the wealth of a nation and its potential to create employment.

An extremely successful entrepreneur is Richard Branson, the Chairman of the Virgin Group, an empire that encompasses travel, communications (books, radio and television stations, computer/video games), retail and hotels. The story of Branson and Virgin is covered in detail on p. 23.

Branson's leadership style is a unique combination of energy, originality and shrewdness. He is the major driving force in the company, a master of motivation, and knows how to get the best out of his people. Furthermore, he is aware of some of his weaknesses and has hired others to compensate for these, having in the process created a highly effective executive constellation made up of people with diverse skills.

Branson, however, is an exception in the way he has taken on the entrepreneurial role. Entrepreneurs are not a homogeneous group. They come in all shapes and sizes, each with his or her own characteristics. In some cases entrepreneurs possess personality quirks that, while they originally may have been a source of great strength, can – when excessive – cause serious problems for the entrepreneur and the enterprise.

The entrepreneur's inner theater
The need for control

A significant theme in the life and personality of many entrepreneurs is the need for control, a preoccupation that inevitably affects the way they deal with power relationships and their consequences for interpersonal action.

Some entrepreneurs are strikingly ambivalent when an issue of control surfaces – they are filled with fantasies of grandiosity, influence, power and authority yet they also feel helpless. They like to be in control but fear being controlled by others.

Some entrepreneurs have serious difficulties addressing issues of dominance and submission and are suspicious toward people in positions of authority. This attitude contrasts greatly with that of managers. While managers seem able to identify in a positive and constructive way with authority figures – using them as role models – many entrepreneurs lack the executive's fluidity in changing from a superior to a subordinate role.

Instead, entrepreneurs often experience authority relationships and the accompanying structures as stifling. They find it difficult to work with others in structured situations unless, of course, *they* created the structure and the work is done on *their* terms.

Listening to entrepreneurs' case histories, one can find many situations where it was their inability to accept authority and organizational rules that drove them to become entrepreneurs in the first place. Many are "misfits" who need to create their own environment.

People who are overly concerned about being in control have little tolerance for subordinates who think for themselves. In an organizational context this desire for control can go to extremes – for example an entrepreneur wanting to be informed about every minute operation of the company. Such micro-management, appropriate as it may be in the start-up phase of a company, will increasingly become a burden as it stifles the information flow, hampers decision making, and inhibits the attraction and retention of capable executives.

The late Robert Maxwell was a good example of an entrepreneur obsessed with control. In his companies there was only one way of doing things. It was his way or the highway. He had to control everything around him, whether people or companies. Everything, however trivial, had to be approved by him. There was no management structure; everything revolved around and depended on him. Through this kind of fragmentation, which created a considerable amount of obscurity, he kept control over all decisions.

A sense of distrust

Closely related to the need for control is a proclivity toward suspicion of others. Some entrepreneurs have a strong distrust of the world around them. They live in fear of being victimized. They want to be ready should disaster strike.

Paradoxically, quite a few feel best when their fortunes are at their lowest. When at the top of the success wave, they imagine themselves incurring the envy of others. No wonder that they respond that business is only "so, so" or "not too bad" when they are asked how things are going. But if their fortunes turn and they are close to bankruptcy, it is as if they have paid the price, done their penance for being successful. As this produces a sense of relief, their predicament can have a positive effect. With the alleviation of anxiety, they have the energy to start anew, which they do with enthusiasm and a sense of purpose.

As some entrepreneurs have a pervasive fear of being victimized, they are continually scanning the environment for confirmation of their suspicions. This behavior pattern does, of course, have its constructive side: it makes them alert to moves by competitors, suppliers, customers or government that affect the industry. Anticipating the actions of others protects them from being taken unaware. But such vigilance can also lead them to lose any sense of proportion. Focussing on certain trouble spots and ignoring others, entrepreneurs may blow up trivial things and lose sight of the reality of the situation.

When a strong sense of distrust assisted by a need for control takes over, the consequences for the organization are serious. Sycophants set the tone, people stop acting independently and political gamesmanship is rampant. Such entrepreneurs can interpret harmless acts as threats to their control and see them as warranting destructive counteractions.

The problem in contending with such a distorted form of reasoning and action is that behind the false perception that leads to fear and suspicion, one can always find some confirmation. Unfortunately, the person who manages in this way forgets the price the company pays in deteriorating morale, low employee satisfaction and declining productivity.

The need for applause

The heroic myth begins with the hero's humble birth, his rapid rise to prominence and power, his conquest of the forces of evil, his vulnerability to the sin of pride and finally his fall through betrayal or heroic sacrifice.

The basic symbolic themes here – of birth, conquest, pride, betrayal and death – are relevant to all of us. Some entrepreneurs act out the same myth, as we have seen, with a Greek chorus in the background applauding their achievements but warning them about pride.

Perhaps the myth explains why so many entrepreneurs live under a great deal of tension. They feel they are living on the edge, that their success will not last (their need for control and their sense of distrust are symptomatic of this anxiety), but they also have an overriding concern to be heard and recognized – to be seen as heroes. Some entrepreneurs experience a strong urge to show others that they amount to something, that they cannot be ignored.

A manifestation of this strong narcissistic need is the interest some entrepreneurs show in building "monuments" as symbols of their achievements. Sometimes the monument is an imposing office building or production facility; sometimes it is a product that takes on a symbolic significance. Maxwell, for example, was indefatigable in seeking (and getting) attention. He constantly needed an entourage and an audience. He was a great self-promoter and was irrepressibly boastful. His objective was to be in the news constantly. The *Daily Mirror* was turned into a kind of family album, with Maxwell writing his own headlines. He even acquired a soccer club, another highly effective way to stay in the public eye.

Defensive operations

Some entrepreneurs resort to some peculiarly primitive defensive processes, which can lead to a great discrepancy between the narrative truth and the historical truth; facts are arranged to suit the individual's needs. Splitting – a behavior pattern whereby everything is seen in extremes, black or white, friend or foe – is a defense mechanism used by some entrepreneurs. Maxwell was no stranger to this way of dealing with others. If you disagreed with him, you were his enemy. He did not take easily to different points of view. He did not forget or forgive his enemies' "crimes." On the contrary, he had a memory like an elephant and would go to great lengths to get even.

Some entrepreneurs also have a tendency to blame others for what goes wrong. They do not see their own responsibility in the matter. Scapegoating is an excellent way of blaming others while feeling virtuous oneself. In assigning blame elsewhere, entrepreneurs may rationalize away whatever responsibility they have for questionable events. Their capacity to delude themselves can be tremendous.

Many entrepreneurs are also incapable of sitting still. There is a cyclical quality to their behavior. They are prone to great mood swings. They have difficulty in controlling their impulses and managing anxiety and depression. They fear that being passive would make them overdependent and in the end fall victim to control by others. Moreover, passivity evokes depressive reactions.

Managing for creativity

We have seen that entrepreneurs come in many different shapes and sizes: some manage for the good, others can become quite destructive. Some of the darker notes of entrepreneurship are quite real, however, and pose serious quandaries for those working for them. Managing an entrepreneur is not always one of the easiest tasks. But although the extremes stand out, most situations do not go that far.

Entrepreneurs do not necessarily have more personal problems than other people, nor do they inevitably have personality disorders. What one can extract from the previous comments, however, is that entrepreneurs have their own unique ways of dealing with the stresses and strains of daily life.

In saying this, I want to emphasize that the boundaries between the very creative and aberrant behavior can be blurred. The mix of creative and irrational is what makes entrepreneurs tick and accounts for many of their positive contributions. Entrepreneurs create new industries and stimulate the economy. Their visionary abilities and leadership qualities make it possible for their employees to transcend petty concerns and accomplish good work.

There are three kinds of people in this world: those who make it happen, those who see it happen, and those who wonder what has happened. We all know where entrepreneurs fit in.

The six dimensions of entrepreneurship

Entrepreneurship, argues **Howard Stevenson**, is neither a set of personality traits nor an economic function. Rather it is a cohesive pattern of managerial behavior that can be measured.

Entrepreneurship is an approach to management that we define as *the pursuit of opportunity without regard to resources currently controlled.* The description can be refined by examining six critical dimensions of business practice: strategic orientation; commitment to opportunity; commitment of resources; control of resources; management structure; and reward philosophy. We shall define these dimensions by examining a range of behaviors.

At one extreme is the "promoter," who feels confident of his or her ability to seize an opportunity regardless of the resources under current control. At the opposite extreme is the "trustee," who emphasizes the efficient utilization of existing resources.

While the promoter and the trustee define the end points of this spectrum, there is a range of managerial behavior that lies between them, and we define (overlapping) portions of the spectrum as entrepreneurial and administrative behavior. Thus, entrepreneurial management is not an extreme example, but rather a range of behavior that consistently falls at one end of the spectrum.

Strategic orientation

Strategic orientation describes the factors that drive a company's formulation of strategy. A promoter is truly opportunity driven. His or her orientation is to say: "I am going to be driven only by my perception of the opportunities that exist in my environment and I will not be constrained by the resources at hand." A trustee, on the other hand, tends to say: "How do I utilize the resources that I control?"

Within these two poles, the administrator's approach recognizes the need to examine the environment for opportunities but is still constrained by a trustee-like focus on resources. An entrepreneurial orientation places the emphasis on opportunity.

It is this dimension that has led to one of the traditional definitions of the entrepreneur as opportunistic or, more favorably, creative and innovative. But the entrepreneur is not necessarily concerned with breaking new ground. Opportunity can also be found in a new mix of old ideas or in the creative application of traditional approaches. We do observe, however, that organizations tend to look for opportunities where their resources are.

The pressures that pull a company towards the entrepreneurial range of behavior include:

■ **Diminishing opportunity streams.** Old opportunity streams have been largely played out. It is no longer possible to succeed merely by adding new options to old products.
■ **Rapid changes in:** technology – creates new opportunities, at the same time it makes old ones obsolete; consumer economics – changes both ability and willingness to pay for new products and services; social values – define new styles and standards; political roles – affect competition through deregulation, product safety and new standards.

Pressures that pull an organization to become more administrative include:

■ **The social contract.** The responsibility to use and employ people, plant, technology and financial resources once they have been acquired.
■ **Performance criteria.** How many executives are fired for not pursuing an opportunity compared with the number that are punished for not meeting return on investment targets?
■ **Planning systems and cycles.** Opportunities do not arrive at the start of a planning cycle and last for the duration of a three- or five-year plan.

Commitment to opportunity

As we move on to the second dimension it becomes clear that the definition of the entrepreneur as creative or innovative is not sufficient. There are innovative thinkers who never get anything done. It is necessary to move beyond the identification of opportunity to its pursuit.

The promoter is willing to act in a very short time frame and to chase an opportunity quickly. The duration of their commitment, not their ability to act, is all that is in doubt. Commitment for the trustee is time consuming and, once made, of long duration. Trustees move so slowly that it sometimes appears they are stationary; once there, they seem frozen.

It is the willingness to get in and out quickly that has led to the entrepreneur's reputation as a gambler. However, the simple act of taking a risk does not lead to success. More critical is knowledge of the territory they operate in. Their familiarity with their chosen field means they have the ability to recognize patterns as they develop and the confidence to assume that missing elements will take shape as they foresee. This early recognition enables them to get a jump on others in commitment to action.

Pressures that pull a business towards this entrepreneurial end of the spectrum include:

- **Action orientation.** Enables an organization to make first claim to customers, employees and financial resources.
- **Short decision windows.** Due to the high costs of late entry, including lack of competitive costs and technology.
- **Risk management.** Involves managing the organization's revenues in such a way that they can be rapidly committed to or withdrawn from new projects.
- **Limited decision constituencies.** Requires a smaller number of responsibilities and permits greater flexibility.

In contrast, administrative behavior is a function of other issues:

- **Multiple decision constituencies.** A greater number of responsibilities, necessitating a more complex, lengthier decision process.
- **Negotiation of strategy.** Compromise in order to reach consensus and resultant evolutionary rather than revolutionary commitment.
- **Risk reduction.** Study and analysis to reduce risk slows the decision-making process.
- **Management of fit.** To assure the continuity and participation of existing players, only those projects that "fit" existing corporate resources are acceptable.

Commitment of resources

Another characteristic we observe in good entrepreneurs is a multi-staged commitment of resources with a minimum commitment at each stage or decision point.

The issue for the entrepreneur is this: what resources are necessary to pursue a given opportunity? There is a constant tension between the amount of resources committed and the potential return. The entrepreneur attempts to maximize value creation by minimizing the resource set and must, of course, accept more risk in the process. On the other hand, the trustee side deals with this challenge by careful analysis and large-scale commitment of resources after the decision to act. Entrepreneurial management requires that you learn to do a little more with a little less.

On this dimension we have the traditional stereotype of the entrepreneur as tentative, uncommitted or temporarily dedicated – an image of unreliability. In times of rapid change, however, this stepped, multi-staged commitment of resources is a definite advantage in responding to changes in competition, the market and technology.

The process of committing resources is pushed towards the entrepreneurial domain by several factors:

- **Lack of predictable resource needs.** Forces the entrepreneur to commit less up front so that more will be available later on if required.
- **Lack of long-term control.** Requires that commitment matches exposure. If control over resources can be removed by environmental, political or technological forces, resource exposure should also be reduced.
- **Social needs.** Multi-staged commitment of resources brings us closer to "small is beautiful" by allowing appropriate levels of resource intensity.
- **International demands.** Pressures that we use no more than our fair share of the world's resources.

The pressures within large corporations, however, are in the other direction, toward resource intensity:

- **Personal risk reduction.** Any individual's risk is reduced by having excess resources available.
- **Incentive compensation.** Excess resources increase short-term returns and minimize the period of cash and profit drains – typically the objects of an incentive compensation system.
- **Managerial turnover.** Creates pressures for steady cash and profits gains, which encourage short-term, visible success.
- **Capital allocation systems.** Generally designed for one-time decision making, these techniques assume that a single decision point is appropriate.
- **Formal planning systems.** Once a project has begun, a request for additional resources returns managers to the morass of analysis and bureaucratic delays. Managers are inclined to avoid this by committing the maximum amount of resources up front.

Control of resources

Entrepreneurs learn to use other people's resources well and to decide over time what resources they need to bring in-house. Good managers also learn that there are certain resources you should never own or employ. Very few real estate companies employ an architect. They may need the best but they do not want to employ him or her because the need for that resource, though critical to the success of the business, is temporary.

The stereotype of the entrepreneur as exploitative derives from this dimension. The entrepreneur is adept at using the skills, talents and ideas of others. Viewed positively, this ability has become increasingly valuable in the changed business environment. It need not be parasitic in the context of a mutually satisfying relationship. Pressures towards this entrepreneurial side come from:

- **Increased resource specialization.** An organization may need a specialized resource such as a high-tech patent attorney or state of the art circuit test equipment, but only for a short time. By using rather than owning, a company reduces its risk and fixed costs.
- **Risk of obsolescence.** Reduced by using rather than owning an expensive resource.
- **Increased flexibility.** The cost of exercising the option to quit is reduced.

Administrative practices are the product of pressures in the other direction:

- **Power, status and financial rewards.** Determined by the extent of resource ownership and control in many corporations.
- **Co-ordination.** The speed of execution is increased because an executive has the right to request certain action without negotiation.
- **Efficiency.** Enables an organization to capture, at least in the short run, all the profits associated with an operation.
- **Inertia and cost of change.** It is commonly believed that it is good management to isolate the technical core of production from external shocks. This requires buffer inventories and control of raw materials and distribution channels. Ownership also creates familiarity and an identifiable chain of command, which becomes stabilized with time.
- **Industry structures.** Encourage ownership to prevent being pre-empted by the competition.

Management structure

The promoter wants knowledge of his or her progress via direct contact with all of the principal actors. The trustee wants relations more formally, with specific rights and responsibilities assigned through the delegation of authority.

The decision to use and rent resources and not to own or employ them requires the development of an informal information network. Only in systems where the relationship with resources is based on ownership or employment can resources be organized in a hierarchy. Informal networks arise when the critical success elements cannot be contained within the bounds of the formal organization.

Many people have attempted to distinguish between the entrepreneur and the administrator by suggesting that being a good entrepreneur precludes being a good manager. The entrepreneur is stereotyped as egocentric and idiosyncratic and thus unable to manage. However, although the managerial task is substantially different from that of the entrepreneur, management skill is nonetheless essential. The variation lies in the choice of appropriate tools.

More entrepreneurial management is a function of several pressures:

- **Need for co-ordination of key non-controlled resources.** Results in need to communicate with, motivate, control and plan for resources outside the organization.
- **Flexibility.** Maximized with a flat and informal organization.
- **Challenge to owner's control.** Classic questions about the rights of ownership as well as governmental, environmental, health and safety restrictions undermine the legitimacy of control.
- **Employees' desire for independence.** Creates an environment where employees are unwilling to accept hierarchical authority in place of authority based on competence and persuasion.

At the other end of the spectrum, pressures pushing towards more administrative behavior include:

- **Need for clearly defined authority and responsibility.** To perform the increasingly complex planning, organizing, co-ordinating, communicating and controlling required in business.
- **Organizational culture.** Often demands that events be made routine.
- **Reward systems.** Encourage and reward breadth and span of control.

Reward philosophy

Finally, entrepreneurial companies differ from administratively managed ones in their philosophy regarding reward and compensation. Entrepreneurial organizations are more explicitly focussed on the creation and harvesting of value. In start-up situations, the financial backers of the organization – as well as the founders themselves – have invested cash and want cash out.

As a corollary of this value-driven philosophy, entrepreneurial companies tend to base compensation on performance (where performance is closely related to value creation). Entrepreneurial companies are also more comfortable rewarding teams.

More administratively managed companies are less often focussed on maximizing and distributing value. They are more often guided in their decision making by the desire to protect their own positions and security. Compensation is often based on individual responsibility (assets or resources under control) and on performance relative to short-term profit targets. Reward in such organizations is often heavily oriented toward promotion to increased responsibility levels.

The pressures that pull companies towards the promoter end of the spectrum include:

- **Individual expectations.** Increasingly, individuals expect to be compensated in proportion to their contribution rather than merely as a function of their performance relative to an arbitrary peer group. In addition, individuals seemingly have higher levels of aspiration for personal wealth.
- **Investor demands.** Financial backers invest cash and expect cash back, and the sooner the better.
- **Competition.** Increased competition for talented people creates pressure for organizations to reward these individuals in proportion to their contributions.

On the other side a variety of pressures pull companies towards more trustee-like behavior:

- **Societal norms.** We still value loyalty to the organization and find it difficult to openly discuss compensation.
- **Impacted information.** It is often difficult to judge the value of an individual's contribution.
- **Demands of public shareholders.** Most public shareholders are simply uncomfortable with compensation that is absolutely high, even if it is in proportion to contribution.

Summary

In developing a behavioral theory of entrepreneurship it becomes clear that entrepreneurship is defined by more than a set of individual traits and is different from an economic function. It is a cohesive pattern of managerial behavior.

This perspective on entrepreneurship highlights what we see as a false dichotomy: the distinction drawn between entrepreneurship and intrapreneurship. Entrepreneurship is an approach to management that can be applied in start-up situations as well as within more established businesses. As our definition suggests, the accumulation of resources that occurs as a business grows is a powerful force that makes entrepreneurial behavior more difficult in a larger company. However, the fundamentals of the behavior required remain the same.

Women entrepreneurs: the way forward

Candida Brush suggests a new approach to women's entrepreneurship.

Name a successful entrepreneur. First to come to mind are most likely Bill Gates (Microsoft) or Richard Branson (the Virgin Group). If pressed, you may mention Michael Dell (Dell Computer), Tom Stemberg (Staples) or maybe Ben and Jerry (Ben Cohen and Jerry Greenfield). But did you think of Donna Karan, Meg Whitman or Lillian Vernon?

So often the first image one has of an entrepreneur is a man. Yet increasingly women are succeeding as entrepreneurs. Consider the following:

- Meg Whitman, founder of the revolutionary internet auction company e-Bay
- Donna Karan, founder of DKNY, a $700 million manufacturer of branded fashions and cosmetics
- Sandra Kurtzig, founder of Ask Computer, and the first woman to take a high-tech company public
- Patricia Gallup, founder of a $700 million direct marketing personal computer and software company
- Anita Roddick, founder of a worldwide retail cosmetic chain that advocates environmental and social values
- Bev McMaster, founder of the franchised We Care Health Services Inc. in Canada, that offers an array of healthcare services at multiple locations
- Candice Carpenter and Nancy Evans, founders of I-village, an internet company that following a $30 million venture capital investment went public within four years of start-up
- Yoshiko Shinohara, founder of Tempstaff Co. Ltd, a $369 million company that provides employees and business services to companies in Asia and the US
- Jean Owen, founder of Owen Healthcare, one of the largest healthcare and pharmacy service providers in the US, with revenues of more than $440 million
- Lillian Vernon, founder of one of the oldest and largest kitchen and household item catalog companies in the US
- Ann Gloag, founder and director of Stagecoach Holdings, which controls about 12 per cent of the public transportation in the United Kingdom.

Growth in women's entrepreneurship

One of the most important factors influencing the global marketplace is the tremendous growth in the number of women entrepreneurs. Women are founding firms in all industry sectors, growing them in geographic scope and size, and contributing significantly to gross national product (GNP) in many countries. The number of women business owners rose during the 1990s in nearly every OECD (Organisation for Economic Co-operation and Development) country.

The US reports that women own 9.1 million firms, which is 38 percent of all businesses. These businesses employ 27.5 million people and generate more than $3.6 trillion in sales annually. Between 1987 and 1999, the number of women-owned firms in the US increased by 103 percent. Approximately 14 percent of all women-owned firms have paid employees compared with 18 percent of all US firms. Although 70 percent of women-owned firms are in services and retail, they are rapidly starting and acquiring businesses in other sectors, including wholesale trade, transportation and communications, agriculture and manufacturing.

In Canada, there are more than 700,000 women-led firms providing 1.7 million jobs, while in Australia, women-owned businesses accounted for about 15 percent of gross domestic product (GDP) in 1996.

What is causing this growth in women's entrepreneurship? There is no single answer, but at a broad level, the environment for women's entrepreneurship is more acceptable today than 20 years ago. For instance, dramatic leaps in information technology make it easier for all entrepreneurs to launch businesses. For women in particular, technology affords them the chance to manage a business and meet family needs, or launch a venture from home.

Furthermore, it is easier for women to be accepted as entrepreneurs because there are more role models, and there is greater sharing of childcare and household responsibilities between men and women. In addition, publications providing specialized information for women such as *Working Woman*, women's entrepreneurship networking groups, websites such as *FWEtalk.com*, research foundations supporting women such as the National Foundation of Women Business Owners, and increased visibility of successful women entrepreneurs in the media all make it easier for women to explore entrepreneurial opportunities.

Another factor is the availability of education and training for women to gain the necessary business planning skills. For example, in the US more than 700 schools now offer entrepreneurship courses at the MBA and undergraduate levels. More than 35 percent of the students taking these classes are women. In addition, the US Small Business Administration offers specialized resources that target women, such as W.NET (the Women's Network for Entrepreneurial Training).

Besides these trends, there are many reasons why women become entrepreneurs. Individuals are influenced to pursue business ownership by "pushes" and "pulls." "Pushes" are defined as negative displacements (i.e. being fired, divorced, widowed, life transitions) whereas "pulls" tend to be positive (i.e. availability of financial support, offer of a partnership, customer contact). Both men and women are motivated by a desire for independence or achievement.[1] However, research also shows men may be motivated by a desire to "be an entrepreneur" or not to work for someone else, whereas women may wish to have flexibility in balancing work and family. Some women are motivated to start a new venture when they reach a corporate glass ceiling, while others believe they can offer a better quality product or serve customers better.

But is the entrepreneurial process different for men and women? To answer this question, it is important to understand key elements needed for venture creation and the external factors influencing these. For venture creation to take place, three central elements are required: an enterprising person, a perceived opportunity, and resources. The *person*, or the entrepreneur(s), is the discoverer of the opportunity in whose mind the possibilities for the new idea or venture come together. The *opportunity* is a perceived or created situation where entrepreneurship might occur. Some might see it as a problem, others might see it as a need that a new product or service can fulfill. *Resources* include physical (plant, equipment), financial (money, credit), technology (technical know-how), human (achieved attributes, education and experience), social (social relationships and networks) and organizational (procedures, policies, alliances).

At the start of a venture, the resources are generally those of the "entrepreneur" – her social contacts, her personal financial contribution, and her education and experience. These basic individual "endowments" provide the starting point for the venture, from which organizational resources are developed into policies, structures, culture and routines; and external financial, physical and technical resources are acquired. Further, these starting endowments, the perception of the opportunity, and the access to resources are shaped by the effects of social structures – work, family and organized social life. For women, the impact of social structures is different than for their male counterparts.

Factors influencing women's entrepreneurship
The workplace
In every country, women's participation in the workforce is limited to certain industrial sectors, they face occupational segregation, are paid lower wages, and are under-represented in upper-level management positions. In the US, women have made significant progress, now being employed in many non-traditional areas such as manufacturing and construction, but they are still heavily concentrated in services (clerical and sales) and administrative positions. In Europe, more than two-thirds of the jobs in health, teaching and domestic service are held by women, and they constitute 66 percent of clerical workers and 12 percent of workers and artisans.[2] The average level of women's pay is below that of men's in all countries because women are employed in lower skill jobs and are paid less for doing the same work.

Besides occupational segregation, women face barriers in rising to executive management positions. In North America and Europe it is reported that more than 95 percent of secretaries are female and 95 percent of managers are male. According to the United Nations, managerial work is segregated by sex in almost every country. In the US, while 25 percent of all managers of Fortune 200 companies are women, the range of women managers in some sectors is as low as 7 percent, but as high as 40 percent in others.

The effect of occupational segregation may limit women's opportunities to start businesses in fast-growing sectors such as high tech, manufacturing, finance or utilities, but it may be a strength in other sectors such as services, communications and education. Salary differentials may impact the amount of money women have available to launch a venture. Less experience at the executive level may limit the leadership skills of women at venture start-up, but greater administrative experience may positively affect their ability to manage people and organizational systems.

Women and the family
Expectations for women's role in the family have changed over past decades, but may still restrict women in terms of time, acceptance as business owners and responsibility for child/dependant care. Most women in OECD countries are expected to manage the household and assume a primary role with the family. In Sweden, women do not receive the same level of support in entrepreneurship from other family members as do their male counterparts, while in Australia women are more likely to perform domestic maintenance and care-giving tasks regardless of involvement in business activities. Young, educated, single Japanese women are

hired with the expectation that they will "retire" into marriage and motherhood within a few years. Even in the US the burden of child and dependant care falls on the shoulders of women who are primarily responsible as caregivers and running the household. A United Nations Report (1991, p.83) states that "women everywhere retain the primary responsibility for unpaid housework."

The expectations for women and their role in the family means they may have less opportunity to devote themselves full time to work endeavors, being subject to time fragmentation, career interruption, and frequently lower expectations for success in entrepreneurial endeavors. Yet women may be better at managing family and work responsibilities, being flexible, and responding to career interruptions as a result of their child-raising responsibilities.

Women and organized social life

Women's role in organized social life also varies from that of their male counterparts. Around the world women's networks tend to be formalized and sex based, whereas informal networks that involve socializing as part of business activities are frequently male-oriented. Research shows that women's networks are larger and more gender and racially diverse, while men's networks are less diverse.[3] In the US, where there are many female associations and network groups of women owners that provide support and channels of information, women are still left out of the "old boys' networks" comprised of high-level executives of large corporations.

Due to interrupted career paths or occupational segregation, women may be excluded from some informal business networks that can affect their access to resources and information. But on the positive side, they may be better at developing formal networking groups designed to encourage exchanges of information among women, that can lead to information and resources.

Approaches to venture creation

The effect of social structures – work, family and organized social life – on women influences the approach taken in venture creation. Clearly the extent and combination of social structure influences differ by country and life situation of the woman entrepreneur, but these impact the women's starting endowments of human and social capital, access to resources and their perception of venture opportunity in business start-up.

The effect of these social structures suggests a new approach – referred to as an "integrated" approach – to venture creation which is different from the "traditional" approach documented by the literature (*see* Table 1). The traditional approach is identified by historical research focussing mostly on studies of male entrepreneurs. Certainly most businesses follow some combination of both patterns. However, evidence shows that males tend to approach venture creation following the "traditional" approach whereas women are more likely to follow an "integrated" approach.

Traditional approach. The traditional approach views the venture as a separate economic entity and structures the organization as a hierarchy. Decision making will be analytical, and the entrepreneur typically will follow set procedures, being authoritarian in management style. The focus will be on task completion through the use of formalized control systems. Goal achievement in terms of economic success is very important. Strategically, traditionalists will prefer to follow strategies emphasizing cost efficiency, and values will be based on competition.

Table 1: Approaches to venture creation[4]

Dimension	Traditional (male)	Integrated (female)
View of business	separate economic entity	co-operative network of relationships
Motives	be independent, be an entrepreneur	create a job, have flexibility in work and family life, respond to social issues
Management style	task oriented, transactional, command/control	people oriented, transformational
Values/assumptions	competition transactional homogeneity	integration of family, work, society reciprocity diversity
Venture creation process	sequential, series of planned steps	simultaneous, construction of relationships
Structure	hierarchy	horizontal, network
Policies/practices	instrumental	nurturing, relational, social
Strategic approach	cost, efficiency	quality, customer service
Decision making	analytical, fact based	intuitive, participative
Goals	economic growth/profit	economic and non-economic social contribution
Performance	financial, economic personal wealth	financial, equally with employee and customer satisfaction, satisfying relationships

Integrated approach. The integrated approach views a venture as a network of co-operative relationships. This approach structures organizations as flat and team-based where decision making is shared and participative. Strong social and employee policies and practices are common, information is widely shared, and strong social values such as diversity and community outreach are common. Performance measures will be both social and economic, and planning will be informal. Family-friendly work rules are typical and strategies emphasize customer service and quality.

Importantly, the approach chosen by a woman entrepreneur will also be influenced by the industry she enters. As noted above, some industries are heavily male dominated, such as mining, construction or agriculture. Male-dominated industries are more likely to value a traditional approach (i.e. auto manufacturing, gas and oil exploration, venture capital, accounting) whereas female-dominated industries (i.e. educational services, childcare, retail trade, real estate) are more likely to accept an integrated approach. This suggests that the woman entrepreneur should consider the "fit" between the approach chosen and the industry.

For example, a woman entrepreneur pursuing a traditional approach in a male-dominated industry may easily be able to identify informal business norms and practices, but she may be perceived as having lower chances of survival. Her success will depend on persistence and adherence to the traditional approach, as well as a strong competitive strategy. For a woman entrepreneur pursuing a traditional approach in a female-dominated industry, there may be a misfit and the woman entrepreneur may be perceived as an anomaly. Her challenge will be to gain acceptance for her traditional approach. Success will depend on successful adaptation of male leadership practices and business policies to the female industry environment.

The woman entrepreneur pursuing an integrated approach in a male-dominated industry must recognize the challenge of trying to break with traditional business practices. Success for this woman entrepreneur is to value her differences, show confident leadership and strong vision. Finally, for the woman entrepreneur following an integrated approach in a female-dominated industry, a fit between the approach and industry is likely. Yet her challenge is to recognize that external stakeholders may consider the venture less serious about economic performance. Success depends on effective environmental scanning and sensitivity to marketplace expectations. Strong publicity and media dissemination of innovative business practices can create further legitimacy.

The future

The domain of entrepreneurship has historically been a male preserve, but this is changing rapidly. While women entrepreneurs in many countries still face significant challenges in launching and growing their ventures, increased social acceptance, influence of technology and targetted assistance programs are making it easier for women to become entrepreneurs. Yet social structures influence personal starting endowments, resource availability and perceptions of what is possible. Women may follow either traditional or integrative approaches, which in combination with industry choice imply different recipes for success.

The number and strength of women entrepreneurs are expected to increase into the next century, meaning the aggregate impact of women on business and society will continue to grow.

1 Brush, C. G. (1992) "Research on women business owners: past trends, a new perspective and future directions," *Entrepreneurship Theory and Practice*, 16:4, 5–30.

2 This trend is true in Sweden and Germany where up to 90 percent of the service jobs, such as typists, nurses and housekeepers, are filled by women. Similarly, in Australia, Finland and Denmark, the labor market remains gender segregated and equal opportunity across occupational sectors has not been achieved.

3 Aldrich, H. (1989) "Networking among women entrepreneurs," in Hagan, O., Rivchun, C. and Sexton, D. (eds) *Women-Owned Businesses*, New York: Praeger pp.103–132.

4 *See* Brush, C. G. (1992) "Research on women business owners: past trends, a new perspective and future directions," *Entrepreneurship Theory and Practice*, 16: 5–30; Brush, C. G. (1998) "A resource perspective on women's entrepreneurship: research, relevance and recognition," *Proceedings of the Organization for Economic Cooperation and Development Conference on Women Entrepreneurs in Small and Medium-Sized Enterprises*, Paris, France; Brush, C. G. (1999) "Women's entrepreneurship," *Proceedings of the Second International Labor Organization Enterprise Forum*, Geneva, Switzerland.

Ten myths about entrepreneurs

Juan Roure details research that shows that, while some entrepreneurs in Europe are thriving, our ideas of entrepreneurial companies in general may need revising.

Which companies are the real job creators in Europe? Who are the entrepreneurs building them? What is the profile of these successful entrepreneurs? What strategies are they following?

These are some of the questions that we have been trying to answer at the European Foundation for Entrepreneurship Research (EFER) since 1987. One of the latest studies conducted by EFER under the patronage of the European Commission – "Europe's 500 dynamic entrepreneurs: the job creators" – has helped confirm many of the general beliefs about entrepreneurship in Europe but also has led us to question some of the more common myths about job creation and growing successful companies.

This article contrasts some of the myths and expectations that we had before starting the study with the realities that we discovered through detailed research results and interviews with 500 successful entrepreneurs, identified from screening ten million companies from 16 countries.

The research sample was limited to mid-sized companies with less than 500 employees in 1989 (the beginning of the period under study) and more than 40 by 1994 (the final year under study). In all the companies the entrepreneur(s) held a significant percentage of ownership.

Myth 1: Small and medium-sized enterprises (SMEs) are the job creators.

Reality: Only a certain type of SME – the "dynamic companies and entrepreneurs" – are the high growers and job generators.

In the period under study, the number of net jobs in Europe, counting all companies, decreased by nearly two million, with most of the losses attributable to large organizations and about 700,000 losses attributable to SMEs. In contrast, the sample of 500 companies that we identified were able to create more than 100,000 jobs. The average annual growth of the "dynamic companies" identified was about 21 percent in employment and 29 percent in turnover. Therefore, in Europe, as supported by a similar study in the US, a small proportion of SMEs is responsible for creating the majority of new jobs.

Myth 2: New companies are the fundamental source of growth in employment.

Reality: High job growth is produced by both old and new companies.

Much attention has been paid to the problems of starting up companies. However, very little is known about managing the "transitions" that are usually linked to strategic moves to new products or markets and to changes in ownership, such as incorporating new partners, family successions or merger and acquisition.

Europe's 500 "dynamic" companies have been in business for 17 years on average. Four companies were actually first established in the 19th century, and only 14 percent were less than five years old by 1994. The spark for growth in many already existing businesses seems to come from the successful management of some of these "transitions" and from a persistence in pursuing new opportunities.

Myth 3: Growing companies come from new and high-growth sectors.
Reality: Dynamic companies come from all sectors.
These results seem to demonstrate that there are no successful sectors but, rather, successful entrepreneurs and organizations. The sectoral distribution of Europe's 500 is quite similar to that of all SMEs. However, the service sector as a whole seems to provide a more fertile ground for growth than manufacturing.

Myth 4: Entrepreneurs of growing companies are young and well-educated.
Reality: Dynamic entrepreneurs are of all ages and educational levels.
Three-quarters of Europe's 500 entrepreneurs are in the 35–65 age range. Only 7 percent are under 34 and 18 percent are over 65. "Dynamic" entrepreneurs come from a wide range of educational backgrounds, with less than one-third having a university degree. These types of entrepreneurs consider themselves as "constantly trained professionals" and rate themselves most highly on skills such as strategy, negotiation and communication.

Myth 5: Growing companies are developed by an energetic and self-sufficient entrepreneur.
Reality: Dynamic companies are built by teams or a partnership of entrepreneurs with a professional approach to management.
Most of the entrepreneurs studied seem to have great self-confidence in their ability to identify and then capitalize on opportunities, overcoming all kinds of obstacles. However, they realize the challenges involved in growing a business in today's competitive environment and, therefore, they form teams or partnerships to complement themselves in managing the company.

Myth 6: Growing companies target large and growing markets.
Reality: Dynamic companies target market segments where they can be leaders or strong challengers.
More than 80 percent of Europe's 500 entrepreneurs consider themselves to be the market "leader" or "challenger" in the segment in which they compete. These companies try to avoid competition by concentrating on segments or "niches," which they sometimes create themselves, where they try to play a significant and influential role by applying proactive strategies.

Myth 7: Growing companies target mainly domestic markets where they can dominate such markets.
Reality: Dynamic companies target a significant proportion of their sales to export markets where they can learn and grow.
About 80 percent of Europe's 500 are active in export markets. On average, the share of exports is 44 percent of turnover, the final destinations mainly being other EU member states. These dynamic companies export a much higher percentage of their turnover than European SMEs in general, using mainly direct distribution channels and, to a much lesser extent, foreign investment, joint ventures or licensing.

Myth 8: Successful growing companies use low-cost strategies to compete.
Reality: Dynamic companies compete with high-quality products and superior service.
Europe's 500 entrepreneurs have opted for differentiation strategies far more

frequently than for low-cost strategies. They seek to differentiate mostly in the quality of their products and in the service that they provide to their customers. These strategies are supported by the high involvement of employees and customers in the improvement process and the high commitment to quality of the entrepreneurs themselves.

Myth 9: Successfully growing companies rely primarily on unique technology.

Reality: Dynamic companies rely primarily on people, whom they carefully recruit, train and develop.

Even though Europe's 500 entrepreneurs consider technological knowledge an important asset to reduce cost and take advantage of new opportunities, they pay a high level of attention to human resources policies, particularly to recruitment, training, employee recognition and team building. Dynamic entrepreneurs, in contrast with other SMEs, may have been stimulated by fast growth in employment, which forced them to adopt a more formal and professional approach to people management.

Myth 10: Growing companies use sophisticated sources of financing to build their companies.

Reality: Dynamic companies are predominantly self-funded, with assistance from bank loans.

Europe's 500 entrepreneurs seek to remain financially independent as much as possible. In 87 percent of the companies, the major entrepreneur controls more than half of the shares. The most important source of financing for this type of company is from retained profits. Bank loans are the only other significant source of finance. Venture capital and private investors had some importance only in approximately 10 percent of the companies that have gone public. However, another 30 percent are considering listing in the future; this may lead to an increased importance being placed on developing capital.

In conclusion, dynamic entrepreneurs have had and expect to continue to have a profound impact on Europe's wealth and job creation. Europe's 500 is only a small sample of a large number of other dynamic entrepreneurs already existing, but hidden, or with the potential of becoming high growers in the future.

The study of these entrepreneurs is still in the early stages. The first results seem to challenge many of the entrepreneurship myths that have been developed through the years. Europe's 500 Association has been created with the purpose of becoming the "voice" and releasing the enormous potential of "dynamic entrepreneurs" in Europe.

Richard Branson: the enigmatic entrepreneur

This case is extracted and edited from "Branson's Virgin: The coming of age of a counter-cultural enterprise" prepared in 1995 by **Robert Dick**, research associate at INSEAD, under the supervision of **Manfred F. R. Kets de Vries**, Raoul de Vitry d'Avaucourt Professor of Human Resource Management at INSEAD.

Family and early life

Richard Branson was born in July 1950, the first child and only son of Ted Branson and his wife Eve. He was later joined by two sisters, Lindi and Vanessa. The family has remained close, all enjoying what Richard was later to describe as a "happy and secure" childhood.

Both Ted and Eve came from comfortable establishment backgrounds. Ted was the son and grandson of eminent lawyers. Eve came from a family of clerics, farmers and stockbrokers, whose womenfolk were expected to have horizons beyond the home.

Eve had decided views on child-rearing. While she was never a martinet, she pushed her children to be self-reliant and responsible, to take control of their own destinies rather than relying on others.

One summer afternoon, as she and four-year-old Richard were on their way home after visiting his grandparents, Eve told Richard to get out of the car and try to find his own way back. The farmhouse where they were staying was not far but Richard got lost, ending up at the neighbor's farm.

Eve Branson now admits that she may have been overly enthusiastic about encouraging Richard's independence but she has never regretted it. She believed that her children's ability to overcome challenges would encourage the kind of spirit she wanted to see in them. Accordingly, she used her considerable energy to organize activities, games and projects for her children that were not only fun but also served a useful purpose.

Holidays, weekends and other free time were used productively. The Branson household had no television since it was "time wasting;" shyness in children was simply bad manners and self-indulgence to be discouraged; if money was short (as it was in the early days when Ted's father cut off his allowance in protest at his precipitate marriage), a solution could always be found in small money-making schemes that Eve thought up.

Ted Branson was never a strict and remote father figure. Sympathetic and supportive by preference, a half-hearted disciplinarian if really necessary, Ted was less directly ambitious for his children than Eve, who expected, for example, that "Richard [would] one day be prime minister."

Richard grew up to be the archetypal naughty boy. Frequently in minor scrapes, scolded for innumerable misdemeanors, and hyperactive in all he did, his parents found him both endearing and fatiguing. According to his father, Branson began his first business venture when he was around 11 or 12 years old. He planted 1,000 seedlings and then went back to school convinced he would make a killing selling Christmas trees. Rabbits ate the trees. About a year later he tried again. This time the scheme involved budgerigars. Another failure.

Richard's parents were particularly concerned about his progress at school, where his main accomplishments were on the sports field, thanks to a strong physique and competitive spirit. His schoolboy heroes were sportsmen, particularly cricketers, and adventurers such as Scott of the Antarctic, the British explorer and a distant relative by marriage.

His indifference to schoolwork (not helped by long-undetected poor eyesight) meant he achieved only average results, which ruled out a legal or other professional career. By contrast, *Student* magazine (Branson's first successful business venture) excited Branson with its possibilities and offered a timely and convenient exit. So, with his parents' reluctant blessing (his father's support was particularly influential), he quit school.

Branson left few friends behind him. While not unpopular, his energetic and single-minded pursuit of that which pleased him left little room for others. His indifference to the contemporary social mores and allegiances common at a school like Stowe (an exclusive private school with a liberal reputation) left him somewhat isolated. His few friends were those inveigled into his various and numerous projects. Commenting on the end of his schooldays, Branson said: "Having left school without going to university, I decided to make money . . . I never considered failure."

The "hippy entrepreneur"

Having in some respects commercialized the anti-establishment lifestyle of the 1960s, it was not surprising that Branson was labeled "the hippy entrepreneur" by the business and musical press. His alternative image was reinforced by the company's operating style where, from the start, informality and equality were essential principles – rarely found in the business world at the time.

When Virgin started out, everyone received the same low salary, there was an absence of hierarchy (Branson was, and is, "Richard" to everyone) and personal attire was casual to the point of idiosyncrasy. Even when the company had expanded massively, this style was very much in evidence; Branson and his staff are rarely seen in conventional business clothes, preferring sweaters and jeans even on formal occasions. Similarly, the company's offices, accumulated over time, were a collection of modest, often dilapidated, buildings scattered about north-west London from which the sound of rock music could usually be heard.

For a long time Branson's office and home was a canal houseboat where he worked alone apart from two secretaries. Eventually Branson was forced to move to a larger home since his two children "started to answer the phones," but he kept the houseboat as an office.

His wife, a down-to-earth Glaswegian from a working-class background, has no interest or role in his business life. This is something of an anomaly at Virgin since Branson, contrary to conventional wisdom, is a great believer in working with family and friends, seeing only the advantages and not the risks. His cousins, aunts, school and childhood friends, parents and former girlfriends have all been drawn into his various business activities. Only his first wife found the situation difficult to accept, but even she is now in a joint venture with Branson developing hotels in Spain.

The charges of nepotism that such arrangements usually engender were muted at Virgin because Branson adopted a promote-from-within policy, giving many of his staff opportunities that their lack of experience and training would have precluded in more conventional companies.

Virgin was unconventional in other ways too. Somehow Branson created the impression that people worked at Virgin for fun and excitement rather than simply as a means of earning a living. Notoriously indifferent to material possessions and unconcerned about everyday financial matters, Branson saw no difficulty in paying modest salaries provided people were enjoying themselves, feeling part of an idiosyncratic enterprise that had a heart. If people were down, a party would revive spirits and, incidentally, give Branson the chance to play a practical joke on newcomers, an embarrassing rite of passage at Virgin that is maintained to this day. Much of this operating style was established not so much by design but by the exigencies of the time when Virgin was getting started. It has proved to be a successful model that Branson can replicate.

His philosophy is to immerse himself in new ventures until he understands the ins and outs of the business and then hand it over to a good managing director and financial controller who are given a stake in it and are then expected to make the company take off.

He knows that expansion through the creation of additional discrete legal entities not only protects the Virgin Group but also gives people a sense of involvement and loyalty, particularly if he trusts them with full authority and offers minority shareholdings to the managers of subsidiaries. He is proud of the fact that Virgin has produced a considerable number of millionaires. He has said that he does not want his best people to leave the company to start a venture outside. He prefers to make millionaires within.

He sees similarities in the Japanese *keiretsu* system (small companies interlocking in a collaborative network) to the structure he has created at Virgin, with more than 500 small companies around the world operating quasi-independently.

The "real" Richard Branson

Richard Branson has become an international celebrity, the subject of numerous profiles in gossip magazines, the business press and television programs. In the UK he has achieved folk-hero status. He is frequently cited as a role model by young people wanting a successful business career that does not compromise personal ethics.

In material terms Branson is undoubtedly successful. He became one of the UK's richest people before he turned 40 and recently ranked as the 11th wealthiest person in the UK, with an estimated net worth of £895 million.

Asked to explain the strategy that got him to this point, he will talk of minimizing risks — "protect the downside, always be ready to walk away" — and seeking out opportunities to build "the largest entertainment group outside the US." Over the years he has made a few strategic statements that, with hindsight, do not relate very much to subsequent events. Most frequently, however, he says he simply wants to enjoy himself.

But can a strategy for fun really explain the creation of a music company by a founder who, paradoxically, has little interest in or knowledge of music? Equally, it is difficult to explain how a shy man, ill at ease when speaking publicly or in private conversation with strangers, can become a supreme self-publicist; how an establishment-born figure with intrinsically conventional views can become the champion of radical and libertarian causes; or how the man who is almost obsessive about fair play can negotiate ferociously for the last penny in a deal.

A London *Sunday Times* report on the British Airways affair (the so-called "dirty tricks" affair) quoted Lord King (at the time BA Chairman) as saying: "If Richard Branson had worn a pair of steel-rimmed glasses, a double-breasted suit and shaved off his beard, I would have taken him seriously. As it was I couldn't . . . I underestimated him."

Perhaps Lord King is not alone in being misled by the hippy entrepreneur image that surrounds Branson. But if that image is not the real Richard Branson, then what is?

The above case is an abridged version. Copies of the complete case may be obtained from the European Case Clearing House, telephone (+44) 01234 750903; fax (+44) 01234 751125; e-mail ECCH@cranfield.ac.uk

THE OPPORTUNITY

2

Contributors

Peter Saunders is Lecturer in Accounting and Entrepreneurship at Imperial College, London.

Sandra Vandermerwe is Professor of Marketing and International Services and Chair of Management at Imperial College Management School, London.

Rita Gunther McGrath is Associate Professor, Management Division, at Columbia Business School, New York. Her research focusses on how competitive advantages are gained through innovation and new venture management.

Stephen Thompson is a venture capitalist with Apax Partners and Co. He is a non-executive director of BioImage A/S and Imperial Innovations. His portfolio includes Lexicon Genetics, Rademacher Group Ltd, RiboTargets, Microscience and SenseTherapeutic Ltd.

Peter Kelly teaches courses in new venture development and entrepreneurial finance at the Helsinki University of Technology. He works with a variety of private technology-based firms on matters related to financial structuring, valuation and capitalization.

Albert Angehrn is Associate Professor and Director of the Center for Advanced Learning Technologies (CALT) at INSEAD.

David Molian is Lecturer in Entrepreneurship at Cranfield School of Management, Cranfield University, UK. His research interests include general marketing, new ventures marketing and the marketing of innovation.

Jean-Louis Barsoux is a senior research fellow in strategy and management at INSEAD.

Stephen Spinelli is the John H. Muller term chair in Entrepreneurship and the Director of the Arthur M. Blank Center for Entrepreneurship at Babson College, Wellesley, Massachusetts. His research interests include franchising, multiple outlet operations, retailing and new venture creation. He is a former franchisee of Jiffy Lube in the US, developing 47 stores in eight years, a founding shareholder of Jiffy Lube International, and founder, Chairman and CEO of American Oil Change Corporation.

Contents

Introduction

Part 2 is concerned with finding a new business opportunity. Clearly, a swift scan of the high street, or any new product catalog, will show that there would appear to be very few new ideas – just old ones repackaged and relaunched. So how do you spot where the opportunity lies, or when a change in legislation has opened a new "window?" How do you decide that e-commerce is the better route to market? This part deals with these questions, with how to assess a new opportunity, and how to decide on the right market entry strategy.

Spotting the market opportunity

Daniel Muzyka looks at the way entrepreneurs identify opportunities. The related question of what makes a good opportunity is tackled in the article on assessing opportunities on p. 56.

The key to entrepreneurship is the ability to identify, pursue and capture the value from business opportunities. Entrepreneurs exist to pursue opportunity. Without it, they have no *raison d'être*. No one can call him- or herself an entrepreneur until they have identified and at least begun the pursuit of an opportunity. No one should call themselves a *successful* entrepreneur until they *have* captured an opportunity.

The problem in addressing the topic of opportunity – and particularly the question "what makes a good opportunity?" – is that it is hard to generalize. The underlying nature of technologies and the way they are adopted by customers and specific industries and competitive dynamics make the construction of a checklist of opportunity characteristics difficult. The emergence of opportunities in "cyber space" makes the characterization of opportunity even more difficult.

It is harder yet to generalize about where entrepreneurs find opportunity. For some entrepreneurs, opportunity comes as a result of extended thought and exploration. For others, it is the product of a fortunate set of circumstances and a quick response to a lucky phone call from a desperate potential customer.

Having said that, we can draw from entrepreneurship research over the past 15 years. We can also draw from research on those who bet on entrepreneurs for a living: private investors and venture capitalists. Their reflections provide us with some guidelines on opportunity. In reviewing these sources, you will find some consistent themes regarding the characteristics of "good" opportunities.

However, we begin our discussion of opportunity with a note of caution. The one thing we do know about entrepreneurial opportunity is that the opportunity models developed by strategy and marketing researchers may not fully apply to new-venture opportunities. More than once, existing strong competitors in industries such as computers (for example IBM) have asked themselves how these young upstarts have been so successful in pursuing opportunities that did not appear on the radar screen of corporate staff groups.

The problem may lie in the underlying source of the models used by large competitors: they were taken from observations of long-run market competition in *established* markets, not from *establishing* markets.

Despite the difficulty in generalizing from the experiences of successful and unsuccessful entrepreneurs regarding opportunity, we will make an attempt to summarize what we know.

What is an opportunity?

Opportunities themselves are something that exist on paper or as an idea. Realized opportunities are those that individuals have turned into profitable and functioning businesses. Opportunity, in practical terms, may therefore be defined as a business concept that, if turned into a tangible product or service offered by a business enterprise, will result in financial profit.

Are there any general points we have learned about opportunity by observing entrepreneurs? The answer comes in a few cautionary points.

Opportunities are about creating value, not necessarily lowering cost

Some would-be entrepreneurs become fixated on whether their product is cost competitive or the lowest-cost product. The name of the game, however, is not necessarily about low cost, despite what some popular production strategy gurus have said. It has been, and always will be, about creating value. Does the opportunity help increase the customers' effectiveness and efficiency? It is simple economics: if it is worth it, people pay. The failure of some entrepreneurs who believe they haven't come in at the right cost is that they have not communicated value.

One example is a productivity software package that came out in the early days of microcomputer software. It was priced below $90 per copy. The company selling the product was doing poorly *vis-à-vis* other packages available. What did consumers tell it? "You cannot provide value since all you do is communicate through price." The company brought the price closer to $120 per copy and used the additional revenue to advertise in order to communicate the value of the product. Turnover climbed precipitously.

Opportunities are not the same for everyone

Many economic and business models suggest that somehow opportunity is "out there" and that it simply "happens." The only problem is who will invest in it and then catch it. Don't get caught in this perspective. If there is one truth that comes from the experience of entrepreneurs, it is that not everyone is equally equipped to perceive or capture an opportunity.

The experience of each individual or team makes them more or less able to identify and capture opportunity. In addition, each individual's perspective (which is a product of their products, services, markets or skills) is different.

What does this mean? It means that although you may be worried that someone else will pursue "your" opportunity, it is not necessarily perceived as an opportunity by anyone else. They may not have your advantages or particular skills in trying to realize its potential. This also means that even though something may be an opportunity for someone else, perhaps you ought to avoid it. In the end, any measure of whether something is a real opportunity must take into account whether you can implement it.

Not everyone pursues opportunities, even if they are obvious

How many times, when someone else started a business and made money out of it, have you said to yourself, "I had the same idea"?

Profit is left to those who wish to show initiative and actually pursue rather than just think about a business opportunity. Creative thought is wonderful but if it does not lead to action it is only an expenditure of energy. Most people and companies do not pursue opportunity, especially if they are reasonably satisfied with the status quo. You must show real initiative to pursue opportunity.

Complex opportunities break down

It unfortunately appears to be a fact of life that the more complex an opportunity is – for example, involving a large number of parties and integrating numerous steps and components for it to work successfully – the more it is *un*likely to come to fruition or to work in the long run.

Some entrepreneurs have ideas but, as they try to pursue them, they find they must involve more and more parties. Sometimes entrepreneurs get caught up in the "artistry" of the opportunity and forget how vulnerable they become when so many components must work together. These are the entrepreneurs whom one subsequently often hears lamenting that they had figured out the opportunity but it was just one little problem that ripped it apart.

Opportunity is not always (rarely?) found in well-documented growth markets

Too many entrepreneurs and venture capitalists have been lured into effort and investment in pursuing opportunities that everybody else has seen. For example, an excessive number of companies were established, virtually simultaneously, in the hard disk drive industry in the US to pursue the new "Winchester drive" technology. Only a few survived.

A simple rule might be that if an opportunity is discussed in all its details on the front page of the *Financial Times,* you might take the time to determine whether it is going to be a real value-added opportunity for you. I always enjoy those advertisements in business journals that note an undiscovered entrepreneurial opportunity that has been successfully pursued by thousands.

Having said all of this, one also needs to carefully distinguish between a growth "trend" and a growth "market." E-commerce isn't a market *per se*, but it represents a trend toward the development of businesses on the internet. As a trend or vehicle for business (i.e. the internet) it will be the home of many new "business to business" and "business to consumer" opportunities.

Opportunities are not necessarily the result of inventions by the entrepreneur

Despite the comment that entrepreneurs are not necessarily inventors, many entrepreneurs are determined to invest their time and effort in searching for opportunities based on some kind of technological breakthrough. This may be admirable, even desirable, but it is not necessary.

Where do opportunities come from?

Entrepreneurial opportunities come in many ways, shapes and forms to those who pursue them. Some individuals are gifted in identifying and throwing off ideas for products and services at a rapid pace. Others conceive how they can make money from an idea they get from a newspaper or hear about from a friend or acquaintance.

Most entrepreneurs have to show a modicum of creativity, although a particularly creative mind is not required. The role of entrepreneurs is not to be people of "ideas." Their role is to be creative in structuring a business around an opportunity and then implementing their ideas.

What we have observed, however, is that the business opportunities they identify are usually related to past experience. It is rare that someone has a lightning bolt out of the blue and identifies a new blockbuster opportunity in a field with which they are not or only slightly familiar. Opportunities are usually related to our work experience, hobbies or social environment.

In other words, ideas for opportunities come from within the realm of our existing knowledge and usually result from our mind connecting seemingly unrelated ideas. The simple rule is: if you want to develop a new concept in a specific, unfamiliar business, go to work in that business so that you know how it functions and can see the linkages.

What types of opportunities are there?

Opportunities are not all the same in either their potential or their risks. We often glorify the individuals who identify and pursue the radical new technologies. However, the reality is that these types of entrepreneurial opportunities are the exceptions and not the rule.

Some individuals seek to identify and pursue such high-potential, high-risk opportunities. Others look for opportunities that have lower risk/return profiles, that is, the entrepreneur accepts somewhat less profit for the sake of a lower-risk project. This may involve not the pursuit of some new high-density, silicon-based chip but the transplanting of a franchise operation from one country to another.

Most successful entrepreneurial opportunities involve the pursuit of relatively simple ideas. For example, entrepreneurs have made significant sums from mass merchandising carpets in more attractive stores, producing appropriate bakery buns locally to supply McDonald's, or locating convenience shops in emerging, high-traffic areas.

In looking for opportunity, consider not only the risk/return relationship but also, and probably more importantly, your own objectives. Some people are looking for the opportunity of a lifetime with massive potential. For them, such an opportunity will define their life. They will pursue it to the fullest. These are often the entrepreneurs we hear about. The Bransons (Virgin) and Gates (Microsoft) of this world fit into this category.

Others are interested in what we often refer to as "lifestyle" opportunities and businesses. If you are looking for a business opportunity that will help you realize a desired pattern in your life, you must be careful to define the limits you wish to impose on the nature of the business that will result from pursuing an opportunity.

There are many people who start everything, from specialist hotels to mail-order firms, because the daily operation of such businesses also enables them to pursue a certain lifestyle. Many individuals who, for example, wish to spend more time, or more structured time, with their families are looking for a different balance between the opportunity and their potential profit.

The search for a good idea

How do you come up with a good business idea? **Peter Saunders** lists some ways to help your creativity.

The aim of this article is to help you build an inventory of creative resources and help you identify a personal strategy for opportunity search.

Essentially there are only two ways in which you can create business ideas – generate your own or develop someone else's. The second is far more common because virtually every successful business is a development of an earlier business concept. These areas, such as management buy-outs/buy-ins, corporate spin-offs, franchising and buying an existing business, are covered in detail in other articles.

In terms of generating business ideas, there are three sources of opportunities: adverts, agents and opportunity spotting, or watching out for businesses that you find match your objectives.

All people and organizations have needs that they fulfill in many different ways. When you can meet these needs better than they are currently being met, you will almost certainly have a business opportunity.

One common route is the employer as an "idea generator" – you might duplicate what your employer is doing, or service a new market that the employer has not bothered to exploit. Other ways of recognizing people's needs include "the complaints department," where you listen to people whingeing to see if you can find ways of reducing their problems; asking yourself "what do people want?"; spotting trends (the growth of home personal computers has led to an enormous number of new businesses from hardware to software, along with magazines and books); and identifying market gaps.

There are some established thinking techniques such as visualization, brainstorming and morphological analysis that can be used to generate ideas.

Visualization is a technique that has been used successfully by many, including Conrad Hilton of Hilton Hotel fame whose autobiography even has a chapter called "You've got to dream." The process is to day-dream – to visualize a picture of your future. Does it include your own company? If so, what is it? Visualization is good at helping determine long-term goals, idea generation and idea evaluation.

Everyone has heard of brainstorming. When used well, it can create large numbers of ideas. To work well, you need between five and ten people and you need to have planned the session in advance. There is insufficient space in this article to cover best practice, so you will need to read up on the topic.

Morphological analysis – dividing a complex problem into elements – can also help generate ideas. As an example one might take skincare products: sun cream, anti-wrinkle cream and tanning lotion, to suggest just three. The potential market for these might be segmented by age – teenage, 20-something and 30-plus. By combining the two, you have nine ideas. Skin tone may be relevant as well. If you have only three skin tones, you are up to 27 ideas already. Once a box has been developed in this way, the more important elements can be simplified into a morphological matrix with only two axes.

Finally, there are some experts in corporate creativity who can help in idea generation. The most well known is Edward de Bono whose book *Opportunities: a*

Pam Murphy had a slurry problem on her farm. The slurry pit was leaching into the local river. So, she had a machine designed that would separate the slurry into solid and liquid. This made storage much easier.

However, leaving a batch of solid for a couple of weeks, she found it had heated up, destroyed all the germs and "cooked" into a perfect, friable fertilizer.

Pam thought: "I am going to sell that" and so the concept of Cowpact was born. In the first year, she sold 25,000 bags by mail order. But that was just the beginning. Pam had a product that could be sold to either the gardener or farmers or both, and the copyright on a process/machine that could be sold in the farm equipment market.

What should she do? Where was the greatest opportunity?

Figure 2

yourself that you would like to have it, so others must too. You would love to have your groceries delivered at 6.30 on a Friday evening, and the internet now makes it possible to place an order. But how many people in your street or locality have access to the internet and could be persuaded to switch their buying habits – and what would they be prepared to pay for the service?

Market share

The potential market may be large and there may be a genuine need, but what percentage of customers do you think you can persuade to switch to your product? Indeed, who are the customers?

We all buy washing powder in the supermarket but we do not decide which brands are displayed on the shelves. That is the role of the supermarket buyer, who may prefer to deal with large suppliers offering a range of reliable, quality products over a new business offering a new, untried product. In other words, you need to think about routes to market and the barriers you may encounter. Of course, this means looking at the competition and their likely reaction to your entry. For example, will they reduce their prices, increase their advertising or develop a similar product in order to try to squeeze you out?

Part of the answer will depend upon how much of a threat you are likely to be to them, and this is often a function of size and market power. Clearly, the more diverse the competition and the smaller your target share, the greater your chances.

How do you find out? You do not need to invest in expensive market surveys – although it may be necessary later on – just ask a few common sense questions. You should be looking to establish the "ball park" to see if it is worth spending time in more detailed market research. You are trying to "prove the concept."

Certainly you will be expected to answer these questions, and many more, if you are seeking to raise money. Investors need to be convinced that you understand your marketplace and are realistic about your chances – and so do you. In the end, however, investors are usually more convinced by names and orders than by market surveys.

Routes to market

Establishing that there is a market is only the first stage. You now need to think about the potential ways to capitalize on the idea – and it may not be to start your own business.

The market may be highly concentrated, dominated by two or three global companies that also control the channels of distribution. So you may be advised to sell the patent, license it, or become a partner in a joint venture. For example, would you advise Pam to set up as a farm equipment manufacturer?

There are two questions to be answered:

- Is there a market?
- Is there potential for an independent business?

If you decide to continue with a new start, remember that competitors are rarely inactive. The best that you can hope for is that they are slow and/or ineffective. You need to think about how much time you may have before competitive reaction will have a serious effect on your business – and what you can do to protect yourself.

Protection

Fundamental to the process of assessing the opportunity is the need to talk to potential suppliers, customers and subcontractors. "But what if they steal my idea?" is a constant concern. "What can I do to protect myself?"

Clearly, being first to market and establishing your brand is one way, as is asking your contacts to sign confidentiality agreements. However, there are three other legal forms of protection to consider:

- **Patents:** this refers to the invention of a tangible item, which incorporates novel features involving an innovative step and which is capable of industrial application. It is particularly important that the entrepreneur understands the prior disclosure regulations since they vary by country. Indeed, patents are granted on a country-by-country basis. Granting of the patent gives the owner a monopoly on its use for a specified number of years.
- **Registered design:** covers designs that are attractive. They may include a shape, configuration or pattern for a specific, manufactured article such as a car.
- **Copyright:** prevents the copying of original works, although in any court action it must be proved that copying has actually taken place. Great minds do sometimes think alike.

Business viability

So far you have been looking at market opportunity. Alongside this you should also be thinking about the business opportunity. Evaluation of this will depend on how you intend to arrange the business – to what extent are you going to subcontract the manufacture of the product or the provision of the service?

Clearly, the answer to these questions will, in turn, depend on issues such as your skills, availability of subcontractors, quality and funding, but eventually it will depend on your financial analysis. Quite simply, you need to know the answer to two deceptively simple questions:

- What are the likely costs of the business and can you sell at a price that will produce a viable profit in the long run? Think about the possible margins. How much room for maneuver do you have if your estimates of either the price or costs are wrong?
- Is the forecast cash flow sustainable? Too many businesses have failed with positive margins but no cash simply because others would not or could not pay in time.

Unfortunately, there are no simple answers to these questions. So you need to think about what may go wrong – sales take longer to take off or amount to only half your expectations, customers take longer to pay, or suppliers are not as reliable in quality or delivery as you had been led to believe, your license to operate as a restaurant does not arrive until after Christmas.

What would these do to the build-up of your sales? In short, what are the critical success factors for your business, how likely are they to happen, how can you mitigate against them, and how fatal could they be?

Is it worth it?

By now you must be wondering. However, remember that you will already know many of the answers or have access to help through your business contacts, friends and family. You simply need to take a cold, hard look at all aspects of your idea in order to convince yourself and others that it might work.

The crawl-out costs

One final question – what are you prepared to lose? What are the crawl-out costs if things go wrong? This is the dreaded issue of risk. There are two types of risk that you should always be aware of – the personal and the business risks. Personal risks may be:

- **Financial:** can you afford to lose your investment?
- **Career:** can you return to your previous job or career?
- **Family and social:** how will it affect your social reputation?
- **Psychic:** how afraid are you of failure?

On the other hand, the business risks include:

- **Market:** will the product sell?
- **Credit:** will the customers pay … and when?
- **Operational:** have I got the right control systems in place?
- **Reputational:** does the market believe that I can do it?

Which of these worries you the most – and would it stop you? In reality, few successful entrepreneurs think in these terms. They simply see the "upside" of an opportunity and provide contingencies to "manage the downside."

Market research

Daniel Muzyka provides a few basic observations regarding market research that are often made by entrepreneurs.

Get your hands dirty
Even if you do have the money to get others to carry out some of your market research, it is better to do at least part of it yourself. By interviewing, speaking with and observing potential customers, you get very important information about their behavior that can help you fine-tune and better sell your concept, both to the customer and to possible sources of finance.

Do your homework
Given the explosion in available information and various computerized techniques for accessing the information, there is no excuse for missing obvious sources of information. Information is available in the form of organized databases as well as on the internet. While it is critical to evaluate the relative importance, relevance and veracity of information gathered, be careful not to ignore or devalue information that contradicts your beliefs.

Focus on the quality rather than quantity of research
You must interview a sufficient number of people concerning your product and market ideas. However, do not just focus on the quantity of individuals you interview. Ask yourself about the quality of the information you are gathering.

Be prepared and flexible in undertaking research
Always be clear about what data you need to gather and whom you wish to speak with. At the same time, be prepared to change techniques (for example, move from surveys to focus groups) and to include others in the process as required. The research is a learning process. All along the way, you may receive information that points you in other directions and to other sources. Follow your instincts and be willing to probe as required.

Construct limited experiments
Often, one of the reasons an opportunity exists is that information is not readily available on it. If it were obvious, others would probably have pursued it. This means that you often have to generate new information. The best way to do this is to look for legitimate parallels (i.e. "someone did this in another industry and learned that ...") or construct experiments that generate new information. Experiments don't have to be large, expensive market research exercises, but since they have a cost, be clear about what you want to learn and be prepared to use the information.

Use an iterative approach
What this means is that you should plan to go out, collect information, return and reflect, and plan to go out again. Do not see your evaluation process as a single event that provides you with a "yes" or "no" answer. Reflection on what you are learning is key.

Even if you are excited, do not lead the witness
One problem entrepreneurs sometimes get trapped by is that they cross the

boundary between testing their ideas with potential customers and selling their idea. You want honest evaluation. If you signal that you are interested only in getting people to accept what you are saying, you will be defeated in your evaluation. You may get positive results but they will be meaningless.

Be prepared to change the product or service

Part of not trying to sell your ideas is that you must be open-minded about the possibility of modifying your product or service. Test alternative combinations of features in the market. Part of the iterative process is that you may modify the product or service during the course of the market research and evaluation.

Do not get frustrated at the lack of data

Do not think of yourself as directly answering a question. You are assembling information to complete a puzzle. It is rare that you will find information directly affecting the evaluation of new opportunities. It should be more not less common that you do not find appropriate information directly impacting your opportunity. In the end, you just want to make sure that you are approximately – not exactly – correct and that you have big margins for error even if your forecast is a little off.

Realize that you also learn after initial introduction

The actual product introduction process is also an opportunity for evaluating opportunity. You should prepare methods of collecting information around the introduction so that you can make quick adjustments that will maximize your potential for success.

The parsimonious path to profit

Rita Gunther McGrath explains how and why entrepreneurs pursue opportunity at the lowest possible cost.

The entrepreneur had a problem. He needed several thousand color advertising brochures in time for a crucial trade show. The best price quote so far had been around $1,500 but even this sum would challenge his already pressured bank account. What was he to do?

The answer eventually presented itself in the form of a forklift truck. Our entrepreneur's uncle, who ran a small manufacturing operation located in an industrial park, possessed a forklift. It also seems that a modest printing company located at the same site did not have a forklift and was in the habit of borrowing the uncle's now and again. A few telephone calls later and our entrepreneur had his brochures, without the daunting price tag.

This story reflects three fundamental habits of successful entrepreneurs. First, a strict discipline of asset parsimony. Second, use of all the resources at the entrepreneur's disposal, in particular social capital. And finally, an approach to making investments of time and money that is analogous to the taking and exercising of financial options.

Asset parsimony

Most start-ups are chronically short of resources. So it is not surprising that entrepreneurs attempt to contain costs. Those of us who study entrepreneurship, however, observe that using the minimum possible amount of assets to deliver their outputs is not something that entrepreneurs do only under situations of cash starvation.

We see even very wealthy entrepreneurs adhere to the same stingy ways with which they began their careers. It seems that being conservative with expenditures is not merely dictated by the situation; it is an overriding philosophy regarding the creative use of assets that permeates the successful start-up.

Consider the case of one of our recent graduates, who decided to get into the import/export business, trading from New York to his native Brazil. The first difficulty was that, being new to the business, it would be difficult to create credibility in the minds of potential customers. Using his small New York City apartment as a base, for example, was unlikely to instill a great sense of confidence in people who would have to entrust him with considerable advance business if he was to succeed. Clearly, a reputable office address seemed called for.

He could of course have simply taken a lease on such a space or rented shared space in one of those multiple-business complexes that have sprung up to serve exactly this kind of need. Doing so, however, violates one of the cardinal rules of asset parsimony: never incur fixed costs if they can be avoided.

How, then, to avoid incurring fixed costs on New York City real estate? The answer appeared in the form of an old schoolfriend from Columbia days with an extremely fashionable Fifth Avenue address. The friend eventually agreed to let our entrepreneur borrow an unused desk and receive mail at his address. Within a month, this was extended to include access to telephone and fax equipment, delivery vans and secretarial support – all paid for but on a strictly variable basis. What is interesting about this arrangement is that both parties benefitted. The entrepreneur acquired a valuable location and his host was paid for underutilized fixed assets.

Where the conventional corporate approach is often oriented toward maximizing returns on a net present value basis, entrepreneurs willingly sacrifice some potential returns in order to minimize fixed investments and maximize flexibility. This has the effect of limiting their exposure if the venture does not succeed as expected.

Successful entrepreneurs show genius at unlocking value tied up in underutilized assets. Renting computer time at night, laboratory equipment during the weekend and access to databases already owned are examples of how entrepreneurs, simply by being flexible enough to work when others aren't, can obtain access to resources at a fraction of what it would otherwise cost.

Successful entrepreneurs are also expert scavengers. Every day, corporations literally throw away valuable assets. One of my favorite stories in this regard is told by Ed Moldt, a former colleague at the Wharton School of the University of

Pennsylvania. At a time when the state of the art in computers was switching from card-read data input and storage to tape-based technology, companies began to aggressively shut down their card-reading operations and throw away the equipment. So anxious were many to get the readers off the premises that not only were they not sold, good money was actually paid to have them removed.

In the midst of all this, Moldt recognized that the conversion from cards was unlikely to be complete and that even the companies making the leap to tape technology were likely to have a need for some card-reading for several years still to come. He then began quietly acquiring card-reading equipment. As he hoped, the need for card-reading had not been eliminated but there were few suppliers left with capacity to do the work, leaving him in possession of a near-monopoly. This is surely a case of asset parsimony taken to the extreme – not only did he not expend capital to acquire his assets, he was actually paid to take them on.

The same philosophy that applies to the use of physical assets can be seen in the entrepreneurial use of human talent as well. Sales people, for example, will often be generously paid but on a commission basis, not a salaried one. Rather than use high-priced consultants to do market studies or develop proposals, entrepreneurs might call on friends or family, or volunteer to sponsor a student project. In these cases, the basic idea is to bring cash flows in before allowing major expenditure.

The moral of the asset parsimony tale is one coined by Ian MacMillan, Director of Wharton's acclaimed Snider Entrepreneurial Center, some years ago:

- Never buy new what can be bought second-hand.
- Never buy what can be rented.
- Never rent what can be borrowed.
- Never borrow what can be begged.
- Never beg what can be salvaged.

Social capital

Together with being choosy about how they invest their money, successful entrepreneurs are brilliant at leveraging social capital into valuable opportunities. They tend to be inveterate, energetic and continuous networkers.

Consider the approach to opportunity spotting utilized by Per Lovgren, a Swedish founder of many companies, based on his knowledge of sophisticated CAD/CAM technology. The worst return on investment Lovgren has ever enjoyed is in excess of 500 percent, to give the reader a sense of the power of his approach.

Lovgren travels extensively and on his travels frequently arranges social evenings with members of his network of management consultant acquaintances. While he is quite happy to pick up the bill for an evening's entertainment, the consultant will be pressed to articulate a problem that his clients are facing that requires a technical solution.

One problem that surfaced on such an occasion was the labor difficulties being experienced by foundry owners in Northern Europe. Foundries are dirty, hot, uncomfortable places to work in and finding labor willing to endure these conditions was becoming increasingly difficult. While a logical alternative would be to automate as far as possible, explained the management consultant, robots don't do well in the foundry environment either. The grit, dust and heat bring their mechanical control systems to a halt in short order.

Lovgren then set out to find whether something like a "robust robot" was technologically viable. He tapped into a second network, this time of professors of engineering. Over breakfast, the professor evaluated the problem, declared the technology to be a non-issue and offered to make a prototype for a budget of something like $300,000. At this juncture, Lovgren could easily have written a personal check and gotten the project under way. But wait – that would have violated the philosophy of asset parsimony.

What he did instead was to use his management consultant network to obtain access to their companies' foundry consultants. Using these contacts, he was able to convince foundry managers to each contribute a small sum to the development of the prototype. Note that not only did this allow him to proceed without investing his own money but it also ensured ready acceptance of the first prototypes and subsequent installation of the final product in a critical mass of foundries.

Memberships in networks, in other words, creates a form of "social" capital which, much like economic capital, can be used to create productive assets.

The options approach

A final observation about entrepreneurial resource acquisition strategies is that they can be likened to the taking and exercising of options. In financial economics, options contracts represent small investments made against an underlying asset that yields the opportunity, but not the obligation, to purchase that asset at a later date. Options thus provide access to opportunities at relatively low cost.

In pursuing their business opportunities, successful entrepreneurs adopt a similar pattern of investment. By building social capital, they begin to lay the foundation for gathering the information, and ultimately insight, that generates new business opportunities. They can then mobilize their networks to acquire resources at minimum cost and subsequently validate their initial assumptions.

This has the effect in real terms of making incrementally more significant commitments to the business as better and better data are revealed. Should the indicators at any point suggest that the business is not viable, the entrepreneur can simply stop pursuing it or redirect attention into other areas without having incurred huge losses in plant and assets.

The options logic allows us to pinpoint how asset parsimony and social capital help create wealth. If assets are acquired sequentially, with minimum possible investment, they limit the downside losses in the event of failure, just as financial options do. By deftly mobilizing their social capital through unique information and friendship networks, entrepreneurs can eliminate uncertainty as to the value of the underlying business in ways that are idiosyncratic to them.

Thus, only someone with Lovgren's access simultaneously to those who could identify the source of the problem (the management consultant), those who could define the technical solution (the engineering professor) and those who could provide financing (the foundry managers) is likely to have started this particular business. Only someone with Lovgren's skill at maintaining rock-bottom investment amounts would enjoy his level of substantial returns on equity. This has the effect of allowing him to build a substantial business from an ordinary-looking labor problem while at the same time preventing competitors from simply copying what he was able to do.

In sum, we see in successful entrepreneurs not so much sudden flashes of inspiration and great good fortune as a consistent set of conscientiously applied disciplines that ensure the minimum possible investment for the maximum possible returns.

The discussion presented here has benefitted enormously from conversations with Ian C. MacMillan of the Wharton School of the University of Pennsylvania and Sue Birley of Imperial College, London.

Catching the punter's eye

Peter Kelly details the criteria venture capitalists and private investors set when they are considering whether or not to risk their cash.

"There is no question that irrespective of the horse (the product), horse race (the market), or odds (financial criteria), it is the jockey (the entrepreneur) who fundamentally determines whether the venture capitalist will place a bet at all."
Professor Ian MacMillan, Wharton School of the University of Pennsylvania

Any experienced "punter" will tell you that there are two fundamental facts of life in trying to predict the outcome of any race. First, it is a simple truth that the future cannot be predicted with accuracy. Second, there is inevitably an element of luck involved in "picking winners."

Having said this, before placing a bet, experienced punters often gather as much information as possible on the condition of the horse, the track and the jockey in the hope that the additional insights will enhance their ability to overcome these given facts.

This horse racing analogy applies equally to the world of the venture capitalist. Any experienced "investor" will tell you that there are two fundamental "facts of life" when trying to determine which ventures to back. First, the only thing that is known for certain is that the projections upon which an investment decision is based are "wrong." Investors and entrepreneurs alike hope that the venture's performance will exceed projections. However, in reality, Murphy's Law often holds true – whatever the problems encountered along the way may be, the venture inevitably takes longer to develop than planned. Second, timing and luck can, and do, influence the level of returns achieved by investors.

Venture capitalists make "informed bets" on the basis of information presented to them in a business plan that outlines the nature of the opportunity, the strategy developed to exploit it profitably and on a sustainable basis, and the credentials of the management team that is going to "make it happen."

In the course of due diligence, investors will seek out additional information to satisfy themselves that:

■ all elements of the plan "hang together"

- relevant risks have been identified and accounted for whenever possible
- prospective returns offered adequately compensate for the risk being borne by the investor and entrepreneur alike and, most importantly
- the management team has the skills, drive and ambition to succeed, particularly in the face of the inevitable pitfalls associated with building and managing a business.

Investors work under the presumption that through gathering additional information and insights, their ability to identify "winners" is enhanced. For an entrepreneur seeking external equity from either venture capitalists or private individuals (so-called "business angels"), it is important to understand the various criteria investors use to evaluate potential investment opportunities.

In many ways, investors are like the Yukon panhandlers of the gold rush days. Panhandlers spent a great deal of time and energy sifting through silt and gravel in search of gold nuggets. Likewise, investors sift through a great number of opportunities to identify those of truly high potential that are worthy of further detailed consideration. A vast majority of proposals, typically 80 percent or more, are rejected after a cursory review of the business plan. When an investor chooses to review a proposal in greater detail, relatively few are actually funded. For every 100 proposals received, perhaps two or three receive backing.

How do investors decide which proposals to back? Venture capitalists and private investors tend to rely on similar decision-making processes in determining which proposals to support. The two markets are in many ways distinct, however, and thus it is useful to discuss the approach of each separately. (The private investment market – so-called "business angels" – is discussed in detail in Part 3 – see p. 110.)

The venture capital perspective

Generally speaking, venture capital funds screen proposals on the basis of a number of generic criteria including: a) the minimum size of the investment they are willing to consider (usually over £1 million); b) the industries that they are prepared to back; c) the stage of development of the business (seed, start-up, expansion); and d) the geographical focus of the venture's operations.

It is important for entrepreneurs seeking venture capital to identify the "right" venture capitalist(s) to approach by ensuring, as far as possible, that their proposal "fits with" the investor's profile. Fortunately for entrepreneurs, venture capital associations in many countries publish comprehensive annual directories that provide contact and fund-specific information to aid the search process.

There has been a marked shift in the industry away from the provision of small amounts of capital (less than £500,000) to ventures in early stages of development to the financing of larger, later-stage management buy-in and buy-out transactions. Having said this, a small number of funds do focus exclusively on small, early-stage deals, and other major market participants, most notably 3i (Investors in Industry) in the UK, continue to invest in these situations.

The message for entrepreneurs seeking relatively modest infusions of capital to finance early-stage development is that it is not impossible to secure venture capital funding but it is highly improbable.

Assuming for the moment that your proposal meets the fund's general screening criteria, venture capital companies are still left with the daunting task of separating the "wheat from the chaff." At this stage of the process, the business plan is briefly reviewed by a fund manager with the aim of forming an opinion on certain key aspects of the plan including:

- the nature of the opportunity
- the potential size of the market
- the strategy proposed to exploit it.

If the investor is not satisfied that the opportunity is in fact "real," that the market growth projections are unrealistic and/or that there is no meaningful basis upon which to create a sustainable and profitable competitive position, the proposal is likely to be rejected.

Simply put, investors will focus their efforts on those few plans that fit their investment criteria, are well thought out and offer the prospect of achieving compound annual returns on investment ranging from 30 percent for management buy-outs to 50 percent or more per annum for early-stage investments.

In the minority of situations where a more detailed investigation is warranted, venture capitalists will invest a great deal of time consulting with internal and external sources of objective information about key aspects of the plan. They will talk to potential customers, suppliers, patent lawyers, technology experts and the like. They will also test out the financial viability of the plan by conducting a sensitivity analysis on the assumptions upon which the plan is based.

During this due diligence phase, the "management capability factor" takes on added importance. Regular meetings are arranged between fund representatives and members of the management team. Aside from being able to question specific aspects of the plan presented to them, through regular interaction with the management team, investors are able to gain a better understanding of the team's true capabilities, their ability to work together as a team, and their commitment to the venture.

Testing management resolve to deal with the inevitable setbacks and challenges associated with building a business is often a decisive factor in the final decision to invest. Additional information obtained in the course of due diligence narrows the opportunity set down even further.

The private investor perspective

Private investors rely on a similar process in deciding which proposals to back. However, unlike venture capital funds, which maintain a highly visible, public presence, private individuals prefer a degree of anonymity, both as a means of controlling the volume of their deal flow and of protecting sensitive personal information pertaining to their private investment activity.

Approaching the "right" individual investor is inevitably a hit-or-miss affair for ventures seeking private equity. From our discussions with private investors, potential investment opportunities are screened on the basis of size, location, and venture needs. In general, private individuals invest:

- in smaller amounts than do venture capital funds (usually between £5,000 and £500,000)
- in ventures that are located in close proximity to their home base of operations
- in situations, often, where the business can directly benefit from the expertise of the investor.

Most private investors have managerial experience in the area of the new venture and are prepared to back promising proposals in a variety of industries, particularly if they choose to invest as part of a syndicate of investors. Entrepreneurs seeking private equity need to be very clear about what contribution they want the investor to make and are well advised to seek out potential investors located in close proximity to their operation.

As the process unfolds, the quality of the entrepreneur/management team becomes an increasingly important consideration. Working as closely as they do with the venture, the personal chemistry developed between the investor and the management team is an absolutely vital consideration. In the words of one investor: "No matter how good the opportunity appears, if I cannot get on with the people, there is *no* deal!"

Advice for entrepreneurs

What is the point of investing the time and resources into developing a business plan if there is only a 2 percent or 3 percent chance that the entrepreneur will be successful in raising funds?

In my experience, a great many business plans fail to pass an initial screen for a number of reasons, some of which can be easily dealt with, others less so. (A checklist of the main issues that need to be covered in a business plan appears in Part 4, p. 155.)

In some cases, it is not altogether clear to the investor what the nature of the opportunity is or, for that matter, how much capital is required and for what purpose. There should be no doubt in the mind of the investor "what" they are being asked to fund. This information should be conveyed in the executive summary of the plan in clear and unambiguous terms.

The real challenge for entrepreneurs is to prepare a plan that "captures the investor's imagination." Business plans are marketing documents – the messages conveyed should encourage the reader to "continue reading."

Many entrepreneurs I have met are passionate believers in their idea or concept. Enthusiasm creates excitement and interest on the part of investors but, when taken to an extreme, passion often gets translated by entrepreneurs in their business plans as "preaching the upside" and "ignoring the downside." In my experience, investors want "a balanced view," assuring themselves in the process that the entrepreneurs:

■ know what they are talking about
■ have identified and considered potential risks from their perspective
■ are committed to seeing the project through.

But a clearly articulated and convincing business plan alone is not enough. The plan must be carefully targetted to the appropriate audience. In guiding their decision to seek venture capital or, alternatively, equity from private individuals, entrepreneurs should address the following questions. Is the amount of capital required large enough to be of interest to venture capital funds? If so, which funds have a stated preference for investing in ventures operating in my industry and/or at my venture's stage of development? If not, do I have a clear idea of what type of expertise and involvement I am seeking from a private investor?

These guidelines are little consolation for the many business plans that fail to secure funding for no other reason than that the two parties hold irreconcilable differences of opinion – situations where the entrepreneur sees an opportunity and the investor does not. In this respect, one can only conclude that opportunity is, indeed, in the "eye of the beholder."

Copyright © Peter Kelly 1997

How to build a strong launch pad

Traditional market entry strategies adopted by large corporations are increasingly unsuitable for today's turbulent times. In this respect, new ventures have some advantages. **David Molian** sets out the position and offers some appropriate new venture strategies.

"Is launching new products harder or easier today than it was ten or twenty years ago?" Ask this question of a brand manager in a large consumer goods company and almost certainly the response will be "harder."

Look for the reasons why, and the usual suspects emerge: intensified competition; consumers who are both more value conscious and less brand loyal; dwindling product lifecycles; and increasingly powerful retailers.

Estimates vary for the rate at which new products fail in the marketplace but the consensus seems to be that most new products in most markets will fall by the wayside. In some industries, such as the software business in the 1980s, the failure rate can be as high as 90 percent. The problem is compounded by the increasing pressure to innovate, partly as a result of fast-changing consumer tastes and behavior and partly because of the possibilities arising from enhanced or novel technologies.

In the case of established brands, managers search for ways to exploit the "equity," or market strength, of a brand through product variants (the mini and maxi chocolate Mars bars, for example) or via diversifications into adjacent segments (Mars milk drinks and Mars ice cream). New products that come to market without a parent brand must make their own way in a world that, if not actively hostile, is usually indifferent.

If market conditions are tough for established organizations, how much more difficult the environment must be for the new venture, especially the start-up. Well, yes and no. Compared with existing businesses, the typical new venture has fewer resources of every kind, fragile or embryonic networks, and a need to build trust and credibility among both customers and suppliers. It carries more inherent risks. Yet it also possesses certain intangible assets that do not appear on the balance sheet.

Speed, or the ability to adapt rapidly, and a capacity for flexibility are two of the more important ones. A management that is hungry is a third asset. And *not* being burdened by the weight of corporate history may well be a fourth.

The management of risk

One of the major themes of *Mastering Entrepreneurship* is the management of risk. How exactly to get into business is frequently one of the major areas of uncertainty in most new ventures. To highlight the options faced by a new venture, it is worth examining how large businesses have traditionally managed the risks associated with entry into new markets or taking new products to market.

For big business, geographical expansion typically followed a pattern: first, importing agencies were used; then, as demand was established, a subsidiary was created or purchased. The overseas businesses would expand through the transfer of product and process technology from the parent as and when the market was ready.

New product introduction, or entry into new market sectors, also followed clear guidelines. Large consumer companies were interested in products with mass market potential, not niche items. The planning, testing and introduction cycle was an extensive one, supported through qualitative and quantitative market research, with the decision to launch normally dependent on a successful "test market," from which national market performance could be predicted. Finally, if the project was sanctioned, large resources in terms of advertising, salesforce and marketing support were committed to minimize the risk of failure.

Not surprisingly, the time between product concept and full-scale launch could be measured in many months if not years. This was acceptable in a stable environment of steadily rising, predictable consumer demand in which all the players played by the same rules – a description that fits the quarter century that followed the Second World War.

Today, relatively few markets (in the developed world at least) conform to that description. Markets that are growing are frequently turbulent and hard to forecast. Those markets that are static – such as mature commodity sectors like soap powder or mass cosmetics – may contain a few pockets of niche activity but are generally a battleground in which a few dominant competitors wrestle each other for an extra quarter percent of market share.

The rules have changed

The upshot of all this is that big business has had to rethink radically its approach to innovation and new product launches. Extended periods of commercialization, where an innovation is handed from research to development to marketing like a baton in a relay race, are just too long. In too many markets the window of opportunity is lost. Yet trying to compress that time to market can create its own risks, as Unilever's experience with Omo Power (Persil in the UK) shows.

In addition, confidence and certainty of success can no longer be attained in the same way. Firepower is no guarantee of victory. IBM's PC Jr and Kodak's Disk Camera are just two examples of failed new product launches supported by hundreds of millions of dollars.

The value chain and opportunity

In turbulent times, market risk is closely tied to the dynamics of the supply or value chain. Within any industry there is a sequence of transactions that takes place between the raw materials producers and the final consumers. This may be complex, as with most manufacturing activities, or it may be simple, as is generally the case with services.

To succeed, the new venture must create value for which a customer is prepared to pay. In each stage of the chain, value is added, the profitability and relative power within the chain varying for each player. The market entry decision is closely related to the position within the value chain that the new venture adopts.

In dynamic markets, opportunity can be seen as the outcome of *changes within* the value chain or the *capacity to create change within* the value chain. Consider two examples. First, the groceries sector. In the UK 30 years ago, creating and sustaining a national grocery brand meant conforming to a certain set of criteria. The manufacturer had to be able to deliver to thousands of small retailers nationwide and to handle the associated invoicing and account management. It also had to create and support national advertising campaigns backed by point-of-sale promotions or neighborhood coupon drops.

Large companies tackled the problem by integrating their activities right along the value or supply chain: from agreeing long-term contracts with suppliers to running fleets of trucks and delivery vans and maintaining a national network of regional and local delivery depots. Smaller organizations used intermediaries such as wholesalers and brokers, which could achieve economies of scale through aggregating product lines and breaking bulk further down the supply chain.

Fast forward to the present day. A small grocery producer can achieve nationwide penetration through supplying just a single big retail account. Delivery can be contracted out and is usually restricted to a handful of large drops each week at the customer's central warehouses. And building brands through million-pound advertising campaigns is not an issue since the retailer is marketing the product under its own label (*see* Figures 1 and 2 for examples of changing value/supply chains).

This transformation has taken place, of course, because of the change in the balance of power between the manufacturer and the retailer in the UK as the grocery trade has become concentrated in the hands of the multiples. Established branded-goods producers see themselves under threat and point to diminishing consumer choice.

But the other side of the equation is that opportunities have been created for literally hundreds of new suppliers to gain entry into the market because the value chain has been transformed. Indeed, certain expanding groceries sectors, such as ethnic foods, are dominated by such enterprises.

The second example illustrates how enterprising new businesses create market opportunities using the potential brought about by shifting social behavior. Mail order has its roots in the 19th century. In the UK, it became primarily a mechanism for providing the poorer classes with cheap credit for clothing. Up until the late 1980s, mail order expenditure by the wealthier ABC1 socio-economic groups remained disproportionately tiny. Then something happened. The middle classes became comfortable with the idea of buying from a catalog.

Large US companies, such as Land's End and LL Bean, began to operate in the UK. Traditional catalog specialists moved up-market and new ventures, such as Cotton Traders, Racing Green and Boden, rapidly carved niches for themselves. This change in social attitudes had lowered the barriers to entry: such companies could get into retailing without tying up their working capital in a high-street presence.

Figure 1: Changing the balance of power in the supply chain

Figure 2: Reconfiguring the value chain: the high street print shop

Risk sharing versus market access

The value chain and risk management can be usefully brought together as a two-dimensional framework in which to view market entry strategy. Given that each new venture occupies a position somewhere in a value chain, a choice has to be made as to how much of the marketing risk the new venture assumes, and how much is in some form shared by other players in the chain.

For all ventures there is a spectrum of risk sharing. At one end are businesses such as biotechnology laboratories whose discoveries are normally licensed to large pharmaceutical houses for downstream exploitation in new drugs. Like an author, this kind of company lives on a royalty income generated by its intellectual property, while the risk of taking the discovery to market is very largely borne by the counterparty.

At the other end of the spectrum are organizations that sell direct to the market, which position themselves in the final section of the value chain, such as catalog retailers. Between the two extremes lies a huge variety of risk-sharing arrangements, covering agencies, wholesaling, franchising, subcontracting, and so on.

The second dimension is access to the market, which also runs along a spectrum from the immediate relationship with the end customer enjoyed by the direct sales company to the very remote connection of the biotechnologist.

As Figure 3 shows, there is typically an inverse relationship between a high degree of risk sharing and access to the market. Note that we are not talking here of *absolute* risk: if the essence of an opportunity is a company's capacity to react swiftly to customer demand, as in the fashion business, assuming the entire marketing risk may well be less dangerous than laying off that risk via a counterparty through whom contact with the customer is filtered. Conversely, if a direct line to the ultimate buyer is of no importance in the business concept, selling direct is unlikely to make much sense.

Equally, we are describing *entry strategies* rather than the long-term shape that a business assumes. It is hard to envisage how an organization could employ business format franchising (for example, instant printing) as a means of getting into business, since the concept has to be tested and made to work before it can be replicated. Franchising is a very effective means of expanding certain kinds of business more rapidly than through organic growth or acquisition. On the other hand, from the perspective of a franchisee, purchasing a franchise can be a very appropriate method of using risk sharing to get into business.

Figure 3

Prototyping and flexibility

Selecting the appropriate risk-sharing arrangement is a *strategic* decision. Marketing risk can also be managed *operationally* by consideration of the process by which a new venture is brought to market.

It was observed earlier that traditional large organization approaches to the innovation process can be too protracted and cumbersome a way of responding to market changes and, in any case, the typical new venture does not have the resources to emulate this process. There is, however, a very important element of good innovation practice that the new venture should focus on, namely the notion of *prototyping*. The term comes from large engineering projects but it has application to all sorts of new ventures. A restaurant business can be prototyped – that is in a format that is acknowledged (by the management at least) as provisional, to be modified in response to market reaction. So can a service.

This concept is valuable for the following reasons:

- Prototyping is a means of containing risk through limiting the commitment of resources. This is especially critical in markets of great uncertainty, such as high-technology sectors, where customer demand or market potential cannot be known or even guestimated in advance of entry.
- Prototyping allows the new venture to test the robustness of the product or service concept, often through giving target customers access in advance of the launch. This is common practice in the software industry, where new software is routinely tested by selected customers (who benefit from privileged access) prior to full release. One of the UK's premier health and fitness clubs adapted this approach. While the club was still under construction, local residents were mailed invitations to tour the site. Those who accepted were shown the plans for the final design and invited to comment, with the result that a number of suggestions were incorporated while it was still possible to do so. The club also, it need hardly be said, acquired a useful database of prospective members.
- Prototyping fosters a mentality of flexibility and responsiveness to customers. Some new ventures start with the advantage of an advance order book. The first wave of customers may represent the core clientele of the business in the medium and even the long term. The first product or service may constitute the main business activity. Equally, neither condition may apply, and within a short space of time the business may be looking both for new customers *and* new products if it is to grow and prosper.
- In many new venture environments, conventional market research methods may not apply. The costs alone of a professional research agency are often prohibitive. But an even greater obstacle may lie in the product/service concept. Where demand is latent (or believed to be latent), the only way to prove it exists is to test the market by offering an early version of the concept in the full knowledge that it may change as a result of customer exposure.

Incremental commercialization

Hand in hand with prototyping goes the notion of incremental commercialization. Traditional modes of innovation are based on a clear separation between development and launch – at a certain point development was frozen and the finished product entered the market.

Clearly, in a manufacturing business (unless it is making bespoke products), a time is reached when mass production to a specification must start. However, even the established approach to new product development includes an element of incremental commercialization in the form of test markets, which allow a company to modify the product either in its physical form or in the way in which it is marketed before a full launch.

For many new ventures, attempting to keep development and launch as distinct processes is inappropriate. For one thing, in line with the rest of the economy, most new ventures today will be service-based at least as much as product-based. Marketing doctrine states that the way to sell a service is to make it, as much as possible, into a product. But the beauty of a service-based business is the speed and flexibility with which the service can be modified in response to the market. At the point of entering the market, the new venture needs to exploit that inherent advantage and avoid undue rigidity in advance of feedback from customers.

A further consideration is that in many sectors the boundaries between research, development and launch are fuzzy because of the nature of the business. Take software, which is a product category in continuous evolution. The point at which a piece of software is "finished" is, in a real sense, arbitrary. Customers are purchasing not a one-off product but a stream of upgrades and new versions, which arrive at ever-shortening intervals.

Summary

A management team should bring to the market entry decision the same skills that characterize the successful entrepreneur – the capacity to determine where in the marketplace the opportunity lies; the ability to work with that opportunity and shape it in response to customers' needs; the feel for managing risk to acceptable levels through the use of partners or suitable intermediaries; and, above all, the ability to smooth the path into the market through the limited exposure offered through techniques such as prototyping and incremental commercialization.

Marking the key points on the opportunity map

Daniel Muzyka provides guidance on what makes a good opportunity.

The name of the game in entrepreneurship is adding value. This includes value added for all parties, especially for the business pursuing the opportunity. The product must add clear value in the eyes of the customer, and distributors and retailers, if they are involved.

How do we measure value added in real terms? The rule of thumb shared by venture capitalists and other risk capital investors is that you should have a gross margin of 35–40 percent or better. This means that in the financial evaluation of an opportunity, the turnover, less the direct cost of labor and materials to produce a product or deliver a service, should produce a number that is at least 40 percent of the turnover. This is the real value added of your product.

Why does this matter? Well, it is obvious that a higher gross margin translates into a higher potential "bottom line." Furthermore, gross margin indicates how much value is being added by unique intellectual, design and marketing resources. If not much value is being added, why do it? Without this value added, you are taking on a significant risk while not creating much, despite the hard entrepreneurial work of assembling people and assets that the opportunity requires.

The magnitude of the opportunity

How big does an opportunity have to be? This question is a little akin to asking how many angels can dance on the head of a pin. The more serious, and right, answer is: "It depends."

It depends on the magnitude of value you wish to create and that will attract and retain your interest. It depends on the size of opportunity that will attract investors who are of interest to you. (Risk capital investors usually have a minimum value in mind.) It depends on the value that is required for you to position yourself in the market to be an effective and growing competitor. It depends on that famous economic factor "minimum efficient scale" – how big do you have to be to be efficient in the use of required assets? And it depends on the magnitude of the business necessary to attract the key team members you require to make the business successful.

Growth-oriented entrepreneurs do not only consider the magnitude of the opportunity but also the basic expected growth rate. True growth-oriented entrepreneurs are very focussed on the potential growth rate. Some realize that too fast a growth rate over an extended period is a negative aspect of opportunities. It is difficult to manage, it attracts competitors like ants at a picnic, and it requires extensive and continuous financing to provide adequate working capital. They also realize that too low a growth rate will not permit them to create their desired value and will not attract key stakeholders.

What are the required growth rates? This varies considerably and obviously depends on the context. However, we can generally say that sustained single digits are too low and sustained triple digits are very difficult. Obviously, this question also depends on just how big a business you want to build. A "lifestyle" opportunity probably should not grow too big.

Another consideration on scale and growth rate relates to whether an opportunity represents a "winner-take-all" situation. In some environments, such as certain markets on the internet, there is not likely to be an opportunity for several competitors to be profitable. This can be the natural consequence of brand recognition, supply contracts, the need for standards and/or restrictions in distribution. Growth rates and the ability to scale up rapidly may be required in this environment in order to close down avenues for competitors to gain the upper hand.

Business economics

In this context this simply means profit. There are two important issues for the would-be entrepreneur: how much profit and where exactly is the profit created? If a business does not add enough value, you cannot have a reasonable profit. Beyond this, the question is: where in the income statement and balance sheet do you create value? How do you make money? Where does the profit come from?

You need to know the key levers in the business that make money for you. You also need to know whether these levers are sustainable. For example, do you make money because you are able to move quickly to supply shops with bread when they under-ordered from their regular suppliers (who visit them once a day only) and their customers are demanding more?

The ability to move quickly and fill spot demand (at a premium price, of course) may be the basis of the business. Understanding these levers makes you understand what your focus should be in managing the business and permits you to test whether it is sustainable and appropriate for you.

One business I knew had a tendency to upgrade every neighborhood it entered. The business itself made a solid though not terribly exciting profit. The entrepreneur would go in, buy a property in which the business was located, upgrade it, start up business and later sell out to a franchise. Other businesses were attracted to the area and would also contribute to upgrading the area. When an evaluation of the worth of the property was made for sale to the franchisee, the entrepreneur would invariably make a large capital gain.

Where did he make his money? In the real estate conversion. He was clear on where he was dedicating his time and energy. He didn't fritter away time on trying to squeeze major improvements in the profitability of the underlying shop. Rather, he would move on to look for new locations.

One of the more interesting phenomena in measuring business value has to do with valuations of unprofitable e-commerce businesses. Valuations are apparently based on very high expectations of future earnings rather than near-term breakeven or profitability. Some entrepreneurial start-ups have maintained very high valuations for years after initial public offering (IPO) without any sign of profitability. While this is an interesting phenomenon today, I would caution entrepreneurs to be conscious of the need to achieve profitability in some reasonable horizon, even if the stock market is fixated on attaching a high premium to the possibility of future earnings.

How long can you pursue the opportunity?

No opportunity lasts for ever. In fact, I encourage you to contact me if you find a highly profitable (legal) opportunity that lasts for ever. First, I might like to invest. Second, I would like to record it so that others would know it. The real question is how long does an opportunity last before everyone else decides to jump in and shift competition to a cost base rather than value base, or worse?

What are the determinants of how long you can uniquely pursue an opportunity? First, do you have some contract that makes a technology uniquely available to you? It may not be a technology that you have unique control of but, rather, a unique source of supply or a unique distribution channel. Second, are you addressing some niche opportunity that substitutes for existing products or provides a strong but unique base for development? Customers whose needs you specifically meet represent a powerful source of competitive advantage. Third, do you have some unique relationship that provides you with a competitive advantage? Fourth, do you have some way of creating "post-entry barriers" (something someone has to spend money on to overcome) for other organizations that follow you into the business?

Your fit and belief in the opportunity

It is often the more emotional side of any opportunity that makes that marginal difference in the success of one entrepreneur and the failure of another. You alone can assess these factors. Do you like the opportunity? Do you really believe in the opportunity? These factors matter because therein lies your level of likely persistence in the face of all the normal difficulties encountered by entrepreneurs.

What are some of the finer aspects of good opportunities?

There are a few lessons about opportunity that long-term successful entrepreneurs have learned.

- **This opportunity leads to others.** To build up a profitable, value-creating business in the long term, an original opportunity must lead to other opportunities. In terms used in finance, an opportunity that creates options on future opportunity has more value.
- **The opportunity helps you build leverageable skills.** Another characteristic of a good opportunity is related to the skills developed and exercised within the organization. Good opportunities are those that force an organization to develop a skill that can be leveraged for the pursuit of many new ideas.
- **Opportunity should not be evaluated or pursued alone.** Investigations of "serial entrepreneurs" and how they identify successive successful opportunities suggests that the saying "two heads are better than one" may be true. Successful serial entrepreneurs usually seek out other individuals with whom they work from business to business. The partner adds new skills to the mix and permits a more robust evaluation and implementation of opportunities.

The final points you may wish to consider encourage you to review the competitive environment and how you compete.

- **Are near competitors "sharks"?** There are some opportunities that involve competition (or near competition) with companies and individuals that are not very aggressive. On the other hand, in some industries, existing competitors "eat their young." Look around and see if there are any new companies that have survived in the broad industry you are considering.
- **How you compete is more important than where you compete.** Worry about your model of competition and don't get fixated on the question of where you are going to compete. Searching for location is important, and needs to be undertaken, but only after you have assessed how you will compete and make money in your business.

The pitfalls and potential of franchising

Stephen Spinelli argues that as long as both sides contribute appropriately, franchising can be a key enterprise success story.

Is franchising entrepreneurship? Certainly, most people would agree that Ray Kroc, founder of the giant restaurant chain McDonald's, or Anita Roddick, The Body Shop founder, were entrepreneurs. But their companies are the franchisers, the owners of the trademark and system. What about the franchisees, those individuals who buy a franchise, implement the concept on a local basis, and serve customers? Are they entrepreneurs?

The answer to the question is based on more than linguistics. The central issue regards the ability of the franchisee to create wealth. Clearly, there are no guarantees of wealth when a new venture is founded. Return *and* risk are the balancing forces controlling the entrepreneurial process and therefore the potential of failure looms in any business start-up, balanced by the prospect of wealth. However, if the buyer of a franchise is simply purchasing employment, then a franchise is no more than an alternative to an employment agency.

Franchising and the economy

Franchising is a major part of the US economy and is substantial in the UK and other western European countries. More than one-third of all retailing in the US, worth over $750 billion annually, is generated through franchised outlets. Franchising accounts for as much as 10 percent of retailing in the UK, France and Australia.

Franchising is generally divided into product franchises and business format franchises. The product franchise is characterized by franchised dealers who concentrate on a company's product line and, to some extent, identify their business with that company. For example, an electronics retailer might carry a differently branded CD player. A car dealer selling one manufacturer's model straddles the line between a product and business format franchise. "Smithtown Ford" merges the franchisee and franchiser brands. The business format franchise accompanies the trademark and distribution rights with information provided by the franchiser to the franchisee on the production processes and delivery system. Business format franchising usually includes a marketing plan, documented and enforced policies and procedures, process assistance, and business development and innovation. This article concentrates on business format franchising.

The belief that franchising is an entrepreneurial venture is supported by the continued success of established franchise systems, the proliferation of new franchises and the profitability reported by franchisees. Recently we have seen an increasing number of multiple outlet franchisees. Some franchisees achieve both growth and diversification by operating multiple franchise concepts.

One of the largest franchisers in the world is UK conglomerate Allied Domecq, which owns Dunkin Donuts, Baskin Robbins and Togo's restaurants. Bob Rosenberg, son of Dunkin Donuts founder Bill Rosenberg, grew the Dunkin system from a few hundred to 3,000 outlets before being acquired by Allied Domecq. He continued to operate Allied Domecq's North American retail operation for ten years. "Allied Domecq's franchise operation can double in the US and the potential in Europe and Asia is exponential," he says.

Allied Domecq is not alone. More than 50 percent of members of the International Franchise Association (an association formed by franchisers) have international departments and 93 percent of those companies expect to increase international expansion. Research indicates that 22 percent of franchisees own more than one outlet. The Kwik Kopy group sees franchising and multiple store franchisees as a key aspect of the growth in entrepreneurship in Europe. The company argues that its franchise owners are with customers every day, focussing on their needs and sharing better ways to fill those needs with their fellow franchisee colleagues. "That is why franchising works. We are not interested in just growing, we want greater success."

Franchisees are becoming larger and more sophisticated. KFC (formerly Kentucky Fried Chicken) has granted franchise rights to Mitsubishi in Japan. In 1991, the European Commission approved a block exemption to anti-trust regulations so that franchisers may now sell in larger geographic territories, allowing franchisees to build a number of outlets.

Keeping the franchisee satisfied?

According to US franchise lawyer Eric Karp: "The relationship is evolving. There is clearly an understanding that building equity is an important aspect of the franchise purchase decision. That means the productive franchisee–franchiser relationship is a long-term strategic relationship that builds wealth for both parties. When franchisees can't do better than a salary, the relationship breaks down."

While the International Franchise Association claims a 95 percent success rate for franchisees, research at Imperial College, London[1] indicates that almost 30 percent of franchisees are dissatisfied (*see* Figure 1). Our research indicates high levels of self-reported profitability for franchisees. Clearly, profit is not the only measure of franchise system satisfaction; it may be more closely linked to the manner in which the relationship is conducted than to finance.

Most franchise contracts are long term (5–20 years). Generally, there is a delineation of responsibilities between the franchiser and the franchisee based on competitive advantages. Those centralized functions that carry economies of scale, such as the acquisition of supply and the creation and purchase of advertising, are

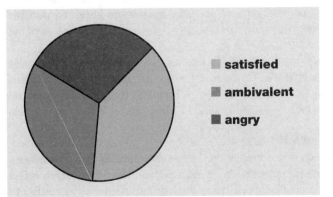

satisfied

ambivalent

angry

Figure 1

Service variable	Importance Mean	Adequacy Mean
Resolving disagreements fairly	4.47	3.02
Effective national advertising	4.46	3.10
Promoting new products & services	4.36	3.10
Developing new products & services	4.33	3.11
Clearly defined operating procedures	4.11	3.38
Market information & analysis	4.07	2.39
Programs & procedures for training employees	4.07	2.94
Access to franchiser management	3.99	3.35
Acting as a supplier of products	3.90	3.36
Training in management skills	3.90	2.58
Organizing local advertising cooperatives	3.77	2.40
Support in new store development	3.76	2.90
Advice on management problems	3.76	2.80
Financial assistance and credit	3.74	2.53
Training in accounting & bookkeeping	3.53	2.48
Advice on financial management	3.52	2.30
Provision of standardized equipment	3.49	3.31
Advice on inventory control	3.45	2.75

Figure 2: Franchiser service variables – importance versus adequacy

assigned to the franchiser. On-site implementation, including the acquisition and development of real estate, human resource management and local promotional effort, is left to the franchisee.

It is not surprising that our research finds most franchisees want more and better services from the franchiser. Figure 2 is a list of the key activities involved in the franchisee–franchiser relationship. Franchisees rank franchiser-provided services for importance and adequacy. We used a scale of 1 (clearly not important or clearly not inadequate) to 5 (most important or completely inadequate). Having conducted this survey with a number of companies in varying industries we see little variance in priorities.

More important in our research was defining which of these service "gaps" caused dissatisfaction in the relationship. Clearly the bundle of marketing functions (national advertising, promoting new products and services, marketing information and analysis and organizing local advertising co-operatives) are the most sensitive concerns for the franchisees. Good franchisers are good marketers in the view of the franchisees. In general, however, franchisees have a clear tolerance zone of acceptable franchiser behavior.

More recently, franchisees have voiced increasing concern about electronic encroachment of exclusive territories. Franchisers are experimenting with shared revenue schemes and creative delivery systems. However, the impact of the internet on franchising is far from settled.

What franchisees should look for

The franchise method of growth is predicated on the assumption that value has been developed through the careful operation, testing and documentation of a commercially viable concept. The essence of franchisee due diligence is to verify the ability of the franchise to create wealth through a business format and for that format to be transferred for local execution.

Prospective franchisees must answer two questions:

- Is risk sufficiently mitigated by the trademark value, operating system, economies of scale and support process of the franchiser to justify sharing equity with the franchiser (via the payment of an up-front franchise fee and on-going royalties)?
- Are personality and management style amenable to sharing decision-making responsibilities with the franchiser and other franchisees?

For those of a more quantitative nature: do the franchise fee and the present value of the royalty payments equal the increased net income from the value of the franchiser trademark? In other words, how many more hamburgers will I sell with the golden arch in front of my restaurant (and the systems and advertising that support the arch) than I would going it alone?

It appears that franchisees tend to be so consumed with start-up, survival and growth in the initial years of operation that building equity is only obliquely regarded as important. But around the seventh year of operation, their piece of brand value seems to take on greater importance. If the franchisee does not internalize the value of the franchise, there is a dramatic increase in dissatisfaction.

A new franchisee should be assured that the franchiser has the income stream and/or capitalization to provide the requisite support services. The list of franchiser-provided services in Figure 2 is an appropriate starting point. Once financial adequacy is proven, the franchisee must look for franchiser resource allocation comensurate with these priorities.

The chronology associated with store development establishes the critical path of service support. Starting with an intimate understanding of the primary target audience, there must be a specifically documented guideline for acquiring (through lease or purchase) an outlet location that allows the franchisee to reach the customer. Then, the franchiser must provide a blueprint to guide the construction and fitting-out process. While the facility is being built, the business format must be taught to the franchisee. Therefore, a training mechanism must be in place.

The methods of training and the level of sophistication among franchisers vary dramatically. This is an extremely important issue. Without effective training the business format cannot be implemented effectively. This extends beyond the franchisees to the franchise staff. The franchisee often becomes the trainer for his or her staff. Long hours are a reality in most entrepreneurial ventures. But poor training schemes may cause a franchisee to spend inordinate time and effort trying to maintain execution quality, draining resources from growth.

The international dimension

A common problem with franchising in Europe is that a trademarked system is "imported" from the US with little attention to the small but significant differences in customer demand. The detailed construction of the business format must adjust to these differences or risk missing the target. The ability of the franchiser to adjust and the commitment of franchiser resources specifically to international development take on even greater importance.

The degree of effort to rationalize differences in adjustments to the business format and having the resources to react to changed customer demand can ameliorate the difficulty of recognizing and reacting to cultural differences. Malls in the US versus the high street in Europe are a distinction of dramatic proportion to the business format franchise. Remember, the marketing services of the franchiser are key to satisfaction. The marketing "bundle" for US application will not necessarily transfer internationally. An understanding of the customer drives marketing. Therefore, misunderstandings, however small, can lead to improper location of outlets and wasted advertising expenditure. If serious financial deficiencies result in early franchise development, the system may never recover. This is especially true if the franchisee is trapped in a bad location or if inappropriate marketing damages the brand.

The importance of information

One of the significant advantages of a franchise is the availability of an abundance of information to complete due diligence of the opportunity. In the US there are numerous federal and state laws regulating franchising. Indeed, some argue that the industry is over-regulated and growth is inhibited. Regardless, the Federal Trade Commission requires the franchiser to file a detailed disclosure document called a Uniform Franchise Offering Circular (UFOC).

There are no similar disclosure requirements in Europe, but European buyers of US franchises are advised to read the UFOC, which includes such information as franchiser-audited financial statements, a list of existing US franchisees, and current franchise litigation. Additionally, visits to existing franchise outlets and interviews with franchisees provide a wealth of information.

Technical issues of support and logistics are easily discovered. However, the more important issue is the way in which the franchise relationship is managed. Our research clearly indicates that the advantages of franchising, including economies of scale in purchasing and marketing, result from rapid growth and overall size and density of the franchiser. Buying power increases and competitive advantages in cost are manifest as the franchise system expands.

It should be noted that international franchise relationships of US companies are often started via a joint venture between the franchiser and a local entrepreneur. Otherwise, the franchiser may develop a company operation that can be franchised at a later date.

Franchisees see themselves as partners with the franchiser in a strategic relationship. Partners require communication to develop decision-making synergy and co-ordination to properly execute plans. When communication and co-operation result in a co-ordinated attack on the marketplace, franchisees are overwhelmingly satisfied. It is essential that investigation of a franchise includes an understanding of the processes by which communications occur and changes are implemented. Often the conduit from the franchiser to the franchisee is a "field representative" of the franchiser.

We began this article with a discussion of wealth creation as a key to entre-preneurship. Our research reveals that many franchisees are making money. The average franchisee in our study at Imperial College had a profit of around £40,000 on an investment of just under £100,000.

1 Stephen Spinelli and Sue Birley (1998) "An Empirical Evaluation of Conflict in the Franchise System," *British Journal of Management*, 9.

Jiffy Lube International Inc.

This is a summary of three case studies – Hindman and Company, Bridge Capital Investors Inc., and Jiffy Lube International Inc. They can be found in *New Venture Creation*, 4th edition, 1994, McGraw Hill/Richard D. Irwin, and 5th edition, 1998, by **Jeffry A. Timmons**, F. W. Olin, Distinguished Professor of Entrepreneurship, Babson College, USA.

After graduating from the University of Minnesota with a master's degree in healthcare administration, Jim Hindman worked for ten years as a hospital administrator. In 1967, he started Hindman Associates, specializing in building nursing homes and, by the mid-1970s, his ownership interests in these and a variety of other unrelated businesses were collectively worth several million dollars. However, after a spell as head football coach of Western Maryland College, he became restless and, by 1979, he was again looking for new business opportunities. Ed Kelly and Steve Spinelli joined him.

The fast oil change business caught his attention. Demand in this market was growing as the number of full-service gas stations had halved over the previous ten years. Jim's brother-in-law knew a man who operated a "Jiffy Lube" franchise and, after several meetings with the owner in Utah, Jim bought the Jiffy Lube trademark and the rights to seven franchises. He then set about growing the business. The goal was to get to 100 units by the end of 1982 through both the sale of new franchises and the acquisition of existing service centers and small franchise chains. Revenues would come from four sources:

1. Royalty fees from franchisees.
2. Rental income on property leased or sub-leased to franchisees.
3. Initial fees from new franchisees.
4. Sales by company-owned centers.

By March 1983, the company was projecting 96 centers in operation. However, this growth was not without its costs. Revenues in 1982 had been $3.5m with losses of $1.4m. Financing of the operation was through a combination of loans and sale of stock to directors, employees and other investors and, most significantly, through the sale of 29 percent of the company to Pennzoil, the supplier of oil for the majority of the Jiffy Lube centers. In return, Pennzoil agreed to guarantee $6.3m of real estate financing.

Unfortunately, the relationship with Pennzoil was far from perfect. They soon discovered that the two companies had different objectives that resulted in different strategies for Jiffy Lube's expansion. Jiffy Lube's business plan emphasized "clustering" and "franchising" while Pennzoil advocated "wide coverage" and company-owned service centers. Hindman decided that the relationship simply wasn't working and he would have to buy Pennzoil's stock and find other sources of finance. With Jiffy Lube's worsening financial status ... "They wanted out. Maybe they thought we were going bankrupt, and they could pick up the service centers when we went under."

Not so. In 1984, the company made a profit for the first time. During the first few years, the company had sold franchises one at a time. But this was not sufficient. Individual sales did not saturate areas quickly enough to achieve name recognition and make advertising cost effective. So, in 1983, it began to sell "area development rights" to investors and entrepreneurs. In return for an up-front, non-refundable fee, Jiffy Lube gave investors the exclusive right to build a certain number of franchises within a specific geographical location. Fees varied depending on the market potential. For example, Tampa, Florida cost $150,000, while San Francisco cost $250,000. In addition, the company continued to collect the initial franchise fee of between $20,000 and $25,000 for each unit developed. As the company grew, management expected the rights to become more valuable, eventually selling for as much as $1 million in larger markets such as Los Angeles.

This sale of large area development rights increased the need for real estate and construction financing. To fund this, Jiffy Lube had signed an agreement in 1983 with Old Court Savings and Loan to provide $16 milliom for the purchase and development of 37 new centers. This was not to end happily. The morning headline on May 6, 1985 – *Local Savings and Loan Collapses, State Takes Over* – saw the closure of Jiffy Lube's primary real estate lender.

Clearly, they couldn't assume that funding from Old Court would resume, nor could they afford to wait. Development of the service centers could not be put on hold since Jiffy Lube would default on real estate purchases if cash payments were not made on time. Contractors were waiting to start, and new franchisees depended on the service centers being completed for their livelihood.

Throughout the summer, the management team battled from one crisis to another using short-term borrowings and stop-gap measures. Unfortunately, their problems were not confined to finance. Competition for market share was getting fierce. In August, Quaker State Oil bought Minit Lube, the number two company in the quick-change industry after Jiffy Lube, for $35 million. Jim Hindman said: "This put us up against the big boys for the first time." But Quaker State had not finished. In September, Jim received a call from the president of the company. "Look, we just bought Minit Lube and I think we should talk." Contingent on future earnings, they made a formal offer of $53.9 million.

Jim's reaction was simple. He must grow. "We will become the McDonald's of the quick oil change business. With approximately 270 service centers open in late 1985, these goals require the opening of over 1,000 new centers by 1990."

But such rapid expansion would need funding, and so in July 1986 the company raised $28 million through an initial public offering and between 1986 and 1987 increased the number of centers from 348 to 561. At the same time, the company broadened the scope of services to franchisees. Training and maintenance of company programs and policies were high priorities; a certification program for technicians was developed; formal procedures were established for employee selection; and a "mystery shopper" scheme was introduced.

Steve Spinelli, now a franchisee owning a significant east coast area and president of the Association of Franchisees, explained: "There are always points of contention in a franchise relationship and we had our fair share. However, Hindman had an ability to intercede personally at strategic moments and to force communications between top management and franchisees. His open door policy included making sure that our door was open too."

Year	Revenue ($'000)	Service centers	
		franchised	company operated
1986	7,683	361	23
1987	10,169	578	31
1988	14,218	805	39
1989	18,840	1,047	47
1990	22,210	1,297	47
1991	23,954	1,427	47

Table 1

The results were dramatic: 1987 sales revenue exceeded the original business plan. In March, the company had become the first quicklube company to advertise nationally. Touting the slogan, "We"ll take care of you like family," a $5 million television campaign featured Dick Van Patten's family. Additionally, regional and local franchisees planned to spend $15 million on local advertising. Just as Jim Hindman had expected, the IPO had raised public awareness and, by 1991, there were more than 1,400 Jiffy Lube outlets operated throughout the US (*see* Table 1).

Postscript

In 1991, Steve Spinelli sold his 47-store franchise to a major oil company. His interest in entrepreneurship and especially franchising led him to pursue his Ph.D. at Imperial College of Science and Technology in London. He graduated in 1995 and now teaches, researches and consults in the fields of new venture creation and franchising at Babson College, USA.

E-commerce – a new opportunity?

Daniel Muzyka and **Sue Birley** look at the new business arena that is creating new horizons for everyone.

We do live in interesting times – indeed, we are in the middle of a technological and entrepreneurial revolution. The world wide web and the evolution of computer and communications technology have made it possible to maintain contact with anyone on Earth, at any time, and anywhere. This sort of access, backed with what would have been viewed 15 years ago as massive processing power available only to large corporations, along with standard interfaces and protocols, has generated a business revolution in this new millennium that is rivaled only by the Industrial Revolution which was led by new forms of transport and energy in the 18th century.

This revolution is beginning to affect all our lives. In fact, it is not clear that one actually needs to leave home to carry on a complete life. One can work efficiently at home, access massive knowledge resources from home, order goods and services from home, and even carry on a social life from home – not that we are necessarily advocating such a confined existence. Actually, "at home" could be replaced with the phrase "from in front of one's computer." This evolution to electronic commerce has created many new opportunities and new businesses, and has led to the beginnings of the demise of some "traditional" industries.

So, does "e-commerce" represent an unassailable arena for business opportunities for everyone? The answer is "yes" and "no." The answer is "yes" in many ways. There is a comparatively low investment required to create an e-commerce site. The practical tools and equipment are all generally available at a reasonable price. There are even service firms that can assist you. In addition, the order fulfillment centers and many of the other services that actually "back" internet interfaces are at one's disposal in the more developed economies.

The answer is "no" in other ways. Building and marketing the business can be costly. Witness the many internet companies that have raised large amounts of capital but have yet to make a profit. Moreover, in many areas, the market is already becoming rapidly saturated. There are many "me-too" sites developing with minor differences. In addition, there are many areas where central sites or service providers (e.g. AOL, MSN, etc.) have subsumed services into their offering, eliminating opportunities for other organizations.

Capturing "mind share" is another issue, as is developing a strategy to keep customers or to improve "stickiness." While there are search engines and directories on the internet, there are many indications that they are not complete. Getting consumers to notice your site and to consistently use it is not a trivial issue. In fact, it is a critical factor for survival and, eventually, success.

There are three issues that are both providing this new opportunity but at the same time may threaten it. First, there are many existing enterprises, such as banks, insurance companies, and food retailers, whose business models are being reinvented by the emergence of e-business, but they have been slow to act. This has provided opportunity to new businesses. However, when they have responded, their existing brand equity has created problems for new e-commerce entrants in some sectors.

Second, an issue that is unanswered at this time relates to appropriate functional strategies for success in the e-business world. There are many prescriptions and textbooks written on how to succeed in the real ("virtual") world of e-business, but there is little in the way of prescriptions on how to create and operate successful e-commerce enterprises. This is both part of the opportunity and part of the challenge for e-commerce entrepreneurs. Quite simply, most entrepreneurs in this field will admit that they are still "making it up as they go along."

The third issue is one of available capital. Currently, the success of many internet IPOs is based on investor expectations for capital growth at the expense of trading profits that are not clearly sustainable in the longer term.

We have four suggestions for those pondering an e-commerce opportunity or who are interested in implementing one.

1. Speed really does appear to be important. It is better to have a site that is "good" up and running quickly than having an "optimal" site running later.
2. Find ways to connect with others, to create value-building alliances. You need other "pointers" to your site, both internet and non-internet. Getting people's attention and building traffic are important.
3. Understand how you are going to make money in this business. We believe that the business or economic model is going to be scrutinized more in the coming years. You need to be able to articulate it clearly in order to attract investors.
4. Be in a position to exploit growth. Some e-commerce businesses have lost position as a result of an inability to deliver.

All of the considerations, concerns and questions concerning the average e-commerce business suggest three functional areas to investigate in defining the business. First, what is your *marketing strategy?* Where is the customer? Where do they "enter" the web? Who currently sees them? What are their other interests? How do we keep them focussed on us? How do I make my presence known to these customers? All of these are legitimate questions. Marketing on the web is an area posing many challenges, such as how to define new market niches given the presence of data but not a physical customer. However, there is significant new research into areas such as customer relationship management, advertising on the web, and data mining (to understand customer behavior and segmentation, an area of keen interest). Given the nature of the web and the ability to capture transaction information and store it easily, there is a wealth of new data.

Second, you need to understand the *supply chain logistics*. While in some e-commerce business areas this is now just a question of finding an order fulfillment service that meets your needs, the questions related to how one delivers a product or service in a reliable, quality manner in other cases is not so obvious. Where do you source the people, products and processes required? Can the services you use ramp up quickly as you experience success? How do you manage your total delivered cost?

Third, you need to address your *systems requirements*. There are still software and hardware issues with the web, especially with the speed of development. More tools to support e-commerce businesses are readily available, but this does not mean that the tools *you* need are necessarily all available. Be clear about *what* you need and *how* you are going to get it. You might also want to ponder how, in the fast-paced world of e-commerce, you are going to keep your tools out of the hands of competitors so that you can secure at least some competitive advantage from them.

Obviously, the marketing strategy, supply chain logistics and systems requirements need to "fit" together in order to realize an opportunity. They need to be compatible with the perceived opportunity and with each other.

One final suggestion we have for would-be e-commerce entrepreneurs is to look carefully for follow-on opportunities and to consider them in the initial design. E-commerce businesses involve significant data collection. You have large amounts of information on customer purchasing behavior. Searching for new opportunities is an even more urgent matter for e-commerce businesses given the turnover in such opportunities and the frothy nature of competition.

Achieving customer focus in the electronic marketplace

Sandra Vandermerwe expands on how to excel in the electronic marketplace.

E-technology offers the entrepreneur opportunities to excel with customers in ways never before imagined by turning ideas into exciting new markets and outpacing the traditionalists still trapped in old thinking and behavior.

Typically, there are four levels for which e-technology can be used:

- **Level 1:** at its most basic, it takes the form of a website catalog or brochure, containing online information about the company and its core products or services.
- **Level 2:** it is used as an alternative channel or tool to promote and sell a firm's wares online.
- **Level 3:** the e-technology offers information that assists customers in making decisions.
- **Level 4:** e-technology is used to help manage customer relationships interactively at each critical point in the customer activity cycle–pre, during and post their experience – thereby facilitating new ways of doing things for and with customers.[1]

At Level 4 the real power of e-technology is unleashed as it is here that the e-technology works to help lock customers on with all of the benefits over time.[2]

How e-technology enables customer focus

Specifically, e-technology enables customer focus in the following ways.

It links benefits

Customers are no longer satisfied with discrete products and services, no matter how good or innovative they may be: they want linked benefits across product, company and industry. This is why Microsoft launched Expedia to provide all the online services to enable people who travel for business or pleasure in the US and Europe to get one integrated experience – what traditionalists had failed to do.

Information is available 24 hours a day, with data updated every half-hour. The range of information includes regional weather reports; arrival times; illustrated guide books; best options to reach a particular business or holiday location; different (and exact) prices; and an insider's guide to the lowest published fares. On many flights, customers can pick the seats they want; find out if rental cars are available at any airport in the world, and reserve them; pay for the trip online or over the phone with a credit card, with tickets delivered overnight. With its dynamic mapping technology, they can click on a part of a city within a stated price range to produce a description of the hotels available and a room can be reserved. By clicking on to Citiscape, Expedia's online worldwide entertainment magazine, they can see what is on in each city in terms of sport, art, food, culture and so on, and self-book where relevant. And they can zoom in to focus on bulletin boards and get information ranging from local bus services to sales tax rates.

E-technology enables the enterprise to take customers through a web experience from the beginning of the customer activity cycle to the end. Corporate entrepreneurs at Ford, for example, have built their entire new strategy around this concept, which starts with need assessment, through to information gathering, procurement, financing, insuring, emergency repairs, maintenance and upgrading. Through single-click access and web-enabled processes, customers are connected virtually to all the participating providers, dealers and the company from a single entry point. The object is to maximize possible opportunities for customers to touch the Ford brand over time in what should be a neverending cycle beginning, through its Y-generation site called Den (Digital Entertainment Network), for the young early on and even before they become drivers.

It personalizes offerings to suit the unique needs of individuals

Ironically, the internet is not a mass medium. It is a one-to-one medium, a powerful tool for customer personalization because, paradoxically, individual customer relationships are not only possible but achievable with millions of people simultaneously.

Linking busy, time-pressed people with a variety of retailers to help them manage their daily chores and home supply needs, Peapod is an example of an enterprise that has gone far beyond just using the technology as an alternative distribution or communication channel to automating the delivery of groceries held in stock or currently being promoted – which is what most retailers are still doing.

Peapod provides shoppers with a virtual supermarket on their screens, organized by any category they want. This virtual supermarket can be laid out in aisles, much as in regular stores, or according to the customer's arrangement, merchandised to accommodate what they like and are interested in. Alternatively, the cyber-supermarket can be arranged by product category or brand, alphabetically by brand, by price, or by specials and promotions. Customers can also shop according to

71

nutritional requirements, such as how much fat, calories, sodium or cholesterol there is in products, with shopping baskets automatically tallying up the customer's set quota.

Expert surrogate shoppers act in the stores for the customers, with specific directions on what to look for, choose and buy in the case of perishables such as vegetables, cuts of meat and so on. Preferences can be added to orders – for instance "I only like ripe tomatoes" – or substitutes can be highlighted in case an item is out of stock. Individuals receive menu-planning assistance and, when a recipe is selected, all the ingredients are automatically placed in their virtual shopping carts unless otherwise directed. Goods are delivered to them around the clock, at a time convenient to them, with coupons accepted by drivers on delivery and help given with special needs such as carrying or storing.

It eliminates old trade-offs

With its powerful and pervasive effects, not only does e-technology allow millions of people online simultaneously, thereby reducing costs, but it also allows the enterprise to get all the benefits of dealing with customers as individuals without any of the trade-offs so typical of the old model.

Auto-by-Tel, the California-based website that links customers to thousands of dealers across brands, took on the entire automotive industry in 1997 and now operates in the UK and Scandinavia, with plans to set up operations in Spain, Brazil and Japan. It arranges to have the car delivered to the customer's house for a test drive; orders the vehicle for them; does the paperwork, including the financing and insurance; and the post-servicing. If the customer opts to buy, the desired vehicle is found at the best price. If the customer is still hesitating, Auto-by-Tel helps them make the right decision. "Information is gathered and given until a customer's needs are assessed, a set of options can be generated, and the best choice can be made," says Karl Nord of the Scandinavian operation.

The cost of having the customer stay online for another minute is extremely low in the electronic marketplace compared with having to dedicate an extra minute to that person face to face or through a call center. In the past, each customer would dominate such a resource, preventing others from using it. But Auto-by-Tel doesn't have to get rid of customers as quickly as possible in order to save money. At point of contact, customers can stay online getting, say, information or making a choice as long as necessary. In fact, this is actively encouraged because customers make better, more informed decisions, thus saving time and money for all concerned.

It enables interactivity

Using e-technology to simply re-engineer what is already being done or just to shave costs is very different from bringing e-technology to individuals and interacting with them so they get exactly what they want. Bill Gates illustrates the significance of interactivity: "One of the things you quickly learn on the internet is that those stories that you just take from the newspaper (for instance) and put up (electronically), people aren't very interested in. Stories where you get interaction and you say OK, under this tax proposal enter what your income is and see how it affects you, or type in your zip code and we'll show you they are giving out a lot of traffic tickets in your area. Things that are interactive and draw on what that person cares about are great."

Interactivity is a powerful tool for customer personalization because it enables the entrepreneur to manage interactively, shaping the offering and learning about the customer. This means that offerings can become more and more proactive and precise, so reinforcing the positive feedback mechanism that locks customers on.

E-technology also enables the company to have multiple links with the company and its partners. Ford talks about two-on-one relationships – in other words, customers are connected to the company site as well as to dealers simultaneously – through its web-based multi-channel applications. But Ford goes further: customers can enter into dialog with employees or partners such as designers about the cars or Ford credit about financing. Similarly, newspapers had only one link with customers in the past – the newsstand. Now a whole range of financial journals allow readers to have links with editorial staff, add their own experiences, get exactly what they want to know in the format they choose, and communicate with special reporters and key figures behind a story.

It mobilizes collective knowledge

The entrepreneur uses e-technology to interact with customers with the express purpose of learning about them, and converting this learning into superior offerings on an on-going basis. E-technology makes this an increasingly easy feat to accomplish because not only can huge quantities of unstructured information be collected, but it can be turned into real-time decision making.

Amazon got its lead because it found a way to add value to customers by taking the hassle out of buying books. But it also provides offerings suited to the unique profile, tastes, habits and on-going needs of individuals. Total knowledge of a person – getting to know them increasingly better – is leveraged to deliver superior value, which is what gets the lock-on that wards off competitors.

Feedback is used to make changes daily to knowledge banks. On the Amazon site customers can click in and add or change their profile at any time. Their files are updated daily, to see what they buy, for whom, and what else could interest them. Amazon is thus able to leverage from the database's ability to "remember" customers, and so treat them as individuals. Customers who visit the website are greeted by name and offered a list of recommended titles based on the books they have already bought. Even without having to visit the site, customers can be kept abreast of the latest publications in their preferred reading areas via "Eyes," Amazon's search agent, which e-mails customers whenever a favorite author comes out with a new book, or something appears which would be of interest to them.

With e-technology the entire collective intelligence of an enterprise and its partners, not just of one person, can come to bear on customer interaction. So when, say, consultants go to a customer, they can take their colleagues or partners, from anywhere in the world, with expertise on any topic, with them. Expanding on this, a member of KPMG's top management says: "Down there on the battlefield every professional that stands in front of a client is [the whole of] KPMG. We are directing the combined intellectual assets of the firm down to a single point."

It connects delivery partners

To deliver the integrated experience requires the connecting of the various delivery partners across product, company and industry. It is easy to establish partners in this way in the electronic marketplace and it can be achieved inexpensively. In fact, the more the integrated community of connected providers grows, the more valuable the network, and each player belonging to it, becomes, thanks to networking externalities which kick in.[3]

Because information can be brought together easily over the internet and intranets, people previously separated can work as one integrated delivery entity, joining processes, combining expertise and sharing infrastructure and resources. Relevant information can go to all partners instantaneously to facilitate both concurrent and real-time decision making. Information from third parties and competitors is also easy to access, which means that companies can offer seamless services and even competitors' products and services to customers. Thus, they become independent advisers, or procurement consultants, rather than just operating in the same old sales mode.

Interactive Investors International (iii), a firm which began in the UK and now has sites in Europe, Hong Kong, South Africa, and offshore, enables customers to look at investment options, compare prices, make decisions, assess the entire range of investment opportunities based on their own needs, transact and monitor share performance. It also helps customers choose with which broker to do business given their budgets and expectations; and customers can use any form of payment. To achieve this, the ideas, knowledge and information of nearly 100 financial service companies and 7,000 financial advisers have been put online by iii, as well as more than 4,500 news organizations worldwide from which 53,000 price/performance investments are monitored.

It drives transparency

Customers are more powerful and informed than ever before because, for the first time, technology allows them to have the information for ease and efficacy of decision making. Wasn't this always the role of the travel agent (anyone can sell air tickets) or the stockbroker (anyone can take an order for stocks)? But traditionalists didn't do it – which gave Sherry Coutu, founder of iii, the gap in the electronic marketplace. She says: "There was a dis-equilibrium between those who knew things, and those who didn't; between those who were making the financial decisions, and those who were on the receiving end of these decisions; between those who held financial power, and those captive to this fact. iii could change this. Anyone could have any information 24 hours a day. This would empower people and liberate them from the financial control of the past, putting the power back with customers."

As more customers go online and chat, the firm becomes more transparent and less able to control its image or influence by traditional marketing means. Individuals can discuss what they feel and what they have experienced with other customers, regardless of geography. Also, customers can influence each other as never before: not only do customers see comments made by the hotel on the Expedia website, but also comments made by guests. Similarly, iii's customers can speak to other customers when choosing the stockbroker they may want to use. In Germany, doctors and medical clinics meet on Praxisline where they can discuss cases, swap experiences, query the experts, compare medical supply prices, and buy health products.

Customer influence can be positive, but it can of course work in the opposite direction as well. As Jeff Bezos of Amazon reminds us: "If you make customers unhappy in the physical world they might each tell six friends. If you make customers unhappy on the internet they can each tell 6,000 friends with one message to a news group."

Entrepreneurs build relationships around this transparency among customers, who become virtual electronic communities, interacting and exchanging information and experiences. They are not afraid of this. Beyond a marketing ploy, the technology is used to enable customers to form a cohesive group and create true communities of value.

It lowers costs

It is essential for customer focus to accomplish both superior value *and* low cost for individuals. If Amazon retains its lead it will not be because of discounts – these can and are being copied. It will be because it has used e-technology to add value at each critical point in the customer activity cycle *and* has lowered the overall price. Peapod customers get a 24-hour, personalized shopping service for which they pay a price for the software applications; a monthly fee; a delivery fee; and a 5 percent surcharge on the order. But this cost is more than offset for them by the savings they make over their total activity cycle. They get more information about products, which helps them make better decisions on what to buy so that they waste less; they save money using more coupons than they normally do. They also do more comparison shopping and less impulse purchasing, use coupons more effectively, and save time, money and energy from not using any transport.

The new economics of e-technology can work to the advantage of customer focus not just because it eliminates many of the heavy overheads of the past, but for several other, more subtle reasons. For instance, ideas, information and knowledge – the growing component in offerings – can be easily, quickly and cheaply transmitted by wire, so making their production and distribution cheap. And given that they are abundant resources (rather than scarce) and grow as they are used and reused, the expenses of producing them again and again are zero or low.

Then there are the costs saved by obtaining input from customers, who pay not only in money but also in value-added opinions, experiences and commentaries. Customers provide solid information on a variety of fronts, including themselves. Moreover, as customers become more familiar with the technology, they are able to participate increasingly in the actual production process, becoming a "key driver of economic value."[4] Additionally, their know-how, when exchanged, shared and disseminated through chat forums, enables customers to train and help each other make purchase decisions, further reducing costs. Amazon customers, for instance, by reviewing books and suggesting what else readers of the book might like to read, become producers, not just consumers.

As the enterprise gets to know customers better, and does more business with them, research has shown that the cost of transactions drops.[5]

Final word

Entrepreneurs won't have the edge simply because they are using e-technology. Nor will they create new markets and wealth if they simply re-engineer what is already being done merely to save costs. If entrepreneurs are to get and stay out ahead in the electronic marketplace in a way that makes it difficult for traditionalists to catch up, it will be because they have used the technology to make customer focus central to their thinking and behavior.

This article is a revised version of the final part of a paper entitled "The Customer Connected Company: the role of e-technology in making it happen," published by Barclays Bank, October 1999.

1 For more on the customer activity cycle, *see* "The customer-focussed mission" in Part 7.

2 For more on customer lock-on and the benefits, *see* "The customer-focussed mission" in Part 7 and Sandra Vandermerwe (1999) *Customer Capitalism: increasing returns in new market spaces*, London, New York, Nicholas Brealey.

3 This tendency for a network to explode in value has come to be known as Metcalfe's law. *See*, for instance, Kevin Kelly (1998) *New Rules for the New Economy*, London, 4th Estate; Carl Shapiro and Hal Varian (1998) *Information Rules*, Boston, Harvard Business School Press; and Thomas Stewart, *Intellectual Capital: the new wealth of organizations* (1997) London, Nicholas Brealey Publishing.

4 Customers as economic drivers is discussed by John Hagel and Arthur Armstrong (1997) *Net gain: expanding markets through virtual communities*, Boston, Harvard Business School Press.

5 The cost of transactions dropping as the company gets to know customers better is discussed by, among others, Frederick Reichheld (1996) *The Loyalty Effect*, Boston, Harvard Business School Press.

Thinking about an internet start-up?

Stephen Thompson gives some guidance on the things an internet entrepreneur should consider.

Internet usage ramped quickly in the US and now it is happening in Europe, with the number of European internet users expected to triple to 100 million over the next four years.[1]

The arrival of the internet has been heralded by some as the start of the third industrial revolution. A principal driver behind this revolution are the relatively low barriers to new entrants, allowing entrepreneurs to spawn internet start-up companies at a phenomenal rate. This rate of entrepreneurship is even more surprising given that many of the conventional parameters for start-up companies are missing. Often there is nothing proprietary about these companies and their financial projections are dominated by substantial losses and modest revenues with breakeven or profitability usually several years away.

Pure-play internet start-up companies face a number of unique challenges as well as the usual ones of other start-up ventures. The issues facing internet start-ups fall into five distinct categories under which they will be reviewed: the business proposition, the route to market, the competitive intensity, management and human capital requirements, and financing the start-up.

The business proposition

The internet is not only having an impact, to a greater or lesser extent, on existing businesses, it is also opening up whole new approaches to the way business can be conducted. These new opportunities arise from the tremendous level of global connectivity and the ability to interact directly with suppliers and customers throughout this new distribution channel.

Internet-based businesses have already explored four distinct broad categories of business: pure infrastructure, software and services, content or aggregation, and retail/commerce. There are many parallels with the PC industry of the early 1980s, where the early winners were the hardware and infrastructure manufacturers; however, over time the value shifted, first to enabling technologies and, ultimately, to programming and content providers.

The next wave of internet businesses are expected to be in the business re-engineering, services and vertical market segments.[2] It is clear though that any internet start-up venture must be based on a business model that has the potential to create value, a demonstrable advantage over traditional bricks-and-mortar businesses, and addresses a market of sufficient size.

Is the business proposition or concept novel?

With there being relatively few barriers to conceiving an internet start-up business, one of the first questions that must be addressed is whether or not somebody else has already had the same idea and started an identical business. It may not be based in the same country but geography is not a big barrier to internet-based businesses.

If somebody else has already set up a comparable internet business, a decision will have to be made as to whether or not the proposed venture should collaborate or merge with the existing business. Alternatively, the basis for competing with the established business must be clearly mapped out.

Does the venture have the potential to create value?

A successful internet business must have identified a way of creating value. Extracting costs, such as from a supply chain by missing out various intermediaries, can create tremendous value. Andersen Consulting has estimated that e-synchronized supply chains can potentially deliver a value proposition of more than $100 million to the average global multinational.[3]

Internet start-up businesses can also create value through transactions, possibly even increasing the overall potential value of a given market. This value can be created by direct interaction with the customer leading to a better understanding of the customer. For instance, Amazon.com uses its direct knowledge of its customers to recommend other books or CDs that may interest them.

Can the internet start-up demonstrate an economic advantage over traditional bricks-and-mortar businesses?

It is not sufficient to be able to demonstrate the potential to create value. Internet start-ups must clearly demonstrate an economic advantage over traditional bricks-and-mortar companies. If an internet business simply proposes to translate what others already do on to the internet it has not understood the potential of the medium. Moreover, it will probably not have raised a sufficient barrier to protect itself from traditional businesses which, once they have woken up, will reconfigure themselves to include internet-based operations. When Barnes & Noble woke up it launched Barnesandnoble.com, its online bookstore.

Another strength of an internet-based business is that once the set-up costs are covered, the business should be infinitely scaleable, with no impact on the operating margin under a given price structure. This is not, however, true of many traditional businesses based around physical assets that usually reach certain operating size constraints.

How will the proposed venture generate its revenues?

Many of the first-generation internet companies relied on selling advertising and, to a lesser extent, on subscriptions as revenue streams. While these may remain modest sources of on-going revenues, it is unlikely that many businesses will be sustainable with these as the sole sources of income.

The simplest way to generate revenues is by transaction fees. In its plainest form, this means the costs extracted from a supply chain can be shared among the supplier(s), internet intermediaries and customers so that everybody wins. The key to transaction-based revenues is first attracting the customer and then generating the transaction(s).

What is the size of the target market?

Key objectives of any start-up business are to identify a target market, determine its size, and estimate the market share the venture should capture. Unlike other start-up businesses, an internet start-up is often global, by definition, as there are no restrictions on access to the start-up's website. While the potential to reach a global market may be attractive, it raises additional fulfillment challenges.

Many business to consumer (B2C) internet businesses are capped by the natural limit on the size of their target market. The online retail purchase of wine is unlikely to be a big business. It is a crowded marketplace with online companies, such as Chateauonline and Orgasmicwines, competing with the established mail-order companies and the traditional high street and superstore suppliers which are also starting to offer online purchasing.

Perceived wisdom is that the largest untapped potential for internet businesses is in business to business (B2B) ventures, estimated to be growing at a compound annual rate of 67.5 percent and expected to be worth $1.5 trillion in 2004, ten times the size of the anticipated B2C market in 2004.[4]

The route to market

Having fleshed out the business model, the next hurdle is implementation. An internet start-up faces a number of specific issues related to technical capability, fulfilment capability, ability to generate traffic and "stickiness," creating a brand, and the regulatory environment.

Are all the required technical capabilities in place?

Andersen Consulting found that there were three main barriers to the development of e-commerce: a lack of robustness of the internet, concerns over security, and concerns over privacy.

Internet entrepreneurs must not fall into the trap of thinking that all they have to do is get a home-made website launched. In the US it is hard to find a competent net-design firm that is able to take on new clients. Aside from having an outstanding website, the venture must factor in alternative emerging access points such as mobile telephones, Psions, Palm Pilots, interactive digital televisions and automatic teller machines. Is all the software adaptable to these emerging access points? Is the software robust and completely scalable at the required rapid pace? Can security and privacy be guaranteed for the user?

Are the fulfillment capabilities in place?

An internet business has to be much more than a web-based front end. The business must be able to fulfill all orders it receives to build brand trust. Users are fickle and are unlikely to return if they have a bad experience. The start-up must avoid establishing an idea in the public mind only to see others reap the reward because it does not have the capacity to serve the marketplace.

This requirement for back-office capabilities such as ordering systems, warehousing and distribution capabilities has created new business opportunities for the traditional catalog retailers and delivery service companies which want to partner with emerging e-commerce concerns. The comparative fortunes of N Brown and Great Universal Stores (GUS) illustrate this. Shares in N Brown, the shovel supplier which offers end-to-end internet fulfillment for e-tailers, rose by more than 95 percent when it announced it was offering fulfillment services to other retailers, while shares in GUS fell by 25 percent as it was unable to clearly articulate an online vision.

Will the venture generate traffic and "stickiness"?

It is essential that the new venture devises a way to draw people to its website. Once users have visited the site it must be "sticky," i.e. experiences must be positive and the site must entice users to come back. beenz.com aims to make websites stickier with beenz, a web-based currency, that can also be used to influence consumer behavior. This is the beginning of the process of achieving what Sandra Vandermerwe has called customer "lock-on," where customers choose a business as their dominant or sole choice on an on-going basis.

How will the internet start-up create a brand?

Building a strong brand name requires forming a game plan from the outset and devoting resources to it. Elaine Rubin, Chairman of Shop.org, says: "It's a game of awareness, the way you generate awareness and credibility, and the way you garner trust among a consumer population is to have your message all over the place, so the consumer says: "Yes, this must be a credible company because I saw it on television."[5] This view is shared by Paul Shalet, Sales and Marketing Director of X-Stream network, who says: "The best way to create a strong online brand is to have a big offline presence."[6]

It is down to spending money with the best advertising agents and this presents additional challenges for the internet start-up. This trend towards massive spending on offline advertising, estimated to be $7.4 billion in 1999, dramatically increases the amount of funding that the venture requires before it achieves breakeven. Then, once the money has been raised, there is a capacity constraint with the better advertising agents coupled with a shortage of physical advertising space, such as billboards, in certain locations.

Are there any regulatory hurdles?

The internet has remained largely unregulated and this poses a number of questions for a venture. How are internet businesses taxed? Where are they domiciled? The recent move of a gaming concern from the UK to Gibraltar is an example of a company moving to a more favorable tax location. Will all internet businesses suddenly become domiciled in tax havens?

The competitive intensity

Internet start-ups have to understand the nature of their competitors and have a strategy for competing in the marketplace. Competitors will appear in two forms:

copycat internet start-ups and the online response of traditional businesses. With both these competitors, a key element of winning is to have and retain the first-mover advantage.

How real is the threat of substitution?

It depends on the number of barriers that the internet start-up can raise to frustrate the efforts of copycat businesses. There is often little that is proprietary in an internet business. Some companies have sued to protect their way of business and Amazon.com and Priceline.com are trying to patent their particular way of doing business. This might not succeed in the patent courts but it will give competitors something to think about.

Another potential barrier that an internet start-up can consider is an exclusive collaboration with another company, an example being fogdog.com which has acquired the rights to sell Nike trainers online.

How will established businesses respond?

Established businesses may have been slow off the mark and may not understand the internet at board level, but they have begun to believe that Andy Grove, Chairman of Intel, was correct when in 1999 he said: "In five years' time, all companies will be internet companies – or they won't be companies."

The management consultancies are helping established businesses respond to the threat of the internet. KPMG's Strategy eBook urges companies to "change the game or change the rules of the game."[7] Andersen Consulting points out that five long-held basic business truths – the wisdom of vertical integration, the earning power of physical assets, the limits of natural growth, the channel power of producers, and the prudence of fast-following – all appear to be crashing down. Both consultancies have, however, identified a number of traditional companies that have responded well to the challenge of the internet.

The message for the internet start-up is that the traditional businesses have woken up and will all be putting the internet at the core of their strategies. "The buggy manufacturers are beginning to shift their strategy; the question is whether they are moving fast enough."

Does the internet start-up have, and can it retain, first-mover advantage?

First-movers in the world of internet start-ups tend to win near-monopolies. It is all about speed and domination. Having established first-mover advantage, the business must scale rapidly and remain agile, keep one step ahead by retaining the first-mover advantage, and become the dominant internet start-up in its defined market space.

Look again at Amazon.com. It was the first online bookseller, it then enhanced the service that could be offered by booksellers with its targetted recommendations. Next it moved into selling CDs and it has established a number of strategic relationships with other e-commerce companies, as it owns the customers. This constant assertion of its first-mover advantage has left internet-based competitors, such as like bol.com and traditional booksellers such as Barnes & Noble, always playing catch-up.

Management and human capital requirements

Some venture capitalists reputedly look for three things in a business: management, management and management. In internet start-ups, because of the accelerated pace at which successful ventures develop, there are additional requirements of management.

Does the management team have relevant industry expertise?

It is essential that management understand their industry. As they will constantly be first-movers they will have to be able to foresee how the internet is restructuring their industry so there is no time in this fast-moving world to learn about an industry. This is especially important with regulated industries, such as healthcare. Would, for example, an online pharmacy be able to sell prescription-only medicines; if so, under what special provisions and granted by which regulatory body?

Has the management team run a big business?

The growth of a successful internet start-up is explosive and management will have to grow rapidly. The management team must have operational experience of managing large concerns, even if at the outset the venture has only five employees and a handful of suppliers and customers. There is little time to train management on the job. These dynamics have created a great demand for experienced management teams.

Does the venture have the necessary online workers to implement the plan?

Find qualified employees. The relative scarcity of management extends to finding and hiring skilled online workers, particularly in internet hot spots. Help is on hand, at least in Silicon Valley, from Guru.com, an online resource for freelance professionals.

Financing the start-up

Every internet start-up venture needs financing. The first round of financing, when there is only a germ of an idea or a draft business plan, is probably the most difficult to raise. Venture capital investors may prefer to invest once the start-up has got off the ground; indeed some funds may only consider investing after the venture has generated six months of revenues. The solution for the seed equity gap and any required advice may be found in one of the internet incubators being set up along the lines of the US-based Idealab.[8]

Can the internet start-up attract a deep-pocketed investor who will add value?

The market is hot and lots of people want to invest in internet start-ups, so who is the most suitable financial partner? The rapid projected growth of internet start-ups dictates that they may spend only a brief time in an incubator or a couple of months on angel seed financing. It will not, however, be long before the venture will require significant amounts of equity financing, over multiple rounds, and this is most likely to come from a venture capital provider.

Times are good for internet start-ups, as the supply of venture capital funds has grown rapidly. European investment in the technology sectors rose from $2.6 billion in 1997 to $4.5 billion in 1998.[9] Over the same period the amount of venture capital invested in start-ups increased by 135 percent to reach $1.7 billion across all industries.

The problem for the internet start-up, with a viable business plan and strong management team, is whose money to accept. This is a trade-off between the cheapest money and strategic investors. The latter should be able to support the venture with the necessary levels of finance, bring valuable experience and contacts, and want to help create a successful large venture.

Are the exit route and timing defined?

The exit must be clearly defined from the outset. The current market dynamics suggest that a successful internet start-up will have either achieved an initial public offering or merged with a larger competitor/strategic partner within 18 months of launch. The entrepreneur must realize that both routes can lead to financial rewards and a small piece of a large pie is often worth more than a large piece of a small pie. The losers are going to be those ventures that fail to become one of the dominant two or three companies in their target market. If this looks likely, the sooner a trade sale or merger is executed, the greater the probability of the entrepreneurs securing their reward.

Issues an internet start-up venture must answer

The business proposition

1. Is the business proposition/concept novel?
2. Does the venture have the potential to create value?
3. What is the economic advantage over traditional businesses?
4. How will the venture generate its revenues?
5. What is the size of the target market?

The route to market

6. Are the required technical capabilities in place?
7. Are the fulfillment capabilities in place?
8. Will the venture generate traffic and "stickiness"?
9. How will the internet start-up create a brand?
10. Are there any regulatory hurdles?

The competitive intensity

11. How real is the threat of substitution?
12. How will established businesses respond?
13. Does the venture have first-mover advantage?

Management and human capital requirements

14. Does the management team have relevant industry expertise?
15. Has the management team run a big business?
16. Does the venture have the necessary skilled online workers?

Financing the start-up

17. Can the venture attract a deep-pocketed, value-adding investor?
18. Are the exit route and timing defined?

1 "The European Internet Report: Déjà Vu?" Morgan Stanley Dean Witter, June 1999.

2 "Internet Overview/Update," Morgan Stanley Dean Witter Technology Team, June 1999.

3 "eEurope Takes Off," Andersen Consulting, Fall 1999.

4 "B2B: 2B or Not 2B?" Goldman Sachs Investment Research, September 1999.

5 "Dot-coms Vie for Attention," *Financial Times*, 17 November 1999.

6 "High–power Advertising pulls the Punters," *New Media Age*, 4 November 1999.

7 "Change the game, Change the Rules of the Game," KPMG's Strategy eBook, K. Patel and G. Damen, December 1999.

8 "Incubators Get Tech Firms up and Running – for a Price," *The Wall Street Journal*, 6 December 1999.

9 "Money for Growth: The European Technology Investment Report," PricewaterhouseCoopers, 1998.

Catching customers on the web

The internet will have a huge impact on the way business is done – especially for small and emerging companies. **Albert Angehrn** and **Jean-Louis Barsoux** explain the ramifications.

For all that has been written about the internet, most managers remain confused regarding its likely strategic impact on their businesses. Our aim, in this article, is not to try to predict the likely technological evolution of the internet but rather to provide managers with a generic framework (the ICDT model) for understanding the opportunities and threats generated by the internet – and for developing a strategy to leverage these. The internet, as this article will make clear, is of particular relevance to small companies and emerging businesses; entrepreneurs cannot afford to ignore it.

What to make of the internet: the ICDT model

The internet, and its related basic services such as electronic mail and the world wide web, have created a new space in which to do business. This has given economic agents, whether individuals or companies, alternative channels for exchanging information, communicating, distributing different types of products and services, and initiating formal business transactions.

The ICDT model (*see* Figure 1) takes its name from the four "virtual spaces" created by the internet: a virtual information space; a virtual communication space; a virtual distribution space; and a virtual transaction space. The four spaces are treated separately because they correspond to different strategic objectives and require different types of investment, and organizational adjustments.

The virtual information space (VIS) is about visibility. It operates like a large billboard. It shows who's who, what's available, how much it costs and so on. It may offer flexible access that allows visitors to "choose their own path" but it remains a one-way communication channel.

The virtual communication space (VCS) is about interaction. Like a café, it provides a "space" for engaging in relationship building, exchange of ideas or opinions. The "space" itself can range from a simple chat-line to a sophisticated 3D space in which individuals "meet." Members of the virtual community can communicate at high speed, low cost and bypass traditional physical and geographical constraints.

The virtual distribution space (VDS) is about service delivery. As with the postal service, there are constraints on the types of items that can be delivered through this channel – it is only suitable for products and services that can be wholly or partly digitalized. Furthermore, the recipient takes "something" away but payment itself happens elsewhere.

The virtual transaction space (VTS) is about trading. It is a bit like a stock exchange in that goods and services are not transferred in this space, only orders, commitments, invoices or transfers of payment.

Figure 1: The four visual business spaces

Access to markets and resources
Information space

In terms of engaging with the environment, the VIS is the virtual space that has attracted the most attention, primarily because it affords instant global access, whether to potential customers or business partners.

For many companies, the internet represents little more than a parallel way of diffusing standard information and their websites mirror the content, not to say the appeal, of their corporate literature. However, simply creating a website does little to stimulate interest. It establishes contact, but if the aim is to connect with other economic agents, the information provided has to be pertinent.

Relevance can be enhanced by customizing the channel to user groups. For example, potential business partners may have very different company or product information needs from potential consumers. But this is not a one-off effort. If a company wants people to return to the site, and to build up an on-going relationship, it needs to update regularly the content of its pages. That requires dedicated personnel and investments in multimedia competencies. Moreover, there is a lot of information to extract from monitoring the flow of visits to the site. Companies that take the trouble to compile and analyze this information may find it a cheap way of understanding customer preferences.

Communication space

The VCS presence of most companies remains underdeveloped because businesses are still not sure what objectives it might serve. Part of the problem is that the interface with customers has traditionally been the responsibility of the marketing department, which is more used to broadcasting to than interacting with customers.

The VCS provides an opportunity to exchange information and opinions through e-mail, in online forum discussions, or more advanced interaction spaces. Discussions among visitors regarding their experiences with the product and ideas relating to its usage may have an unforeseen pay-off for the company. Besides helping to differentiate the product, it may also yield unexpected insights on possible product adaptations or highlight untapped market segments. There is also a case for opening similar sites for corporate users – potential partners, suppliers or distributors from within the same industry – who might interact in closed user groups, discuss industry trends via online forums, and formulate requests for meetings with company representatives.

Distribution space

Exploiting the VDS potential of the internet is primarily aimed at cutting costs and lead times. Of course, software and publishing companies have been particularly quick to latch on to the possibilities of dispensing with intermediaries and delivering their products directly.

But the internet can also be used to distribute to customers auxiliary services associated with "physical" products such as cars. Instruction manuals, customer support and consulting services, product-related training and updates – including digital pictures and music – can all be provided over the web in ways that "augment" the value of the "core" product.

What is more, the internet creates the possibility of offering new value-adding services. Some companies have found that they can repackage the information they use to control their processes and make this information available to customers as a service. A typical example is the magazine or newspaper that gives outside access to its archives, initially designed to support its journalists. Another example is the Federal Express service that allows customers to track their parcels online. This reduces the number of expensive calls to customer service representatives and has increased customer loyalty in a fiercely competitive market.

Transaction space

The objective here is clear: to engage in business-to-business or business-to-customer transactions such as ordering, invoicing and payment. This has both revenue-generation and cost-reduction potential in that it facilitates order processing and shortens lead times. The cost of an internet transaction in banking, for example, is a fraction of the same transaction at a bank branch. Business-to-business transactions have benefitted considerably from this channel. It allows companies to trigger automatic ordering, to invoice, and make payments easily. This has been facilitated by electronic data interchange (EDI) platforms, which provide a high level of security. In fact, many businesses are insisting that potential suppliers install EDI if they want to be considered.

Business-to-consumer transactions do not yet benefit from the same kind of security or reliability as offered by the EDI system, with the huge potential for wide-reaching commercial activity with consumers being stifled by legal, security and reliability concerns. Commercial activity so far has been limited to low-value

Figure 2: Virtual Vineyards is a web-based wine and speciality food shop

purchases such as software, books, music and magazines. One such example is Virtual Vineyards, a web-based wine and speciality food shop (*see* Figure 2). Visitors can purchase directly from the company using an online form.

A more secure system is proposed by IBM which enables visitors to browse through a catalog of products via the web and then place orders interactively via a secure credit card information form. Many companies are looking into ways of improving security so it is only a matter of time before online transactions explode. Once security can be guaranteed, a company will simply need to hook up its internet site with its internal accounting system or other transaction-processing systems. This is an advanced type of application that will demand heavy investments.

Internal websites

Internal websites, known as intranets, offer businesses most of the same functions as groupware at a lower price, and without the need to tie themselves in to a single groupware vendor. They make it easier for employees to access and share internal information. Although covered in detail in the original paper on which this article is based, they are not detailed here.

Changing the rules

So far, the internet has had limited impact on how most companies operate and its strategic impact has been weak. However, once it fulfills its potential, the cumulative influence of the internet within the four virtual spaces may produce a different order of change altogether. The full exploitation of the communication and transaction spaces, in particular, may upset a lot of our basic strategic assumptions about how best to absorb, process and leverage information. This assertion is based on what remains a little documented phenomenon: the emergence, thanks to the internet, of a new breed of business, the global start-up.

The most embryonic start-up becomes a multinational company, at low cost, simply by virtue of setting up a website. As the joke says: "The great thing about the internet is that no one knows you're really a dog." But many of these new entrants are not dogs at all. The internet has done much more than magnify their visibility. It has provided them with a low-cost distribution network, with a way of searching for business partners, and of collecting critical information about distant markets and resources.

The internet does more than simply let new entrants compete on a par with established companies; it can sometimes give them the edge. Consider the challenge of accessing resources. The China Internet Company, backed by the Xinhua News Agency, has established a network of internet sites for 40 industrial cities. This is accompanied by a complete catalog of Chinese laws relating to trade and export, a translation service and news. Given the paucity of a physical infrastructure for information about exports, the internet will quickly become the key channel for companies wishing to do business with Chinese suppliers.

Similarly, where companies are offering a specialized product or service, the internet serves to trawl for customers worldwide. It has the capacity to transform former niche markets into mass markets. Moreover, the low cost of distribution on the internet makes it viable to serve whole new market segments. For example, online newspapers have created a new readership among expatriates living in remote locations who were previously neglected.

The internet also allows small companies to conduct forms of market research that would previously have been prohibitively expensive even for big companies. As already mentioned, this can be done by tracking the behavior and preferences of visitors to websites. Furthermore, the internet allows companies to conduct cut-price surveys that are much more effective than phone or mail surveys in that they allow branching (that is, different questions based on different responses to previous questions).

While a virtual marketspace creates new business opportunities, at the same time much of the conventional wisdom of business is threatened. For example, the size of a business will no longer be much indication of the scope of its geographical activities. The traditional concern with "where to do business?" is superseded by the concept of "how to do business?"

A well-established network of physical assets may no longer be of much use; indeed, it may even get in the way of speedy strategic reconfiguration. The key competencies embodied by a company will no longer relate to products but rather to processes and particularly the capacity to link up quickly and effectively with different types of network.

Of course it all raises a new set of practical issues. How do you build up trust and commitment without face-to-face contact? How do you increase the motivation to share information where the outcome is uncertain? How do you anticipate the key networks and make the right learning connections?

Companies hoping to leverage the potential of the internet will also have to create new roles or even whole functions: a scanning function to monitor and influence internet opinion; a new service development function to think up ways of creating value for customers; liaison roles to support networks of remote members; usage analysts to perform market research on the web; and archivists responsible for keeping track of content generated on the company's websites.

The winners will be those companies that organize themselves to capitalize on the internet's capacity to increase sensitivity to resource and market opportunities worldwide and to share knowledge and experience internally.

CASE STUDY

Amazon.com: unleashing the power of e-technology to focus on customers

Jeff Bezos probably hadn't figured on sore knees and an aching back when he decided to leave his high-powered job to begin an entirely new career and business. Just 30, he had until then followed the whizzkid's classic path: a summa cum laude Princeton University graduate in computer science and electrical engineering, the youngest ever Senior Vice-President in a Wall Street investment bank, and fast becoming one of the city's leading money and hedge fund managers, he was seemingly destined for the corporate fast track. Then in 1994, everything changed.

During a casual read, Jeff Bezos came across a startling statistic to do with the internet: usage of the new medium was growing at 2,300 percent a year. His reaction was quick and decisive: "It was my wake-up call." Anything that was growing that fast was going to be an opportunity for market creation and growth.

Thanks to the bonuses he had made in his brief yet successful Wall Street career, Bezos decided to quit his job. The next few months he spent studying the key factors necessary for success on the net. He soon narrowed his list down from about 20 potential products to just two: music and books. Possibly because he loved reading, possibly because his wife was an aspiring novelist, and definitely because of the innumerable hassles encountered by customers at any traditional book retail outlet, he chose books.

He called the business – what he intended to be the world's biggest bookstore – after the world's longest river. Using some of the $11 million he had managed to raise thanks to his contacts on Wall Street and through his intensive networking among West Coast venture capitalists, he set up his headquarters in July 1995 in a 400 sq ft storeroom, three floors above an art gallery in a slightly seedy street in Seattle. It was furnished with a refrigerator-sized box running the computer hardware for the Amazon.com website. Bezos and his workers would kneel on the floor, late into the night, packing books to ship off to their growing number of customers – hence the sore knees and aching back.

From the outset, Bezos's objective was to build an online store that was customer friendly and easy to navigate. The idea behind Amazon.com was not to replicate, or even do better, on the web what bricks and mortar bookstores did: sell books. None of the traditional outlets had the goal of having every book in print in stock – a concept Bezos visualized for Amazon from the start, a cross between a library, an information bureau and a retail store. He wanted to provide a different and enhanced experience for customers and thus get as many as possible back again and again. So the immediate priority was to identify and remove the hassles of book buying, including getting to the store; looking for a book; waiting to be served; standing in a line to pay; waiting weeks for out-of-stock books; lack of feedback and follow-up when these books did arrive; and, last but not least, paying inflated prices for physical and personnel infrastructures.

Bezos was determined to show that being online did not mean less service, it meant more. "If you make customers unhappy in the physical world, they might each tell six friends. If you make customers unhappy on the internet, they can each tell 6,000 friends with one message to a newsgroup. If you make them really happy, they can tell 6,000 people about you. You want every customer to become an evangelist for you."

Amazon sought to get to know individual customers better. Employees were trained to spend as much time, money and energy on service and building relationships as they did on selling and shipping books. They were encouraged to go to greater lengths to exceed expected standards when a customer needed assistance on, say, a queried title, a mistaken address and so on. When a customer wanted help, the humans took over from the machines – 20 percent of Amazon staff did nothing but answer queries from the e-mail center. "We want Amazon.com to be the right store for you as an individual," commented Bezos. "If we have 4.5 million customers, we should have 4.5 million stores."

Because Amazon had effectively done away with activities and expenses that were not adding value to the customer experience – looking for prime physical sites; decorating, redesigning and promoting them; as well as a huge administrative and sales staff – it was initially able to take 30 percent off the price of selected hardbacks, and 20 percent off paperbacks. But while being able to offer books for less was an important element in the Amazon strategy, it wouldn't be enough to ensure that customers came back to the site over and over again. To achieve that, customers had to feel they were getting superior and personalized value. The Amazon.com site went beyond being an extensive catalog. Typically, a brief synopsis of the book would be included, as well as reviews, from leading journals, such as *The New York Times*, as well as from other readers. Visitors to the site were encouraged to write and submit reviews of books they had read.

Bezos's intention had always been to grow the market, rather than just cannibalize existing sales. When customers looked up a book on the Amazon site, they were told of two or three other titles purchased by other people who had bought the same book. Customers were signed up through a personal notification service, called "Eyes," which meant that they could indicate what kinds of book, either in terms of subjects or authors, they liked to read. They received regular e-mails with reviews of what Amazon's editors considered "exceptional" books in these categories. Customers could modify or add to their reading profiles whenever they wanted by e-mailing the customer service desk. Paying for books was done by entering credit card information, which was specially encrypted to ensure privacy and security.

Bezos also pioneered the concept of an "Associates" program. He knew about networking effects, one of the precepts of the modern economy, and that the value of an infrastructure increased exponentially as more members joined it who produced customer value. And that meant more for everyone, including customers. The objective was to get as many others as possible to join the Amazon network, rather than to keep it proprietary. That way, customers could find exactly what they wanted irrespective of its location on the web, and get to that site quickly and seamlessly at the click of an icon. For example, for readers interested in cooking, Amazon provided a direct link to Starchefs, which specialized in books for gourmets. Through this collaborative concept, website owners also recommended books to be purchased at Amazon.com, in return for which they earned referral fees of up to 15 percent. By the beginning of 1999, the number of Associates had grown to 200,000.

In the second half of 1998, Amazon spent $250 million on purchasing two internet companies: PlanetAll, a provider of highly personalized online services for 1.5 million subscribers that enabled customers automatically to update their address books, calendars and reminders on a minute-for-minute basis; and Junglee Corp., a maker of database systems which let customers find any kind of merchandise on the net, and which shared its revenues with the portals that co-branded its services. The Junglee technology enabled Amazon to stretch its brands even further into e-merchandising. The PlanetAll connection gave it access to the names and addresses of people to whom Amazon customers might want to send such merchandise, for example as gifts.

Amazon also formally entered the European market with the launch of two websites, one in the UK – Amazon.co.uk, following its acquisition of Bookpages – and the other in Germany – Amazon.de, after acquiring Telebook. Bezos explained his thinking: "We want to make it possible for anybody in the world to order a German-language book, a Japanese-language book, not just an English-language book. So we need to have local customer service operations, local distribution centers, to really service those markets as if we were a local company there."

One of the drawbacks of an online bookstore like Amazon.com was that it could not offer comfy sofas and cappuccinos to those who browsed through its virtual aisles. So Bezos determinedly set about finding innovative ways to enhance the overall customer experience. For example, an agreement in July 1997 with Pulitzer prize-winning author John Updike led to Updike writing the beginning of an original story (entitled *Murder Makes the Magazine*) exclusively for Amazon. Over the next 44 days, visitors to the site could write and submit their suggestions for continuing the story. The writers of paragraphs selected by the Amazon editorial staff to continue the story each received $1,000. In all, 400,000 people participated.

Hand in hand with such "fun" initiatives, Amazon.com continuously enhanced and upgraded its customer interface technologies and infrastructures. It launched a "recommendation center" on its website, offering individuals personalized book recommendations based on their specific profiles and interests and on the ratings of other customers. Since many people didn't know precisely what they wanted to read next, an "if you like this author" selection gave them a suggested list of other authors. Bezos and his team also began working on highly sophisticated systems that would help individuals find the precise books that "would change the world for them. If you can do that you are creating real value," he said.

Amazon developed and launched a technology called 1-Click, which gave customers the ability to make purchases with a single click of the mouse, eliminating the need for them to give order information every time. Bezos claimed that 1-Click represented a "new standard for ease of buying on or off the web," irrespective of product. In another innovative application of technology, Amazon began work with a company called NuvoMedia on a handheld device allowing readers to download the books they wanted directly from the web.

In June 1998, its presence now firmly established in the marketplace, Amazon expanded into music. More than 125,000 CDs were offered, ten times the selection of the average music store, at discounts of up to 40 percent. Music fans could search by CD title, artist, song title or label, and listen to more than 225,000 songs. There were expert and customer reviews, interviews with artists, essential lists, news, and an updated index of the hottest CDs. A few weeks later, at customer request, the site was expanded to include 42,000 classical and opera CDs.

Also based on demand and feedback from customers, the company launched a "mini store," aimed specifically at children, called Amazon.com Kids. This featured a catalog of more than 100,000 books for children, teens and their parents. In addition, the mini site had in-depth articles, reviews, interviews, and special search and recommendation services.

Bezos was determined to build what he called a "literary stock market," from which both readers and writers could benefit. Authors, accustomed to getting royalty statements once a year from publishers, could check to see how their new book was doing on a daily basis from a globally assembled listing, continually updated. Students and others seeking information could use this as a reference site.

Bezos follows the mantra of "GBF" (Get Big Fast). He explains: "This is a scale business. And what happens is that the fixed costs of doing this business are very high, and the variable costs of doing this business are extremely low. As a result, our major strategic objective has always been GBF. At the same time, we are investing significant amounts of money in advertising and marketing in order to introduce ourselves to as many customers as possible, as soon as possible ... We spend marketing dollars at a level which is disproportionate to a company of our size. And we do that because we believe this is a critical ... time where, roughly speaking, maybe a dollar spent on advertising today is worth $10 spent on advertising next year."

Amazon is able to boost sales simply by persuading more people to visit its online store, rather than having to follow the normal retail route of opening new outlets. As Chief Financial Officer Joy Covey explained: "I don't think we could have grown a physical store base four times in one year."

Throughout 1997 and into 1998, Amazon worked on several levels in order to achieve this "GBF" growth objective. It also began tapping outside sources of finance. In May 1997, it went public with an initial public offering of three million shares at a price of $18 per share. By early August, the price had jumped to $28.75. A few months later, Amazon negotiated a $75 million, three-year credit facility from a bank consortium led by Deutsche Morgan Grenfell.

By the first quarter of 1999, Amazon had become the third largest bookseller in the US in revenue terms, and the leading online shopping site. It had also become the number one bookseller in the UK and Germany. It had 6.2 million customers in more than 160 countries, with 64 percent repeat buyers. Its share price had sky-rocketed by 1,300 percent in 12 months and, though it had not yet reported its first dollar of profit, investors had put its market value at $11 billion, much higher than many of the traditional "greats" of retailing.

Notwithstanding the enormity of competitive reaction on a global scale to Amazon's revolution, a *BusinessWeek* article in December 1998 commented: "Even though Amazon is still a long way from making a profit, its basic economics suggest the upstart will someday look more like a fat-cat software company than a scrambling-for-profits retailer. Once Amazon gets enough customers and sales to pay off its initial marketing and technology investments – and as that technology pays off in falling ... costs – additional revenue drops to the bottom line."

The Amazon story is yet to be fully played out. But it illustrates the potential power of e-technology once it is focussed on customers.

The above case is taken from *Customer Capitalism: increasing returns in new market spaces* by Sandra Vandermerwe, Nicholas Brealey Publishing, 1999.

"Amazon.com: marketing a new electronic go-between service provider," case study written by Sandra Vandermerwe and Marika Taishoff, available from European Case Clearing House, ref. 598-069-1.

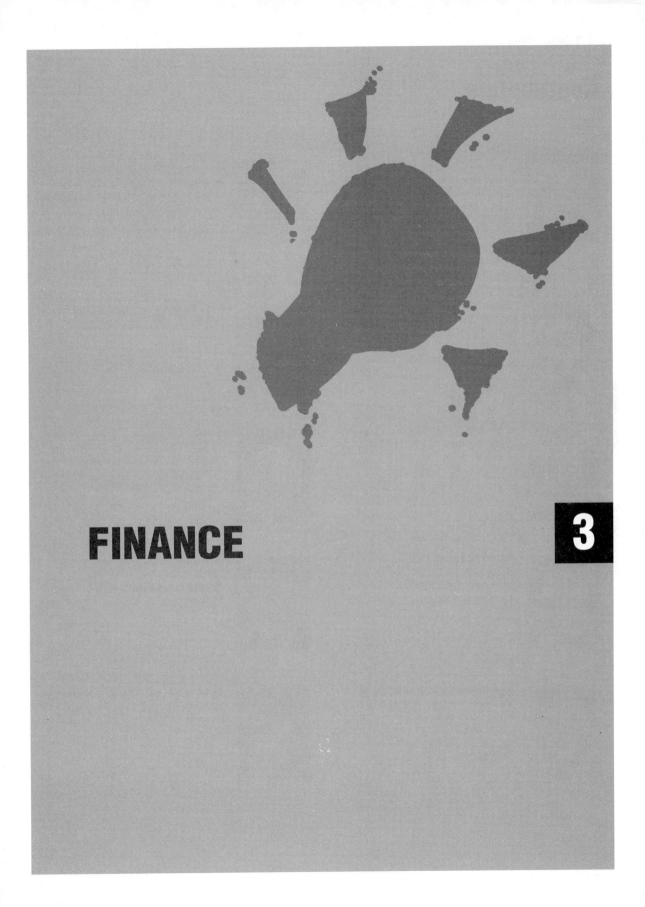

FINANCE

3

Contributors

William D. Bygrave is the Frederic C. Hamilton Professor for Free Enterprise and former Director of the Center for Entrepreneurial Studies at Babson College, Wellesley, Massachusetts. He has been a Visiting Professor at the London Business School, INSEAD, France, and Special Professor at the University of Nottingham, UK. He teaches and researches entrepreneurship, especially financing of start-up and growing ventures.

Jonathan Levie is a member of the Strathclyde Entrepreneurship Initiative at the University of Strathclyde, Scotland.

Colin Mason is Professor of Economic Geography at the University of Southampton.

Richard Harrison is Professor of Management Studies and Director of the Entrepreneurship Centre at the University of Aberdeen, Scotland.

Harry Sapienza is Assistant Professor, Management Program Area, at the Darla Moore School of Business, University of South Carolina, Columbia. His main research areas are top management teams, strategies implementation, and entrepreneurship.

Benoît Leleux is the S. Schmidheiny Chair in Entrepreneurship and Finance at the International Institute for Management Development (IMD), Lausanne, Switzerland.

Hugh Richards is a director of 3i and is responsible for 3i's investment business in London.

Herwig M. Langohr is Professor of Finance and Banking at INSEAD, Fontainebleau. His research interests include corporate finance, money and banking.

Martin Binks is Senior Lecturer in Economics and Entrepreneurship in the School of Management and Finance at the University of Nottingham.

Christine Ennew is Professor of Marketing in the School of Management and Finance at the University of Nottingham.

Contents

Introduction

Part 3 is about the various sources of money which you may need to start a new venture. The part is in two sections. First, the authors discuss the merits of sources such as family and friends, bankers, venture capitalists, and business angels. Their articles also give some handy hints as to the criteria which each of these "lenders" may use in assessing business. The second section looks at the overall financial structuring of the emerging business.

Calling on family and friends for start-up cash

William Bygrave provides an overview of the kinds of financing decisions that need to be faced by the new entrepreneur.

For would-be entrepreneurs, there are two types of start-up capital: debt and equity. Simply put, with debt they do not have to give up any ownership of their businesses but they have to pay current interest and eventually repay the principal; with equity they have to give up some of the ownership to get it but they may never have to repay it or even pay a dividend. So it is a trade-off between paying interest or giving up some of the ownership. Debt and equity funding are discussed separately on pp. 99 and 105.

In practice, what usually happens depends on how much of each type of capital an entrepreneur can raise. Most start-up entrepreneurs do not have much flexibility in their choice of financing. If it is a risky business with little or no assets, it is impossible to get any bank debt without putting up some collateral other than the business's assets – most likely that collateral is personal assets. Even if entrepreneurs are willing to guarantee the whole loan with their personal assets, the bank expects them to put some equity into the business, probably equal to 25 percent of the amount of the loan.

It is no surprise that the vast majority of entrepreneurs have to start their businesses on a shoestring and leverage their savings and labor. And they start with remarkably little capital. For example, one quarter of the *Inc. 500 – Inc.* magazine's annual list of its 500 US small business stars – began with less than $5,000, half with less than $25,000, and three-quarters with less than $100,000. Fewer than 5 percent began with more than $1 million.

Typically, entrepreneurs start their businesses with "sweat equity" and personal savings. Sweat equity is ownership earned in lieu of wages. Then a wealthy investor who knows something about the entrepreneurs or the industry, or both – sometimes called an informal investor or "business angel" – invests some personal money in return for equity.

When the company is selling a product, it may be able to get a bank line of credit secured by its inventory and accounts receivable. If the company is growing fast in a large market, it may be able to raise capital from a formal venture capital company in return for equity. Further expansion capital may come from venture capitalists or from a public stock offering or a merger with a larger company.

Most new companies are not high-potential businesses and will never be candidates for formal venture capital. Nevertheless, they must find some equity capital. In most cases, it comes from the 4Fs – the Founders initially dig deeply into their personal savings (often to the point of exhausting them), then they turn to Family, Friends and Foolhardy investors.

It can be a scary business. Entrepreneurs often find themselves with all their personal net worth tied up in the same business that provides all their income. It is double jeopardy because if their businesses fail they lose both their savings and their means of support. Risk of that sort can be justified only if the profit potential is high enough to yield a commensurate rate of return.

How can the owners of private companies get a satisfactory return on their investments without making their companies public or selling them? The two ingredients that determine return on investment are the amount invested and the annual amount earned on that investment. Hence, entrepreneurs should invest as little as possible to start their businesses and make sure that their companies will be able to pay them a "dividend" big enough to yield an appropriate annual rate of return.

For income tax purposes, that "dividend" may be in the form of a salary bonus or fringe benefits rather than an actual dividend paid out of retained earnings. Of course, a prudent company ought to be generating cash from its operations – rather than by borrowing more money externally – before that "dividend" is paid.

It is said that happiness for an entrepreneur is positive cash flow. However, if a company is growing rapidly, every penny of internally generated cash is plowed back into the enterprise to sustain its growth, leaving nothing to be distributed to the entrepreneur and the investors.

Perhaps it is more correct to say that real happiness for an entrepreneur is free cash flow – the internal generation of more cash than a business needs to sustain its optimum growth rate. Free cash flow can be distributed as dividends to the owners or used to buy back shares from owners who want to realize their investment in the company or be retained in the business.

No wonder Bill Gates is smiling a lot these days. Microsoft, the company he started on a shoestring in the late 1970s, generated so much free cash flow in 1999 that it added $2.5 million hourly to its $17 billion war chest.

Convincing the cash-conscious banker

Jonathan Levie describes some of the sensitive issues involved in persuading a bank to part with money to fund a new venture.

Most large banks provide excellent information packs on how to open a new business account and how to make a loan proposal.

Here we aim to shed light on these issues so that the entrepreneur can take informed decisions on whether and how to seek debt finance and present a proposal in the best possible way. The following sections describe the nature of lending; the benefits, costs and risks involved to both parties; and critical success factors in forging a banking relationship for a new venture.

The nature of lending

Few entrepreneurs understand the nature of lending. As Adam Smith noted more than 200 years ago, they tend to think that banks could and should "extend their credits to whatever sum might be wanted without incurring any other expense besides that of a few reams of paper."

This view enrages bankers, who typically reply: "If you become successful we cannot share in your success, so why should we lose if you lose?" In this long-running shouting match, both sides miss the point.

Banks make most of their profits on net interest income. This is the difference between the interest they pay on money "borrowed" from depositors or other banks and the interest they receive on *the same money* "lent" to borrowers (such as entrepreneurs). Very little (say 5 percent or so) of the asset base of a bank consists of shareholders' funds, or equity, and they operate on very narrow net interest margins.

For example, let's assume that, for commercial lending, fees cover expenses and that the net interest margin is 3 percent. A customer defaults on a one-year term loan and the entire principal (amount loaned) is lost. As the bank must repay its depositors, the loss reduces the equity portion of the bank's balance sheet. Even worse, because it is allowed to lend only in proportion to its equity base, the loss reduces its ability to lend.

Yet to just make up the principal in that one bad loan, the banker must earn the full 3 percent net interest margin on more than *33 new loans* of the same type. (It takes more than 33 three-hundredths to make one.) This is why bankers do not like high-risk loan proposals, why loans must be repaid, and why security in support of an advance is often sought "just in case."

Experience and statistics have led bankers to believe that new ventures are, on average, relatively high-risk lending propositions. However, the long-term rewards to bankers on new venture lending can be high. A young company that grows into a successful strong business creates an ever-increasing potential source of income to its bank – from fees, loan interest, deposit interest, foreign exchange, leasing, factoring, venture capital, merchant banking, insurance, extra personal accounts for an expanding and increasingly wealthy workforce, and increases in local business activity.

Bankers are well aware of this and attempts to poach "star" accounts in the medium-sized corporate sector are legion. However, research has indicated that in some countries, entrepreneurs who have a good banking relationship are surprisingly loyal to the banker who helped them to start up and that attempts to poach are often resisted.

No one can predict precisely which new businesses will succeed; banks may well have to accept an increased level of bad debts among their new venture accounts in order to capture the stars of tomorrow. The good news is that failure rates are highest early on, when the amount of debt a company carries is relatively small.

Benefits, costs and risks

Why should entrepreneurs borrow? Debt finance makes sense only if the returns to be made on the extra business financed by the debt considerably exceed the costs and risks of borrowing. In that case, the entrepreneur can make more money with bank finance than without it and can even write off the interest against tax.

The costs of borrowing include search costs, interest costs, and fees and conditions attached to the use of the debt. These conditions can place considerable restrictions on the future management of the business and even on the private life of the entrepreneur's family.

The risks of borrowing include wasted time in shopping around to no avail, interest rate rises, unexpected charges, a new bank manager with a different perspective, a change in bank policy, and the bank's reaction to a "temporary" downturn in the business (which might include freezing the current and deposit accounts and calling the loan in early).

Bankers are constantly asked to put up virtually all of the finance for a new venture. This suggests that the real reason why so many entrepreneurs seek debt finance is that they desire to minimize their own financial investment while maximizing their "control," defined as share ownership. Bankers are well aware of this. If a banker does entertain such a proposal, the loan will have so many conditions attached to it that the banker will not just "control" the business but also the entrepreneur.

Critical success factors

Personal loans are now routinely screened in many countries using computerized credit scoring techniques. Commercial loan decisions, in contrast, are still heavily influenced by the personal impression the entrepreneur leaves on the loan officer, although this varies a lot from bank to bank, and even from sector to sector within the same bank.

Research suggests that bankers form an impression of an individual quickly and tend to stick to it. It is for this reason that the entrepreneur must impress at the first meeting. The aim should be to project confident professionalism. Entrepreneurs should dress conservatively, turn up on time, emphasize their relevant experience and management skills, be ready to produce documentary evidence to support their argument, articulately argue the case for debt finance using the banker's language, and not give in too easily.

Remember the banker needs to be sure that the entrepreneur can negotiate with his/her other resource providers and overcome unforeseen obstacles to pay back the loan. Asking tough questions is one way of testing these skills. Research also shows that overblown attempts to impress can leave a negative impression.

The banker's language is the language of finance, and surprisingly few entrepreneurs speak it. This means that the financially literate and articulate entrepreneur has a real competitive advantage in the market for debt finance. In the interview, the banker will probably question key assumptions behind the numbers in the financial plan. They are well aware that projected sales figures can be derived to cover the loan instead of the other way around. Financial honesty is just as important as financial literacy.

Bankers often assess debt proposals using simple checklists. Figure 1 shows two widely used checklists. Some banks have introduced more complex checklists that are closer to credit scoring systems. They assess the management, market, strategy and general competitive environment using a statistically determined weighted scoring system. Opinions vary as to the value of these for new venture proposals. Many bankers place more weight on their judgement of how the entrepreneur will cope in any eventuality than on their assessment of the venture's strategy, which may evolve considerably.

Remolding the proposal

The banker may suggest changes in the entrepreneur's proposal to reduce the bank's exposure to acceptable levels. In debt/equity terms, "acceptable" usually means roughly equal contributions to the capital base of the business by the promoters and the bank.

Bankers need to see that the entrepreneur is putting as much as is necessary into the company. They also need to be sure that the finance is actually needed in the amount and type requested. Although factoring (the sale of receivables) is not usually an option for a new venture, the leasing of some assets may be and leasing can sometimes improve cash flow and the debt/equity ratio.

Security

Security is probably the most contentious issue in the entrepreneur/banker relationship. Bankers need at least one and preferably two alternative sources of repaying the loan other than cash flow. Land, buildings, vehicles, government stocks, quoted shares, insurance policies, stocks and receivables all have security potential but only at their distress sale value. Often the only fall-back security

The 5 Cs
Character of borrower
Capacity to repay
Conditions (product, industry, economy)
Capital provided (debt/equity ratio)
Collateral, or security

CAMPARI
Character of borrower
Ability to borrow and repay
Margin to profit
Purpose of the loan
Amount of the loan
Repayment terms
Insurance against non-payment (security)

Figure 1: Two common banker's checklists

available at start-up is in the form of a personal guarantee backed by assets, usually the family home.

The practice of requesting personal guarantees varies from country to country. Entrepreneurs hate them because they wipe out the advantages of limited liability. Bankers like them because they feel the entrepreneur will work that much harder to ensure the loan is repaid. On the other hand, having to call on a personal guarantee in the event of a shortfall from the sale of business assets is one of the most difficult and stressful calls a banker must make.

Bankers tend to be skeptical of government-backed business loan guarantee schemes for situations where insufficient security is available. They infringe on their profession, may have politically-motivated conditions attached, carry a higher paperwork load, and have a higher failure rate.

It may be smarter to portray a proposal as a "regular" banking proposal, in which sufficient security is available, and keep the personal guarantee option open initially in the hope of negotiating it away later. Creative thinking about security, such as obtaining options from suppliers to repurchase assets in principle, getting revaluations on land or buildings, or positive data on the marketability of assets, can help meet the banker's requirements. Separating cash flows into "definite" (for example, secured orders, royalty or service payments from secured orders) and "probable" (future sales) may reduce the amount of security required.

To offset the risk and security issues in a new venture proposition, the entrepreneur should ensure that the banker recognizes all the profit possibilities to be gained from this new account.

Negotiating hard on fees or the interest rate may not be in the entrepreneur's best interest. If the banker stands to gain, say, 30 percent more interest income by charging 1 percent more, and if that 1 percent represents only 10 percent of the entrepreneur's tax-deductible interest charges, why should it stand in the way of securing the loan?

Aftercare of bankers

Let's assume that after shopping around, and several near misses, an entrepreneur has secured a loan commitment. The banker's enjoyment of the up-front fees will soon fade and nervousness will set in. Bankers hate "surprises" and often assume the worst when they hear nothing. To offset this, the entrepreneur must keep up a steady stream of good news and warn the banker of possible bad news before it happens.

The banker will probably want regular (such as monthly) balance sheets, profit and loss, and cash flow accounts. The entrepreneur should also send press releases, customer endorsements, export sales leads, invitations to exhibitions, whatever good news he or she can muster. Enquiries related to other high-margin banking products, which have some likelihood of being needed (such as large foreign exchange transactions or letters of credit), will keep the banker focussed on the future profitability of the account rather than on its present riskiness.

If an entrepreneur has continued to keep the bank abreast of developments, and the worst happens, the banker will at least feel informed. In addition, if the banker moves on and a new banker takes over, the file will show that some progress is being made. Often, what entrepreneurs need in a crisis is a little more time from their banker. Time is granted on trust. Keeping up that stream of information can create a small reserve of trust, which one day could save the life of the business.

What venture capitalists look for

Daniel Muzyka and **Sue Birley** describe the factors venture capitalists look at when they consider investing.

One group that spends a great deal of time screening business ventures for appropriate opportunities is the venture capital industry. Indeed, they may review as many as 100 before investing in one. During this process, as is the case with any professional group, they develop implicit models of what makes a good opportunity.

Entrepreneurs need to recognize and understand these models as part of their search for funding. Even though venture capital in Europe and the US represents only a small percentage of total capital invested in entrepreneurial business, and may not be directly relevant to all entrepreneurs, these investors have had a major impact in influencing the evaluation models of other classes of risk-capital investors simply because of their experience. As such, they provide guidance as to the relevant factors to consider when evaluating an opportunity.

This is a complex area with multiple factors to be taken into account – and, of course, every business is different. So the investor is likely to be faced with the need to weigh up the relative importance of, for example, market potential, forecast financial performance, and management skills.

Curious as to whether there was some generalized decision model used in the industry, we asked a number of venture capitalists to tell us about the factors they considered – and the trade-offs they made – in their investment decisions. As we review these factors, it is important to keep the phrase "all else being equal" in mind since we assume that there is data available to support each of the criteria listed. A lack of information on any may arouse suspicions and propel it to number one for purposes of evaluation. The criteria used are listed under seven headings:

- **Product-market factors** involving various aspects of the nature of the product and the market, such as projected market size, growth and seasonality.
- **Strategic-competitive factors** related to the classic notions of strategy and competitive dynamics and including the nature and degree of competition, strength of suppliers and distributors, and the ability to create "post-entry" barriers (the ability to block others from coming into a market).
- **Management team factors** involving the leadership capabilities and track record of the lead entrepreneur and the management team.
- **Management competence factors** including organizational and administrative abilities, marketing, sales, and production capabilities.
- **Financial factors** including, for example, time to breakeven and the projected rate of return.
- **Fund factors** reflecting the relationship of the opportunity to the nature and location of the fund. Venture capitalists must be conscious of their portfolio and the commitments they have made to their investors regarding the type of investments they will consider (for example, early-stage start-ups, management buy-outs and so on).

■ **Deal factors** relating to the specific nature of the investment, the stage of development of the business, and the ability to syndicate the deal and to invest in later rounds (that is, at later stages in the growth of the investment).

Is there a common view and, if so, what is the relative importance of each of these factors when venture capitalists are asked to trade one off against another? The answer to the first is "yes." European and American venture capitalists generally have the same model for evaluating potential investment, whatever the stage of development of the business, and this is the same as that used by their colleagues around the world. Figure 1 lists the overall rankings and indicates that venture capitalists are primarily interested in whether the lead entrepreneur and the team have the required leadership and managerial capacity to be able to deliver the opportunity. Their logic is clear. If these qualities are absent, everything else is problematic.

Financial projections receive some weight but are overwhelmed by considerations of the team and the market opportunity. Again, this makes intuitive sense. Financial projections are realized only when a good business proposition becomes a reality, not when it is forecast. The actual nature and degree of competition in the market are less important than the team's apparent ability to sustain and protect market share.

The implications for entrepreneurs when seeking external finance are clear. Who implements what is most important. How and where they will implement it are secondary. So entrepreneurs need to worry about themselves, their skills and the fit of the management team in relation to their proposed venture. They need to make sure they can convincingly demonstrate leadership ability and the appropriate competencies to potential investors.

1 Leadership potential of lead entrepreneur.
2 Leadership potential of management team.
3 Recognized industry expertise in management team.
4 Track record of lead entrepreneur.
5 Track record of management team.
6 Sustained share position.
7 Marketing/sales capabilities of team.
8 Organizational/administrative capabilities of team.
9 Ability to get the cash out of the investment.
10 Degree of product-market understanding.
11 Expected rate of return (return on investment)
12 Time to breakeven.
13 Financial/accounting capabilities of team.
14 Ability to create post-entry barriers.
15 Business meets funds constraints.
16 Process/production capabilities of team.
17 Uniqueness of product and technology.
18 Market growth and attractiveness.
19 Degree of market already established.
20 Time required to pay back the investment.
21 Ability to influence nature of business.
22 Importance of unclear assumptions.
23 Stage of investment required.
24 Ease of market entry.
25 Strength of suppliers and distributors.
26 Nature and degree of competition.
27 Location of business.
28 Business and product fit with venture capitalist's portfolio of investments.
29 Projected market size.
30 Sensitivity to economic cycles.
31 Ability to syndicate (or bring others into the investment) deal.
32 Number and nature of co-investors already in the deal.
33 Seasonality of product market.
34 Scale and chance of later financing rounds.
35 Location of business relative to fund.

Figure 1: Order of factors considered in assessing venture capital opportunities

They should focus on presenting a clear product-market strategy, incorporating a unique product or service that can create post-entry barriers. In addition they must make sure they have credible financial projections that are clear about the time to operating breakeven (which for venture capitalists should be relatively short) and show a way for investors to get their money out (the all-important exit route). The entrepreneur should not become obsessive about presenting copious, well-packaged financial information. Real risk capital investors know that these are all fantasy without the rest of the opportunity being in line.

In fact, these guidelines are relevant whatever the situation, whether you are seeking funding from a bank, from a private risk capital investor or venture "angel," from your family and friends, or whether you are simply trying to convince yourself of the viability of your proposal. After all, you have almost certainly invested time and probably money already and it makes sense to see if it is worth continuing.

Having suggested that there is a relatively common view, you should know that there are some differences among investors. Their differences are going to be a product of their history and deal experience. Knowing the relative importance of the overall factors of evaluation are important. We would also suggest that you get to know something about each of the venture capitalists you approach and their investment patterns – it may make all the difference in getting to "yes."

For a full report of the study, see Muzyka, Birley and Leleux (1996) "Tradeoffs in the investment decisions of European venture capitalists," *Journal of Business Venturing*, Vol. 11, No. 4, July, 273–288.

How the venture capitalists work out the financial odds

Equity financing is the riskiest form of new venture investment and investors require significant provisions to reduce their risk. **William Bygrave** explains.

Every business has equity financing. Initially it is money that entrepreneurs put into their ventures to get them launched. Some entrepreneurs augment their personal capital with money invested by family and friends. A few expand the equity in their business by selling shares to business angels. A tiny elite group of high potentials raise equity capital from formal venture capital companies.

Of the two million or so ventures started annually in the US, about 95 percent get all their equity funding from the founding entrepreneurs and their immediate family and friends. No more than 5 percent get funding from angels; and less than .05 percent get it from formal venture capitalists.

The most sophisticated private equity investors are professional venture capitalists. By examining how they evaluate, value and finance entrepreneurial companies, we can learn a lot about the process of private equity investing. Granted, this is a group of sophisticated investors, but they set the standards for good practice when it comes to equity investments in private companies.

Entrepreneurial folklore says that professional venture capitalists do not invest in a company until their rising greed overcomes their declining fear. Put differently, it means that they do not put money into a company until they are convinced that there is a reasonable probability that the potential financial returns measure up to the risks. As a rule of thumb, this means that they expect to get a return of between five and ten times their initial investment in about five to seven years. In an ideal case the company will grow rapidly and make an initial public offering of its shares within five years of the first venture capital investment.

Common shares are the riskiest equity – none more so than shares in a young, private company. Besides the fact that common shareholders stand last in line to get paid when a company fails, investment in a private company lacks liquidity because there is no public stock market where the shares can be readily traded. But there are many other risks to contend with.

Consider the example of Apple Computer. Founder Steve Jobs first approached a professional venture capitalist in the fall of 1976. At that time, the company was selling Apple I microcomputers to hobbyists. The total market for microcomputers was minuscule and no company had a commercially viable product. What's more, Jobs and partner Stephan Wozniak were college drop-outs with modest work experience. The venture capitalist turned them down because Jobs and Wozniak were neophyte entrepreneurs, without significant management experience, with an introductory product in an embryonic market.

At the venture capitalist's suggestion, they approached Mike Markkula, a semi-retired Intel veteran, who made an angel investment in Apple and brought much-needed management savvy. The company introduced the Apple II in 1977. The following year, when Apple sales were about $10 million a year, the first professional venture capital was invested. By then the infant microcomputer industry, propelled by the VisiCalc spreadsheet, was no longer exclusively the domain of nerds; early adopters were actually using microcomputers for real business applications.

When venture capital was invested in Apple, the management, market and technological risks, although still high, were much lower than they had been 18 months earlier and were outweighed by the potential financial returns. How do venture capitalists evaluate those risks and what kind of returns do they expect from the companies in which they invest?

First and foremost, venture capitalists invest only in companies with first-class entrepreneurial leaders in markets that are big enough for a company's sales to grow to at least $50 million with pre-tax profit of 20 percent within five years. Experience shows that a company like that will be able to go public, or be bought by a larger company, and will return five to ten times the venture capitalist's original investment. A tenfold return in five years yields an annual rate of return of 58 percent and a fivefold yields 39 percent, which are within the range of satisfactory risk-adjusted returns.

Next, venture capitalists hedge their bet by staging the financing in more than one round. Suppose an early-stage company projects that it requires $5 million of equity financing before it will be able to go public. If a venture capital group decides to invest, it will usually split the financing into two rounds of, say, $2.5 million each.

Provided that the company meets its projected sales and profit milestone with the first round of $2.5 million, the venture capitalist will almost certainly want to invest the second $2.5 million. Typically, if the first round is sold at $1 per share, the second round will be about $3 per share. Hence, with two rounds of financing, the company sells only 3,333,333 shares (2.5 million plus 833,333) to raise $5 million, rather than 5,000,000, if it had raised all the financing in one round.

However, if the company falls hopelessly short of its milestone, the venture capitalist most likely will not invest any more money and, in the worst case, will be prepared to write off the first $2.5 million. So by staging the investment, the venture capitalist hedges his risk, and the company, provided that it meets its projections, reduces the number of shares that it sells.

If this were a real-world case, it's likely that the venture capitalist would syndicate the deal with two other venture groups, because another way that venture capitalists manage their total financial risk is by investing in a portfolio of different companies.

Finally, venture capitalists reduce their financial risk by purchasing convertible preferred shares, which give them very specific rights and preferences compared with holders of common shares. The final investment agreement can run to 200 or more pages but the key provisions of the agreement are summarized in a term sheet of a few pages. Those provisions protect the venture capitalist's investment in the event of both negative and positive future events. The venture capitalists have rights to convert preferred shares to common shares, dividend rights, redemption rights, registration rights, protection from ownership dilution in a recapitalization, rights to maintain pro rata ownership in future rounds of private financing, and rights to approve the issue of any equity security, the liquidation of the company and the acquisition of or investment in another company.

They also have ways of controlling the company through both ownership of equity and seats on the board of directors. If they hold 51 percent of the common shares, they have outright voting control. Although they initially might not have a majority of the board seats, they have the right to appoint a majority of the board of directors if specified negative events happen.

In addition, the term sheet places significant requirements on the management and employees of the company. These include issuing timely annual audited financial statements and monthly or quarterly unaudited statements, non-compete agreements, key person life insurance, a stock vesting agreement that any employee who leaves prematurely has to sell a portion of his or her shares back to the company at their nominal price, an agreement that while the company is private any employee cannot sell shares to a third party without first offering them to the preferred shareholders, a limitation on the stock option pool, and limits on managers' salaries.

Due diligence, financial prudence and legal agreements notwithstanding, it is impossible to eliminate the risk inherent in equity investing. In general, investments in younger companies are riskier than those in older ones because they have shorter track records and investments in them have to be held longer. Hence, venture capitalists classify companies according to their stage of development.

A *seed-stage* company is one with not much more than a concept; a *start-up* company is one that is already in business and is developing a prototype but has not

Stage	Expected annual return
Seed	80%
Startup	60%
First-stage	50%
Second-stage	40%
Third-stage/Mezzanine	30%
Bridge	25%

Figure 1: Expected returns on venture capital equity investments

sold it in significant commercial quantities; a *first-stage* company has developed and market tested a product and needs capital to initiate full-scale production. *Second-stage, third-stage and mezzanine* financing fuels growing companies; and *bridge* financing may be needed to support a company while it is between rounds of financing, often while it waits to go public.

The younger a company, the greater the risk and the higher the expected return. The expected annual return declines from about 80 percent for seed-stage financing to about 30 percent for a third-stage financing (*see* Figure 1). It is the expected return, combined with the valuation of a company, that determines the price per share a venture capitalist will be willing to pay to buy equity in it. Since venture capital is invested in growing companies, the venture capitalist wants to know what the value of the company is likely to be at some future time when it can sell its investment and realize a capital gain. It estimates the valuation of the company at some future date then discounts it back to its present value.

Here is a simplified illustration of the most commonly used method. A one-year-old company is seeking $2 million of start-up financing. Its projections show that it will have earnings (net income) of $5 million five years in the future. The venture capital group believes that the company can have an initial public offering in five years and that the price to earnings (P/E) ratio will be 20. Thus, the future total valuation of the company will be $100 million (20 × $5 million).

The venture capitalist wants a 60 percent rate of return; so the present value of the company is $9.54 million [$100,000,000/$(1.6)^5$]. Hence, for an investment of $2 million, the venture capital group needs 21 percent [($2/$9.54) × 100] of the company's equity to achieve a 60 percent return. There are huge uncertainties in that computation. The earnings are only projections and even if the company achieves its projections five years hence it might not be able to go public if the market for initial public offerings is in a slump. And who is wise enough to foresee what the P/E ratio will be five years in the future?

Figure 2 shows how the percentage ownership required to yield a 60 percent return on a $2 million investment varies with the future valuation of a company and the holding period. It contains some simple messages for entrepreneurs seeking venture capital. First, they should think big enough when making their projections because the greater the future valuation of the company, the less equity they will have to sell to raise their venture capital. Second, they should propose an early public offering because the shorter the expected holding period for the investment, the less equity they will need to sell. Third, they should grow their companies as big as possible before raising venture capital because the longer they wait, the lower the required rate of return and the shorter the holding time to harvest the investment.

In this example, if the company were a first-stage instead of a start-up investment, the required rate of return would be 50 percent instead of 60 percent,

Holding period	Future valuation of the company ($ million)				
	20	40	60	80	100
2 years	26%	13%	9%	6%	5%
3	41	20	14	10	8
4	66	33	22	16	13
5	NA	52	35	26	21
6	NA	84	56	42	34
7	NA	NA	89	67	54
8	NA	NA	NA	NA	86

Figure 2: Percentage equity required to yield a 60% annual rate of return on a $2 million investment

and it might be ready to go public in four years instead of five. Hence, the company would need to sell only 10 percent of its equity instead of 21 percent.

Target annual returns that can go as high as 80 percent seem to be outrageously exorbitant to new entrepreneurs. But they have to keep in mind that returns from good investments have to compensate for losses on bad ones. In a successful venture capital portfolio, out of every ten investments, two will make or exceed the target rate of return, two will be total write-offs, and the remaining six will range from the "walking dead," where the companies never get big enough for a significant harvest, to the "walking wounded" that need refinancing if they are to have a chance of making it.

The average annual returns on venture capital since the birth of the professional industry in 1946 have been, at best, in the mid-teens, which suggests that this industry is not making excessive returns on a risk-adjusted basis. Indeed, some financial observers might argue that the returns are not adequate compensation for the risk involved.

No doubt about it, private equity is the most expensive type of capital for entrepreneurs. What's more, when it comes from sophisticated investors, such as professional venture capitalists, it has numerous covenants and restrictions. When things go badly wrong, venture capitalists exercise their rights and intervene in managing the company, often removing one or more of the founding entrepreneurs in the process. It's those situations that lead to the derogatory term "vulture capitalist."

However, when things go well, everyone wins. Entrepreneurs get the capital that enables them to grow their companies faster; venture capitalists get a return commensurate with the risks they take; and society gets exciting new products and high-quality jobs. What's more, the best venture capitalists, such as Arthur Rock, John Doerr, and Ben Rosen, bring much more than money to the deal. They bring the wisdom, earned by advising and observing entrepreneurs in whom they invested, to build tiny companies such as Apple, Sun Microsystems, Netscape, Amazon.com, Lotus and Compaq into industry giants.

Business angels are the answer to the entrepreneur's prayer

Most funding for new business ventures comes not from venture funds but from private investors. **Colin Mason** and **Richard Harrison** explain.

Contrary to the widely held perception among entrepreneurs, venture capital funds are not the main source of start-up finance. The reality is that venture capital funds specialize in making large investments in companies that have got beyond the start-up stage. Indeed, there is a paradox in that as more and more money has flowed into venture capital funds from the financial institutions, so the size of investments made by venture capital funds has risen sharply. This is because venture capital funds have not increased the number of partners at the same rate, and so do not have the human capital to manage lots of smaller investments requiring hands-on involvement. Morgan Jones, a leading East Coast venture capitalist, therefore advises entrepreneurs not to "come to us wanting $1 million. We only do $3 million to $12 million deals." On the West Coast, John Doerr, a leading Silicon Valley venture capitalist, makes the same point: "The garage start-up is dead. We want to be able to invest $4 million in a start-up."

The so-called informal venture capital market is the main source of risk capital for companies at their seed and start-up stages. This market comprises high net worth individuals, the majority of whom are cashed-out entrepreneurs with substantial business experience, who are prepared to invest either on their own or with others directly in entrepreneurial businesses. Because of their substantial involvement in the businesses in which they invest, most can only manage a few investments at a time. Consequently, most are relatively infrequent investors, investing no more than once a year, although a small minority are considerably more active.

Most business angels strive to preserve their anonymity, although some have a high profile. There are no directories which list business angels and there are no public records of their investments. It is therefore impossible to say how many business angels there are or how much they invest in aggregate. However, it is clear that the number of business angels has grown in recent years as a result of the increasing number of millionaires that have been produced by the entrepreneurial revolution of the 1980s and 1990s. The best estimate of the scale of the informal venture capital market from the Center for Venture Research at the University of New Hampshire, which specializes in monitoring this marketplace, suggests there are about 250,000 business angels in the US who invest $20 billion every year in around 30,000 ventures. This is about twice the amount invested by the institutional venture capital market in terms of dollars invested and is at least 20 times larger in terms of the number of ventures financed.

Business angels are a heterogeneous group, and making generalizations about them and their investments is problematic. However, based on research in North America and Europe, the following statements about angel investments can be made.

Size of investment

Business angels invest from as little as $10,000 up to around $500,000, although the typical investment is less than $200,000. However, the majority of business angel investments involve co-investors, usually other business angels (generally trusted friends and business associates), but occasionally venture capital funds, and thus deal sizes can be larger. Business angels may also provide additional follow-on finance.

Business characteristics

Business angels invest predominantly at the seed and start-up stages of business development, and make investments in virtually all industry sectors.

Investment structure

The majority of investments involve equity finance. However, business angel investments may also involve loans (generally unsecured), guarantees, and debt-equity arrangements either alongside equity finance or on their own. Equity investments typically involve straightforward financing instruments (ordinary shares). More complex instruments (e.g. types of preference shares) are relatively unusual, except in larger investments.

Business angels normally do not take a controlling interest. It is more common in larger deals, which typically involve more than one investor, for the investor(s) to take a majority shareholding. However, these deals are often structured in a way that allows the entrepreneurs to regain majority control if the business meets performance targets.

Value-added contribution

Informal venture capital is "smart money." Business angels are value-added investors, thus the benefit for the entrepreneur is not just money but the advice and counsel of the business angel, and the doors that they can open. Business angels contribute their commercial skills, entrepreneurial experience, business know-how and contacts through a variety of hands-on roles to make a wide range of strategic, monitoring and supportive inputs.

Entrepreneurs who have raised finance from business angels report that their most valuable contribution is as a sounding board for the management team. Despite the obvious potential for this involvement by business angels to lead to interpersonal conflicts with the entrepreneur, the available evidence suggests that in most cases the relationships are consensual and productive.

Geographical distribution

The informal venture capital market is primarily a local marketplace. Business angels can be found in virtually every town and city, unlike institutional venture capital which is geographically concentrated in just a few states. Thus, in many parts of the US informal venture capital is the only type of venture capital available.

The majority of business angel investments are local, typically within two hours' traveling time of where they live. This is because of the hands-on nature of their investing and consequent need for frequent contact with their investee businesses. However, business angels who have very specialist investment preferences (e.g. a particular sector or technology) are likely to invest over longer distances.

Holding period

Business angels are fairly patient investors, with a majority willing to hold their investments for more than five years. Successful exits are normally achieved through a trade sale, and only occasionally through an IPO.

Motives

Business angels are not altruistic. They are motivated first and foremost by the opportunity for capital gain. Thus, they are interested in investing only in fast-growing businesses which have the potential to generate returns of at least 20 percent per annum (averaged over the life of an investment). Some investors also seek income from their investment, either by working full-time in the business or else by being paid a regular fee for their value-added contribution to the business.

However, business angels are also motivated, in part, by non-financial considerations. They derive "psychological" income from the satisfaction and excitement of being involved with a new business, helping it to get started and grow, and mentoring the next generation of entrepreneurs. Some business angels are also motivated by various "hot buttons," for example an interest in a particular technology. Altruistic considerations also play a role: these include the opportunity to bring a socially useful product or service to market, assisting in the economic development of their community, and supporting the free market system that enabled them to prosper by assisting the next generation of entrepreneurs.

Approach to investing

The approach of business angels to investing is influenced by three key considerations. First, they are investing their own money and so are free from outside pressure to achieve a target rate of return, to justify their investment decision to anyone else or to refer decisions to others for approval. Second, they typically allocate only a relatively small proportion of their wealth to their informal investments. Thus, it will not seriously affect their lifestyle if they lose their money. Equally, they are sufficiently wealthy so as not to *need* the returns from a successful investment. Third, the business experience and financial sophistication of most business angels means that they are capable of evaluating the merits and risks of prospective investments, especially those in industries in which they have had experience.

Investment process

The investment decision of business angels is a three-stage process. At the *initial screening stage* the angel comes across an investment opportunity and decides whether it is of sufficient interest to invest some time to investigate it in detail or to reject it out of hand. More than 90 percent of investment proposals are rejected at this stage, in many cases simply because the opportunity is not a good fit with the types of investments that the business angel is interested in investing in (e.g. in terms of industry, location, amount of funding required). For those investment proposals that pass the initial screening, the investor will invest time in a *detailed examination* of the business plan or proposal outline, including one or more meeting with the principals. At this stage the investor is deciding whether or not to invest in principle. The final stage involves *negotiating* with the entrepreneur concerning the terms and conditions of the investment.

Investment criteria

In their evaluation of investment opportunities business angels aim to satisfy themselves with regard to four key questions. First, is there a *market* for the product or service, is it growing and how competitive is it? Second, will the *product or service* be competitive? What is its unique selling proposition (USP) and how will this be maintained? Business angels are not interested in investing in firms which are simply providing "me-too" products. Third, is the *entrepreneurial team* credible? Investors place greatest emphasis on the experience and track record of the management team. Finally, what is the *upside potential* of the opportunity, why is the money being sought, and what will it be used for? Angels also want to see that the entrepreneurs have committed themselves financially to their business.

Advantages and disadvantages of raising finance from business angels

Raising finance from business angels has a number of attractions. First, although they seek a financial return on their investments in the form of capital appreciation, they are, nevertheless, often partially motivated by non-financial considerations and so may be willing to accept lower returns if they expect to receive "psychological" income. Second, business angels have a short decision cycle. The time to elapse between first meeting and receipt of funds is less for private investors than venture capitalists (2.5 months compared with 4.5 months) and their investment decision is normally made in weeks rather than months, and is even sometimes made in days. Third, business angels require less formalistic investment documents, which limits the involvement of professional advisers (e.g. accountants, lawyers) and so keeps the costs down for the entrepreneur. Fourth, business angels play a hands-on role in the companies in which they invest. Thus, entrepreneurs are able to benefit from the substantial commercial skills, entrepreneurial experience, know-how and contacts of their investors. Fifth, business angels can help groom the business to attract follow-on finance from a venture capital fund and may even provide the introduction.

But there are also some disadvantages that should not be ignored. Their pockets are not as deep as those of venture capital funds and so they are less likely to become involved in later financing rounds. Their hands-on involvement may become meddlesome. Some business angels may turn out to be "devils," with ulterior motives for investing.

How to find a business angel

Most business angels rely upon networks of trusted friends and business associates to identify investment opportunities and are more likely to invest in opportunities that come from these sources. Other referral sources include accountants and, less often, bankers, lawyers and stockbrokers. Some angels also identify investment opportunities through personal search.

Entrepreneurs can maximize their chances of finding business angels by using the following strategies:

- search locally
- look for successful entrepreneurs who are familiar with the industry or market
- many business angels are active in charitable and civic affairs
- participate in networking organizations such as business clubs, industry and professional associations, university alumni associations as well as social organizations such as golf and tennis clubs
- use "gatekeepers" such as lawyers, accountants and venture capitalists.

The good news for entrepreneurs is that the search for business angels is becoming easier with the creation of *networks* which seek to connect investors and entrepreneurs. These take various forms:

- AceNet: a national computer-matching service sponsored by the US Small Business Administration
- angel networks: local matching services run on a non-profit basis by economic development bodies and universities; some commercial angel networks have also emerged, with garage.com having a particularly high profile
- angel clubs: high-profile business angel syndicates, the best known of which is the Band of Angels in Silicon Valley
- venture capital clubs/forums: less formal breakfast/luncheon clubs of investors.

These networks are regularly listed in the business media and most also have their own websites.

What to expect from venture capitalists

Harry J. Sapienza looks at what investors will want to see for their money.

Do you really want venture capital? Or, more to the point, do you want what venture capital inevitably entails – partnering, decision consulting, discipline, and high expectations? By this point, you have a pretty clear idea of what venture capitalists look for in an investment prospect. You know that they are looking for a business with great potential for growth, run by a highly skilled, motivated, and resilient entrepreneurial management team. If you pass this screening, and if you are particularly lucky, they seem to be implying, you might – just might – get an investment offer.

It is easy for me to say that if you don't really want what venture capital entails, you shouldn't take it. I know, you know, and *they* know that sometimes the temptation to accept a large chunk of desperately needed money with no immediate obligation to pay it back is too strong even for the most sensible of us to resist. However, if you do take it, you should be aware of what it entails so that you can make the most of what it does for you and minimize the worst of what it might do to you.

Trends in venture capital[1]

The image of venture capital that has lingered over time is one of industry-creating, early-stage, high-tech entrepreneurs partnered by a highly involved syndicate of savvy venture capitalists. Much has changed. From the entrepreneur's perspective, some of the change has been favorable, some not so favorable. Who gains and who loses? First of all, the presence of venture capital has spread from the US to virtually every major economy. Not only has formal private venture capital become more available in more places, but in most countries government-backed venture funds and private investors have joined the fray. Furthermore, venture capital firms have become more willing to cross borders, offering their money and their expertise to hot prospects as far as the increasing sophistication of communication technology will take them.

There has been a trend away from syndicating investments; thus, entrepreneurs have to deal with fewer outsiders. More money has become available for low-technology ventures, for later-stage expansion, for management buy-ins and buy-outs, and for a variety of other high-growth prospects. The size of individual capital infusions has grown as well.

One of the few downsides of these trends is that less money is going into new ventures, especially outside of the US. While many policy-makers are scrambling to find ways to stimulate significant venture capital availability for high-potential new ventures, thus far newer ventures have too often had bootstrap or combine bootstrapping with aid from private investors to fuel early growth. Nonetheless, many venture capital firms still focus on backing early-stage ventures, and others provide the needed follow-on from bootstrapping and angel investing.

The following sections provide a brief overview of (1) what venture capitalists consider beyond the capabilities of the entrepreneurial team and the market opportunity in making investment decisions; (2) commonalities across venture capital presence; (3) variations from normal involvement; and (4) sources of friction. The final section summarizes the key points and offers some advice for considering whether to take the money and how to manage the relationship if you do.

Are you a suitable partner?

Needless to say, venture capitalists must be convinced of the capabilities of your entrepreneurial team and the opportunity for explosive growth before they even consider your venture as an investment.[2] However, the last critical judgement they make is whether they want to go into a deal with you and your team. Venture capitalists are keenly aware that entrepreneurs do not generally seek venture capital because they need another business partner. They know that, in general, entrepreneurs want the money, without hassles. Unfortunately, this is an unacceptable arrangement for them. They are investing significant amounts of their own, their partners' and their limited partners' money in a risky investment. They have a fiduciary responsibility to oversee strategic decisions affecting the disposition of these funds. Further, they undoubtedly feel that the experience they have accumulated with dozens and perhaps hundreds of launchings may just be of use to you. First and foremost, then, they wish to invest in an entrepreneur who understands, accepts, and even looks forward to availing themselves of the venture capitalists' advice.

Much of what venture capitalists do during the due diligence and negotiation phases is geared toward assessing whether you are really ready to "accept" what venture capital entails. In many ways, this assessment is critical simply because many of the other factors vital to success are impossible to predict. Quite reasonably, venture capitalists want to avoid entrepreneurs who really don't want them to be involved. Before deciding whether to proceed, they look for subtle signals of the entrepreneurs' partnering characteristics, especially their openness to outside views and their true motives. Unfortunately, as I said earlier, powerful incentives to complete the deal may cause either you or them to ignore or gloss over signals that the deal probably should not go forward.

However enamored venture capitalists may be, they will structure the deal to protect themselves if their assessments of your "willingness" to partner were wrong. They will specify board seats, reporting requirements, performance targets, and staged financing to ensure that they have adequate say in the development of the venture. Further, they will make it clear that this is a marriage intended to end. Explicitly or implicitly, the parties agree that the venture capitalist has the right to seek means to exit the relationship, collecting their portion of the value of the venture at that time.

They showed you the money – now what?

Suppose you get the money – what can you expect? While there are significant variations between preferences of individual venture capitalists, there are a number of similarities no matter what country, industry, or stage of development your venture is in. Venture capital investors impose a type of regularity and discipline on entrepreneurial companies that they might not otherwise impose upon themselves.

First, expect a regular schedule of board meetings, formal strategic and financial reporting requirements, challenging performance targets, and tightly controlled, "staged" financing. Typically, one representative from each venture capital firm with significant funds in your company will stay "semi-involved" with the workings of your business. In some cases, one "lead investor" may keep tabs for a syndicate of investors, but usually all will want some direct and meaningful contact. By "semi-involved" I mean to express the idea that they will almost never be purely passive investors, nor, on the other hand, do they have the time or inclination to become steeped in operating details and decisions. It is important to remember that venture capitalists want you to run your business.

Important formal involvement and strategic debate occur at board meetings, but you can expect investors to be in touch with you and with other members between meetings to shape decisions before they arise in the more public forum of the boardroom. Usually the lead investor will take the position of chairman of the board, though not always. Odds are that you will welcome the help in structuring meetings because the burden of preparing the reports and presentation of data is not trivial. Furthermore, this arrangement also imposes a discipline on the investor to remain abreast of issues and developments. Many entrepreneurs find it overwhelming to try both to run a business and to prepare "updates" for outsiders.

Typically, board meetings will occur anywhere from once a month to once a quarter, depending on the stage and circumstances of the venture. Some venture capital firms have very clear guidelines for the format and substance of the meetings, but many do not. If no clear guidelines are available, it is a good idea to confer with the lead investor about what form of information and presentation is preferred.

For most venture capitalists, the quality of your written financial and strategic reports will be of vital interest. Especially important will be the comparison of projections with actual performance, along with your synopsis of the reasons for variance from targets.

An important way that venture capitalists limit their exposure and test you out is by "staging" the financing (i.e. providing only an amount of funding sufficient to cover needs for a very limited period of time). Both you and the investor expect follow-on rounds of financing. However, the investor will want to watch how you handle the money provided, how well you predict and meet performance marks, and what the nature and focus of your efforts will be. While both sides expect additional rounds of financing to be forthcoming, the timing and "price" of such infusions inevitably spark serious if not contentious debate. The volatility of such sessions is undoubtedly enhanced by the fact that venture capitalists often provide as little capital as possible between financing rounds.

Research has shown that the roles played by venture capitalists are a bit different from what casual observers expect and what is often promoted by venture capital firms themselves. In short, while they will do some networking for the venture (including, for example, managerial recruiting and providing professional customer leads), this sort of involvement is sporadic and takes a back seat to the strategic and personal support provided. Clearly, both venture capitalists and entrepreneurs believe that venture capitalists' most important role is as a sounding board for strategic and financial issues. However, both apparently also recognize the psychological and physical stress that entrepreneurs routinely endure. Therefore, it is perhaps not surprising that venture capitalists and entrepreneurs alike see the provision of interpersonal support (e.g. being a coach, a confidant, or a friend) as a highly important role.[3]

Lastly, you should expect that conflict will be a part of the relationship. The stakes are high. The venture's path is unclear. And different ideas regarding priorities and how to achieve them inevitably arise. Successful relationships will be those that are able to surface the potentially useful different perspectives on how to achieve ends while minimizing interpersonal friction that may undermine the ability of the investor-entrepreneur team to work together effectively.[4]

Given the high stakes, the uncertainty, and the differences in preferences and motivations, potentially destructive conflict lurks close beneath the surface. It is no wonder, then, that successful venture capitalists try to assess the type of partner the entrepreneur will be before they go in and that they work hard to establish a good relationship once they are in. Nonetheless, while the relationship is important, it must be remembered that it is primarily a means to an end – that of realizing a significant return on investment. The bottom line is still the bottom line. However, although bad relationships can result in good returns and vice versa, the better the rapport between entrepreneur and investor, the greater the chances that the provision of capital, advice, and support will be there when it is needed.

Variations in intensity of involvement[5]

The prior section implies that, generally speaking, venture capitalists seek to stay well informed about the goings-on of your business, to keep operating decisions firmly in your hands, and to push you hard to achieve significant progress while limiting the extent to which this progress is generated primarily by "throwing money" at your problems. Conflict is inevitable, but seasoned venture capitalists try to minimize the extent to which conflict is about personalities. They understand the value of supporting and encouraging you. Ultimately, however, if you can't do the job, they will want somebody in there who can. And they will work toward getting you to see things this way, too. Their preferences play a role in how close they get to you and how they manage their inner conflict between loyalty to you and loyalty to the investment they have made.

Beyond variations caused by personal preferences, several factors will cause the level of involvement to increase, decrease, or change somewhat in nature. Greatest involvement appears to occur around significant changes in the ownership structure of the venture, just after initial investment as the investor gets to know you and your business thoroughly, around new rounds of financing, and when the investor is preparing to exit the relationship. Further, if the investor's stake in the venture rises significantly over time as a result of multiple rounds of financing, this can offset their tendency to reduce involvement as the relationship and venture stabilize.

Early-stage ventures usually require greater attention because their viability is still in doubt and because minor errors can be of such great consequence to them. Distance can be an impediment to involvement; however, venture capitalists tend to avoid investing in ventures at greater distances if they believe significant involvement will be needed.

If the venture is in a technically sophisticated industry, the venture capitalist may spend more time learning the ins and outs of the industry. In fact, the level of conflict between the venture capitalist and the entrepreneurial management team may be greatest in highly technical businesses. Venture capitalists often stay deeply involved in high-potential technology ventures for a variety of reasons. Not only do the investors need to work harder in these firms to understand them, but investors recognize that the culture of such firms often promotes values that are at odds with the investors' goals. Often, these ventures are run by technical people more interested in scientific discovery or technical perfection than in growth or profitability. Even when they are interested in explosive growth, however, they may not have the business experience to understand how to realize the potential.

The upshot of these factors is that venture capitalists often try to stay more involved in the early development of such ventures. Inevitably, entrepreneurs in such firms become frustrated with the investors' lack of understanding of their product and their emphasis on mundane business concerns, whereas the investors tend to become frustrated with the entrepreneurs' lack of appreciation for sales and marketing. When these relationships work, however, they are often the most productive because of the complement of perspectives and skills.

Finally, venture performance can influence the general level of involvement. If the venture is struggling and the investors still believe they can make a significant difference, they may step up involvement. From the entrepreneur's perspective, however, this may be a two-edged sword in that there is a danger under these circumstances that the investors may attribute failing to the entrepreneur's incompetence and will seek to put someone else at the helm of the venture. If the prospects for the venture are fairly hopeless, the likelihood is that the investors will try to minimize the effort put into the venture. At the other extreme, when the venture is doing very well, venture capitalists stay active, trying to discover ways to maximize this potential and to promote its potential for public offering or trade sale. The lowest level of involvement can be expected when the venture is surviving comfortably but does not appear destined to realize the potential originally hoped for.

Pet peeves of investors and entrepreneurs

I have emphasized the importance of a good relationship in both parties achieving their goals, and my research has indicated that despite the popular belief that these relationships tend to be contentious, one-sided, and unpleasant, this is not the case. That does not mean that good relationships ensure the success of these ventures: many ventures with venture capital backing fail or fail to realize the type of growth necessary to compensate the parties for the effort expended. What it does mean is that the participants generally feel that the parties involved worked hard and co-operatively to achieve desired ends and that they believe the working relationship enhanced rather than harmed their chances to succeed.

At the same time, there are some recurring "pet peeves" that investors and entrepreneurs have about one another. Perhaps if you are aware of these, you can avoid some of the problems, or take them in stride.

Investors get annoyed when board meetings are no more than what they call "dog and pony shows" put on by entrepreneurs because they have failed to carefully prepare the meeting or because they wish to avoid providing real information. Hiding, delaying, and misrepresenting information are the deadliest sins an entrepreneur can commit. At times, of course, the entrepreneur will feel that preparation for the board meeting should be secondary to actually running the business and keeping it afloat. The investor can buy this – once, perhaps. The other thing that can annoy investors is a spoken or unspoken attitude that the venture is the entrepreneur's "baby" and that the investor has little right to require, to advise, or to question much of anything that the entrepreneur has carefully thought out. Equity, the entrepreneur must realize, means partnering attitudes and actions.

Investors can be equally, if not more, annoying. At times, they give the appearance of second-guessing, of refusing to acknowledge their role in strategic decisions that didn't work out, and of underestimating the impact of the unpredictability of market conditions. Nothing will annoy an entrepreneur more than an investor who comes to a board meeting without having carefully examined the reports and then asks questions that display this ignorance. Related to these complaints are those about board members who perform "undue" diligence and nit-pick during the meetings about minor inconsistencies or errors; these complaints are exacerbated when the investor appears to put no effort into trying to become more learned about the venture's product or market.

Entrepreneurs also complain about the investor–investor disputes that can at times undermine all progress at board meetings; these disputes are at times self-interested spats about valuation or exit timing and at others simply personality or ego conflicts. Finally, entrepreneurs become annoyed if strategic decisions are negotiated among investors outside board meetings without their knowledge or input.

Conclusion

At its most powerful and effective, venture capital investing brings together deep-pocketed investors who have a wealth of experience in launching rapidly growing businesses with entrepreneurs possessing unique skills and technical knowledge but in need of money and advice to fuel their enterprise. In many ways, the partnering, discipline, decision consulting, and high expectations of the venture capitalists are just what the entrepreneurs need to realize their highest potential.

The problem is that there are some inherent conflicts in this arrangement that can best be overcome with an adjustment of attitude on the entrepreneur's part and the development of an effective, co-operative partnership through the efforts of both.

A primary adjustment required of you is likely to be one of attitude. Entrepreneurs, by their very nature, tend to be confident, creative and independent. Such attitudes are necessary for new venture creation in the first place, but they must be tempered to some degree if entrepreneurs are going to enter into partnerships with venture capitalists. And make no mistake about it, venture capitalists may not expect to be fully active partners in the venture, but they insist on being partners. If you cannot truly accept a role for the venture capitalist beyond that of funds provider, the deal should not go forward.

The difficult part of this adjustment is emotional rather than rational. Intellectually, you will find it easy to understand that the investor is purchasing a partnership share; whether you can really accept that over time is another question. In any event, some people are easier to partner with than others. Therefore, you should do your own due diligence regarding the venture capitalist and the kind of partner he or she is. Further, you should find out what kind of say you might have in choosing a replacement should that venture capitalist leave the venture capital firm or be assigned elsewhere.

Expect conflict. Expect to be questioned. Expect to be supported. It is critical for you to settle the appropriate flow of information and to establish a level of honesty and openness that creates the type of respect, trust, and mutual respect critical to this partnership. If you have partnered with an experienced venture capitalist, odds are that he or she is skilled in the kind of constructive interaction that I have emphasized. However, some may not be as skilled as you would like. In such cases, you should help communicate the norms of honesty, respect, and trust you expect.

If you just want money, don't take venture capital. It is too expensive if that is all you get out of the deal.

1 The trends described in this section are based on the reviews of Manigart and Sapienza (1999) and Wright and Robbie (1998).

2 An extensive literature exists on venture capitalist selection criteria but few new insights have developed since Macmillan *et al.*'s 1987 report that managerial team ability, market opportunity, and risk are the key criteria.

3 Research conducted by myself and my colleagues in the US, Europe, and Asia demonstrates the same pattern of results. For greater detail *see*, for example, Sapienza, Manigart and Vermeil, 1996.

4 Higashide, H. and Birley, S. (1999) "Conflict in the entrepreneur-venture capitalist relationship," *Frontiers of Entrepreneurship Research*, Babson, Mass. The authors find that high levels of idea or "cognitive" disagreement are associated with high performance in investor-entrepreneur relationships, but that high levels of interpersonal conflict are associated with low performance. The trick is to encourage idea disputes while maintaining a healthy interpersonal respect and trust.

5 In this section I discuss factors that appear to cause an increase or decrease in the amount of venture capital involvement. However, these increases or decreases are more likely to be realized in the US, the UK, and Asia where the average amount of involvement is higher than it is in continental Europe. Sapienza and colleagues have found that venture capitalists in the US and Asia tend to spend about 200 hours per year on a given venture, compared to about 150 in the UK, and about 90 in continental Europe.

Stantret: a private cargo airline in the USSR

This case was originally prepared by **Dr Igor Touline** of the Institute of World Economy and International Relations, Moscow. It was subsequently edited by **Dr Abby Hansen** in collaboration with Professor **Derek Abell**, IMD. Financial support was provided by the European Foundation for Entrepreneurship Research (EFER).

In the early 1990s all forms of transport in the USSR had become severely inadequate. Railways were in need of modernization; roads were in disrepair; in the trucking and civil aviation industries there was a serious lack of both spare parts and gasoline. Aeroflot, the largest air carrier in the world, put little emphasis on maintenance and flew its planes until they wore out. Moreover, these inefficiencies were not confined to transport. The food storage and processing facilities were also in poor condition. In the spring of 1990, all these problems were thrown into stark relief when it became clear that the country was likely to reap a bumper harvest. Vegetables and fruit grown in the Crimea would be left to rot while distant places like Siberia suffered from shortages.

This was an ideal opportunity for Sergei Slepstov. Aged 25, he had risen from a factory worker in his native town in the Urals to become a senior marketing manager with a construction concern that was participating in the creation of a computer information network. Its role was to disseminate supply and demand information about surpluses and shortages of construction materials around the country. Working with this information gave him an idea.

The idea of organizing an effective brokerage activity got stuck in my mind. Nothing could be more straightforward. If someone has a surplus of something and another person or organization has a shortage of the same thing, all one has to do is to organize a mutually beneficial exchange.

Sergei concluded that sellers and buyers could profit handsomely if swift transportation of produce could be ensured. But how could he make it work? Quite simply, he found an "angel." Within days of conceiving the idea for an air transport service, friends introduced him to Ustas Lamin, president of Stanlet, a large Soviet-American joint venture in the entertainment business. Sergei recalled that Ustas said to him:

I shall give you the possibility but nothing else.

Stantret was established as a subsidiary of Stanlet and, with this as a credible business base, Sergei approached the bank for a 600,000 rouble, three-month credit facility. He had forecast that, given the difference in price between tomatoes in the north and south, one aircraft could make enough deliveries in three months to yield 141,000 roubles in earnings. All he had to do was to find an aircraft, pilots, fuel, flight paths, landing slots and, of course, customers.

He first went to ARI, a subsidiary of the Ministry of Aviation Industries [MAI], located near Moscow, which had several dozen planes sitting idle most of the time. He told the ARI managers that he had a large order to ship fruit and if they could provide an equipped plane and arrange its reception along the route, they could share the profits. After some delay they agreed.

Lack of fuel was, however, a major problem. But Sergei knew that report-padding and double counting were routine and he suspected that fuel reported as having been consumed was, in fact, still available. So he decided to barter. In northern parts, he offered fresh produce and elsewhere consumer goods such as video equipment, which he bought in Moscow using the company's bank credit.

When putting together a deal with a large-scale buyer of agricultural produce he would arrange for the free use of one or two tons of a 40-ton shipment of fruit in the interests of "ensuring the smooth operation of the air bridge." The one or two tons cost little to the buyer, compared with the selling price in the north and, in return, the buyer was guaranteed a timely delivery. U. Umarov, managing director of a large joint venture in Tashkent:

When I attempted to use an Aeroflot plane there was such a prolonged delay that I never dispatched the consignment of fruit. When I tried sending another consignment by motor transport, two trucks disappeared and I had to hire guards and sustain losses. With Slepstov, there was neither problem, nor any losses ... With Aeroflot, arrival on time is an exception. Even when Slepstov charges more than Aeroflot, I gain.

By September 1990, Stantret had far exceeded the forecasts in the business plan, flying the aircraft for twice the number of hours projected; and by the end of the first quarter 1991, the company was showing a gross profit of 18,410,100 roubles. During this time, Sergei had continued to arrange the cargo flights with creative deals that often involved an *ad hoc* mix of regular payments and barter, a skill which he later taught his employees. However, this was part of his downfall.

At the end of April 1991, he noticed that two large contracts showed a customer price 5 percent below the price he had negotiated and, upon close inspection, he found that the rest of the contracts included similar discounts. Checking with friends at the bank, he found that large sums had been paid to the accounts of managers responsible for his air shipment operations:

It was a real blow. I didn't catch them red-handed, but I could no longer believe them. I still can't see what went wrong.

The final blow came when he learned that a new joint-stock company, Volga-Dnieper, had accumulated 270 million roubles – enough to buy several large cargo planes. Even more worrisome, it had forged relationships with MAI.

Sergei faced a major strategic decision. Should he turn Stantret into a joint-stock company and orient it toward long-term projects? Should he accept the invitation of a US commercial company to become its official representative in the USSR? Should he leave the company, raise money on the strength of his good name, and start a new business? Where was the new opportunity?

The above case is an abridged version. Copies of the complete case may be obtained from the European Case Clearing House, telephone (+44) 01234 750903; fax (+44) 01234 751125; e-mail ECCH@cranfield.ac.uk

Resourcing the entrepreneurial business: it's not just about money[1]

Benoît Leleux looks at the range of resources an entrepreneur has at his fingertips.

A valuable entrepreneurial opportunity should finance itself, right? In a world of perfect information and endless financial and managerial resources, it would seem natural that a worthy investment would find its ideal financier under most circumstances. Unfortunately, the world of entrepreneurship is not one of complete information and predictability, nor endless resources: it is a world of constrained allocations under massive uncertainties. Furthermore, growth is an integral part of the definition of entrepreneurship, and growth is a big consumer of resources, both financial and human ones.

The combination of higher risk and uncertainty, smaller scale, and superior growth potential is a pretty potent cocktail, but one that leaves the fundraising entrepreneur with a world-class hangover. So, what are the key issues in financing the growing firm?

The resource gap

A fundamental characteristic of many entrepreneurial ventures is the imbalance between the resources needed to capitalize on the opportunities and those available. The gap includes cash but also management skills, distribution channels, networks, technology, etc. The problem faced is then rarely about money alone. We resort here to the term "resourcing" rather than "financing" to reflect the fact that most high-growth firms face a number of constraints, not just a lack of money. Understanding the full scale of resource requirements is a required first step in assembling a successful deal.

The bundled resource dilemma

Where most established firms can segment their respective needs into separate components, and hire or buy the appropriate resources (such as consultants, lawyers, engineering and R&D firms, distributors, shelf space, etc.), young, high-growth companies often face what we refer to as a "bundled offer." For example, they may not be able to develop their own marketing channels, or have the credibility to sign agreements with companies with their established channels. Raising money from a reputed venture capitalist may provide not only some necessary financial resources but may also open the door to these channels of distribution that otherwise would have remained inaccessible. This is what we mean by bundled resources: financing is not an end in itself but a means used by the firm to satisfy some of its other fundamental needs, such as locking in some critical strategic partners, or gaining the visibility required for a successful product launch.

Resources for the growing business go far beyond financial requirements. Risk and growth interact, for example, to create difficulties in recruiting the corporate and technical talent required in such circumstances. People of exceptional quality need to be brought in at all levels, and yet financial resources are heavily constrained. Designing incentive and compensation packages then becomes another fundamental task of the original venture group.

Resourcing the entrepreneurial business, irrespective of size, becomes a multi-faceted exercise where financial elements will have to be balanced against other non-financial dimensions that are equally critical to the success of the venture. Without the means to shop around for each need individually, entrepreneurs have to be more creative to assemble the same combination of key success factors at a smaller cost and scale.

Unbundling the resources: resource maps

A convenient method to assess the multiple dimensions and contributions of a particular source of financing is the use of the concept of *resource maps*, radial diagrams highlighting the relative "score" of each potential source of financing on a set of fundamental criteria. We propose in Table 1 a set of 12 fundamental characteristics of financing sources that need to be investigated when creating an optimal resourcing package. Half of these characteristics would be considered as primarily financial, the other half deal with issues of governance, flexibility, industry knowledge, and management skills.

Table 1: General parameters of the resource maps framework

Financial characteristics	Non-financial characteristics
Cost of money (required rate of return)	Management skills
Fund-raising expenses	Speed of decision
Depth of pockets	Industry/product knowledge
Collateral requirements	Flexibility
Risk-bearing abilities	Other resources provided
Reputation/signaling	Control tendencies

Required rates of returns vary by source depending on perceived levels of risk and the ability of each one to actually manage that perceived risk. Similarly, the costs of raising the funds vary greatly, from relatively insignificant costs in the case of friends and family to 10–20 percent of the sums raised in the case of public offerings of equity. Investors also differ in the extent to which they may be able to continue financing the growth of the firm (the depth of pocket variable), how much collateral they will require, how comfortable they are taking the risk, and the signal their investment may send to other investors. On the non-financial dimensions, investors differ as to their speed of decision (which may be critical to certain firms), the industry knowledge and management skills they bring to the table (directly or indirectly), their flexibility in terms of the future, and how involved they like to get with the company management.

Financing ecotypes

With the 12-dimensional framework in hand, and a good understanding of what these dimensions imply, it is now possible not only to map the package presented by each source of financing, referred to as the resource maps, but to identify their

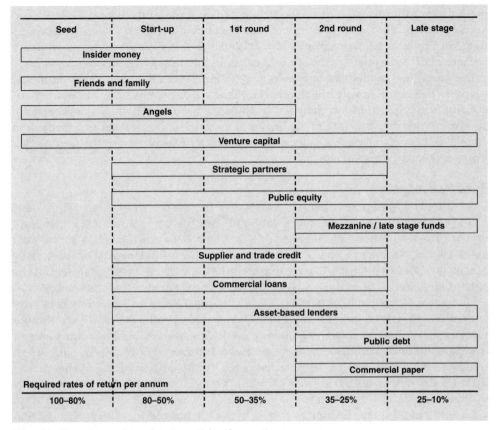

Figure 1: Financing ecotypes by stage of development

optimal ecological biotypes, referred to as *financing ecotypes,* the circumstances under which a particular financing source is most likely to invest and be called upon by entrepreneurs.

The combination of resource maps, illustrating the mixture of characteristics exhibited by each possible source of financing, and financing ecotypes, or set of circumstances under which they are most likely to be optimal, offers an innovative way to look at the entrepreneurial financing activities. Even though the details of the ultimate financing package will very much depend on idiosyncratic circumstances, the combination of tools provided here are invaluable in guiding the initial draft financing package.

We present in Figure 1 a model of financing ecotypes driven by two fundamental variables: the firm's stage of development and the level of information availability. To the extent that the second variable is very much correlated to the first, this model can actually be seen as one-dimensional. The model indicates a significant overlap of financing sources in each major stage of development of the venture. For example, seed financing is shown to be financed alternatively by the entrepreneur's own resources, friends and family, angels or high net worth individuals, or even venture capital. With the money used essentially to build a "proof of concept" of the product or service opportunity, there is indeed little chance of using debt capital for that purpose: the high level of risk, the non-existence of cash flows, and the lack of marketable collaterals point to the use of equity-type capital from the less risk-averse sources. With a proof of concept and solid business plan in hand, a start-up round of financing faces a significantly enlarged pool of capital suppliers, adding a number of debt suppliers to the seed-stage equity providers.

The simplified model can only take you so far. In other words, for a financing source to be identified with the appropriate stage of development is a necessary but not sufficient condition for inclusion in the entrepreneur's financing package. To determine the relevant mix of resources to be used, it is necessary to analyze in more detail the offer by each major source of capital. This is done in the next section through the use of resource maps.

Resource maps

The 12 fundamental dimensions of the resource framework were described in Table 1. To facilitate the cognitive identification of the "best fit" source of financing, we propose the use of a simple table (Table 2) which lists the relative score of each major source of financing on these 12 dimensions. Each fundamental characteristic is ranked from 1 to 10, with 1 indicating that the characteristic is not present in the particular source of financing and 10 indicating an extremely strong presence.

Let us look for example at friends and family first. These investors rely primarily on trust and friendship to counter information asymmetries. Even though sometimes limited in resources (money, skills, networks, industry knowledge), friends and family can also create tensions with prized relatives, especially when things don't turn out for the best. As indicated by one entrepreneur, raising money from relatives has its advantages but can turn Christmas dinners into pretty acrimonious shareholders' meetings.

Beyond the immediate family circle, it is also possible to raise money from individuals willing and able to invest in entrepreneurial companies. These individuals, known as angels or informal private equity investors,[2] include former or current entrepreneurs, professionals (lawyers, doctors, consultants, etc.), or wealthy families. These individuals invest on a variety of grounds, from identification to the

Table 2: Resource maps scores for major financing sources

| Sourcing of financing | VC | | Angels | | F&F | | Public equity | | Trade credit | | Asset loans | | Government | | John's project | |
Relative score	low	high	low	high	low	high	low	high	low	high	low	high	low	high	low	high
Cost of money	8	10	6	8	5	8	2	5	0	2	1	3	0	3	5	9
Fund-raising expenses	0	2	4	6	3	6	7	10	0	2	3	5	6	9	1	5
Depth of pocket	7	9	5	7	3	5	8	10	0	3	1	4	1	4	6	9
Collateral requirements	0	2	1	3	1	3	0	3	2	5	7	10	0	3	0	2
Risk-bearing abilities	7	10	6	8	3	6	5	8	0	2	0	3	3	6	7	10
Reputation and signaling	8	10	5	7	0	3	5	8	0	3	0	3	0	2	3	6
Management skills	7	10	5	7	0	4	0	5	0	2	0	3	0	3	7	10
Speed of decision	7	9	5	7	3	5	3	6	6	9	7	10	6	10	7	10
Industry/product knowledge	7	9	5	7	1	5	1	4	6	9	5	8	0	3	7	10
Flexibility	7	9	6	8	5	8	1	4	0	3	0	3	0	3	7	10
Other resources	7	9	5	7	2	5	1	4	0	3	0	3	1	4	7	9
Control tendencies	7	9	5	7	3	6	1	3	0	2	0	2	1	4	2	5

F&F: Friends and family; **VC:** Venture capital; **Angels:** informal venture capital investors; **Asset loans:** asset-based lending;
Government: public financing programs; **John's project:** described below

entrepreneur ("I remember these early days in my career ..."), a proxy for entrepreneurial thrills ("I can't do it myself but at least I will be part of it"), or as an extra layer of diversification in an investment portfolio. They also bring very different resources to the table, from none to a high degree of industry knowledge and extensive networks.

Private equity investors operate mainly at the early stages of the company, where their more limited resources can buy larger ownership stakes. Their required rates of return are in line with those required for these stages of development, often falling at the lower end of the scale when non-financial benefits are present for investors.

Angels have also taken advantage of new technologies such as the internet to develop a more organized approach to deal search: formal networks such as AceNet or AngelNet provide direct access to them for entrepreneurs.

Venture capital firms, or professional equity investors, raise money from institutions, individuals or even public entities[3] to target equity investments in firms at all stages of development, from seed to buy-outs and bridge financing. As a group, the industry presents a heterogeneous profile, with funds specializing by stage of development and industries. Whereas a significant percentage of investments by US venture capitalists is committed to early-stage deals, their European counterparts target most of theirs to late-stage deals, as shown most recently by Leleux and Surlemont (2000).[4]

Venture capitalists share their professional approach to investments, running extensive due diligences and bringing to the table internal and external expertise when needed. Known for their hard-nosed approach to projects, they are also unusually able to take on risk and provide management expertise.[5] The reputation of some long-existing venture capitalists is second to none, and their presence in the capital structure sends a strong signal to other investors and stakeholders.

When considering the investors' depth of pocket, nobody beats public markets with their ability to raise large sums of money on a repeated basis. Public stock markets provide a well-organized forum for fundraising activities. The posted price they provide constantly for a firm's equity is also invaluable in evaluating management's actions and designing effective incentive plans, and provides a convenient means of payment for acquisitions. Unfortunately, the process of going public is convoluted and expensive, requiring extensive disclosures and the costs associated with the use of reputed advisers. It also imposes on-going disclosure costs for as long as the firm remains publicly owned. Government regulation is intrusive, designed to protect the ubiquitous "uninformed" public investors from the less scrupulous managers, forcing regular disclosures.

The availability of public equity markets differs markedly by country: where the US has always cultivated the notion of "public venture capital," with market investors willing to capitalize firms at very early stages of development, European investors have proved more conservative and less willing to take on equity risks.[6]

From resource maps to deal structuring

The two frameworks presented above, namely the financing ecotypes and resource maps, provide invaluable help in designing an appropriate financing plan, structuring what is otherwise perceived as an art form. To move from these frameworks to actual deal structures, one must start with mapping the firm's resource requirements. For this purpose, the map used above for financing sources can be implemented, and is now referred to as the *resource requirement map* for a particular project. By superposing the resource requirement map with the specific resource maps for each possible source of financing, it is possible to identify not only the sources that provide the best match but also to detect areas where there may be weak or insufficient coverage, indicating a need to source such characteristics independently of the financing.

To illustrate the process, let's investigate the situation faced by a 30-year-old entrepreneur called John, who is trying to launch an internet-based charter plane reservation system for the corporate market. With a background in business administration and consulting, and having helped some companies establish commercial websites, but limited experience in the aviation market, John has access to $50,000 of personal resources, not including the second mortgage he could get on his house, possibly worth another $50,000. In his spare time, John has already developed a working prototype of the internet site that would provide business travelers with a quick and efficient way to tap the private charter market. He has also incorporated the company in the State of Maryland as WebPlanes.COM. What is missing at this point are relationships with charter plane companies, full development of the site, and an aggressive marketing campaign to make the service known to both business travelers and charter plane companies. All in all, he estimates his needs at $1 million, two-thirds of which would be to market the service to companies and individuals.

John's company is stuck somewhere between the seed and the start-up stage. With signed commitments from service providers (charter plane companies), a more polished product, and a solid business plan, John's project would more squarely be labeled a pure start-up. Based on financing ecotypes (Figure 1), this stage of development calls mainly for equity-type financing, given the level of risk faced and the lack of information available at this point about the probability of this project becoming viable. Practically, this would call for insider seed money, friends and family, angels, venture capitalists, strategic partners or the public equity markets.

John would first need to sit down and evaluate as realistically as possible his portfolio of resource needs. Besides money, he clearly lacks connections to the plane rental industry and the charter companies, as well as management skills in that sector. Speed of decision is of the essence since there is, according to him, a clear first-mover advantage in this business. With little money to spend in searching for investors, and little collateral to offer beyond his house, fundraising expenses should be as limited as possible. On the other hand, it is quite clear that further rounds of fundraising may be required, so depth of pocket is important as well as flexibility. At this stage, the project risk remains very high, so investors willing to bear such risk are called for.

With all these non-monetary needs, the cost of the money may be less relevant since the project seems to have very significant profit potential on paper. John clearly knows that he would resent intrusion into management, so some arm's length relationship is preferred.

With this resource requirement map in hand, it is now possible to check which financing sources have the maps most closely matching the project's needs. Friends and family may be short on depth of pocket, risk-bearing abilities, reputation and signaling, management skills, speed of decision, industry and product knowledge and other resources, and long on control tendencies. Not the best match, but they may still provide the base on which to build the rest of the deal structure.

High net worth individuals potentially provide a better fit, in particular if selected with a background in the airline or travel industries. They can provide the management expertise and the industry knowledge, while remaining flexible and making decisions fast. As long as control tendencies are kept in check, and these individuals can be identified, contacted, and convinced relatively easily, these would provide many skills and resources needed for the venture to succeed.

Venture capitalists would also make strong candidates for the deal, if they can be convinced to join. Their reputation can help attract other investors and key personnel, and their managerial expertise would be a useful addition. Of course, they will be expensive and intrusive, but their ability to move fast and move others may be critical here.

Public equity markets would fail to provide the needed expertise in many areas, and would be too costly and slow to obtain.

Strategic partners may provide another valid alternative, as long as it is recognized that they may not help solve the management problem and that their investment may later jeopardize the independence of the company. On the positive side, they may be able to provide technical expertise and relatively cheap capital to bring the project to market fast.

What would then be an ideal financing package? This is where the entrepreneur-cum-chef comes into play, balancing the contributions of each for the benefit of all. At this early stage, business angels with industry experience and venture capitalists would constitute the main course, with strategic partners providing attractive trimmings. The objective is not to obtain the absolute lowest-cost package but one that offers the most desirable balance of resources, now and when required in the future, with the attributes most needed to make the project succeed. The failure to recognize the other needs of the business leads to a large number of unnecessary business failures.

Conclusion

We highlighted the difficulty in separating financial from non-financial resource needs for entrepreneurial firms. We referred to this problem as the bundling of resources and offered a very simple framework to analyze the resourcing issue for entrepreneurial companies. With the resource and resource requirement maps in hand, individuals should be better able to map their course in the jungle of start-up financing.

These tools will come in handy but will not completely eliminate the need to expend vast efforts in reaching the final financing plan. In a sense, they offer the maps, the GPS and machete to direct your guerrilla financing efforts, but they will not fight the battles for you. It is in those fights that the entrepreneurial drive and spirit will reveal itself, and in a more productive fashion than simply tracking down the wrong type of financing.

1 This article is based on "Resource Maps and Financial Ecotypes: A Visual Approach to Resourcing the Entrepreneurial Business," *Babson Entrepreneurial Review*, Spring 1999. A modified version of the article is forthcoming as Chapter 7 of a book entitled "Entrepreneurial Management" by Benoît Leleux, Daniel Muzyka and Neil Churchill, to be published in 2001 by McGraw-Hill. I want to acknowledge here the financial support for this project obtained from the IAF Chair in Entrepreneurship and the R&D

Department at INSEAD, the Glavin Center at the F.W. Olin Graduate School of Business at Babson College and IMD.

2 The term informal is unfortunately inappropriate since it tends to imply a less professional approach to the investment. Angels are very heterogeneous in their professionalism but some of them are as professional as venture capitalists in their due diligence and their ability to evaluate deals.

3 One such example is the Small Business Investment Corporation (SBIC) which can get a lot of its resources from the Small Business Administration in the United States.

4 Leleux, B. and Surlemont, B. (2000) "Public versus private venture capital: seeding or crowding out? A pan-European analysis," *Journal of Business Venturing* (forthcoming).

5 For some recent evidence on venture capital behavior, *see* Lerner, J. (1995) "Venture capitalists and the oversight of private firms," *Journal of Finance,* 50(1): 301–318; Birley, S., Leleux, B., *et al.* (1996) "Trade-offs in the investment decisions of European venture capitalists," *Journal of Business Venturing,* 11: 273–287; Brav, A. and Gompers, P. A. (1997) "Myth or reality? The long-run underperformance of initial public offerings: evidence from venture and non-venture capital-backed companies," *Journal of Finance,* 52(5): 1791–1821; Gompers, P. and Lerner, J. (1997) *Money Chasing Deals? The impact of fund inflows on private equity valuations,* Cambridge, MA; Gompers, P. and Lerner, J. (1997) *The Valuation of Private Equity Investments,* Cambridge, MA; Gompers, P. A. and Lerner, J. (1997) *Venture Capital Fundraising, Firm Performance and the Capital Gains Tax,* Cambridge, MA; Gompers, P. A. (1994) *Optimal Investment, Monitoring, and the Staging of Venture Capital,* Chicago, IL, University of Chicago, Graduate School of Business; Gompers, P. A. (1997) *An Examination of Convertible Securities in Venture Capital Investments,* Cambridge, MA; Leleux, B. F. and Muzyka, D. F. (2000), "Courting the European growth equity: a survey of attitudes towards listing alternatives," *Venture Capital,* 2(1).

6 It is interesting to note that until 1995, most IPOs in Paris were not raising any capital, but simply listing previously existing shares. In this case, the money raised actually goes directly to previous owners, with no direct effect on the company. For an overview of the issues facing European issuers, *see* Leleux B., Muzyka, D. and Guégon, N. (1998) "European new issue markets: preliminary review," 3i *QED* (December).

Recipe for a capital cake

Hugh Richards explains how financial structures for new ventures are put together.

Much of the classic thinking about financial structuring was developed for large, stable businesses, particularly quoted ones. It tends to draw heavily on historical track record and stock volatility in determining the cost of capital. That thinking has little place in helping a young company, where the uncertainty is such that informed guesswork and compromises are the order of the day. This article will examine some of the ground rules and then look at practical examples by way of illustration.

The starting point is to establish how much capital is required and for what purpose. This may sound obvious, but the younger the business, the higher the level of uncertainty and the more difficult the funding requirement is to estimate.

We can start in the classic business planning sense by considering the market and the likely level of sales, and work back through variable costs of sales to fixed-cost requirements. This builds up a picture of the overall cash requirement, for what purposes it will be required, and how its shape will change over time. These cash flows can then be tested by working a series of "what if" scenarios and examining the impact on the funding requirement.

The key principle in funding is matching – the provision of capital must mirror the purpose to which it is being put. Put simply, you would not wish to finance a major factory development with three-year money, or a personal computer with a 25-year mortgage. Most businesses have some more or less permanent requirement for capital, best funded by equity and retained earnings, some longer-dated requirements best matched by term debt, and some fluctuating requirements most easily funded by overdraft.

Business owners are concerned to keep the cost of capital to a minimum. The principal choice is between debt and equity (discussed in detail on pp. 99 and 105) although in practice the cost can be altered by mixing the two in varying quantities. To recap briefly. Debt is cheap, usually costing 1–3 percent over the bank's cost of capital. Though cheap, it also has teeth and the old adage – "debt gets you up in the morning, equity lets you sleep in late" – is relevant. Debt brings with it obligations – interest payments and capital redemptions that have to be made – and the consequences for not meeting these are severe.

So there must be a sensible and prudent relationship between the reliability of a series of cash flows and the amount of debt being used to finance them. For example, a fully let portfolio of 12 office properties let to good-quality tenants could be financed almost entirely with debt, while the long-term working capital requirement for the launch of a new product in an overseas market would be more prudently financed with a high level of equity.

The principal difficulty with equity is that it is expensive. It is the most valuable resource that the owner has to sell and once sold is difficult to repurchase. To make the sale worthwhile, the owner has to believe that he can use external capital to build a business more quickly and more soundly, ensuring that his reduced level of shareholding in a bigger business is more valuable than the retention of all of it in a smaller one.

Risk and return

The provider of capital starts by analyzing the various risks that he or she faces. Perhaps the most important is one that the entrepreneur rarely considers, and if he does, even more rarely has a full perspective on: *managerial risk*. To what extent does the team have the ability to deliver? There must be a mix of relevant skills, the experience and the determination to succeed. Much better a good team with a marginal idea than a marginal team with a good one. The former will survive, the latter probably will not. (These issues will be considered in Part 5, p. 189.)

Despite large amounts of work, there is little evidence of correlations between particular backgrounds and entrepreneurial success. The biggest danger is the temptation to back people with similar backgrounds to your own or people that you like. This is almost universally disastrous. There is a limited amount that you can deduce in an interview type of environment. You have to see people *in situ* in their businesses, talk to their team, to those around them, to those for whom they have worked in the past.

Where you believe you have identified shortcomings, it is important to fill them with complementary skills from others rather than hoping that people will change fundamentally. This may require full-time additions to the team or support of a more non-executive variety. The single most critical appointment from an investor's perspective is that of chairman. That person's responsibility is to ensure the competence and capability of the team as a whole and he is more likely to have a proper perspective than a shareholder alone.

The *commercial risk* that an investor faces is a function of a company's circumstances and potential within its particular environment and is identical to that of the entrepreneur.

The *financial risk* is not the same, if only because the amount of capital and the forms in which an investor proposes to make it available will be different to those of the entrepreneur. The key from the investor's perspective is to understand the potential returns from an investment and to weigh those against the amount placed at risk on the one hand and the chances of losing it on the other.

Returns to investors can be by way of income (for example, interest on loan stocks, dividends) and/or capital (for example, redemptions, profit on sale of shares). But usually the potential for a capital profit on an eventual sale of the investment is by far the most significant of these.

Shareholdings, particularly minority ones, in unquoted companies are usually wholly illiquid so an assessment of the potential value of the company as a whole at some stage in the future needs to be made. If the investment is a minority one, then equally importantly the chances of the majority wishing to sell at all needs to be assessed. That potential must be weighed against the risks.

First, the quantum of exposure needs to be understood. If the investee company fails, how much would be lost? The answer is almost invariably the whole of the investment. It may be possible, however, to enjoy security for at least part of the investment, for example a loan secured on a factory or on the company's debtor ledger. The chances of realizing that loss links back into the assessment of the managerial and commercial risks that an investor faces.

Examples

Let us now look at applying these ideas in two strongly contrasting situations. First, the start-up company, where the risks are at their greatest. Managerially, you probably have a group of people who have not worked together before and who have not started up a company before. Commercially, you will be unclear about the product's potential in the market; you may not know whether the product "will work," you may not even know whether the company can manufacture or supply it.

3i's practical experience is that such companies usually take three separate rounds of finance and an average of seven years before they become independently cash positive. One in eight is a huge success; two in eight fail within a short timescale; and five in eight limp along. As a rough rule of thumb, an investor must believe that there is the possibility of multiplying his or her original investment by a factor of ten, if everything goes according to plan, to justify taking risks of this magnitude.

Take Geoconference Limited as an example, a start-up backed by 3i in 1996. Teleconferencing is the process by which three or more parties are involved in the same phone call, using either normal audio phones or video facilities. The company aims to provide a service co-ordinating such calls, which can be a logistical headache for companies even when few parties are involved. Where more than four or five parties are connected, normal corporate exchanges fail to cope and a third-party agent is required. Calls of several hundred parties can be accommodated with the aid of special equipment. The company proposed to use a top-of-the-range bought-in "bridge" to provide its service.

Geoconference's clients were to be predominantly large corporations. In 1995, the UK audio market was worth around £13 million and was reported to be growing at 50 percent per annum. The video market was still nascent, but with the wider incorporation of cameras into desktop PCs, the potential could be considerable. Competition came from the large international telephone companies, and Geoconference intended to compete by offering a wider range of add-on services and, most importantly, by providing a better quality of service.

The management was a key attraction. The proposed managing and operations directors had worked together in the telecommunications industry for the past 16 years, and were keen to build a business of their own. A sales manager and financial controller had been identified, and a chairman with previous start-up experience had been appointed.

Demand was almost impossible to forecast with any accuracy, but the directors believed that sales could reach more than £5 million per annum within four years. To fund capital expenditure and initial losses, £2 million was required. The directors had £100,000 available to invest. Would you have provided the balance, and if so, on what basis?

It should be clear by now that decisions such as this are not straightforward. Commercial risks include extended delays in getting new equipment operational, the need to recruit suitable staff quickly and, critically, how rapidly new customers can be gained. Existing service providers could respond by cutting price and new entrants could enter the market.

The potential, however, in a growing market was considerable and the experience of the management is encouraging. So, if we were inclined to invest, what terms would have been appropriate?

A proportion of the requirement could be met with a Regional Selective Assistance grant from the Scottish Office. The balance of around £1.5 million was to be subscribed in a mix of equity and loan stock by 3i and one other institution in exchange for a 60 percent shareholding. Thus our risk was some six times that of the management for an equivalent level of equity. A good investment? So far, so good! The company's turnover is now approaching £5 million and it remains well positioned in a market which is continuing to grow.

Compare the start-up situation with that of a management buy-out of an existing concern. The buy-out is the process by which incumbent management effect the purchase of the business for which they are presently working. (Buy-outs are covered in detail in Part 8.)

There are two principles common to all buy-outs. The first is that the management team invariably has only a fraction of the amount of money required, so it effectively borrows the balance. The second is that it is the cash flow of the company concerned that is utilized to pay for and redeem the capital that was borrowed to effect the purchase. So there must be a sensible and prudent relationship between the purchase price of the business and its underlying ability to generate cash that is surplus to its on-going requirements. In contrast to the start-up situation, there is a management team with an established track record, and the commercial circumstances of the company do not change.

The risks are principally financial ones, a function of the new leveraged structure that is being imposed on the company. As a guide, eight out of ten of all buy-outs backed by 3i are broadly successful and the possibility of doubling your money if everything goes according to plan would be a practical rule of thumb.

Take CareCo, a company that operates nine homes for elderly dependent patients, with a total of 360 beds. They are located in "character" properties and the company aims to provide a premium quality of care to private patients and those able to top up state-provided funding. Occupancy levels reached 95 percent three years ago but have fallen to 87 percent, affected in part by the uncertainties surrounding new legal requirements.

A number of the homes would benefit from capital expenditure, with the opportunity to take the number of beds up from 360 to 410. In the medium term, modest growth is forecast from the acquisition of additional homes on the back of demand arising from the company's reputation with municipal authorities.

The management team is long established and has been responsible for building the business over the years. The matrons in charge of each of the homes play a key role and are heavily committed to CareCo's philosophy.

Turnover in recent years has been broadly static at £5.1 million, with falling occupancy levels matched by a tight control on costs. Profits of about £1 million look to be a maintainable minimum, rising progressively over five years to £2 million as a consequence of the capital expenditure program. An acquisition price of £7.5 million has been set by the vendor. A further £3.1 million is needed for capital expenditure, and the management has £200,000 to invest.

The key to the financing of this business is the strength and reliability of its cash flow. The maintainable earnings of £1 million a year translate entirely into free cash flow, enabling a bank loan repayable over 12 years at a fixed rate of 9 percent per annum to be accommodated comfortably. The balance of £2.3 million to effect the purchase must come from the management's backers. But on what basis? More debt would not be appropriate but nor do the growth prospects for the business justify locking up large amounts of ordinary share capital.

In practice, the majority of the requirement is invested by way of preference shares, offering a cost of money yield and redemption over five years, starting in five years' time. The core equity is made up of the management stake of £200,000 for 40 percent, and £300,000 from 3i for 60 percent. The capital expenditure requirement would be met by providing a mix of bank debt and additional preference capital.

The effect of this structure is to provide the bank with a well-covered loan, the investor with a total investment of £2.3 million, composed in the main by preference capital but including a stake of 60 percent in CareCo, and the management with a highly leveraged stake of 40 percent at a cost of £200,000.

The relationship between the management's cost of equity and that effectively paid by the investor (in this case, a factor of around seven) is often known as the envy ratio, for obvious reasons. If all goes according to plan, the bank loan and then the preference capital will be progressively redeemed, providing for a rapid rise in the value of the core equity holding.

Leverage of course also works in reverse. If the company struggles to achieve its forecasts, the yield on the preference capital will be threatened and then potentially the company's ability to redeem it at all. The value of the core equity would be worthless.

To sum up, the potential for entrepreneurial companies and the uncertainties that they face make traditional structuring techniques inappropriate. The important principles are to match the funding profile with the requirement and to weigh the potential for returns against the risks that are faced.

Valuation as a source of insight

Herwig Langohr explains how discounted free cash flow valuation works and its important relationship to business realities.

Entrepreneurs are in business to build value. The question is: how much value is actually being built?

Valuation is a process that assists the formation of an answer based on business judgement. More than a technique, it is a benchmarking exercise, typically done before making major decisions such as selecting a business strategy, starting a new line of business, expanding an existing one, or before entering important transactions such as buying or selling a business, spinning off a bundle of activities from a larger organization, getting outside shareholders in for the first time, attracting a strategic partner, raising new equity, or going public.

What the entrepreneur needs to realize is that he or she will typically know much more about the business than the equity investors he or she is trying to attract. This, one might think, should be reassuring to investors. In fact, it is often frightening to them. Why? Because the entrepreneur may not only know the good news about the business much better but also the bad news. While investors know that there will always be some lemons around, they don't always know which they are.

Valuation is part of the due diligence process that tries to sift the wheat from the chaff. It therefore helps parties to reach agreement about a price at which they are willing to transact without being clairvoyant about the true risks and returns of doing so.

Principles

The key in the valuation process is the point of view of investors. The decision to part or not to part with their money in exchange for a security is theirs. They are fully aware of the information asymmetry in the situation. This perspective generates our seven valuation principles.

1. **The purpose of valuation is to gain understanding** – not to get a number. No diligent investor will pay a number without understanding what is behind it. Once understood why, how and when the business is expected to make profit, the problem of what value to place on the profit stream is already largely solved.

   Through analyzing the profit equation, valuation helps reach a sound business judgement about the value of the business. Therefore, it cannot be disconnected from the critical aspects of the business context and requires due transparency of the profit drivers and their mechanics. Otherwise, valuation is a garbage-in and garbage-out exercise not worth undertaking.

2. **For investors, only the future pays – never the past.** Valuation attempts to simulate the future, not to settle up the past. Information about the business past and the management track record help in assessing expected future performance but the buyer will only pay for the future.

The entrepreneur has probably made considerable sacrifices and entrepreneurial efforts. Investors count only the business prospects these create, not their costs. That is why these are called sunk costs. In entrepreneurship, endeavors bear no entitlement for compensation; only prospective benefits do. It is sometimes hard for entrepreneurs to come to terms with this merciless reality. If some errors have been made in the past or bad luck has struck, it could very well be that prospective value falls considerably short of historical value.

The worst that could happen then is that the entrepreneur sticks to these sunk costs as value benchmarks. This could prevent the business from attracting the equity oxygen it needs to grow, to develop, sometimes even to survive. More than one business has run into this ground of sunk costs. It is always better to cash an actual market price that is low than not to cash a historical value that is high.

3. **Cash is king.** For the purpose of valuation, the prospects of the business must be laid out in cash flow terms. Again, this is because we look at the business from investors' perspectives.

To buy business assets or shares in the business, the investor gives up a scarce resource: cash. If financed with a loan, the investor uses the cash purchased with the loan to pay for the investment. Even if the means of payment is a security given up in exchange for the investment, the resource cost that the investor sacrifices in this transaction is the cash value of the security handed over the day the deal is executed. Buying into a business is in that sense no different than buying groceries: you don't pay with accounting numbers but with cash.

What the investor wants back eventually is also cash. He or she needs to know how much cash the business is expected to free up that could be returned to investors while maintaining the business in optimal shape. This is called free cash flow (FCF). Valuation must provide insight into the FCF generating power of the business and determine its current market price for the investor. Accounting data will be useful inputs in this process but are not the output.

4. **Cash today is worth more than cash tomorrow.** No entrepreneur acutely aware of his or her immediate cash needs will argue with that. So future FCFs must be discounted back to the present to determine what they are worth today, that is, their present value (PV). Discounting means computing how much cash is needed now to produce the expected FCFs through interest, interest on interest, and returning the cash invested. The PV is an amount that produces a cash flow stream equal to the FCF stream.

Of course, the higher the interest rates, the lower the PV. This "time value of money," which incorporates inflation, is given by the yield on a default-free government bond with equal length as the FCF stream. For a five-year pound sterling stream, this would be around 7 percent, making £1,000 in five years worth £713 today, and £1,000 during five years in a row, £4,100.

5. **To take more risk, investors want higher expected return.** In other words, there is no free lunch. Again, no entrepreneur will take offense at this. But an interesting paradox arises. Where is the risk if you get higher return? The answer is that while we are pretty sure about the amount of the risk that we are taking now – that is, the amount that could be lost and the likelihood of losing it – we remain pretty uncertain about what the actual future return is

going to be. The price is what you part with and risk. The return is only what you expect.

The higher these risks, the poorer the quality of the FCFs and the more the market will downgrade these to a low PV. The deeper PV is downgraded for poor quality, the higher the expected return that these cash flows represent relative to that PV. In other words, the worse the possible downside, the higher the upside must be to offer an attractive deal. It is not unusual to find discount rates of 60–80 percent per year for start-ups or first-round equity financing to reflect these uncertainties (*see How the venture capitalists work out the financial odds*, p. 105).

Risk-adjusted discount rates are what are called the cost of capital, known as "k," or the expected return after corporate income taxes that a prospect must offer to attract investors. Investors establish their requirements on the basis of the alternative risk return opportunities available in the market, the actual marketability of the project, and their relationship to its management.

To compensate for general equity risk, the market has paid on average over the past 70 years an arithmetic premium of around 7.5 percent over the bond rate. To compensate for the risk of a particular company relative to the stock market, that premium must be adjusted by a factor from 0.40 for businesses with relatively highly stable revenues and low operating leverage to 2 for equity that is highly exposed to the business cycle because of commercial, operating and financial risks. A "safe" project would command a "k" of around 10 percent, a "risky" one 22 percent.

But entrepreneurial projects are more often than not illiquid. Selling them may require considerable time and effort. This illiquidity imposes additional costs and risks to investors for which they want additional compensation. This can easily increase the discount rate by 5–10 percent.

In addition, suppliers of risk capital often offer advisory, monitoring and networking services along with their capital. These consume a lot of time and could risk damage to reputations. They must be compensated. Fees are out of the question. Capital gains are not. This adds an additional 20–40 percent to the discount rate.

In short, the illiquidity, service and reputation considerations tend to swamp competitive capital market risk return requirements in the downgrading of expected FCFs to determine the PV of an entrepreneurial project.

6. **The business entity creates the value, not the securities that distribute it.** This simple but powerful principle helped two famous economists, Miller and Modigliani, earn the Nobel prize.

    The entity approach to valuation starts with valuation of the business as a business, regardless of how it is financed. It discounts the FCF from operations at the "k" of the business cost to obtain the PV of the business entity. In the absence of any financial debt, this would correspond to the value of the company's shareholder equity. In the presence of such debt, its market value is deducted from the business entity value to obtain the PV of the equity.

7. **While it is good to be with the right company, it is better to do the right thing.** Investment bankers and dealmakers typically use some form of "comparables" to price cash flow forecasts. This valuation against peers is a legitimate due diligence consideration for intermediaries and a useful consistency check. But it should not become an alibi for lack of scrutiny.

The entrepreneur sells a unique proposition and the investor expects to collect returns from a specific business. While market-based, the valuation method should provide sufficient insight into these unique characteristics.

Application

The discounted FCF approach applies these principles extensively and involves six steps:

- forecast FCFs during the forecast horizon
- estimate "k"
- estimate the continuing value, that is, the value at the horizon
- discount all these to the present to get the business PV
- add cash and marketable securities
- deduct financial debt to get the equity PV.

This building block approach makes transparent where value comes from and is therefore popular. It also links easily to regular business information and circumstances.

For example, the FCF of a particular period is nothing more than net operating profits minus taxes paid on these (NOPLAT), plus depreciation minus the investments that had to be made during the period to generate the cash. These investments are the increase in working capital requirement (the investment necessary to operate the fixed assets, such as increases in receivables or inventory, which tend to be proportionate to sales) plus net capital expenditures. In other words, the FCF approach recognizes realistically that to create more value, most businesses require investment. No investor can eat the cake (withdraw cash) and have it too (leave cash in the business to create more value).

Take as another example a company that stops growing after a few years. At the horizon, the company plans simply to replace assets without any further investment. In this case, FCF will coincide with NOPLAT and NOPLAT will never grow. It becomes like a perpetuity and its value at the horizon is simply NOPLAT divided by "k." If the company is expected to grow after the horizon, a realistic long-term sustainable growth rate of FCF will have to be built in to estimate continuing value.

Further, consider a company that operates under perfect competition – unlikely for start-ups or initial financings but not unrealistic sometime down the line. In that case, you pay for what you get and get what you pay for: the cost of further expansion investments (I) will be equal to the PV of the FCFs that these investments will generate. This is like buying bonds in an efficient bond market: they earn the competitive return but nothing more.

The cost of such investments is equal to the present value of their expected free cash flows: I = PV(FCF). The difference between the PV(FCF) and I is called the net present value (NPV) or, synonymously, the economic value added (EVA) of an investment. Under perfect competition or in an efficient bond market it is zero: NPV = EVA = PV(FCF) – I = 0. Under these circumstances, expansion does not add value and FCF is also equal to NOPLAT. It is as if the company were only replacing its existing assets.

Alternatives: the comparables approaches

While discounted cash flow is the best way of organizing valuation according to our seven principles, price to earnings (P/E) and price to book value (P/B) ratios are second best variants to it.

The P/E ratio tells how "expensive" one unit of earnings really is. Naturally, i) the more that unit of earnings can grow without asking for more cash from the shareholders, ii) the more that unit pays out in cash to the shareholders without reducing its future growth, and iii) the lower the "k", the better the quality of that earnings unit and the more expensive it will be.

The P/B ratio tells how many currency units of shareholder value one currency unit of shareholder investment has created. It is a measure of what management has done with a unit of shareholders' money: create value (P/B>1) or destroy it (P/B<1). Naturally, i) the more the prospective profitability of the business exceeds its "k", and ii) the more there are such profitable investment opportunities, the higher the market value of that capital will be relative to its original cost.

The comparables approach to valuation multiplies the earnings (E) or book value (B) of the business to be valued with the P/E or P/B ratio of a "comparable" company to determine what the business would be worth if it would command these P/E or P/B ratios.

If applied properly, these approaches should reach similar valuation results because they also work with forecasts about the business, its cash flows to investors, growth, and cost of capital. Unfortunately, they rely extensively on accounting numbers and are used often as an alternative to proper analysis by simply plugging in a P/E or P/B ratio without due investigation of the true comparability between the businesses. Further, because accounting data involve many discretionary adjustments and few businesses are really comparable at all times, this method can lead to confusions.

Actually, P/E and P/B ratios are highly variable within industries and over time. Companies in the publishing sector in the Netherlands recently had P/E ratios ranging from 8.3 to 24. Between 1949 and 1995, the average S&P 500 P/E ratio was 13.9, ranging between about 6.9 in 1980 and 22.5 in 1961. The S&P 400 P/B ratio ranged from about 0.4 to 1.9 between 1960 and 1994 with an average of slightly less than 1.1.

Conclusion

Discounted FCF, P/E and P/B approaches should all lead to the same valuation results if applied equally analytically. The more a situation is complex, the more the profit equation and the uncertainties surrounding it require thorough analysis to gain insight. The discounted FCF method forces that analysis. That is why some people criticize it for requiring too many estimates and approximations and for being "too academic." But in our opinion, it is always better to be approximately right than to be exactly wrong. Diligent investors know this. That is why the more complicated the discounted FCF is, the less they will be satisfied with shortcut methods.

The financials of a business plan are a check on its overall consistency and attractiveness. Discounted FCF analysis is a simple exercise to help determine how much value the business is actually expected to build. And isn't this what valuation is all about?

Profiting from a closer banking link

Most enterprises are funded by the banking sector. **Martin Binks** and **Christine Ennew** explain the importance of a two-way information flow to maintaining a good relationship.

However well developed a local venture capital industry may be, it is still the banking sector that is the main supplier of finance to growing businesses. The dependence on bank finance is evident in both the UK and the US, where there are well-developed venture capital providers, and is even more extensive in countries such as Germany and Japan where venture capital is less well established.

This heavy reliance on bank finance (in the form of either long- or short-term debt or some mixture of the two) means that any problems or inefficiencies in the provision of such finance can result in the loss of growth potential from enterprising businesses. Aside from the negative impacts that this may have on individual entrepreneurs, there may also be a significant cost to the economy if such businesses are unable to grow and develop.

When banks consider the provision of debt to an entrepreneur, they are effectively making an investment in the enterprise concerned and looking for a return in the form of interest payments and the repayment of the initial capital. In deciding whether to provide finance, a bank must evaluate the potential of the proposed project and the likely commitment of the management to ensuring the success of the project.

This process is by no means straightforward and provides a classic example of the problems that may arise when contracts (e.g. the provision of debt finance) are being negotiated in the presence of what economists refer to as "asymmetric information." Asymmetric information is a situation in which one of the parties to a contract does not know or cannot observe some of the information that is necessary to the contracting process.

In the case of bank finance, asymmetric information is present because a bank typically cannot perceive the true abilities of the entrepreneur and the real prospects for the proposed project. This is a problem that arises when the project is evaluated but it may be compounded by monitoring problems once finance has been provided. Specifically, having provided finance, a bank may not be able to ascertain whether the entrepreneur is actually devoting the necessary amount of effort to ensuring the success of the project. These information problems are not unique to entrepreneurial companies but are considerably more prevalent because such businesses tend to be smaller and the costs of information collection higher.

Credit rationing

Economists have evaluated the existence of these information problems and their implications for the provision of debt finance from both theoretical and empirical standpoints. One perspective suggests that some form of credit rationing will arise and that potentially viable projects will fail to obtain funding. However, an alternative viewpoint argues that the result will be an oversupply of credit rather than a "debt gap." Others have suggested that the extent of these problems may be

A cautionary tale of collateral

In many countries, banks make significant use of collateral to ease the information problems associated with a lending decision. As well as signaling the quality of a project and incentivizing managers, collateral also provides a means of recovering at least some of their investment should a venture fail.

In practice, realizing security in the event of default can be difficult and may attract adverse publicity. Banks are nevertheless careful to ensure that the realizable value of collateral is greater than or equal to the value of the loan.

This can present problems, particularly in relation to business assets. In the event of default these commonly command a much lower price (at auction for example) than their value to the company as a going concern.

Thus the value of collateral required will often be much greater than the finance provided. One consequence is that companies purchasing plant and equipment add far more to their costs than they do to the value of business assets for collateral purposes.

The more rapidly companies expand, the larger the gap between the two and the more likely their proprietors are to rely on personal assets (houses, shares etc.) to secure additional debt.

Businesses often resist the idea of surrendering control over personal assets, particularly where this means limited liability status is eroded. Table 1 shows the pattern of "collateral taking" in the UK over the past ten years based on data provided by the Forum of Private Business; further evidence for Canadian businesses is provided from a study by the Canadian Bankers Association.

overstated and that decisions to lend or not and the price of funds only reflect a bank's knowledge of the entrepreneur and his or her business.

Clearly, the state of our knowledge is very partial and there is a need for further work to understand the existence and effects of information asymmetries. However, there is evidence to suggest that some of the apparently conflicting views may not be mutually exclusive. A study of lending decisions to smaller US businesses, for example, suggests that while the macro effects of credit rationing may be small, credit may still be rationed to some entrepreneurs and be more readily available to others. In particular, this result may be related to the role of collateral in debt finance.

Companies may overcome bank uncertainty by offering sufficient collateral to both secure the debt and provide reassurance that the business will perform to the best of its abilities in undertaking the project. Offering collateral, in the form of either personal or business assets, can be seen as an entrepreneur signaling the quality of a project; and the willingness to accept the risk of surrendering collateral in the event of failure ensures that he or she is fully committed to the venture.

However, if collateral is in limited supply, debt gaps may still exist and valuable projects may be lost. Lack of collateral may be particularly prevalent among smaller and more enterprising businesses. In addition, the provision of personal collateral in the form of a guarantee or house deeds effectively erodes limited liability status and may discourage investment at the margin, given the additional personal risk it implies.

Information flow

While collateral provides one mechanism by which the problems of debt access may be reduced, an alternative approach is to consider how to improve the quantity and quality of information flows between the bank and the business.

Although perfect information is an unobtainable goal, the quantity and quality of information available to a bank will be influenced by the nature of the relationship with each business. A close relationship has the potential to provide a bank with a better understanding of the operating environment facing a particular business, a clearer picture of the managerial attributes of the owner, and a more accurate overview of the prospects for the business. Thus, from the perspective of the bank, the relationship provides the basis for understanding customer needs and resources and identifying the most appropriate ways of meeting needs.

An effective relationship is not just one-way; it requires a positive contribution from both parties. The ability of a bank to meet customer needs requires that the owner/manager provides the bank with appropriate and timely information and is receptive to suggestions and advice from the bank. This process imposes costs on both sides, and each party may be prepared to invest in the development of a relationship only if the benefits are expected to outweigh the costs. Furthermore, a close relationship may not be necessary or appropriate for all businesses. The established, stable, smaller business with no aspirations for growth and limited financing needs may have little to gain from investing in improving the flow of information to its bank and indeed may actively prefer an arm's-length relationship.

However, for the entrepreneurial business with significant financing needs to fund growth, a close and supportive relationship may be essential for success. Equally, banks may perceive significant benefits from investing in the development of a relationship with such a business because of the impact of its current and future success on bank performance.

The importance of the banking relationship and the provision of finance for enterprising businesses is such that interested parties (governments, banks, business organizations) monitor its status and development regularly. In the UK, the relationship between small businesses and their banks has been closely monitored since the Committee to Review the Functioning of Financial Institutions (the Wilson Committee) reported in 1979. This monitoring has been continued through regular surveys of the membership of the Forum of Private Business (FPB), which have taken place every two years since 1988. The National Federation of Independent Businesses (NFIB) in the US has undertaken similar surveys, as have both representative organizations and bankers in Canada.

Despite a variety of locations (US, UK, Canada), these surveys tend to show a remarkable degree of similarity; respondents are heavily reliant on debt finance and banks make extensive use of collateral (especially personal collateral) in granting loans. Levels of satisfaction with banking relationships vary and most surveys tend to report areas such as pricing and availability of credit as particular concerns. Where surveys have been conducted over a period of time (as in the UK) there is evidence of an initially poor relationship (and a lack of differentiation in services offered) which improves over time as banks become more responsive to business needs.

Interestingly, in those instances in which banks appear to provide a closer and more interactive relationship (and firms respond) there is evidence to suggest that this outcome is beneficial to both bank and business. The 1998 FPB survey received responses from more than 4,000 companies. On the basis of these it is possible to categorize companies and their banks into participative (P) and non-participative (NP) and observe the respective financing conditions (*see* Figure 1). This evidence would suggest that there is the potential for both sides to gain from being active participants in a relationship.

As established above, the relationship is seen to be important because it determines the effectiveness of communication between the two parties and, therefore, the exchange of information. In the past much has been made of the contrasting experiences of Anglo-Saxon banking methods in the UK and US and a

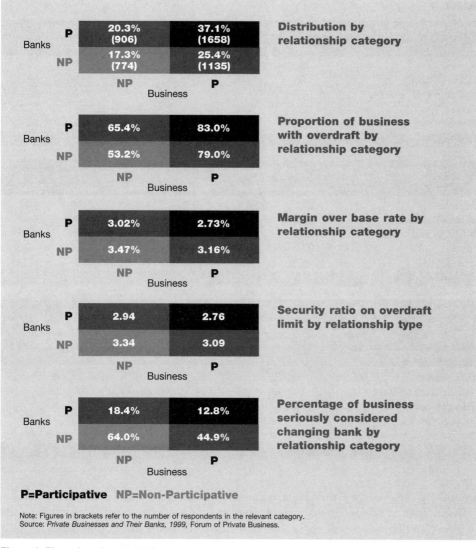

Note: Figures in brackets refer to the number of respondents in the relevant category.
Source: *Private Businesses and Their Banks, 1999,* Forum of Private Business.

Figure 1: Financing characteristics

more relationship-based "industrial banking" approach such as that operating in Germany, Japan and, to some extent, France.

Some of the claims for the supremacy of the industrial banking systems have been exaggerated in that the benefits of such a longer-term approach were usually enjoyed more by medium and larger-sized businesses than by smaller entrepreneurial organizations. Nevertheless, these traditions have appeared to engender a longer-term perspective on the growth and development of businesses as well as more highly qualified bank staff. The actual outcome of these alternative approaches to banking relationships is hard to measure but should be apparent in qualitative differences in the exchange of information undertaken by banks and entrepreneurs. Certainly there is evidence to suggest that information flows in bank/business relationships are improving and developments in information technology have the potential to enhance this process significantly, both by

Table 1

Type of collateral on overdraft (% of respondents)						
	1988	1990	1992	1994	1996	1998
Personal	n/a	31.8	32.4	30.2	24.4	23.4
Business assets	n/a	24.9	28.2	25.1	26.9	29.5
Business and personal	n/a	25.5	30.7	30.3	32.0	29.9
None	n/a	19.9	8.7	14.4	16.7	17.2
Number	n/a	3315	4692	3486	2642	3205
Collateral ratio on overdraft	-	4.78	3.48	2.35	3.14	3.00

Type of collateral on loan (% of respondents)						
	1988	1990	1992	1994	1996	1998
Personal	23.2	28.5	27.1	25.8	21.2	19.8
Business assets	27.2	31.5	32.3	31.3	31.7	35.7
Business and personal	22.4	23.5	29.4	32.2	35.8	33.7
None	27.3	16.5	11.2	10.7	11.3	10.8
Number	872	1721	2603	2142	1371	1778
Collateral ratio on loan	-	3.85	2.09	1.92	2.00	1.83

Patterns of collateral taking in Canada				
	Whole sample	Male owned	<5 Employees	Turnover <$250,000
% required to provide	n=950	n=471	n=338	n=236
No collateral	35	36	28	32
Any guarantee/assets	65	64	72	68
Personal guarantee	57	57	59	62
Personal assets	37	34	46	34
Sponsored guarantee	21	13	18	13
(% sum is greater than 100 because of multiple guarantees				

improving the quality of information sharing and by reducing the costs of so doing.

The impact of new technology on the banking industry has been augmented by the growing emphasis on cost reduction as a result of increasing competition in their traditional markets. At the same time, the pressures toward engendering a more effective relationship have also grown. Looking to the future, there are signs to suggest that with developments in information technology, banks are increasingly able to offer more personalized relationships to some companies while providing a more arm's length service (online banking and credit scoring) to others.

Countries such as Germany, in which banking relationships were traditionally more effective, may be slower to embrace the potential offered by new technologies. Changes in the UK and the US may lead to the integration of information exchange between entrepreneurs and their banks with rapidly developing management information systems, credit-scoring decision-support models, and expert or knowledge-based systems. This may enable businesses and banks to be much more accurate in tailoring the closeness of the relationship to the needs of both parties. The resulting efficiency gains could lead to significant advances in the competitiveness, both of the banking industry and the enterprises they serve.

Lernout & Hauspie Speech Products, NV

In early November 1995, a month after filing their request for registration, the Securities and Exchange Commission (SEC) gave Jo Lernout and Pol Hauspie the final permission for the planned introduction of their company, Lernout & Hauspie Speech Products NV (L&H), on the NASDAQ stock market. If the IPO was successful, L&H would be the first Belgian company ever to list on NASDAQ, alongside industry heavyweights such as Microsoft, Netscape and Intel.

For L&H, the IPO was a milestone in its remarkable history. Since its inception in 1987, the company had on many occasions teetered on the verge of bankruptcy, rescued only by the financial acumen of a management team that demonstrated on many occasions its ability to tap a wide range of financing sources, some traditional, such as venture capital, government subsidies, bank loans, and private investors, and some much less so. The IPO would not only solve the company's most urgent capital needs but would give a lot of publicity and credibility among US investors and potential clients. As such it was viewed as a critical element of the firm's financial and commercial strategies.

Even though the founders had a positive impression after a series of roadshows, the success of the IPO was still largely uncertain. In its eight years of operations, L&H had never been able to make a profit and had accumulated losses of $72 million (*see* Tables 1 and 2 for selected consolidated financial data). In addition, a great deal of uncertainty remained as to the potential size of the market for speech recognition products, the main staple of L&H, and competition within these markets promised to be intense, with many large, deep-pocketed international players showing a desire to enter the game. Finally, December 1995 promised to be a peak month in IPO activity on the NASDAQ, with 76 announced issues. Competition for capital among the various IPOs was increasing, and in November many companies had already had to grant discounts as high as 20 percent on their estimated price ranges (compared to 14 percent and 7 percent for September and October respectively).

The company and its technologies

Lernout & Hauspie Speech Products, NV was incorporated in the Flanders region of Belgium in December 1987 to develop and license advanced speech technologies. These technologies combine advanced signal processing algorithms and proprietary software, using linguistic rules and databases of speech profiles developed through the sampling of thousands of native speakers under various acoustical conditions. These technologies enable L&H's customers to develop products which:

- employ a natural language user interface (LUI) which can recognize naturally spoken speech (*automatic speech recognition or ASR*)
- create speech from text and data and respond to voice commands with speech (*text-to-speech synthesis or TTS*)
- efficiently store, transmit, and replay speech (*digital speech compression or DSC*).

Table 1 Consolidated income statement of Lernout & Hauspie Speech Products, NV

Figures in $1,000	Full years ended 12/31		9 months ended 9/30	
	1993	**1994**	**1994**	**1995**
Revenues	**180**	**2,381**	**1,569**	**4,467**
Operating expenses				
Cost of license revenues	1,442	4,693	4,005	696
Cost of engineering revenues	125	739	575	1,153
Selling, general and administrative	3,985	8,856	5,824	8,546
Research and development	3,081	3,362	1,804	3,022
Total operating expenses	10,633	17,650	12,208	13,417
Interest and other financing expenses	2,149	3,593	2,668	2,349
Net loss	(12,602)	(18,862)	(13,307)	(11,299)

Table 2. Consolidated balance sheeet of Lernout & Hauspie Speech Products, NV

	Dec 31 1993	Dec 31 1994	Sept 30 1995
Assets			
Current assets			
Cash, and cash equivalents	13	2,048	3,115
Accounts receivable	428	1,013	3,116
Prepaid expenses and other current assets	275	662	997
Total current assets	716	3,723	7,395
Deferred financing costs	0	895	638
Property and equipment, net	1,664	1,686	2,567
Software development costs, net	3,873	732	222
Total assets	6,253	7,036	10,822
Liabilities and shareholders' equity			
Current liabilities			
Notes payable	10,829	10,168	12,523
Current portion of long-term debt	1,464	1,915	1,697
Accounts payable	2,986	2,086	2,640
Others	3,734	2,678	1,625
Total current liabilities	27,869	25,763	27,708
Long-term debt less current portion	4,796	20,584	22,803
Total liabilities	32,632	46,347	50,511
Shareholders' equity			
Preferred shares	702	702	12,801
Common shares, no par value	13,895	23,298	24,559
Accumulated deficit	(41,910)	(60,722)	(72,071)
Currency translation adjustment	934	(2,539)	(4,978)
Total shareholders' equity	(26,379)	(39,311)	(39,689)

Even though speech-related technologies had been around for years, the speech technology market in 1995 was still considered to be in a relatively early stage of development. These technologies were computer-intensive, requiring massive storage capacities and speedy processors, and not very robust to the many artifacts of the sounds, intonation, and pronunciation of natural speech. Furthermore, the bulkiness of digital speech data made real-time manipulations difficult and storage expensive. Such limitations put speech products out of reach for mass consumer markets.

In 1994, advances in expert systems and the emergence of powerful processors, cheaper memory chips and storage components facilitated the resurgence of the market for speech-related products, with sales reaching $165 million in that year alone and industry sources estimating the 1998 figure to reach the magic $1 billion. All three branches of the speech technology market (ASR, TTS, DSC) benefitted from the computer-led rebound fueled by the rapid development of voice-related products.

The industry structure had proved volatile and subject to major shifts. Entries by small and large players were frequent. Few proved commercially or technologically successful, resulting in many early exits. Survivors focussed on market niches such as speaker-independent, small-vocabulary speech recognition over the telephone. Most players specialize in one of the three main branches of speech technologies, seldom developing competencies spanning the other related areas. L&H believed that, even though it might not have the best technology in each and every segment, the ability to deliver customized solutions for all three branches, in many languages, and for multiple computer platforms, was a definite competitive advantage. Building on this unique selling proposition, L&H management believed it could capture between 15 and 20 percent of the total market for speech recognition products.

The products

L&H's uniqueness is embodied in the *Language Factory*, a unique development methodology. This software assembly line pulls together pieces of audio segments from its speech database and uses its expert systems (linguistic, rule-based artificial intelligence) and proprietary algorithms to deliver the expected final product: the ability to recognize new audio fragments, to generate audio samples from texts, or to compress digital audio data to fractions of their original size. The modular nature and efficient regrouping and pattern matching by the Language Factory lie at the heart of the company's perceived competitive advantage: the ability to develop applications embedding all three technologies, in any language, in any direction (speech-to-text, text-to-speech), and for any computer.

The company has targetted four principal markets for licensing its multi-lingual, multi-platform speech technologies:

1. computers and multimedia
2. telecommunications
3. automotive electronics
4. consumer electronics.

The company licenses its technologies to original equipment manufacturers (OEMs), specialized semiconductor component manufacturers, and software vendors for use in a broad range of applications. The licensees include industry stalwarts such as AT&T, Microsoft, Novell, Philips Car Systems, and Samsung Electronics.

The founders

Jo Lernout, 47, and Pol Hauspie, 44, had been friends for years when they decided in the mid-1980s to "start up something together." Jo Lernout began his career as a teacher in a hotel management school, but quickly grew tired of the repetitive nature of the job. After attending an MBA program at the Vlerick School of Management (Gent, Belgium), he worked for five years as a sales manager in the office automation branch of Wang Laboratories Belgium, until he was promoted in 1985 to national commercial director.

Pol Hauspie is a self-taught individual. He inherited his father's accounting firm, but soon started writing his own software programs in the evenings. In 1977 he founded HPP Computer Center, a developer and marketer of software for accountants and financial advisers. In 1986, he sold HPPCC and took a sabbatical year to visit Japan and Taiwan, where he was introduced to voice recognition products.

Getting started

After returning to Belgium, Pol and Jo visited Belgian universities in search for state of the art research on speech recognition. They found three laboratories meeting their criteria, in essence demonstrating world-class competence in a specific field of speech processing: text-to-speech in Gent, speech recognition in Leuven, and speech compression in Mons. After negotiating specific licensing agreements with each of these labs for the commercialization of their respective technologies, Pol and Jo were ready to start their major (ad)venture.

To finance initial R&D activities, equipment purchases, and working capital needs, Jo Lernout explored a wide range of sources of financing. Following the first round of contacts, Lernout & Hauspie Speech Products, NV was formally incorporated in December 1987: the capital was fully subscribed by the two founders and nine private investors. The initial capital lasted the company only 12 months, so a first round of outside private equity was called for.

Commitments were obtained from the Flemish Regional Investment Fund GIMV, as well as two other Belgian venture capital firms. Each investor took one-third of the new offering. The company was recapitalized in July 1989, with $750,000 raised for one million new shares. The original founders were diluted down to 28 percent of the total shares outstanding.

Strategic differences quickly arose on the board of directors between the founders and the new outside investors, which had to be replaced by a group of angel investors in June 1990. At the same time, L&H Holding Co. purchased two million new L&H shares at the price of $0.75 each, injecting a badly needed $1.5 million of fresh equity into L&H.

Faced with an ever-increasing burn rate, the cash injection did not last very long either. For the full 1990 fiscal year, the net loss amounted to an impressive $5.3 million. In order to survive the ordeal, the founders turned to ever newer sources of financing. First of all, some of the R&D expenditures found financing through grants provided by the Belgian government and the national telephone company, for a total of $2.5 million. Guerilla financing tactics were also brought to bear, such as dramatic stretching of some of the accounts payable.

In March 1992, L&H sold its applications business to refocus all its efforts on the development of the core speech technology. The sale brought in $752,000 of cash and future royalties on the applications were estimated to potentially generate $3.2 million in revenues.

In November 1992, the company made a third private equity placement, raising $11.5 million by issuing around 3.8 million shares at $3.0 each to a group of angels and venture capitalists. The company hired an experienced and respected finance manager who specialized in the financing of entrepreneurial ventures and introduced a stock option program for key employees. One million warrants were distributed among key personnel, followed in 1994 and 1995 by another two million. Upon exercise, these warrants could potentially represent up to 20 percent of the outstanding shares.

From early 1993, L&H started searching for an international strategic partner among potential users of its technologies. AT&T, the largest potential customer and an important competitor with extensive self-funded research facilities, quickly emerged as a prime candidate. In September 1993, following eight months of due diligence work, AT&T and L&H announced a deal in which AT&T invested in excess of $10.0 million in exchange for a strategic say in the company. The deal was a major milestone in raising the international credibility of L&H (a "voicelilliputter" in the words of some industry insiders). Such increased visibility significantly improved the commercial prospects of the company: in a matter of months, L&H sold licenses to a number of telecoms giants, including Northern Telecom and Deutsche Telekom.

Guerrilla financing

The now well-established pattern of no revenues and significant R&D expenses ($3 million for 1992) carried over into 1993, resulting in a net loss of $12.6 million for the year. Another round of private equity financing was closed in June 1994, with the company raising $6.4 million.

In parallel, the company issued $20 million of automatic convertible bonds (ACOs) to smaller, domestic private equity investors. These bonds would automatically convert into L&H common stock in case of an IPO before their stated 1997 maturity.

Finally, in September and October 1995, L&H signed investment agreements with four foreign strategic partners: the Egyptian language expert Al Alamiah; the Israeli Venture Capital Firm Evergreen; the US software company Quarterdeck; and the Japanese technology giants Yamaha/Intec. These committed $15 million contingent on L&H setting up joint ventures with each of them and contributing its technology to the development of language-specific applications, e.g. Arabic with the Egyptian partner or Japanese with Yamaha/Intec.

With the private placement obstacle cleared, the road to NASDAQ seemed to be wide open. L&H was anxiously contemplating the historical opportunity of being the first Belgian company quoted on NASDAQ. It filed for registration with the SEC on October 11, 1995.

In early November 1995 the SEC gave its formal approval to the L&H prospectus. During a three-week roadshow, L&H and its underwriters had to convince a wide range of investors, both in the US and Europe. L&H was not exactly an easy sell to investors. The company had not turned a profit in seven years and both the market and product developments were still uncertain. This clearly put L&H in the speculative category, with serious risk exposure. To make things more difficult,

Renaissance Capital in its *IPO Intelligence Report* gave rather negative advice (it rated the company 5 on a scale of 0–12, where 12 is the top-rated IPO). Other analyst services, such as *IPOMaven*, were slightly less pessimistic, but none was a blank endorsement of the introduction.

Equally threatening was the high level of activity on NASDAQ. Much in contrast with the preceding summer, November 1995 had been one of the hottest months in history for NASDAQ, with an average of about three IPOs per day, and December promised to be even busier. An analysts' survey predicted that the fourth quarter of 1995 would be the best ever, with more than $12 billion raised, putting 1995 back in serious contention with 1993 for the best IPO year ever.

On the one hand, this could be interpreted as good news for L&H, indicating the market's willingness to absorb high-risk stocks. On the other hand, competition for capital was bound to be rather fierce. Another negative factor was the dismal performance in the past few weeks of companies active in the speech technology sector. Stock prices of L&H competitors, such as DSP Group, Voice Powered Technology and Kurtzweil Applied, had tumbled by 38 percent, 17 percent and 12 percent respectively since the beginning of 1995.

The introduction price was still not finalized. The company expected to raise between $30 and $40 million, with an estimated price bracket of $10–$14 put forward by Hambrecht & Quist. This implied that around 3.5 million shares would have to be offered. Setting the introduction price was no easy matter. Too high a price could damage the offer's acceptance but would maximize the proceeds to the company and to the underwriters. Conversely, too low a price would attract many investors and result in rapid price increases during early trading, a common "success" measure for investors. ACO owners were also anxiously watching the IPO price setting since their bonds would be automatically converted into shares at 85 percent of the introduction price, but with a minimum price of $14.74. The ownership structure of L&H would again dramatically change with the IPO. The L&H Holding company would retain about 34 percent of the shares. Publicly-traded shares would represent 26 percent of the outstanding equity.

On November 27, 1995, three days before the introduction, L&H management received a fax from H&Q in San Francisco, outlining H&Q's final proposal for the offering. The proposed share price of $11 was clearly at the low end of the estimation range. Despite reservations, Jo Lernout and Pol Hauspie knew they had to provide a definitive answer to the offer by the end of the day. Once more, they considered all possible consequences and outcomes, taking into account not only their personal interests but those of the ACO holders, existing shareholders, and the management team. Should they push ahead with the IPO under the present conditions?

The above case was written by Professor Benoît Leleux of the IMD for class discussion rather than to illustrate either effective or ineffective handling of an administrative situation. This version is based on a case written with Professor Herwig Langohr of INSEAD.

GETTING STARTED

4

Contributors

Alice de Koning is an Assistant Professor at the Stockholm School of Entrepreneurship, associated with Stockholm School of Economics, Sweden.

Robert M. Johnson is a successful entrepreneur in both the US and the UK.

David Grayson is Director of Business in the Community, London, and Chairman of the Business Link Accreditation Board in the UK.

David Norburn is Director of Imperial College Management School and London University Inaugural Professor of Management. His research focusses on corporate governance, cross-border acquisitions and joint ventures. He is a director of two entrepreneurial companies, Whurr Publishing and com.medica.

Howard E. Aldrich is Kenan Professor of Sociology at the University of North Carolina, USA. In his study of the role of social networks in entrepreneurship, he focusses particularly on gender differences.

Amanda Brickman Elam is a graduate student in sociology at the University of North Carolina, USA. Having worked several years for a start-up software firm in the Research Triangle Area of North Carolina, she takes a special interest in business ownership.

Contents

Introduction

Part 4 deals with the process of getting started and the various stumbling blocks along the way. The authors remind you of some simple but crucial universal truths – that it always takes longer than you think, that you will inevitably face many obstacles, that you need to think about corporate governance issues, that there is always help around, and that often that help comes from your personal and social network, your family and friends. You are also reminded of new "network" opportunities through which to market your services – the internet.

A business plan to entice backers

Alice de Koning provides a checklist for what to put into a business plan and how to present it.

Not all successful entrepreneurs prepare a business plan before launching a new business or deciding to buy an existing company. Some would-be entrepreneurs prepare very good business plans – but fail in their implementation. So why prepare a business plan at all?

Business plans have two main purposes. First, a business plan is a sales tool, so that you as an entrepreneur can attract customers, investors, or others to support your new business. Second, a business plan is an exercise to sharpen your thinking.

Through gathering and organizing information into a business plan, you are required to think through your ideas in more detail. Ideally, this thinking process should help you improve your ideas. Define how your company will add value to your customers, and show how the company will deliver that value. While you do this, you should look for potential problems and creative tactics to improve your business model.

The biggest criticism of writing a business plan is that people get caught in "analysis paralysis." How can you avoid this? One way is to avoid excessive reliance on libraries and magazines for information. Don't hesitate to talk to experts in the industry and professionals – a "dumb" question to an expert can sometimes yield better insights than any internet search engine. Another way is to take concrete actions and see how others react. For example, try to sell something or get other solid commitments – information based on real transactions is better than empty promises of support. For instance, Idea Lab sets up "fake" websites to sell new products and services. For a day or a week they watch their "sales," using that information to refine the business plan.

Gather the information first

A business plan includes many elements, most of which will require careful research. Depending on the country or region you live in, you will be able to rely on a combination of libraries, government databases open to the public, lawyers or accountants, and personal contacts. Interviews with potential customers and suppliers give your plan credibility and will probably improve your business idea and strategy.

The easiest way to build the business plan is to collect the information first, before writing the plan. European Venture Capital Association suggests this list:

- resumés of founders and key managers
- statistics relating to sales and markets
- names of potential customers and anticipated demand
- names of and information about your competitors and your assessment of them
- financial information required to support your project
- research and development information

- production process and sources of supply
- information on requirements for factory and plant
- magazine and newspaper articles about your business and industry
- regulations and laws that could affect your business
- product and process protection (patents, copyrights, trademarks).

Why are you writing a business plan?

Remember to write for your readers. Who will read your plan? Is it potential investors; customers? Think about what questions they will have and what aspects of the business are important to them. When you write the sections and design the layout of the plan, imagine you are speaking to your audience.

Business plans are useful for existing businesses, too. If you plan to turn around a business or start a new phase of growth for your existing business, a business plan is a great tool to articulate your ideas while at the same time convincing investors and other people to support your project.

Communicate your passion. Whatever your great concept, it's your responsibility to explain the idea in a clear and lively fashion. Let others catch your enthusiasm. In fact, the very process of researching and writing the business plan for a specific audience should help you clarify your ideas.

Most important, don't let your audience get bored: keep it interesting and concise, all the way through.

Make it look good

The business plan speaks for you. The better it looks and the clearer the ideas in it, the more results you'll get. A clean professional look means your business plan will be read seriously. If you don't have the computer skills to prepare the plan, hire a service that does.

A business plan isn't a novel – try to keep it within 20 to 40 pages, including a three- to five-page summary (see below). Obviously, a sophisticated high-technology manufacturing business may require extra pages to cover the necessary details. Include just enough detail to demonstrate you have done your homework and you understand the market and the business. Remember, if your audience are venture capitalists, you just need to convince them to invest.

Start off the business plan with the executive summary, which should give the essential elements and excitement, to entice the reader into looking at the full plan. Investors get lots of proposals – they won't read for more than five minutes if you can't intrigue them.

Organize the information into logical and clear sections. Short sections of two to three paragraphs with informative headings are easier to read and to review. A detailed table of contents also helps.

The contents of the plan

Use the business plan to help your readers "see" your business in the future. By including all the critical elements (which are here organized in four main sections) the business plan should answer your readers' unspoken questions about how your business will actually work. These sections are summarized from EVCA research, which asked venture capitalists what they wanted to see in a business plan.

Management and organization information – who are the people?

Like potential employers, potential investors need to be convinced that you and the other people in the venture team have experience, skills, talents and integrity. A synopsis of each person's background, with special attention to any successes in managing high-growth projects, should be included.

Besides the people you have, what specific skills are missing in the management team? Acknowledge the gaps and show you understand what kind of people the business needs to succeed. In fact, your readers might be able to help you find that key person.

How will you structure the organization? In terms of the board, what kind of directors do you need or want? In terms of employees, describe your vision of reporting relationships, incentives and recruiting.

Product information – what is the product or service?

Describe both the features and the benefits to the customer of the product. Insert a photograph or artist's impression. Relate your product or service to existing products and technology and clarify the distinctions. If you have a technological idea, explain the product and its uses in plain language.

Is more R&D required? Write up a research plan, including specific development objectives, a budget and schedule. What are the risks in the technology? How likely is it that another company is working on similar ideas? Can this R&D be leveraged into a range of products? What about patents?

How will you deliver the product? A detailed analysis and plan for producing the product should be generated. Don't just include the factory or shop but also describe how and where you will get your raw materials and notice whether any problems might occur (for example, delay in overseas delivery). What will be the production costs? How will you control quality?

Review government regulations for your product (national and at least regional) and be sure to identify required approvals or environmental restrictions. What plan do you have for getting approvals or permits?

Marketing information – how will you market your product?

The bottom line for any business is converting an idea into a product that people will buy. Is there a market for your product? Do you understand the market forces that will affect your business? Do you have the ability and resources to sell and distribute your product?

- **The market:** The first priority is to clearly specify the target market segments, explain why your product is suitable and what advantages it offers over existing products.

How will you position your product for the target segments? Discuss all the relevant factors – your proposed marketing policy for the price, quality and design of the product, the type, style and content of advertising and public relations, the sales force, service and so on.

Estimate both the size of the market, and the cost in people and finances for reaching it. The marketing strategy and customer benefits should work together. For example, your pricing strategy should be based on the value of the product to the customer, not on your manufacturing costs.

- **The competition:** The business plan must describe who your (potential) competitors are, including companies overseas. You should also prepare a defensive strategy based on probable reactions of your future competitors. Beware of competitors with lots of money – they have the resources to fight hard and long if they decide you threaten their future.
- **Sales and distribution:** The first decision is whether to work with outside agents or to have your own sales force and distribution system. Both have advantages and disadvantages.

Think about ease of reaching customers, size of orders, number of customers and need for customer support as you decide on a system. If you will depend on only a few customers for most of your sales, you must plan how you will manage that relationship profitably.

Consider export sales separately – the costs and benefits of outsourcing distribution may be very different. Many private companies and public services can help your business expand internationally at a reasonable cost.

- **Advertising and public relations:** Many products require advertising to create sales. Explain your advertising philosophy, budget and plan, making sure to link the advertising to your overall market positioning strategy.

Your options include using public media for "free" advertising. An agency can help create a winning strategy but select an advertising or PR agency carefully – check the work they have done in your industry.

Financial information – how will you finance the business?

The amount of financial information in the business plan depends on how much money you seek and the stage of your financing. The plan should include three elements:

- **The funding request:** State how much money you need, why you need it and what you will do with the funds. Don't try to keep the amount as small as possible – allow enough for contingencies.
- **Financial statements:** If your company is already operating, include the latest audited accounts and comment on trends and fluctuations.
- **Forecasts:** Use the information you have gathered on the market, product and costs and make realistic assumptions to build a scenario of the next several years for your business.

The financial forecasts should include profit and loss statements, cash flow and pro forma balance sheets for up to five years. The level of detail (monthly, quarterly or annual) should depend on the type of business. Seasonal businesses usually have high financing needs for specific periods of time, for example just before the snow falls for ski businesses. Your forecasts should show the peaks and troughs of your business.

Time pressures "can cloud the mind"

Daniel Muzyka and **Sue Birley** point to the huge time commitments that beginning a new venture involves.

It always takes longer than you think – isn't that always the case, almost a rule of nature? Yes, and as one experienced entrepreneur we know always says, "take your initial estimate of how long it will take you to start the business, double it and add 50 percent."

Why is this so? As you would expect, it is a mixture of things, partly to do with process and partly to do with the entrepreneurial spirit. The "trouble" is that entrepreneurial opportunities are usually captured by entrepreneurs who, by their very nature, are optimists. This optimism extends to the time taken to accomplish tasks – the problem is that the rest of the world is not as engaged with our ideas, does not accept the need for urgency and takes its own time.

Of course there is a learning curve effect. The second time you are sure to be much better at setting realistic timescales and priorities – assuming there is a second time. So find a surrogate – talk to those who have gone through this before you and check your expectations with them.

The consequences of getting the wrong time frame are clear. You and your team can become unduly frustrated at the wrong moments and abandon a perfectly viable opportunity. Even worse, you may accept a disadvantageous funding deal, buy a bad business or sign a lease on a poor location just because it was the path of least resistance. Time pressures can cloud the mind.

This can also be fatal financially. If your sequencing of costs and revenues is badly mis-timed, you can enter the "Valley of Death" earlier, and stay in longer, than is sustainable. This is not to say that you have to get it absolutely right. Nobody does. But as we have said earlier in *Mastering Entrepreneurship*, many profitable businesses fail because they run out of time (*see* Figure 1).

So here are a few of the common sources of delay in starting a business – as seen through the eyes of an impatient entrepreneur.

Figure 1

Figure 2: F International *the first eight years*

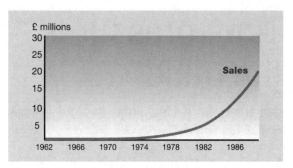

Figure 3: F International *the first 19 years*

Customers

Most entrepreneurs assume that finding customers will be quick and easy. After all, they are offering a novel product with new value-added to the market. Why wouldn't potential customers switch their buying habits?

Unfortunately, and not unexpectedly, this is rarely the case. It takes time to identify the right customers – the supermarket buyer, the building specifier, the specialist niche consumer group. It takes time to communicate with them – their diaries are likely to be much fuller than yours and they have priorities that may not include you. It takes time for them to try your product or service and time to decide that they will introduce it – maybe next year. It takes time for customers to move from low level experimentation with a new product or service to being a regular customer.

You can bootstrap this process by focussing on "opinion leaders" early on and leveraging their enthusiasm into the rest of the market. However, examination of the growth path of most new ventures will show a long period of establishment and consolidation – often with only a few customers – before the venture finally takes off. Take, for example, the case of F International. The sales path for the first eight years looks strong and positive (*see* Figure 2) but put against the next 19 years it is almost horizontal (*see* Figure 3).

Of course, the reverse can also happen. Customers are falling over themselves to buy your products. You begin to over-trade, controls slip, quality slips, credibility declines ... and the customers fall away. Getting the timing right is one of the many things out of your control but the one thing your must get right. At the very minimum, you must have contingency plans in place for either event.

Suppliers and distributors

Getting the right suppliers and distributors is critical to success. Yet at the start the entrepreneur is in a position of relative weakness – he or she does not have a trading business, just a potential business. Moreover, you may want them to do some development work for you or arrange special terms for delivery or payment.

It will take time to find those prepared to talk and to negotiate a deal. You will probably have to meet many people in order to share your ideas and convince them of your intent. Incidentally, this applies not only to independent start-ups but also to existing businesses. A management buy-out, for example, is a new venture as far as suppliers are concerned. You are no longer a "blue chip" company with a reliable payment record and you may find the "terms of business" change accordingly.

Having said that, leveraging past experiences with established businesses and maintenance of a professional demeanor during negotiations can lead you to more favorable outcomes.

Securing a location

For many businesses, certainly those in retailing, finding the right location is key. It can also be frustrating, demoralizing, time-consuming and expensive. Indeed, this is even the case for "virtual" internet companies. Amazon still needs a computer nerve center and book storage. So, if you have never dealt in the commercial real estate market, we have one word for you – beware. This can be far worse than buying a house. For example, we know of one entrepreneurial team setting up a chain of shops and it took over one year to sign a deal on the first site. They then discovered it would be another six months before all the leasehold improvements could be put in place so that they could open their doors – and that was just a builder's estimate. How often, in your experience, have they delivered on time!

Regulations

Where do we start? Clearly you cannot avoid them and, depending on your industry, they can be legion. Even in the best circumstances where the rules are clear and the bureaucrats helpful, you can find that the relevant committees only meet once a quarter, you have just missed the last one and there is a waiting list. That is assuming that you will need only one round.

Let it suffice for us to give you just one example of the creative problems posed by bureaucracy. One entrepreneur who was trying to start a food processing business in Germany was faced with two sets of codes from two different government departments. Each of the codes, while a bit ambiguous, seemed to suggest to the bureaucrats in charge that certification was required from the *other* department first in order for them to proceed. But neither was willing to contact the other – after all, it was not their problem. And there was no provision for inter-departmental contact without permission "from above."

How did the entrepreneur deal with this? At first, not well. Six months went by and nothing had happened. In the end, entrepreneurial creativity led him to invite each to lunch at the same time without the other knowing. He arranged an exchange of documents over lunch. The problem was solved, honor was preserved and the bureaucratic machine was undamaged.

Team development

On p. 206 Simon Stockley talks about how to build a team for a growing business. We would simply add to this by stating the obvious – it takes not only time but also commitment and tolerance.

You need to attract the right people and keep them interested in the new challenges they will face almost every day. This can be particularly difficult in the early days when you are assembling the business. Many interpersonal issues and personal concerns, especially those about effort and rewards, tend to become apparent over time.

It will take time to negotiate an acceptable agreement, particularly if there is equity involved, and then it may take months before they are ready to join you. Alternatively, you may find a much needed person leaving the team half way through negotiations for funding or just as you have landed your first major sale – and you do not have anyone else to take their place.

Technological developments

This is a subject all on its own. Even if you have a piece of technology that works on the laboratory bench, how do you know it will survive the ravages of the consumer world? Even if you believe a certain new technology is the answer, will technological progress in your discipline stop and an even better technology for your application be introduced in another part of the world?

Take the example of a new type of catamaran that has passed all the laboratory simulations. Fine, but now you are going to have to try it out at sea – not just once but many times (you need to know about longevity) and under different weather conditions (you need to know about safety and strength). These tests will almost certainly throw up more technological problems you had not predicted – and you cannot plan for what you do not know.

The search for money

During all this process of assembling the resources of your business you will be trying to work out how much money you need and how to raise it.

As earlier parts of *Mastering Entrepreneurship* have made clear, identifying potential funding sources, communicating with them, capturing their interest, helping them to pursue their due diligence, negotiating a deal and discussing the formal documents with lawyers are likely to take some time. Moreover, you are likely to be dealing with more than one source of funding.

So if you are looking for venture capital, it can easily take six months from the first meeting to the time when you finally receive a check. Of course you will hear of someone who raised their finance in a couple of weeks, but they will have forgotten to tell you that they had floated the idea with potential investors six months ago.

Energy and commitment

As any psychologist will tell you, you cannot "burn your engines at the red line" constantly without a break. Yes, you can sustain extended periods of energetic engagement in pursuit of an idea, but most people cannot run continuously without some balance, some time to recharge both physically and emotionally and some time to see their family occasionally.

Take, for example, the end (or rather the beginning) of a management buy-out. The team has worked non-stop for six months or a year negotiating the deal and at the same time doing their "day jobs" running the company. The deal is done, the relief is enormous, reaction sets in and you finally realize how exhausted you really are. Clearly you need a holiday. But that is not possible – the new venture needs your undivided attention.

Are we being over-dramatic? After all, we hear all the time of investment bankers who work non-stop, almost day and night, to close deals or of corporate executives almost sleeping on the factory floor to solve a production crisis. But these stories do not compare with the time and effort that are needed to get a new venture off the ground. The investment bankers have fixed requirements to meet, deal with a limited number of individuals in negotiations and, for the most part, have clear, known targets; executives have the resources of their corporation to help them. The entrepreneur is unlikely to have a rich relative to bail him or her out. The business is yours to manage – as are your health and energy.

Relationships

We know of no definitive studies of divorce rates or the break-up of relationships among entrepreneurs. But experience suggests that they are all too common. It may seem trite, and indeed perfectly obvious, to remind entrepreneurs that their families might like to see them some time, but as one venture capitalist we know has observed when asked why profitable businesses are offered for sale: "The entrepreneur has decided to go home and introduce himself to his wife and children – if they are still there."

Taking care of time

Are you discouraged by now? That was not our intention. All we are asking for is a dose of reality. So try to:

- establish a realistic time frame for all your plans. Try to work out where delays are likely to cause you the greatest problems and set up contingency plans.
- set realistic expectations for the members of your team, and those you depend upon for emotional and financial support – and that includes both your management team and your family (who are also part of the team).
- if you are intending to start a new venture, think about what can be done while you are still employed. Getting the core members of your team in place or thinking about your business plan will take time and effort but need not interfere with your job.
- Think about the funds you need to support your basic lifestyle – you may have to think about personally "downsizing." You really do not want to have to worry about this while you are closing critical parts of a deal or working 80 hours a week getting the office or factory together.

In short, successful entrepreneurs are usually good time managers as well. That is how they manage to do 48 hours' work in 24.

Negotiating the start-up obstacle course

Robert Johnson describes the difficulties encountered in starting a business and how to tackle them.

One of the difficulties in understanding start-ups is that there are few theories that one can derive from studying them. Without living it oneself, one can only examine anecdotal evidence of what the entrepreneur can expect when starting a business. Yet there has rarely been a successful start-up that has not encountered major difficulties along the way and a number of these problems are common to most start-ups.

By understanding what to expect, the entrepreneur can at least be better prepared to deal with what often seems to be an unending parade of crises that have to be resolved yesterday. Here, then, are the problems which I believe are most critical as well as most common to entrepreneurs in starting up a business.

Everything takes longer than planned

This is unquestionably the most pervasive problem as it underlies many of the others as well. Despite genuine attempts to "be conservative" in their plans, entrepreneurs always underestimate how long it takes to get things done (*see* p. 159).

A common mistake is failing to understand fully the sales cycle for their product or service – in the first instance, the time it takes just to get to the real decision maker(s); then the time it takes to close the critical initial sales; and finally the time it takes to roll out sales and achieve more aggressive targets. Another common mistake is underestimating the time it will take to develop a new product and actually get it to market, often involving countless stages, tests and approval processes that can drag on endlessly.

Yet the problem is not limited to the big, obvious areas of risk in a new business, for even the smallest things take time. Entrepreneurs don't often realize the time it will take them to set up an office, to get communications and IT equipment and then make it work properly, to establish sound operating procedures and many more seemingly mundane things.

Often the entrepreneur has come from a larger organization where such things were simply handled by someone else; now he or she has to do everything, from buying toner for the copier, to setting up the price sheet for the product line, from negotiating a supply agreement to franking and posting the mail. The multitude of tasks, big and small, are never-ending and simply take time.

Thus the entrepreneur must be very clear about what deadlines are the most critical and focus on achieving them, because many things will take a lot longer than expected.

Gaining market credibility is very difficult

Virtually every new venture starts out with little credibility. Even people with lots of experience and visibility in an industry will find their credibility tested when they set out on their own.

This problem is exacerbated when one has to educate the market on a revolutionary product or service. Changing buying behavior is one of the most difficult challenges any business faces, and it is even more so when the company is a new kid on the block.

Often there are false starts, dead-ends and adjustments before the company gets its marketing right and begins to gain the credibility so necessary to build the business. This is one reason why you often hear the advice to stick with products, technologies and markets that you know well. Having the knowledge of, and a network in, an industry and then building on that network are important factors in bridging the credibility gap.

Forecasts are rarely accurate

In many new ventures one can project costs reasonably well; but trying to forecast sales can be exasperating – no one gets it right. When David Potter introduced the first Psion organiser, there was no way to predict what initial sales would be. There were no comparable products, and it was difficult to explain to people the benefits of a product that they did not know they might want or need. Fortunately, Potter's timing was right and a new industry was spawned; others have not been so fortunate.

Others have encountered higher costs than expected, particularly when the venture has involved extensive product or systems development. The net result of such problems is that most new ventures run out of cash; and if there is one rule that entrepreneurs must heed, it is: "don't run out of cash."

Certainly profit and loss are important but in a start-up the key is to stay on top of your cashflow. Indeed, for the first four years of our company's life, we ran the business from a cashflow statement.

Increasing turnover (by itself) does not always solve the problem

Many entrepreneurs are good salespeople; and when things get tough, they do what they do best – sell more. This often helps, but there are some things to beware.

Sometimes sales increase at the expense of margin, and often a business can never regain its higher margins once they have begun to fall. Prices are often set too low initially and margins can get squeezed. Sometimes the focus on turnover leads to relaxed financial disciplines and ultimately to credit or even cost control problems.

In my own information business, a premature sales push led us to lose focus on building the supply of our data, which resulted a year later in a lower level of information available to sell and thus even more pressure on sales.

The moral: protect your margins and keep your focus while building turnover (*see* p. 337).

Supplier relationships are demanding

Just as a new business encounters credibility problems in the marketplace, so it will find developing relationships with suppliers difficult. Sometimes just identifying suitable suppliers takes longer than you expect.

Entrepreneurs are often surprised to find a supplier with whom he or she had regular dealings in their former company taking a tougher stance now that the entrepreneur is running a new business. It is not easy to establish creditworthiness, and securing favorable terms usually comes only with time. Likewise, ensuring quality and timely supply requires diligent oversight.

You will need good reasons to persuade suppliers they can benefit from having a relationship with your company. Be prepared to spend time on initiating and building relationships with them.

Getting paid is not always easy

It is no secret that small businesses are often the victims of the credit payment policies of larger companies. But in many instances the real problem lies inside the new business itself. Credit control is often *ad hoc* and lax, pressures to build turnover lead to poorer quality customers and people find countless reasons not to push their customers to pay. Yet it need not be that way. Establish tight credit and collection methods from the start and you can help avoid unnecessary cash crises.

Premises produce headaches

Growing businesses rarely have enough space to grow, yet they cannot afford to commit to excess space. Thus the entrepreneur finds him- or herself constantly struggling with how to plan and provide for space needs. It can lead to long-term commitments, involve requests for personal guarantees (which should be resisted) and tie up valuable cash.

The best solution is to be wary of long-term commitments early on and even pay a premium, if necessary, to retain flexibility.

Building a good team is difficult and time-consuming

The quality of the management team is crucial to the success of any business, yet few new ventures start with more than one or two people, let alone a complete team. Building and developing that team is very difficult. It is hard to find the right people (another reason why one's network in an industry is so important), and the process demands a lot of the entrepreneur's time. (*See* p. 206.)

One agonizing decision for many entrepreneurs involves whether to pay the fees and use a search firm. But for some key positions, outside help is needed. Also, in the end not every person works out well, so the process begins again.

Despite the difficulties, this is one of the most important tasks that the entrepreneur must handle – it takes a real team to build a significant business. Do not compromise on key appointments. If it is taking longer than you want, persevere and go for the best people you can find. It will pay off at the end of the day.

Managing people is the biggest challenge

The entrepreneur finds him- or herself selling to customers, negotiating with suppliers or subcontractors, working with an advertising agency, dealing with banks and investors, and doing a myriad other things outside the company. Yet the toughest task – and indeed the most time-consuming (at least mentally) – is managing people. This is the true test of an entrepreneur in trying to build a significant company.

This is also a test of one's leadership – the ability to get others to buy into the entrepreneur's vision, to motivate them and sustain their commitment to the business idea and to get them to work together to achieve the goals set for the company. It involves leading and exerting authority while also learning to delegate and empower. It means welding together and molding the team while also addressing conflict head on. It also involves painful decisions and lots of time spent talking with people.

The message is simple: be prepared to spend the time required on people issues and be prepared to make difficult people decisions.

There will be conflicts among partners and investors

Entrepreneurs often are so committed to their business idea that they see their company as a kind of family. So it can be devastating when conflict arises with one of their key partners.

Yet such conflicts inevitably occur along the way in a developing business, centered on such issues as whether people share the same vision and sense of purpose, whether key executives are growing with the business and bearing the load equally, whether individuals and investors share compatible exit goals and many other such matters.

These are not easy problems in the best of companies and it can be even more difficult for the entrepreneur who thinks of his team as a family with common goals. This is where communication among all parties is mandatory and where listening skills are critical. Don't wait until such conflicts occur to ensure that open and effective communications are part of your corporate culture.

The pressures on the entrepreneur are relentless

The entrepreneur often finds him- or herself immersed in every aspect of the business, often fire-fighting at the expense of planning, feeling responsible for everything and everyone, and "living the business" to the exclusion of nearly everything else. There is no question that the pressures are heavy and constant and decisions have to be made with the reactions of a fighter pilot. I've even heard some successful entrepreneurs say that if they had known in advance what they were going to go through, they probably would not have done it. Yet many not only survive, they thrive.

I believe that one of the keys to survival and success is for the entrepreneur to find a way to achieve some sense of "balance" in his or her life. That may sound odd, since everything discussed above suggests that such a goal is not achievable; but I think it is essential. The entrepreneur must maintain a "real life," taking the time (difficult though it may be) to be with the family, to stay in touch with friends, to look after his or her health, to develop spiritually and to find other interests besides work that can help sustain him or her as an individual. If an entrepreneur can do this, then he or she will find it easier to deal with the other problems discussed above and hopefully will ultimately enjoy the fruits of success in a business venture.

Building a network for business co-operation

David Grayson outlines the roles for government in helping small business.

Many national governments have established their own business advice agencies. One of the most substantial and long established is the US Small Business Administration, created in 1953. It provides financial, technological and management assistance to Americans wanting to start, run and grow their businesses. In 1998, it provided assistance to more than one million business owners. The SBA's portfolio of business loans, loan guarantees and disaster loans – worth more than $40 billion – makes the SBA the largest single financial backer of small business in the US (www.sbaonline.sba.gov).

Business – especially a small business – is inherently suspicious of government and is therefore wary of any business advice services provided by government. Whatever the objective quality of the advice, there will always be the suspicion that information given in confidence to a business adviser will somehow find its way into the hands of tax and regulatory authorities. Conversely, business support organizations that are clearly seen to be run by and for business are much more likely to win the confidence of small business clients.

Beyond sound and stable macro-economic policies and a reasonable regulatory framework for business, the most effective government contribution is, therefore, to engage business people in the provision of its own business information and support services. This involves government in a number of roles:

- **Funder:** pump-priming and providing core funds for services that are desirable for improving business performance but which small businesses are unable to pay for – or certainly unable to cover the full cost. Specifically, funding services where there is market failure.
- **Cajoler and catalyst:** to bring different organizations together and to provide a forum where they can agree on common standards and services. This may sometimes involve banging heads together or rewarding good collaboration between business organizations that are being asked to work together.
- **Champion:** to encourage quality and continuous improvement; encouraging benchmarking between business support organizations and establishing an authoritative accreditation and certification system to ensure quality – either through voluntary self-policing or statutory means.
- **Stimulator:** to help business organizations develop a long-term vision of how the external environment is changing, how this will affect small companies and, therefore, to help business support agencies respond both in terms of what they do and how they provide it.

Government also needs regularly to ask itself whether any direct assistance that it provides to business could be better provided through independent business support services either commercially or with the help of subsidies. The growth of the internet and the growing use of new information and communications technologies by entrepreneurs mean that government can provide a great deal more information online and, in particular, can publicise regulatory requirements for different categories of business through the internet. The SBA website, for example, allows small businesses to identify regulations affecting them. Singapore's Productivity and Standards Board (www.psb.gov.sg) and its Trade Development Board offer substantial information via the internet – as part of the overall Singapore government "thinking island" strategy (www.ecitizen.gov.sg). The UK government's plans for a Small Business Service, due to start in Spring 2001, include a strong emphasis both on e-commerce and on making advice and information available electronically.

Additionally, government has its own unique channels – for example, embassies around the world – which can provide additional advice and support for businesses wanting to trade internationally.

The UK government's network of one-stop shops for small business support – Business Links (www.businesslinks.co.uk) – and the US network of Manufacturing Extension Centers specifically designed to help small manufacturing businesses (www.nep.nist.gov), are both based on local partnerships of existing publicly funded/subsidized support services under local business leadership. In the case of Business Links this has involved chambers of commerce, Training & Enterprise Councils, local enterprise agencies and local councils.

These one-stop shop initiatives have a number of aims:

- raising the quality of service to small businesses
- bringing together a range of different organizations' services
- developing new services
- reaching more businesses
- changing the primary focus for publicly supported business development agencies (from an almost exclusive emphasis on the self-employed and micro-enterprises towards a greater balance, including a concentration on companies that have the aspiration and the potential to grow, recognizing these will include some start-ups)
- proactively going out to find this new primary target audience
- reducing the duplication between agencies and thereby freeing up resources for new service development
- moving from producer-led to customer-focussed activities
- taking from government control a range of business services
- anchoring business support more firmly into a coherent economic development strategy for a locality.

A key innovation has been the introduction of personal business advisers (PBAs) in the UK Business Links system and "engineers" in the US Manufacturing Extension Centers. Analogous to account managers in an advertising agency, or a relationship manager in a corporate finance house, these are the gate-keepers to a range of help both from within the centers and from commercial services nationally and internationally. A recent census of the 500 PBAs now working in Business Links shows that 89 percent of them have previously run their own business or worked in a small business. They bring a wide range of expertise to the network.

Video-conferencing

In the UK the government has quite consciously funded state-of-the-art information technology for Business Links because the fast-growing small businesses that it wants to attract know the value of fast communications and market intelligence. Business Links is offering video-conferencing facilities in some UK embassies and consulates to help small companies make direct contact with overseas customers and suppliers. This will become part of a set of integrated international trade services.

Government-subsidized business support services should not and cannot replace the market, however. They are there to help owner-managed businesses to make the transition to team-based organizations, to experience the added value that competent external advisers can bring and to help start-ups/early-stage businesses that are not yet able to pay for such services commercially. Publicly supported services can also introduce small businesses to new forms of support: for example, to help first-time and passive exporters, or to help them to understand the value of design. This is not picking winners – but if they have worked with a businessman or woman over an extended period, experienced business advisers are usually able to spot those with the aspiration and the potential to grow.

There is a strong argument that government-backed business support agencies should be charging for some of their services. First, because this will generate extra resources that can be ploughed back into the development and extension of services. Second, and arguably at this stage even more important, charging is about credibility, demonstrating value and setting the right culture. There is growing evidence to show that small companies value much more those services for which they are paying. If business support services are to succeed, they must be run in a business-like way and operate commercially (albeit with a clear public purpose). Both the UK's Business Links and the US Manufacturing Extension Centers aim to generate at least 25 percent of their income from their clients.

International support

National support services also need to provide international business support, and the characteristics of world-class business support are very similar to those of successful international companies.

Services must be customer-focussed, entrepreneurial, forward-looking, open to change and improving continuously, networked to a wide variety of external partners, their help tailored to meet the needs of individual customers rather than being based on "schemes" with pre-determined qualification criteria.

Achieving this can be measured against a number of benchmarks:

- positive impact on customers
- the percentage of total budget that is generated from clients' fees
- the quality of these earnings: is there a genuine increase in "real" customer billings (not just recycling public grants)
- percentage of the primary target audience that is regularly using the service
- numbers of clients who are repeat business
- introduction of new clients by existing clients
- numbers of two-way referrals with banks and management consultancies
- percentage increase in first-time exporters and in passive to active exporters.

Business Links

Wendy McCouaig and **Steve Tillet** both turned their business ideas into reality with the help of Business Link Kent in the UK.

Wendy's project was the result of a visit to the US where the buggies for hire in shopping malls caught her eye. She decided that it would be a good idea to introduce the buggy to large UK shopping centers. Wendy had a prototype KiddyKar buggy designed and built, and it was given the seal of approval by her 22-month-old son Donnie and by Thurrock Lakeside shopping center which quickly placed the first order.

Steve needed finance to expand his racing seat manufacturing company, and he, like Wendy, turned to Business Link Kent for help. An adviser helped him draw up a three-year business plan and make a successful application for a business innovation grant. The grant, he said, enabled him to switch from making seats by hand to manufacturing them.

There are a number of international examples to draw on. The German Steinbeis Foundation focusses on sectoral expertise – especially for technology businesses – by connecting small companies to experts in more than 370 Steinbeis Transfer Centers at education establishments and corporate R&D centers (they have a pool of more than 3,400 experts, www.ste.de). The US Manufacturing Extension Centers mobilize the expertise and resources of individual partner organizations. The New Zealand TRADENZ agency is strong in integrated international trade services, helping small companies with market intelligence and so on. In continental Europe, the Danish Technological Institute (www.technologisk.com) and the Emilia Romagna district of northern Italy have promoted and supported networking in the small business sector by building business support services around clusters of small companies in particular sectors.

Business support services face a number of challenges:

- finding how to measure the impact they have on their clients
- reconciling the different timescales in which politicians and the media expect to see results, compared with the time it really takes to change culture and practice
- accounting properly for the use of public funds without shackling the entrepreneurial drive and enthusiasm of business-led local partnerships
- establishing credibility with clients by showing an understanding of the needs of their business.
- achieving the right balance between bottom-up flexibility and responsiveness to genuine local market differences, with the economies of scale and assurance of minimum quality standards that a national business support brand has to have.

There is now an exciting opportunity to build on the initial success of support services such as Business Links by, for example, working with big companies to develop the capacity of their small business suppliers; by getting groups of small businesses working together to achieve quality standards (perhaps to exploit a particular overseas market or to develop staff training programs); and through supporting the commercialization of technological innovations, either in new small businesses or through helping innovators to find licensing opportunities and joint ventures.

In particular, business support services can play a key role in building an "infrastructure for collaboration" between government, successful technology entrepreneurs, big business, universities and centers of technical expertise. All this becomes far easier with widespread use of the internet.

The bandwagon of corporate governance

David Norburn looks at the relevance – or otherwise – of the debate on corporate governance, especially non-executive directors, in the growing business.

"Daddy, daddy, will I be like you when I grow up?" "Of course, son. You'll start shaving, behave badly but soon you'll be responsible. You have to think of others – the stakeholders in the family. What you will need is a set of rules, of responsibilities. What you need is corporate governance."

In parental eyes, how apt that the child should ape its elders; the entrepreneur managing the growing company seeking the acclaim of maturity, and governance the vestment. But what is governance and how applicable is it to the growing company? Is it necessary and, if so, when should it be adopted in the corporate life-cycle?

Primarily, governance is the structural mechanism that attempts to ensure the long-term wealth of the business for the benefit of the shareholders. After all, the shareholders are the owners of the business. The question is, how should it be introduced? And what are the systems and procedures appropriate to make it happen?

Take the UK as an example. Following alleged directors' abuse – in cases such as BCCI and the Maxwell affair – and concern over the large remuneration packages of a number of corporate managers, Sir Adrian Cadbury chaired the Committee on the Financial Aspects of Corporate Governance. The elements of his recommendations in 1992 were:

- the separation of the roles of chairman and CEO.
- full disclosure of and criteria for the chairman's remuneration.
- no service contract beyond three years without shareholder approval.
- a separate audit committee staffed exclusively by non-executive directors (NXDs).
- a separate remuneration committee staffed by a majority of NXDs.
- interim financial statements with full auditor discussion.
- NXDs to have full paid access to independent advice.

Three years later the Greenbury Committee added:

- remuneration committees should be non-executive and independent.
- remuneration committees should adopt a policy of full transparency on directors' pay packages.
- share options should be phased over time and fully disclosed.

While the specific details of these recommendations are peculiar to the UK, the underlying theme is common in many countries and, on the surface, seems sensible. Yet the debate is fierce.

Sir Arnold Weinstock, in his speech on retiring as chairman of GEC of the UK, commented: "I don"t like non-executives being set against executive directors as Cadbury seems to imply. It destroys the cohesion of the board. They should be supported by non-executives not held in suspicion by them." In other words, Sir Arnold saw non-executive directors as boardroom policemen. Warming to his theme, he continued: "One or two of the Greenbury provisions are a bit peculiar. They are used as an excuse to virtually persecute directors. Trust must exist in a democratic capitalist society between shareholders and the people who run their company."

Interestingly, similar concerns were also expressed by a significant shareholder. The UK's largest pension fund, Mercury Asset Management, was quoted in *The Independent* newspaper in September 1996: "We do not believe that blanket implementation of the various codes of practice is necessarily effective or desirable … the introduction of a code of best practice cannot of itself ensure that companies are managed with competence and integrity and each company needs to be analyzed on an individual basis." Yet in the last three years the global bandwagon of corporate governance has accelerated: Proposition 211 (US); The Peters' Report (The Netherlands); the Confederation of Indian Industry; the Kuala Lumpur Stock Exchange; Turnbull (UK) all strongly recommend codification and guidelines for structure, process, and risk exposure.

What has this to do with owner-managed businesses?

It is a fair question. After all, the guidelines are intended to protect the interests of the diverse shareholdings to be found in quoted companies. In the entrepreneurial business, control and sovereignty are much more tightly held.

The shareholders and the directors are almost always one and the same, certainly in the early days. Entrepreneurs as managers have an obvious dual interest in protecting shareholders' (their) interests while growing their wealth. External investors with a significant shareholding have the option of appointing a director to the board. So why should there be any discussion about corporate governance for this sector?

The answer is twofold:

- There is an increasing call for the growing business to appoint non-executive directors, primarily because it is felt that they will add skills not to be found within the firm. These include, for example, a different but complementary strategic perspective and guidance as to "best practice" in managing the larger business. Moreover, they are seen as an important "sounding board" and referee for the chief executive as he or she struggles with the problems of delegation and succession.
- As the growing company develops aspirations to become publicly quoted, those who consider the "child" to have reached maturity require that it adopt "grown-

up" behavior. So stock exchange regulations in most countries will require some system of checks and balances on the activities of the executive managers – and these will often involve a view as to the appropriate constitution of the board and the balance between executive and non-executive directors.

Are NXDs really necessary?

There is a fundamental question about the type of person to be appointed – should they be "truly independent" or not? – and it is a debate still unresolved in the larger company arena.

Some feel that independence, which usually means someone who is not connected to the business or to the incumbent directors, is crucial if the monitoring role is to work; others feel that knowledge of the company or industry from another standpoint is an important new perspective.

Of course, the larger company can afford the luxury of both. But for the entrepreneurial company, this may not be relevant or affordable. Certainly, as the company grows, enters new markets and creates new structures, those who have experience elsewhere can be invaluable members of the team but on an incremental and individual basis.

Who should NXDs be?

Quite simply, in any organization, people, not structures and rules, make decisions. The development of strong corporate governance in the growing company should be based on animate skills not inanimate structural imposition. The first non-executive director is a very special person, requiring empathy, complementary skills and a clear understanding of the needs and motivations of the entrepreneurial business.

They are not easy to find and entrepreneurs should beware of ageing warriors from large organizations seeking their own corporate Valhalla of the trophy directorship, often proposed by commercial marriage brokers. After all, the past may not be relevant and there is a danger that these corporate executives may bring approaches that are inappropriate and culturally alien to the growing business. What relevance can a 1970s' managerial grooming have to companies such as E*Trade?

The solution, as is often the case, can usually be found closer to home. All the research in the field of entrepreneurship reinforces personal networks, not structural groupings. At the end of the day, the owner(s) will only listen to, and pay for, advice and assistance that they respect and trust – and that usually comes from those they have known for some time.

However well intentioned, the bandwagon of corporate governance, laudably promoted by those concerned about directors' potential abuse of their positions, is not a blanket solution for the growing company. The "child" may well know best.

"Daddy, daddy, should I be like you when I grow up?" "Don't be silly, son. Times have changed. I don't understand the internet. I'm too old to learn new tricks."

A guide to surfing the social networks

Networking can help the individual and the business as a whole, say **Howard Aldrich** and **Amanda Brickman Elam**.

Importance of networking for entrepreneurs

New businesses are founded as a result of motivated entrepreneurs gaining access to resources and finding niches in opportunity structures. From the beginning, social networks are crucial assets for business owners struggling to make a place for themselves in competitive markets. Entrepreneurs try to build successful businesses by maximizing the opportunities they find and minimizing the obstacles they confront. Networking allows entrepreneurs to enlarge their span of action, gain access to resources and opportunities otherwise unavailable, and avoid obstacles.

In this article, we propose a framework for thinking about networks in a more systematic fashion. We offer an expanded vocabulary for describing your networks, emphasizing subtle but important distinctions between types of network relationships. By understanding the difference between types of ties, you will be better prepared to choose a networking strategy that fits your particular circumstances.

Network composition

Entrepreneurs are embedded in networks of social relationships. Some are personal, such as ties to family, friends, and neighbors, and others are business-related, such as ties to customers, vendors, and creditors. Social relations are, to varying extents, purposive: some arise because of accidental or unplanned encounters with individuals, some are created via organizational memberships, and others emerge as planned interactions for obtaining access to specific information. In this sense, then, all entrepreneurs construct networks of social relations in the process of obtaining resources for their firms.

A personal network consists of all those persons with whom an entrepreneur has direct relations – for example, partners, suppliers, customers, bankers, family and friends. The simplest kind of personal network includes people whom we meet on a face-to-face basis and from whom we obtain various services, including tangible goods, advice, information, and moral support.

Networking as an activity can be distinguished from normal business behavior by focussing on the nature of the transaction. So, for example, a single, brief, market-mediated transaction, such as buying a newspaper, usually involves two people who might never expect to see each other again. We will describe such transactions as "contacts," rather than network "ties." By contrast, taking a customer to lunch is contact between two people who may well expect to be starting a long-term relationship and, as such, the activity is a first step toward building a network tie. "Ties," rather than "contacts," are the basis of "networking."

We can think more systematically about networking if we organize the types of relationships that make up a person's total set of relations into three embedded

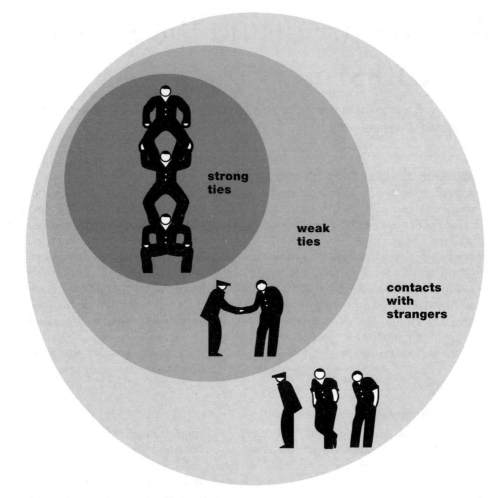

Figure 1: Framework of network relationships

circles, according to the strength of the relationship – strong, weak, and inconsequential (dealing with complete strangers), as shown in Figure 1. The innermost circle represents strong ties, the middle circle includes weak ties, and the outermost circle covers contacts with strangers.

Strong ties

The most durable and reliable relationships in a personal network are strong ties. Strong ties are usually of long duration and are based on a principle of implicit reciprocity. In other words, they are long-term, two-way relationships, with something to be gained by both sides. Consequently, strong ties are typically more reliable than other ties and involve a strong degree of trust and emotional closeness. Individuals tend to make heavy investments in this type of relationship, requiring fairly frequent contact with the other person.

Because of the effort involved in creating and sustaining a strong tie, most people have only about five or six strong ties in their network. Ten strong ties would be very unusual, and twenty would be truly heroic! We rely on strong ties for advice, assistance, and support in all areas of our lives. An example of a strong tie would be a person you feel comfortable turning to for advice about an ethical dilemma you face at work, or perhaps asking someone to watch your children for you on short notice. An entrepreneur's strong tie network is usually composed of a majority of business associates, a few close friends, and one or two family members.

Strong ties are especially important for business owners, as they provide a means of avoiding the opportunism and uncertainty inherent in typical market-mediated transactions. In social situations where people expect to deal with each other over an extended period, strong ties yield three benefits: trust, predictability and voice. Trust is a crucial component of business dealings, as it tells us who we can count on in difficult situations, and it substantially enhances predictability in relations. Predictability refers to how the other party will behave if situations change. And, finally, voice means making your complaints known and negotiating over them, rather than silently sneaking away. Each of these benefits is enhanced in long-term relationships. Hence, strong ties carry substantial benefits for entrepreneurs who work in challenging environments where people expect to interact frequently over a long time span.

Weak ties

Whereas strong ties are based on trust, weak ties are superficial or casual and typically involve little emotional investment. Weak-tie relationships are typically of shorter duration and involve lower frequency of contact. They are also less reliable and more uncertain than strong ties and often fade into dormancy, only to be revived when assistance is required. As shown in Figure 1, they can be thought of as arm's-length relations, involving persons whose handshake we seek but whose full support we cannot count on.

Individuals have many more weak ties than strong ties. A quick look in your address book and business card collection can give an approximate count of your weak ties. Younger and more junior people typically have fifty to one hundred weak ties in their networks. By contrast, older, more senior people may easily have one hundred or more. Examples of weak ties include the relationships you may have with a customer or client, with a supplier or investor, and even with your family doctor.

In contrast to strong ties, weak ties are characterized by opportunism, uncertainty, and exit. Opportunism is inherent in typical market-like transactions, which are generally driven by self-interest and leave little or no room for trust. Uncertainty means you have difficulty in predicting the weak tie's actions. And, lastly, exit refers to the notion that, when you are faced with opportunism and uncertainty, it is probably easier to go elsewhere to complete a transaction involving a weak tie, rather than to negotiate for a better deal.

Weak ties do not carry the same secure benefits that strong ties do, but they do have a major benefit of their own, namely that of diversity. Relations with weak ties can expose entrepreneurs to channels of information not available through strong ties, as we will point out.

Contacts with strangers

A third type of network relationship can better be described as contacts, rather than ties. These types of network relations are entered into for pragmatic purposes and usually occur with strangers or individuals with whom no prior relations have existed. Contacts with strangers are typically fleeting in duration and require little or no emotional involvement. An example of a contact with a stranger would be buying a piece of equipment from a person who advertised in a trade publication.

We have only a limited understanding of the relative value and importance of these pragmatic contacts with strangers. Arm's-length, self-interested transactions are at the core of economic models of markets and, for that reason, are taken for granted. In fact, very little is known about how they are established, because their existence is simply assumed in economic models of how markets work.

Models of entrepreneurship and business life-cycles emphasize the context-dependent nature of the three types of relations we portray in Figure 1. For entrepreneurs, strong and weak ties may be more important than contacts with strangers for the mobilization of resources occurring in the early stages of business development. Later, when a newly founded business is on its feet, arm's-length transactions and contacts with strangers assume more importance.

This framework helps to clarify the types of relationships found in personal networks. In reality, of course, the boundaries between categories are not so easily defined. The differences between strong ties and weak ties are the easiest to distinguish. Differences between weak ties (which may involve infrequent contacts with others who are barely known) and contacts with strangers (who are completely unknown) are a little more difficult to recognize. Consequently, most current research addresses strong ties, few studies touch on weak ties, and none really focusses on contacts with strangers.

Effective networking

Effective networking is a challenge for most entrepreneurs, for whom time is a valuable resource. The foremost questions concern where to focus your energies, how to expand your network, and how to keep track of your ties. We offer three general suggestions on how to improve your networking: strengthen direct ties, cultivate diversity, and systematically plan and monitor your ties.

Strengthen direct ties

Networking with your weak ties to turn them into strong ones is a way of overcoming the weaknesses inherent in pure market-like transactions, of strengthening the resource base of your business, and expanding your circle of trust. Strong ties are important because they encourage the development of trust, predictability, and voice in network relations. These benefits help to mediate the risks inherent in building new businesses. However, time and resource constraints mean that you'll probably never have more than five to ten strong tie relations, and so you must pay strategic attention to weak ties.

Cultivate diversity

Diversity is crucial for entrepreneurs, as it provides access to critical information, such as potential markets, new business locations, innovations, sources of capital, and potential investors. There are two ways to cultivate diversity: use your strong ties or expand your weak ties. The first way is to cultivate strong ties with people who have ties to very different parts of the business environment in which you operate, opening up channels of information otherwise inaccessible. Entrepreneurs can leverage their direct relations by a judicious choice of strong ties who have access to others quite unlike themselves.

A second way to gain access to new information is to expand your weak ties. While strong ties are clearly important, a network made up of all strong ties will be of limited value to an entrepreneur. The reason is straightforward. Because people tend toward emotional and personal balance in their strong ties, their inner circle tends to be fairly homogeneous. For example, according to research we have conducted, male business owners almost never have women in their strong tie circles. In homogeneous networks, information known to one person is rapidly diffused to others and interpreted in similar ways, and an entrepreneur gains little new information from talking to more than one strong tie.

By contrast, people are less concerned with balance in their large circle of weak ties. The persons with whom we have weak ties, such as casual acquaintances, are less likely to know each other than are those with whom we have strong ties, such as close friends. Heterogeneity is both more likely and more tolerated among a person's weak ties. Contacts with casual acquaintances, different from yourself, link you to diverse others, each of whom has a close circle of persons unknown to you. If these strangers have information, or resources, of value, then you can gain access to them indirectly through the diversity of your weak ties. (You could also accomplish the same goal by diversifying your strong ties, but that requires very intense and often unsettling maneuvering.) So, in essence, a large set of diverse ties may be better than a small set of overlapping ties because you achieve better access to critical information.

"Brokers" – people who facilitate links between persons who are not themselves directly connected – are central to the expansion of many personal networks. For example, venture capitalists often play broker roles because they bring together technical experts, management consultants and financial planners to supplement an entrepreneur's limited knowledge and experience. Some social settings facilitate the activities of brokers, such as bars and restaurants in Silicon Valley, California, which serve as central meeting points and support a complex pattern of social relationships stimulating high start-up rates. Finding and using brokers can help an entrepreneur cultivate diversity by expanding weak ties.

More systematically plan and monitor network ties

Personal networks which are of real value to an entrepreneur must include a balance of both strong and weak ties, that is, of strength and diversity. Effective entrepreneurs are usually to be found in positions that are connected to lots of diverse information sources, as well as in positions benefitting from a reliable set of strong ties. The challenge of effective networking is to find ways of more systematically organizing your personal networks to maximize the flow of resources that are so critical to business development after startup.

Effective networking involves three steps. The first is to collect the contact information about your network ties in one central repository. People organize information about their network ties in various ways. Some people compile it into one address book or business card file, while others keep bits and pieces of it tucked away in file drawers. Some people even go as far as setting up computer databases to track the information. Whatever you do, become more methodical in how your network information is categorized and organized.

The second step is to create a feedback loop for monitoring and pruning this collection of ties to keep information manageable and productive. This means reviewing your collection of ties at regular intervals. Your review will provide descriptive information on frequency of contact, results from past contacts, and other information on the state of the relationship. Based on your review, you should trim those ties that are out-of-date or no longer useful.

The third step involves some strategic thinking. How balanced is your network? Is your network helpful in providing you with the resources you need? How can you improve your network? Do you need to devote more time to maintaining strong ties? Which of your weak ties is worth the effort of developing into a strong tie? Do you need to increase your weak ties or are you trying to keep up with too many?

Conclusion

The picture which we have drawn shows entrepreneurs embedded in a social context, channeled and facilitated, or constrained and inhibited, by their positions in social networks. Effective networks are crucial to business success because they increase your span of action, economize on time and other resources, and possibly help you to control an unstable business environment. Networks balanced between strength and diversity, strong and weak ties, are of the most real value to entrepreneurs. The challenge is to find ways of more systematically planning, monitoring, and pruning network information.

Meeting people to shape opportunities – the entrepreneur's way

Alice de Koning considers how much an entrepreneur can gain simply by talking to people.

An entrepreneur I met recently told me this story about how he started his third company.

"I decided to earn my MBA while I was running a company which sold plastic manufacturing machines. I wasn't interested in taking a job in consulting or management, but I participated in the interview process anyway, to make contacts. One company in particular interested me. I knew, through my contacts and through chatting with their representatives during a campus visit, that they had a packaging problem for an upcoming new product.

"I went through the job interview process, until I was finally scheduled an interview with the key vice-president. As soon as our first interview began, I told him I wasn't interested in working for him, but I did want to solve his packaging problem.

That meeting led to further meetings, as I proposed an innovative new package concept. To prepare a convincing proposal, I needed to hire an engineer, and work with him to develop the technical aspects of the product and process. I got the order.

"Deliveries were supposed to start in two months, and I didn't have a plant, financing, staff – nothing but me and the engineer. These were in the days before venture capitalists existed, and nothing was straightforward or easy. I immediately contacted former customers and consultants I had met over the years, and a number of successful colleagues who graduated with me from an elite engineering school. I managed to find an appropriate plant which I could use, leased the equipment, and got financing for raw materials based on the signed contract. I was in business."

Stories like this one highlight the magic of entrepreneurship. Against the odds, pursuing a new idea, the individual starts a new company and wins! But there is more to this story than struggling against the odds. The story shows how much time the entrepreneur spent talking to other people, working with others to develop his ideas and access the necessary resources.

I have taken a particular interest in collecting stories of how successful entrepreneurs shape ideas into business opportunities, because I think we can learn something important about that "magic." I talked to successful serial entrepreneurs, people who had started at least three companies, were successful in almost all their ventures, and had achieved a significant increase in wealth or assets.

I expected to learn about the entrepreneurs' unique thinking patterns or special analysis tricks for discovering opportunities. Instead, I discovered that opportunities are formed over several months or even years, and that these entrepreneurs form their opportunities through discussions with people. The process of opportunity formation is essentially a *social* process, with the individual or team working through and with people.

The contrast between our common myths of instant opportunity recognition and this picture of a slower opportunity formation process could not be greater. Just the phrase "opportunity recognition," used by researchers and entrepreneurs alike, can be misleading. Opportunity recognition suggests that good ideas for new businesses are waiting to be discovered by an astute observer. We often believe that the discovery of the opportunity can be identified at a precise moment, as a sudden intellectual inspiration when an idea suddenly comes. And, in fact, these moments do happen – all the entrepreneurs I met could remember specific moments or incidents, when they had a sudden insight. But these moments exist within the broader process of opportunity formation, in which the entrepreneurs gather information and re-shape the ideas to create an improved business concept. In fact, sometimes an entrepreneur could recall five or six moments of opportunity recognition, all related to the evolution of one idea.

Opportunity formation happens in a series of encounters with people, which are used to shape and develop an idea. Ideas change as the entrepreneurs learn more about the market, the industry, the technology, the resources available, the customers, and any other relevant aspects. The entrepreneurs try to build a business concept which they are confident will be feasible and profitable.

In some cases, the original idea must change dramatically. For example, one entrepreneur I met "recognized" an opportunity in leasing water treatment systems to smaller municipalities. As he talked to people, however, he realized his only potential supplier was unreliable and the government tended to be a slow customer.

He eventually settled on leasing sewage treatment to private companies, complete with a range of profitable services. In the process of arriving at this business concept, he spoke to potential customers, consulting engineers, bankers, environmental agencies, suppliers and potential employees. At each step, he gathered more information, tested the feasibility of aspects of his concept with these "experts," and assessed what resources were available at what price. In fact, this process is ongoing, as the business expands into related markets and products.

What are some of the key aspects of opportunity formation? I like to distinguish two main aspects, information gathering and concept creation. Information gathering includes scanning and seeking or research. Serial entrepreneurs tend to be on the look-out for opportunity information all the time. Whether they are reading the paper, having a casual conversation, or deciding whether to attend a gathering of business people or alumni, they are always looking for certain kinds of information. Researchers have named this characteristic "alertness" or "mindfulness," to describe how people have an unconscious mental attitude which filters in high-priority information. Information seeking is more active, when entrepreneurs have questions they want answered and they seek out answers. The combined quality of information scanning and seeking is dependent on the quality of the entrepreneurs' network. That's why the most successful entrepreneurs I met seemed to have extensive ties within their industries and often with their fellow alumni (often business or engineering school graduates). Also, the most successful entrepreneurs did not hesitate to approach any expert with their questions, even if they had to pay for their time. High-quality information resulted from their high-quality contacts.

Concept creation, in my model of opportunity formation, includes thinking and assessing resources. Thinking is obviously a necessary ingredient, but surprisingly much of the thinking happened during discussions with other people. The entrepreneurs often told me that they were talking to a colleague when they realized a new approach to a problem. Many researchers have found that dialog is an important part of thinking – Karl Weick quotes a girl who said: "How can I know what I think until I see myself say it?"

Assessing resources is a fundamental part of creating a business concept. Critical resources varied from one opportunity to the next, but might have included personnel, customers, financing, plant and equipment, suppliers, lawyers, etc. As the entrepreneurs explored their options, the ideas were re-shaped to reflect what resources they could access. Over time and with success, most of the entrepreneurs had a much easier time accessing any resources they wanted, but they were still careful to match the evolving business concept with the available resources. One entrepreneur, for example, specialized in turning around low technology manufacturing, but had no interest in day-to-day management of the operations. His critical resource was potential partners, who were capable of managing a small manufacturing company. The skills and knowledge of the potential partners were critical to how he evaluated take-over targets and planned to re-shape their product markets. In opportunity formation, the evolution of the ideas is intertwined with discovering and organizing the necessary resources.

Why do entrepreneurs prefer to talk to people, rather than check databases and libraries? Successful entrepreneurs do not like to waste their time. Most felt greater efficiency was achieved by asking experts questions and picking up details as they met people throughout the day. In some cases, the "experts" were truck drivers and small-scale customers who provided a detailed understanding of how products and services were used. In other cases, top names in a specific industry or technology were sought out. According to one entrepreneur, it was critical to talk to people all the time. Another entrepreneur noted that he never hesitated to ask questions, although he certainly wouldn't waste long dinner meetings just to get two or three tidbits.

The entrepreneurs seemed to share two reasons for using people to gain information: one, people are more efficient information filters, and two, experts often know more than they realize. Through a dialog, the entrepreneur can elicit both hard facts and expert intuition. One entrepreneur did not hesitate to ask "dumb" questions of experts: he found his outsider perspective often identified new solutions to industry problems, and the expert was skilled enough to verify immediately whether the idea would work.

Why do they think and access resources through people? Like information gathering, concept creation through people is efficient. The entrepreneurs needed to do more than just identify resources, though. If they decided on certain resources, they invariably needed the co-operation and trust of people to access those resources. An obvious example is convincing a new employee to join a non-existent company, as in the opening vignette. But even money is delivered by a human being, and building the right relationship is important.

Recent research has shown that entrepreneurs often obtain resources cheaply (that is, less than market price), because of their social skills. Social skills aren't about being "nice," but being effective in relationships. For example, an entrepreneur who shares contacts and information with an industry consultant is more likely to gain access to potential customers and new ideas from that person in the future – and probably for free.

Entrepreneurs also need to inspire people, to motivate them to believe in their business concept. Sometimes the entrepreneurs' reputation will give them credibility with others, but even experienced and successful entrepreneurs described critical conversations when they worked hard to win the support of key people.

CASE STUDY

Swift@rt

"... And the winner of the 1999 European Business Plan Competition is SwiftART!" Alberto Geneletti, Robin Dell, Francesco Lazzarini and David Millan from the MIEM program at SDA Bocconi had transmitted their enthusiasm in their business idea to the judges gathered at INSEAD and beaten competition from 13 student groups selected from the leading European business schools. Alberto had a degree in electronic engineering and three years' work experience in the multimedia industry; Francesco was a computer engineer with experience as software tools manager with VLSI Technology; Robin had graduated from the London School of Economics and was a marketing and IT expert; while David had a degree in economics from Princeton and had worked in an investment bank.

SwiftART's mission was to become a world-class animation studio, combining creative talents and technology to create great characters for the next century. The group felt the time was right to start up a new company located in Europe for several reasons:

- **Overall audio-visual industry revenues are growing fast.** A study on future audio-visual markets carried out for the European Commission in 1997 estimated that *the industry's overall revenues will grow by about 70 percent by the year 2005*, due to the dramatic growth in outlets, in particular multiplex theaters, multi-channel television and VCRs.
- **Content providers will have the opportunity to capture a large share of these revenues.** The study, "Economic Implications of New Communication Technologies on the Audio Visual Markets," shows that free-to-air TV is the engine behind the European audio-visual industry with a projected growth, in real terms, from €7,500 million in 1995 to €10,400 million in 2005.
- **A market is opening for low-cost productions**, as supply of high-cost products tends to be directed to larger audiences at peak hours and new specialized TV channels require programs to fill non-peak hours.
- **New market opportunities are particularly appealing for European producers**, as online as well as off-line products share a boom with pay-TV and home video. In these areas, European companies have traditionally performed less strongly than their US counterparts; however, the growth of pay-TV is likely to put a major emphasis on domestic content, thus putting European content providers – who are already quite strong in multimedia production – at an advantage.

Figure 1 shows expected growth of different forms of broadcast media; these are expected to represent 35 percent of content providers' revenues by 2005.

- **Online advertising is likely to grow**, as new online content providers look for new sources of revenues.
- **Traditional advertising is going to be attracted by high-quality animation.** The ever-rising cost of making live-action movies is pushing studios more towards animation; at the same time, computer-generated animation is getting increasingly cheaper. According to the founder of Apple Computers, Steve

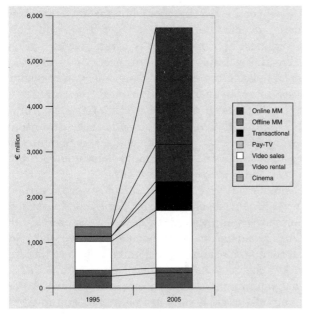

Figure 1: Expected growth of different forms of broadcast media

Jobs, Pixar is the lowest-cost producer of high-quality animation in the business. With traditional techniques, an animated movie costs $100 million–$125 million. Pixar can do it for $75 million–$100 million. Whereas a traditional animation can employ up to 600 animators, Pixar does the job with 200 animators and software programmers. The use of computer animation in advertising is going to be particularly appealing for consumer goods manufacturers, as they can exploit the potential of animated characters for merchandising to the younger generation and to families.

These market openings combine with technological opportunities:

- **Computing power grows as costs fall**. The equipment necessary to produce *Toy Story* – the first computer-animated movie, made in 1994 – would today cost one sixth of what it did then.
- **Digitalization of movies allows for new, low-cost diffusion channels**. The introduction of digital television services not only offers more free-to-air opportunities, but will also determine the market growth for pay-TV services and extend the sector into a new world of pay-per-view. Moreover, the increased functionality of digital products, combined with the lower distribution costs of video-on-demand products, should allow service providers (and ultimately content providers) to extract higher margins.
- **Digital film distribution in theaters will offer competitive advantage to computer animation studios**, since the expensive transfer from digital to photographic film will no longer be needed.

Given the cost advantages associated with computer-animated films as opposed to traditional films, and the success at the box office as well as in the home video market of computer-animated movies – such as *Toy Story*, *Antz* and *A Bug's Life* –

the four partners in SwiftART decided the timing was right for starting up a company specialized in the production of computer-animated characters; a difficult task, however, was to determine the most appropriate entry strategy. One option was to focus initially on the advertising industry and to make 3D animated commercials or videoclips in order to develop the necessary know-how and register patents, and then, after a couple of years, to seek venture capital financing for a movie. Alternatively, the company could focus on the development of a movie – or a TV series – from the beginning, this being riskier but potentially more rewarding and appealing to institutional investors. Moreover, the four friends were planning to seek support from the European Union's MEDIA II program to help fund both the development of videoclips and movies, and the associated software.

Competition was fierce. In the commercial area, three companies were regarded as benchmarks at international level. One was very strong in the US and virtually non-existent in Europe, had 250 employees and was particularly strong on real-life effects and technological ability. The second one, based in London, was two years old and a force in the production of 3D commercials; design and animation were its core strengths, together with a network of agencies both in Europe and the US. There were rumors that the company was planning to develop a movie. The third player was a very low-cost producer, using off-the-shelf software packages, and ideal to help projects with tight budgets.

In the computer-animated movie area, two companies were dominant. Pixar was the oldest in the market; founded in 1986, it employs approximately 430 people. Pixar animation, it is said, "combines the creativity of some of the world's leading animators and story-writers with an entirely new, three-dimensional animated look." Pixar's first full-length movie, *Toy Story*, released by Walt Disney in November 1995 and the world's first fully computer-animated movie, was the highest earner that year. Pixar's *Toy Story II* has also been released. The company uses three proprietary software systems: (i) Marionette, an animation software system for modeling, animating and lighting; (ii) Ringmaster, a production management software system for scheduling, co-ordinating and tracking a computer animation project; and (iii) Renderman, a software system for high-quality, photo-realistic image synthesis that Pixar uses internally and licenses to third parties. Pixar continues to invest heavily in these software systems and believes that further advancement will lead to additional productivity and quality improvements. Pixar's relationship with Walt Disney dates back to 1987; the two companies entered a three-picture production deal in 1991 with *Toy Story* the first film and *A Bug's Life* the second. Disney – which markets the films and the associated products – gets around 90 percent of the profit on the first three movies.

Pixar's rival is Pacific Data Images, a computer animation studio specializing in high-end 3D animation and visual effects for the entertainment industry; the company was started in 1980 and has grown to have a staff of over 260. Its mission is to mix artistry and innovative technology to bring characters to life in works of pure imagination. It has designed, directed, produced or animated hundreds of films, commercials and music videos. Production credits include Warner Bros' *Batman & Robin*, Universal Pictures' *A Simple Wish*, and DreamWorks' *The Peacemaker* and *Antz*. It has also developed 3D characters for *Batman Forever*, *The Arrival* and *The Simpsons*. Commercial work includes spots for Jet Dry, Gatorade and Circle K. PDI popularized "morphing" techniques with the effects created for

Michael Jackson's music video, *Black or White*. It has developed proprietary tools that allow precise control and positioning of each body part to help animators create complex movement in their characters. It has developed techniques for both human and creature animation, including lip-sync, as well as realistic hair and fur. In March 1996, PDI signed a co-production deal with DreamWorks to create original, computer-animated movies. PDI's computer animation is 40 percent owned by DreamWorks and 60 percent by its founders.

SwiftART concluded that it could benefit by focussing on the development of commercials using off-the-shelf software packages as well as on the production of fully computer-animated commercials, in order to create a distinctive cartoon-like look and feel. The development of commercials would be instrumental in creating a brand image. At the same time, the company would develop proprietary rendering software necessary to improve quality, increase differentiation and sharply reduce production costs.

Postscript

The students graduated from SDA Bocconi in December 1999. Alberto identified two software specialists as partners for the company, and is going to produce a serial for a TV channel. SwiftART aimed to begin operations in spring 2000.

PEOPLE, FAMILIES AND TEAMS

5

Contributors

Alden G. Lank is the Stephan Schmidheiny Professor of Family Enterprises at IMD in Lausanne, Switzerland. He is the founding executive director of the Family Business Network and its president and a member of its executive board.

Dennis W. N. Ng is a doctoral graduate of Imperial College Management School and family business successor with interests in London and Asia.

Laura Kellogg is a consultant with Sibson & Company, a leading management consulting firm with ten locations worldwide, specializing in organizational effectiveness and remuneration. Her expertise includes organizational change and design, professional service firms, and salesforce effectiveness.

Simon Stockley is lecturer in entrepreneurship in the Science Enterprise Centre, Imperial College Management School.

Sue Cartwright is Senior Lecturer in Organizational Psychology at the Manchester School of Management, University of Manchester Institute of Science and Technology.

Cary L. Cooper is BUPA Professor of Organizational Psychology and Health at the Manchester School of Management, and Pro-Vice Chancellor (External Activities) at the University of Manchester Institute of Science and Technology (UMIST). His research interests include occupational stress, women at work and industrial and organizational psychology.

Contents

Introduction

Part 5 returns to people. But this time we are looking at groups. First, we confront the family. It is trite but true that anyone who has both a family and a business inevitably has a family business and must confront and manage the tensions and choices which have to be made. One tension which is particularly difficult for most is the choice and timing of a successor – and this is so all over the world, as we see so clearly when we look at the "bamboo network." The second group of players we look at are the management team and our authors discuss the issues of selecting and building a "goal-scoring" team.

Making sure the dynasty does not become a Dallas

Alden Lank explains why so many family businesses tend to break up.

Many of the 300-plus delegates at the seventh world conference of the Family Business Network held in Edinburgh in September 1995 were astonished by what they were hearing. More than one speaker underlined the fact that only a small minority of family enterprises survive beyond the first generation in the hands of the founding family. Yet a significant number in the audience represented second and subsequent generations. What had gone wrong with all the others? Why had they been so fragile?

Studies on the longevity of family organizations made in several countries all come to the same conclusion. While it is impossible to make exact transnational comparisons (there are as many definitions of "family enterprise" as there are researchers in the field), the general tendency is clear: between two-thirds and three-quarters of family businesses either die or are sold out of the founding family during the first generation's tenure. Only 5–15 percent continue into the third generation in the hands of the descendants. These figures compare unfavorably with the staying power of equivalent non-family controlled companies.

As family enterprises are a – if not *the* – major contributor to the economic and social well-being of all capitalist societies, this fragility is a cause for concern. What factors can explain the lack of longevity?

First of all, there can be little doubt that family enterprises are the most complex form of business organization. At first sight, this statement may seem preposterous. However, reflect on Figure 1. It depicts in highly simplified form a model of a typical (all but the smallest) corporation.

The chief executive officer (CEO), holding Role 7, is faced with managing all seven sets of roles in a synergistic manner in pursuit of the business's mission and objectives – no sinecure under the best of circumstances. Figure 2 adds but one dimension: family. Note that by so doing, the number of roles to be managed by the CEO in position 15 has more than doubled – a significant increase in complexity.

This conception of the family-controlled corporation begins to explain some of the negative dynamics commonly associated with family organizations. Popular television series such as *Dynasty* and *Dallas*, for example, delight in highlighting the squabbles between and within generations. These conflicts are often attributed to "personality differences." Yet an analysis of Figure 2 shows that the basis of the differences may be related more to role than personality.

A good example is the important, frequently emotionally-charged decision concerning the dividend pay-out ratio. A person sitting in Role 15, let us say as chairman of the board/CEO/owner/family, quite logically can have a very different opinion from the younger sister occupying Role 5, with no seat on the board and not being employed by the family's enterprise. In the former case, one could expect a strong desire to maximize reinvestment of profits in the business, while the sister might like to see higher figures on her dividend check.

The inevitable overlapping of family with the three circles in Figure 2 leads to

Roles
1 Just management/employees
2 Just owner
3 Just board of directors
4 Management – board of directors
5 Management – owners
6 Owners – board of directors
7 Management – owners – board of directors

© Alden G Lank

Figure 1: A typical corporation

challenges which no totally publicly held corporation has to face. Here is one all-too-common scenario taken from a real family enterprise.

Georges, 64, is CEO, sole owner and member of the board. His son Jean, 31 and a bachelor, is vice-president manufacturing and technology and likewise member of the board. Daughter Marie, 34 and married with one son (Marcel, 12), is vice-president sales and marketing and a board member.

Marie and Jean detest each other and have been in sibling conflict since early childhood. Both expect to be nominated CEO and take voting control whenever Georges decides to retire. Marcel is an outstanding student and already has shown entrepreneurial skills and an interest in the business. In his mother's mind, there is no doubt that he will replace her as head of the family organization when she steps down.

There is a board meeting scheduled for next Friday to decide on certain strategic investments which will start to impact the bottom line ten years from now. It is not far-fetched to suppose that the next board meeting will be hardly typical of what one could expect in a publicly held corporation. The family's emotional dynamics, in all probability, will either covertly or overtly rule their discussions on what, in theory, should be a purely rational business decision. Yes, family businesses are different.

Beyond the inherent enhanced complexity, what other factors explain the fragility of family companies? What causes them to leave the founding family's control or go bankrupt? There are two parts to the answer. First, they disappear for the same reasons as any corporation, including:

■ opportunity to sell out at an attractive price (in a capitalistic economy this provokes no automatic opprobrium)
■ inability to anticipate or adjust to changes in the marketplace
■ insufficient investment in R&D
■ inadequate control of costs

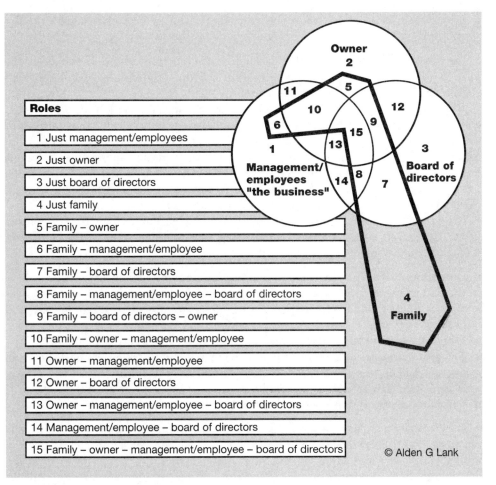

Roles

1 Just management/employees	
2 Just owner	
3 Just board of directors	
4 Just family	
5 Family – owner	
6 Family – management/employee	
7 Family – board of directors	
8 Family – management/employee – board of directors	
9 Family – board of directors – owner	
10 Family – owner – management/employee	
11 Owner – management/employee	
12 Owner – board of directors	
13 Owner – management/employee – board of directors	
14 Management/employee – board of directors	
15 Family – owner – management/employee – board of directors	

© Alden G Lank

Figure 2: A typical family corporation

- lack of access to affordable capital
- other poor management practices.

However, not surprisingly, family enterprises also face certain challenges specific to themselves, such as:

- failure to find capital for growth without diluting the family's equity (total ownership control being a sacrosanct principle for many families)
- inability to balance optimally the family's needs for liquidity and the business's need for cash
- poor estate planning and the inability of the next generation to pay inheritance taxes
- lack of willingness of the older generation to "let go" of ownership and management power at an appropriate moment
- inability to attract and retain competent and motivated family successors
- unchecked sibling rivalries with no consensus on the chosen successor
- inability to attract and retain competent senior non-family professional managers

■ unmanaged conflict between the cultures of the family, the board and the business.

The above list is striking for the predominance of factors related to managing the process of ownership and management succession – the single most important reason for the fragility of family enterprises.

What does research on the experience of long-lived, multi-generational family companies tell us about how to manage the inherent fragility of this most prevalent and oldest form of business organization? Families that are aware of the special complexities of being managers and/or owners of their own company already have a head start. For example, being able to see that conflicts may stem from the differing perspectives of the various roles described in Figure 2, each of which may have a rational basis, could defuse a highly emotional situation.

The probability of maintaining a healthy and vigorous enterprise (as well as family) will also be enhanced if the owning family accepts the truth of the six following conflict-management propositions:

■ Over time, conflict is inevitable in families and in family businesses
■ Conflict can be healthy or unhealthy, functional or dysfunctional
■ How conflict is managed is one of the key determinants of effective families and family businesses
■ While there are several conflict management strategies, there is no panacea
■ The goal in conflict management should be to maximize win–win situations for all parties and to arrive at the best decision, given the family's and the family business's mission, goals and objectives
■ Pre-establishment of the "rules of the game" can obviate many conflicts.

These propositions put conflict in perspective and remind us that conflict *per se* is not negative. In fact, a company or a family with no conflict has probably lost the ability to innovate and adjust to changing circumstances.

Figure 3 outlines three broad categories of options or strategies of conflict management. (I am defining conflict as a type of behavior which occurs when two or more parties are in opposition or in battle as a result of a perceived deprivation whose cause is attributed to the other party or parties.)

The first category (**Avoidance**) groups those approaches which attempt to avoid coming to grips with the grievances or issues separating the parties.

■ **Ignorance** may be a simple reflection of the reality or a deliberate attempt to keep one's head in the sand.
■ **Withdrawal** implies a recognition of conflict as well as a decision to move back from the fray.
■ **Denial** permits fooling oneself and others (at least in the short term) into believing that a conflict does not exist, while knowing full well at the conscious or subconscious level that something is wrong in a relationship.

Avoidance mechanisms have limited long-term usefulness except in the most minor of cases.

■ *Referral* strategies basically place the responsibility for conflict management in someone else's hands.
■ *Triangulation* is all too common in family businesses. Here a third party – often

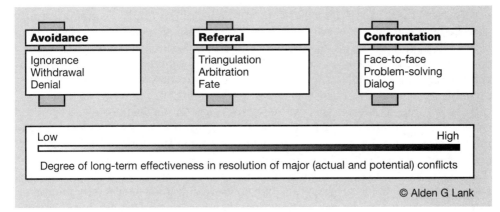

Figure 3: Conflict management options

Mom – acts as a message carrier between the warring parties, for example sibling versus sibling, Dad versus daughter and so on. This strategy may keep the lid on the situation for a short period but it puts Mom into a highly unenviable position. In any case, once Mom is out of the picture (for example dies), one can expect a major explosion with few survivors.

■ *Fate* refers actual or incipient conflict to God or chance. The reasoning goes: "Eventually this problem will go away. Why talk to Dad about succession? He will just get angry and evade seeking a solution. He's already 78 and can't last for ever." This line of thought explains why so many succession issues are resolved in family businesses by the lawyer and accountant while riding in the limousine en route to the cemetery to bury Dad.

■ *Confrontation* strategies acknowledge the existence of conflict and require the parties to work together to find a mutually beneficial solution. On occasion, an outside professional facilitator may be very useful in creating the conditions for positive *problem-solving dialog*.

Experience shows that the earlier the confrontation, the better. One highly successful first-generation husband–wife team recently explained the two most important reasons for their success. "As co-CEOs there must be absolute clarity in and outside the company concerning how roles are divided. And we do not allow anything to fester between us for more than 4–12 hours." Families which allow 4–12 *years* of hurt and frustration to develop (a not uncommon phenomenon) may find that not even skillful confrontation will save them.

Source of wealth

Increasingly, families in business are rediscovering the wisdom of the maxim: "an ounce of prevention is worth a pound of cure." In the context of conflict management, this means achieving consensus around the "rules of the game" in regard to the family, its enterprise and the interface between the two before the issues in question become a problem. The labels given to the (preferably written) text vary from family protocol, strategy and mission to credo, philosophy and values.

No two families ever produce the same texts and there are huge disparities in the degree of detail and prescription. Typical topics include the roles of the different governance institutions (such as family assembly, family council, family shareholders' committee, board of directors and executive management), behavioral norms for the family and businesses (for example no washing of family dirty linen in public, no bribing of public officials by the company's representatives), employment policies for family members (rules of entry and exit, how they are to be treated compared to non-family employees) and who represents the family on the board.

Many of these manifestos specify the family's view on the business as its source of wealth (for example the current generation of owners acts as steward of the inherited capital for the next generation), guidelines for dividend policy, philanthropical objectives, the workings of the internal stock market and so on.

As important as the final document is the process used to produce it. The very discussion of broad concerns such as "what do we stand for as a family *and* as an owning family" bring the generations together around the fundamental *raisons d'être* of their familial relationship.

Once the "rules of the game" are on paper, many potential conflicts will be defused on the basis of the criterion that "the family has already decided that . . ." This does not mean that the key principles are engraved in stone. They can be revisited periodically by the family as circumstances change.

Earlier it was stated that the single most important cause of the fragility of the family business was the inability to manage the succession process. Let me conclude by focussing on management succession, making several recommendations to the outgoing (successee) and incoming (successor) generations in regard to management succession.

From the potential successor, I would ask for a careful analysis of the reasons for joining the family company. Is it because it is the only job available? Is it only because that is what your parents expect of you? Is it because you fear you will be disinherited if you decide to go elsewhere? Is it because you figure that the working hours would give you more time to play golf? If the answer is yes to any of these questions, it may be wiser for all concerned for you to look for another company.

Have you the required education for entering the business? Have you had experience outside the family enterprise? There are at least three good reasons for working elsewhere before joining the family's enterprise. First, it will give you an indication of your true market worth. Second, if you succeed, you will be able to enter the family enterprise, should you so desire, with a proven track record. Third, if you fail, there will be less negative fall-out for you and the family if it happens in someone else's company.

If you have met the above criteria for entry, are you active in designing the career path which will maximize your chances of being a valid candidate to replace the outgoing generation? Are you insisting on receiving objective feedback on your performance and opportunities for training and development? Are you sure that you are the most qualified candidate?

My recommendations to the successee are predicated on one primary conviction: the final choice must be made on the basis of who has manifested the most competence to lead the family's enterprise into the future. This may mean that your sentimental favorite, based on kinship, will have to give way to a non-family successor, difficult as this may be for you.

As the current leader of the organization, it is the successee who has the fundamental responsibility for managing the succession process. My advice would include the following:

- never force the potential successor to enter or stay with the business against his/her will
- see that a career path is built which will provide the potential successor(s) with challenging assignments, diverse experiences, realistic objectives and standards, quality feedback on performance, opportunities for continuing education and training, appropriate rewards
- manifest interest and concern
- share your hopes and desires for the future (without expecting that the successor will automatically accept them)
- involve others (be they family, board members or outsiders) in advising on the final choice and try to maximize consensus
- announce your intention of phasing out with the timing made explicit
- stick to your intentions
- ensure that you have a game plan for your retirement period.

There are, of course, many other recommendations which could be made to successees, including, importantly, deciding on what their departure *style* will be. Here are some archetypes (originally formulated by Sommerfeld and Spence, *Family Business Review*, Vol. 2, No. 4, Winter 1989):

- **monarch:** refuses to depart voluntarily and typically dies on the job
- **general:** agrees to depart but spends most of his time plotting to return to power
- **ambassador:** gives up the CEO post, may stay on the board, represents the enterprise externally in industry associations and so on
- **reborn entrepreneur:** keeps contact with the company but starts a new, non-competitive venture
- **hedonist:** cuts ties with the company and spends time doing things he or she never had time to do earlier – sports, hobbies and so on.

Unfortunately, there are too many monarchs and generals (particularly successees of the founding generation) and too few of the others.

Letting go can indeed be difficult, if not impossible. Yet this is the final test of greatness for the outgoing generation. If more of them could do the necessary planning for this critical transition and honor the established process, the inherent fragility of family companies would be transformed into increased robustness and health – to the advantage of both the family and its enterprise.

Succession in the "bamboo network"

Family businesses run by Overseas Chinese have been the engine of economic success in the Pacific Rim but, says **Dennis Ng**, succession problems could arise as Western and Chinese cultures clash.

An economic miracle

Over the past 30 years, many have studied the reasons for the success of the Pacific Rim economies. In particular, the Overseas Chinese's dominant participation in the development of these economies has been the subject of much academic and media attention.

The economic strength of the Overseas Chinese in this region is substantial (*see* Figure 1). The 55 million Overseas Chinese control $2 trillion in cash or liquid assets, and are the biggest direct investors in China, with investments totaling more than $26.5 billion in 1997: 58 percent of the total foreign investment in China. To put these figures in context, these 55 million people, taking into account their officially acknowledged power in the Asean (Association of South East Asian Nations) economies, constitute 10 percent of the region's population and around 70 percent of the region's economy. The Overseas Chinese produce nine out of ten of the region's billionaires and around two-thirds of the retail industry. It is worth noting that the majority of their businesses are family businesses.

The main explanations for the economic success of the Overseas Chinese have always returned to one answer: culture. The reasoning was that there were other countries in similar circumstances but which did not enjoy the same economic miracle. Better management as an explanation would not hold as an argument as the quality of management is dependent on the quality of the people managed. Hence, culture must be the missing link. The Overseas Chinese's cultural make-up, with their emphasis on tradition and Confucian roots, served the Chinese family businesses well against a variety of economic policies implemented by the host governments, and provided the flexibility to be competitive in changing economic climates. With greater collectivism, centralized control and clear vertical order, the Overseas Chinese family businesses have managed to generate the co-ordination and control needed to stimulate massive growth as latecomers to the world economy and capitalism.

Succession and unaccompanied minors

Despite all the success achieved, the Overseas Chinese, often referred to as the "bamboo network" due to their unique characteristics, are now being tested as they have never been before. The test will come from the passing of the founding generation of the businesses.

Traditionally, due to the ingrained respect for authority, the succession process for Chinese family businesses has been less problematic than their western counterparts. Nevertheless, past experiences have shown that it does suffer from similar problems to western family businesses, such as successor incompetence and

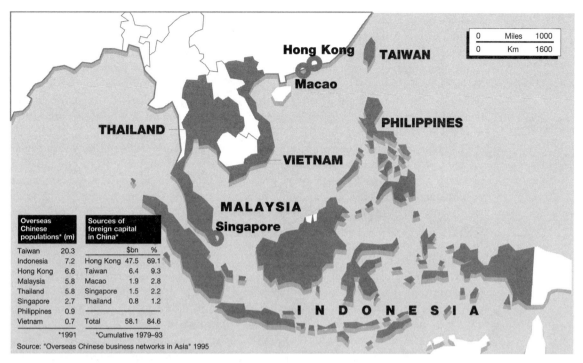

Figure 1: Overseas Chinese in South-East Asia

generation differences in opinion. To complicate the situation, due to the accumulated wealth of the Overseas Chinese, and the effects of western influence, many families have sent their children abroad to study at a very tender age, with some leaving home as early as the age of six. These children, often referred to as unaccompanied minors by psychologists (and airlines, who came up with the term), will be the successors of the bamboo network, but will possess a different cultural make-up. The different cultural make-up is an extra consideration which previously did not pose any threat for the Overseas Chinese family business succession.

The scramble for western qualifications is due not only to western influence and economic prosperity. In the past, the Asian economic climate has favored the opportunistic and dashing entrepreneurs, but the circumstances are changing, and there is now a greater need for organizational and management skills. Many Overseas Chinese parents hope that one day, their children will return to the family business with a western MBA. What is ironic is that the process of a western education may cause complications to the unaccompanied minors' succession of the family businesses, to the extent that succession may never take place due to cultural differences between the parents and the unaccompanied minors.

Cultural identities

The issue of a possible cultural gap arises because unaccompanied minors live at the juncture between two cultures. Their "marginality," as identified by psychologists, gives them certain psychological properties. One of the main properties has been identified as "double-consciousness:" the simultaneous awareness of oneself as being a member and an alien of two or more cultures. Unaccompanied minors, being adolescents leaving home to study abroad in a different culture for an extended period of time, are "marginal" people, and perhaps the effects are more exaggerated since they leave home at an age when self-identity has barely had time to form. Their "marginality" occurs because unaccompanied minors, while being influenced by western values during their time abroad, usually return to their families for holidays, and hence their Chinese values are reinforced during that period. This bombardment by two different cultures has implications on the unaccompanied minors' cultural identity.

The issue of cultural identity has been studied in America on Chinese-American adolescents. For unaccompanied minors, it is possible for more than one cultural identity to exist. A spectrum of identities has been identified by American psychologists studying Chinese unaccompanied minors, ranging from the individual who rejects all aspects of being Chinese in an anxiety to identify with a western culture (the so-called "banana" type – yellow on the outside but white on the inside), to a radical individual who may espouse a new "Asian" consciousness who rejects both Chinese and western cultures.

Five models can be used to show where marginal people arrive on the spectrum (*see* Figure 2). These are assimilation, acculturation, alternation, multiculturalism and fusion. The first two models involve the individual acquiring a different culture. The two cultures form a hierarchical relationship, with the newer culture dominating. The difference between the assimilation and acculturation models is that the acculturation process is an involuntary one, and that the individual, while being a competent participant of the dominating culture, will always be identified as a member of the minority culture. The first two models will result in the "banana" end of the spectrum.

The fusion model suggests a new form of culture being formed by fusing the existing and the new culture. The result is likely to be towards the new "Asian" consciousness end of the spectrum. In the middle of the spectrum is the category of bicultural competence or biculturalism, achieved by the alternation or multiculturalism model. The alternation model suggests that an individual can alter his/her behavior accordingly to suit the cultural context. The alternation model suggests that it is possible for an individual to maintain a positive relationship with both cultures without having to choose between them. The multiculturalism model assumes that an individual can maintain his/her identity while developing another positive identity within the new culture.

Bicultural competence

By definition, a person is considered culturally competent (for one culture) if he/she appreciates and internalizes the basic beliefs of a given culture. This implies the ability to accept a culture's basic worldview and act within the constraints of such a worldview. To be biculturally competent implies being culturally competent in two cultures simultaneously.

"Banana" -------------------------	Biculturalism -----------------------	New "Asian"
from	from	from
assimilation/acculturation	alternation/multiculturalism	fusion

Figure 2: Spectrum of identities and coping models of unaccompanied minors

Whether an unaccompanied minor is biculturally competent or not is vital for effective succession within the Overseas Chinese family businesses. I have found that virtually all of my research sample of Overseas Chinese unaccompanied minors who managed the succession process effectively are biculturally competent and adopt the alternation model. The reason is that the "banana" types suffer problems adapting back to their original culture, and hence usually avoid returning to their originating country. Those who do return usually report frustration in the family business and confrontations with the parents due to their cultural differences. The ones who adopt the fusion model usually refuse to return to the family businesses, and prefer to do their own thing. It has to be said that only a handful of unaccompanied minors adopt the fusion model.

An intriguing finding is that there are discrepancies according to where the unaccompanied minor goes to study. An emerging pattern indicates that unaccompanied minors in the United States tend to be less biculturally competent than those who study in other countries. The Chinese culture, when encountering the US culture, appears to cause the most "cultural confusion" among unaccompanied minors who are exposed to both. Many unaccompanied minors who studied in the United States say they feel "too Chinese to be western, and too westernized to be Oriental."

From the biculturally competent unaccompanied minors' point of view, by experiencing different cultures they have become more aware of their own cultural make-up, and can consciously deal with any psychological dissonance which may occur. Biculturalism has provided these unaccompanied minors with an advantage in business too. By being aware of more than one culture, the unaccompanied minors can be more effective as managers and leaders of international businesses.

Further, with Overseas Chinese family businesses growing in size and geographical influence, the traditional Chinese methods of conducting businesses require adaptation and change. Biculturally competent unaccompanied minors can draw on their experiences in both cultures to extract the benefits of western cultures and western management, while retaining the secrets of the Overseas Chinese economic culture.

Conclusion

It can therefore be argued that biculturalism is an important characteristic for Overseas Chinese unaccompanied minors to possess in the succession of family businesses. Further, as we already know, western cultures are not homogenous. Each western culture influences unaccompanied minors differently, with some cultures being more dominating than others. This has an effect on the unaccompanied minors' ability to become biculturally competent. In other words, when Overseas Chinese parents decide to send their children to different countries, they may have unconsciously already made the decision as to who will be the successor to their family business.

From my experience with Overseas Chinese family businesses, the most pressing problem faced by these businesses is succession. The scenario of a biculturally incompetent successor is almost always the case. The resulting conflict causes emotional distress among the family members, and in the worst cases can threaten the very existence of the family firm.

However, all is not lost: with effective open communication and mutual respect of the cultural make-up of all family members involved, there is no reason why the Overseas Chinese family businesses, with their brilliant track record in adapting to difficult circumstances, should fail to cross the succession hurdle. It is possible for unaccompanied minors to become company majors, but they cannot do it alone.

Critical link between business and organization

Laura Kellogg explains the importance of managing the human dimension in start-up and high-growth companies.

In a rapidly growing entrepreneurial company, sustained success reflects how well the business and the organization are in concert. It is far too easy, during a phase of high growth, for a company to risk subordinating or ignoring organizational and human resource issues for short-term business challenges.

However, human resource management is not just the administration of remuneration, benefits and personnel issues: it encompasses the strategic management of human capital, which over time makes or breaks a business. Successful human resource management enables a seamless, explicit integration of business and organization. To achieve this integration, the entrepreneur must answer (in order) the following questions:

- What is the company? (mission and values statement)
- Where does it want to go? (goals)
- How will it get there? (strategy)
- What does it need for the journey? (organizational capabilities)
- How will it recognize the destination? (vision of success)

Integrating the business and the organization, especially during rapid growth, requires flexibility and foresight. One broadly applicable approach, helping the entrepreneur identify how to manage human resources, is to depict how the company will grow through discrete strategic eras across key dimensions that characterize the business. That is, develop a series of snapshots, including the "start-up" (current) high-growth phase and near to mid-term future. Next, map out the organizational capabilities required to support each era.

The kinds of dimensions on which to characterize the business might include:

- business objective (build brand awareness, commercialize technology)
- competitive premise (product excellence, creative solutions)
- nature of customer relationship (transaction-oriented, consultative)

- investment priorities (expand through acquisition, secure organizational capabilities)
- role of management (low involvement, goal-setting focus, high priests of culture).

Other relevant dimensions are the nature of business risk, role of technology, client portfolio and so on. Pick six to eight dimensions that best describe the company and define each at distinct points in time.

Making the critical link between business and organization entails characterizing the human resources requirements. Assess and define the company's need during each era for:

- **structure:** to support the business. In general, look from the outside in and let customer-facing activities shape structure. Determine the balance between formal and informal structures, the role(s) of teams and so on. How can the structure be flexible to support growth?
- **work and job design:** to get the work done. Determine what kind of job positions will be needed to do the work and how those jobs fit in the structure. How will growth impact what work needs to get done and when could scale dictate a different design of the work itself?
- **staffing:** to ensure that people have needed skills and competencies. Determine the profiles that fill the jobs. How different are profiles during the start-up and during high growth, and when must generalists begin to specialize?
- **support systems:** for the staff, including performance management, training and development, and recognition and rewards. When does "one size fits all" no longer suffice and what messages should systems reinforce for the near and longer term?
- **behaviors:** how the company's values manifest themselves in the internal work environment. How is risk taking viewed or what characteristics of the start-up are critical (versus detrimental) for the future?
- **leadership and management style:** to have vision and to build and mobilize the organization to execute strategy. Will the founder be the right leader in one, three, six years?

One of the greatest challenges for a leader of a rapidly growing entrepreneurial company is managing that alignment between business and the people. Successful management of the human resource dimension means integrating business strategy and organizational capabilities to achieve company goals.

Building and maintaining the entrepreneurial team – a critical competence for venture growth

Simon Stockley considers the importance of team working.

If there is one issue on which the majority of theorists and practitioners agree, it is that a high-quality management team is a key ingredient in the success of many high-growth ventures. Conversely, a growing body of venture capital research suggests that most of the reasons for failure may be traced to specific flaws in the venture team.

The difficulty, of course, is that the quality of a team depends on the context in which it operates and this context may be highly dynamic. This observation is hardly new, for as Edith Penrose observed four decades ago, the balance of capabilities and critical skills required in an organization often shifts dramatically as it grows and/or as its external environment changes. One implication of this is that both the *nature* and *composition* of the management team may need to change if the firm is to evolve within its environment. The alternative, of course, may be extinction.

Clearly, then, for the founder (or the founding team) seeking to grow their business in a dynamic environment, building and maintaining a team capable of creating stakeholder value is a matter of the utmost importance. However, what in theory appears to be straightforward can be anything but in practice. The purpose of this article, therefore, is to highlight some of the key issues that may be encountered on this journey.

The nature of teams

Before we begin we should first be clear about what we mean by an entrepreneurial team. In much of the literature, the entrepreneurial team is defined in terms of "two or more people who establish and share ownership of the new organization." The trouble is that these definitions limit membership of the entrepreneurial team to those in place prior to the founding of the venture. Our view is that entrepreneurial activity does not stop once the business is established and that team members who join at a later stage can, and should, contribute to the firm's repertoire of entrepreneurial behaviors.

A more insightful approach may be to consider how teams actually form in practice. Recent research suggests that teams frequently form in layers.[1] The founding team, often small and bound by personal relationships, forms a "nucleus" around which additional members are recruited as the business grows (*see* Figure 1). In many cases, the late joiners form an "outer team," which may feel (or actually be) distanced from the inner workings of the organization. The central challenge of entrepreneurial *leadership* is to weld the inner core and outer team together to form

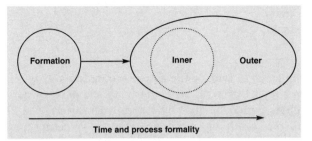

Figure 1: Team formation (after Vyakarnam *et al.* 1999)

an integrated whole. This is not necessarily the task of a single leader, nor are the boundaries of the team impermeable. However, the team thus created should be better able to exhibit the cohesive patterns of managerial behavior so ably described by Howard Stevenson in Part 1 (pp. 8–13).

We should also bear in mind that a world of difference exists between a pseudo-team of senior figures at the apex of a hierarchy and a "real" team. McKinsey & Co.'s Jon Katzenbach defines the latter as: "a small number of people with complementary skills who are committed to a common purpose, performance goals and an approach for which they hold themselves mutually accountable."

Thus, a team that has growth (or value creation) as its dominant purpose and which displays entrepreneurial behavior can be considered to be an *entrepreneurial team*. The important thing to understand, however, is that teams must be able to display a variety of appropriate behaviors. After all, it is not always helpful to be entrepreneurial when dealing with H. M. Inspector of Taxes or the I.R.S.!

Are teams of value?

We now turn our attention to what it is that entrepreneurial teams actually do and to those factors that are known to affect the team's ability to accomplish these tasks.

A particularly helpful perspective on this question is provided by Dan Muzyka, Michael Hay and Sue Birley's article on what MBO-MBI investors look for when screening new proposals (*see* p. 321). The authors conclude that management team factors reign supreme on the list of opportunity evaluation factors. For investors, the top ten team criteria are:

1. Effectiveness of group decision making
2. Ability to lead the organization
3. Previous profitable track record
4. Success in managing business-related conflicts
5. Trust within the team
6. Commitment to group goals
7. Ability to manage interpersonal conflicts
8. Balance of team skills
9. Level of collective motivation
10. Team understanding of investors' needs.

Similar criteria, or their behavioral antecedents, factor in virtually every published study of venture capital decision making. Given that these characteristics and behaviors matter, what can be done to ensure that they are optimized? Two broad types of action are possible:

1. Change the composition of the team
2. Develop the capabilities of the team.

Team composition

Early in the life of the venture, changes to team composition are most likely when new members are being hired to support growth. With maturity the pattern may change, with existing team members being replaced by others with different skill sets. Either way, the following factors are likely to be important in selecting new team members:

- expertise and technical competence – are they competent and do they fill a gap in the team?
- do they have relevant industry experience in a growth (or other relevant) environment?
- will they have credibility with employees and in the marketplace?
- will they fit within the team and the culture of the organization?
- are they trustworthy and sufficiently motivated?
- do they bring funding or a valuable network of contacts and customers?

Recruitment and selection are notoriously difficult tasks and it is easy to make mistakes, particularly in judging criteria such as fit, motivation and trustworthiness that may become apparent only with time. For this reason it is not unusual for entrepreneurs to recruit key team members from within their network of contacts. Aside from recruiting full-time executive members, it may be helpful to consider the use of non-executive directors, informal mentors and paid consultants to address imbalances and skill shortages within the team. Equity investors are also likely to offer their expertise (for a fee) as part of a funding package. The value of non-executive directors can be considerable (as demonstrated by Sloan School professors supporting MIT spin-outs) but do pick them just as carefully as you would a full-time team member.

Process capability development

Our consideration of capability development will assume that the team already possesses the "hard" technical skills required in their specific functions (e.g. finance, marketing, R&D, production). Clearly, in practice it may not, but this is usually a relatively straightforward matter to deal with. Instead we will examine three "group process" issues that affect the effectiveness and the efficiency of the team:

- group decision making
- conflict management
- group cohesion (trust, collective motivation, and commitment to group goals).

The reader will be aware that each issue is related, in some way, to the other. Consequently, a shortfall in one area can easily affect the group's performance in another.

A central theme in developing team process capabilities is the concept of *awareness*. Individual team members need to understand themselves (self-awareness), each other (group awareness), and the goals of the organization (strategic awareness). Further, it is useful to have an awareness of group dynamics and the pathologies that affect these processes. It is to this area that we turn first.

Decision-making groups

In theory, a group should make better decisions than individual group members working alone. Research suggests,[2] however, that groups are subject to social processes which undermine their decision-making effectiveness. Team members should remain alert to, and guard against, the following behaviors:

- **risky shift** – groups tend to make more extreme decisions (either risky or conservative) than the average of their members' decisions. They also tend to be less creative
- **groupthink** – groupthink may occur when achieving consensus becomes more important than the quality of the decision. Those with power may coerce other team members into conformity even though they have private reservations
- **satisficing behavior** – a tendency of groups to make minimally acceptable decisions
- **egocentric behavior** – senior individuals may refuse to consider opinions or accept knowledge that runs counter to their own
- **status effects** – the views of senior executives tend to be valued and acted upon disproportionately
- **individual dominance** – although sometimes justified (by expertise) the danger exists that a verbose individual will disproportionately influence the group
- **communication bias** – differences in ability to communicate tend to influence the weight given to contributions.

It is helpful from the outset to be clear about the nature of the decision to be made (in terms of its complexity, its political sensitivity and its strategic importance), the speed with which the decision is required, and the ultimate quality sought. The team might also consider which decisions really need to be made by a group and the possibility of varying the membership depending on the issue to be processed. A number of aids to group decision making have been developed including brainstorming, the Delphi technique, and decision conferencing, although evidence of their effectiveness is mixed.

When conflict is helpful

The pressure to achieve consensus in group decision making, and for people to conform in group situations, is particularly strong and can be highly detrimental to decision quality. Research suggests that the introduction of conflict into the decision-making process, through a process known as *"devil's advocacy,"* can help to overcome the damaging effects of these behaviors. It is crucial, however, to distinguish between two very different types of conflict:

- **cognitive conflict** – cognitive or "task conflict" exists when there are disagreements among group members about the content of a task or decision, including differences in viewpoints, ideas and opinions
- **affective conflict** – affective or "relationship" conflict exists when there are interpersonal incompatibilities within the team. These typically include tension, animosity and annoyance among group members.

There is substantial evidence to suggest that affective conflict and interpersonal attacks seriously limit group-level performance and productivity as well as individual performance. Affective conflict is usually damaging and has to be carefully managed. Cognitive conflict, by way of contrast, facilitates the critical evaluation that is important in overcoming "groupthink."

The message for the entrepreneurial team making a strategic decision is apparently straightforward: each team member should be encouraged to express their opinions openly and to challenge the ideas of others in a constructive manner. In practice, however, care is needed. Not only can too much cognitive conflict generate feelings of annoyance and anger, it can also slow down (or halt) the decision-making process. This is particularly damaging in high-velocity environments where the speed of a decision may be crucial. So, the relationship between the level of cognitive conflict and decision quality is not linear but is heavily influenced by group norms and the nature of the decision being made. The level of conflict required for optimal or "vigilant" decision making requires judgement on the part of the group. This judgement will be facilitated by the establishment of conflict and decision-making norms within the team. It is helpful to discuss these and to make them explicit.

Managing conflict

Agreeing group norms about conflict and decision making can help to avoid the affective conflict that is potentially so damaging to the cohesion of the team. Occasionally, however, affective conflict may surface. This is often viewed as an inevitable part of organizational life. The extent to which affective conflict represents a problem clearly depends on many factors (including its source, nature and intensity) but it is useful for the reader to be aware that individuals have preferred strategies for managing conflict.[3] Each strategy, based on differing levels of assertiveness (A) and co-operation (C), is useful in a different set of circumstances (*see* Table 1). The ability of the group to manage cognitive conflict will be facilitated by a collective understanding of its members' preferred strategies and the understanding that different behaviors are appropriate in different circumstances. There is no "one best way" and often a blend of styles may be needed.

The management of affective conflict is important in maintaining the trust, commitment and collective motivation within the group. The development of these important group characteristics, which manifest themselves as a strong team spirit, are discussed by Sue Cartwright and Cary Cooper in the following article. Their paper highlights the importance of investing time in building relationships within

Table 1: Conflict management strategies

Strategy	Useful when
Competition High A, Low C	Quick decisions have to be made, the survival of the organization is under threat
Collaboration High A, High C	Commitment and consensus are required. Difficult or serious problems are being tackled
Avoidance Low A, Low C	There is no chance of winning in a competition. People are angry
Accommodation Low A, High C	Losses need minimizing
Compromise Mid A, Mid C	Stalemate situations, temporary settlement is required

Source: Thomas (1976)

the team. This is certainly necessary but too often overlooked, perhaps because time is such a scarce commodity, particularly in a high-growth environment. So is there anything that can be done to speed up the process? The answer is a qualified yes.

Individual and team awareness

As relationships develop we gain an awareness of the personality, motivations and behavioral characteristics of other people, and they of us. This awareness, however, is usually far from complete, a situation compounded by the fact that many individuals have low levels of self-awareness.

Fortunately, a number of tools have been developed which, if used with care, can help team members to better understand themselves and each other. Examples include the Myers–Briggs Type Indicator (a psychological profile) and Schein's "Career Anchors" (a career motivation diagnostic). These tools should, however, be administered and interpreted with the assistance of a trained professional – in view of the fact that they tend to lay bare the individual (at least in a psychological sense), they are not a DIY proposition. The objective should be to gain an appreciation of each team member's personality, key motivators and their personal and career goals (what makes them tick, what gives them a buzz, what they actively dislike). Armed with this understanding, the members of the group should be better able to build and maintain working relationships with each other.

The paradox of consensus

This brings us to our final issue: the extent to which the goals of individual team members are congruent with those of the group, and of the organization. Here we are fortunate in being informed by a sizeable body of research that has investigated the relationship between top team consensus about the goals of the organization (its "ends"), the content of the strategy employed to achieve these goals (its "means") and venture performance. It is perhaps, then, ironic that little consensus exists within the literature that examines this topic. For example, some studies find that means–ends consensus is positively related to performance, others find that consensus on either means or ends is beneficial, while others conclude that consensus has a negative impact. So what are we to believe?

First, it is clear that a paradox exists. A high level of consensus, particularly when decisions are being made, begins to look like "groupthink." The management team has one worldview and may be blind to new ideas outside the group's dominant logic. The resulting decisions may be less effective than those that take account of divergent opinions. The alternative view is that consensus makes the implementation of decisions more efficient. On the face of it, this appears to be a classic effectiveness–efficiency dichotomy. What appears likely, however, is that consensus may be more important during certain phases of the venture's life than in others. Before periods of transition or corporate reorientation, a divergence of opinion is seen as beneficial. Once the decisions have been made it may be helpful (up to a point) if agreement exists about the way forward. In highly dynamic environments, however, complete agreement within the team may not be desirable.

A final point to note is that team members frequently have different perceptions about what the goals and the strategy of the organization actually are. Thus, lack of consensus may actually result from alternative mental models rather than real disagreement about ends and means. Either way, it may be helpful if these matters are discussed within the team and made explicit, particularly before talking to investors.

To conclude, I am reminded of my former chief executive's favorite saying: "Nothing manages itself." Nowhere is this truer than in building and maintaining a high-performance entrepreneurial team, yet this is often overlooked in the race to get the product to market. So, be aware, be vigilant, be deliberate, invest in relationships, and manage this aspect of the venture. The results will not disappoint you.

1 *See* Vyakarnam, Jacobs and Handelberg (1999) *Journal of Small Business and Enterprise Development*, Vol. 6, No. 2, pp. 153–165.
2 West, M. A. (1998) "Group decision making," in N. Nicholson (ed.) *Blackwell Encyclopaedic Dictionary of Organizational Behaviour*, Blackwell, Oxford.
3 Thomas, K. (1976) "Conflict and conflict management," in M. D. Dunnette (ed.) *Handbook of Industrial and Organizarional Psychology*, Rand-McNally, Chicago.

Distilling a strong team spirit

Teams do not always work as well as they can or should. **Sue Cartwright** and **Cary Cooper** offer some suggestions on making them more effective.

Theoretically, teams should produce more ideas, make better-evaluated decisions and be more successful in implementing those decisions than individuals working alone.

So why is it that teams often spend excessive time (and money) only to come up with rather "tired" designs and schemes, overly complicated systems and procedures, or unworkable solutions that never see the light of day or create more problems than they solve?

Working in teams ought to be energizing and provide an opportunity for individual members to broaden their professional knowledge and personal skills. Yet team meetings frequently become a forum to play games, a chance to assert individual superiority and put other people down. Despite their resources and initial dynamism, even top teams can run out of steam or become paralyzed by disagreements and an inability to reach a consensus.

Teams are perceived to have the advantage over individuals because they can draw on collective resources and expertise. This assumes that:

■ there is, in fact, some expertise within the group – a selection issue
■ individuals will willingly pool their expertise and work together to pursue a common goal – a process issue.

If all the available resources in a team are to be utilized, it is important that team members feel comfortable about opening up and sharing information with each other. As this may mean admitting what you do not know as well as asserting what you do know, team members must not feel intimidated by others or consider that in being honest they may provide political advantage to others. This is still often a major stumbling block for the most able of teams.

It is part of the culture of business for individuals to compete with one another, particularly in uncertain and ambiguous circumstances. In the case of cross-functional, international or very senior teams, there is bound to be a strong element of competition. After all, individuals will have succeeded and secured their membership to a "top" team by rising through the organizational ranks, going it alone and standing out from the crowd.

Pressure driven

To develop sufficient trust to be able to function effectively as an entrepreneurial team, team members need to spend time together to get to know each other. The England football team should, in theory, reflect the best individual footballing skills in the country. Yet it is frequently said that the England team underperforms because team members have little time to train together, to get to know each other, to be able to recognize each other's strengths and weaknesses, style of play and so on.

The theory of group development as a four-stage process of "forming, storming, norming and performing" is familiar to most managers. However, in practice, most teams are so driven by pressure to meet the project deadline and get on with the "performing" as quickly as possible that the relevance of process and relationship issues are overlooked.

Typically, the first signs of any potential dissent or interpersonal difficulties within the team are ignored or smoothed over by the majority rather than confronted. The team has not got time "to get bogged down" in issues that are perceived to detract from the task. But unless fully aired and resolved, grievances or bad feelings within a team invariably escalate into conflict or cause individuals to withdraw psychologically from the team.

For teams to work together, sufficient time needs to be set aside for building relationships. Ideally this should involve the team in social activities away from the workplace. Some organizations have returned to T-group type techniques as a means of improving team relationships. This involves getting together teams on a non-task driven basis to meet and explore work relationships without a specific business agenda. Others place a strong emphasis on activities, such as outdoor events, that help teams learn the value of co-operation. As organizations increasingly move towards the concept of "virtual" teams, linked by technology, opportunities for face-to-face contact need to be created and are of great importance.

While most team-building initiatives focus on developing cohesiveness, this should not be at the expense of stifling challenge in a team. Constructive criticism and debate in teams is healthy and positive, provided members confine their criticism to the issues and behavior of others, rather than attacking personalities. Behavior can be changed; personality is more difficult. Therefore some training in conflict-resolution techniques and the giving and receiving of criticism is another important aspect of making teams work well.

Given the importance of the decision-making process in teams and of obtaining team members' commitment, it is clearly necessary to be able to assess participation and involvement within the group. In their book *Organizations and the Psychological Contract* (1996, BPS Books, Leicester, UK), Makin, Cooper and Cox suggest a range of decision-making behaviors that can dictate team effectiveness (in ascending order of effectiveness):

- **apathy:** no one contributes to group discussion, not because they are in agreement but because they are totally disillusioned
- **"plops":** a suggestion is made but totally ignored
- **dominance:** one particular individual dominates the meeting. This is often accompanied by apathy
- **pairing:** this is the simplest form of groups within a group. The psychological support offered by pairing is considerable
- **voting:** this is sometimes the only way to resolve disagreements. There are times, however, when it is appropriate and others when it is inappropriate
- **false consensus:** if agreement cannot be reached, one way out of the impasse is to couch a decision in such broad terms that a number of interpretations are possible. A false consensus becomes apparent when the time comes for the decision to be implemented. Each side has a different understanding of what was agreed
- **consensus:** this is the most desirable conclusion. Genuine agreement leads to genuine commitment.

There are also practical steps that can be used to make teams work:

- regularly changing the venue and seating arrangements at team meetings. Teams can get set into patterns of thinking – and interacting – if they always meet in the same room and sit in the same place. Changing seating arrangements also avoids cliques or pairings developing
- hold "second-chance" meetings before a final decision is made so that the team has time to reflect rationally and come back on issues. This avoids the danger of making rash decisions that were carried more by enthusiasm or time pressure than sound judgement
- record minutes of team meetings with the name of the person required to take action alongside. This ensures that everyone is clear about what has been agreed and what they are required to do
- highly creative and energetic teams often come up with lots of ideas and actions but are poor at allocating the role of "completer/finisher" to progress them. They should provide teams with regular feedback on their performance
- celebrate team successes.

ALTERNATIVE
PERSPECTIVES

6

Contributors

Max Boisot is Senior Research Fellow at the Sol Snider Center at the Wharton School, University of Pennsylvania. From 1984 to 1989 he was Dean and Director of the first MBA program to be run in the People's Republic of China in Beijing.

Sarath Kodithuwakku is Director of the MBA program at the Department of Agricultural Economics, University of Peradeniya, Sri Lanka.

Pedro Nueno is Bertran Foundation Professor of Entrepreneurial Management at IESE Business School, University of Navarra, Barcelona. He is also a member of the board of directors and Chairman of the academic council of the China Europe International Business School in Shanghai.

Gordon Redding is Professor Emeritus at the University of Hong Kong, where he was founding director of its business school. He is also Affiliate Professor of Asian Business at INSEAD. His current research is focussed on comparative systems of capitalism, with an emphasis on those of Asia.

Michael G. Scott (d. 1998) was Professor of Entrepreneurial Studies in the Department of Management and Organization at the University of Stirling. His research interests included entrepreneurial career aspirations, small business failure, the impact of legislation and "portfolio" entrepreneurs.

Bert Twaalfhoven is Founder of the European Foundation for Enterprise Research.

Akin Fadahunsi is Senior Research Officer at the Centre for Enterprise and Economic Development, Middlesex University Business School.

Contents

Introduction

Part 6 roams the world. It is important to recognize that much of the literature in the field of entrepreneurship is from the US and Europe and thus based upon western values and cultures. Therefore, this part explores enterprise activities and the impact of national and religious culture in other communities – China, Japan, Korea, Sri Lanka, Nigeria, and the emerging countries of Eastern Europe.

A corporate culture in a world of global villages

As an introduction to a part devoted entirely to enterprise in an international context, **Max Boisot** examines the meaning of cultures and their implications for growing businesses.

The Buddhist and the broker

Imagine two characters, each faced with a communication task. The first is a Zen master concerned to impart to his disciples how to reach *satori*, or enlightenment. His knowledge is of the fuzzy and elusive kind, hard to codify, easy to misinterpret. It cannot easily be put into words and for that reason can only effectively be transmitted in face-to-face situations by force of example. It requires time, a high degree of trust and a sharing of values.

The second is a bond trader about to purchase commercial paper. He (or she) sits in front of a screen and enters his instructions on a machine. He transacts with a seller whom he has never met and who sits on the other side of the globe. His purchasing decision is readily codified as so many bonds at a given price. It registers as a small movement in the bond price that transmits worldwide in seconds.

If we are given to stereotyping, we can suppose that our Zen master lives in the ancient Japanese city of Kyoto and that our bond trader lives in New York, the heartland of American capitalism. Each inhabits a distinctive type of culture, shaped by the extent to which its critical knowledge can be structured and shared.

Culture as information flows

What our two, highly caricatured examples bring out is that the extent to which we can codify our knowledge determines how far we can share with others. Numbers move faster and further than words, and words, in turn, transmit more readily than images or the atmosphere of a meeting. This relationship between the codification and diffusion of knowledge can be illustrated by means of a simple diagram (*see* Figure 1) known as a "culture space", or C-space.

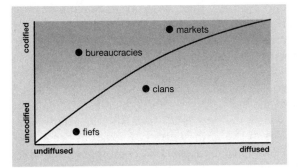

Figure 1: The C-space

	2 – bureaucracies	**3 – markets**
codified information	● Information diffusion limited under central control ● Relationships impersonal and hierarchical ● Submission to superordinate goals ● Hierarchical coordination ● No necessity to share values and beliefs	● Information widely diffused, no control ● Relationships impersonal and competitive ● No superordinate goals – each one for himself ● Horizontal co-ordination through self-regulation ● No necessity to share values and beliefs
	1 – fiefs	**4 – clans**
uncodified information	● Information diffusion limited by lack of codification to face-to-face relationship ● Relationships personal and hierarchical (feudal/charismatic) ● Submission to superordinate goals ● Hierarchical coordination ● Necessity to share values and beliefs	● Information is diffused, but is still limited by lack of codification to face-to-face relationship ● Relationships personal but non-hierarchical ● Goals are shared through a process of negotiation ● Horizontal coordination through negotiation ● Necessity to share values and beliefs

Table 1: Transactions in the C-space

Cultures are shaped by the structuring and sharing within groups of critical social knowledge. Four distinct types of culture are represented as points in the diagram. Their location is a function of the codification and diffusion properties of the information they draw on. Table 1 relates these properties to certain cultural features.

Of course, there are potentially as many types of culture as there are ways of grouping people together and these are often overlaid. The culture of a street-corner gang, for example, is embedded in the wider urban culture; that of a corporate board in the culture of the enterprise; and so on.

Two types that increasingly preoccupy managers today are national culture and corporate culture. They are also interested in how they influence each other. Understanding this can be critical to a company's foreign operations. Many a western enterprise operating in a highly codified manner, for example, has come to grief in countries whose culture is located in the lower regions of the C-space. The question is: who should do the adapting? The enterprise that wants to sell or the host country that wants to modernize?

Do cultures converge?

The popular assumption is that globalization is moving us into a world in which the broker's culture will gradually eclipse that of the Zen master. Instantaneous communication is creating a global village, a world in which the word "global" will count for more than the word "village."

But this is just another way of arguing that societal development and modernization gradually move cultures up the C-space and that, as they do so, they move them to the right, into a region of the space where information is highly codified and hence rapidly diffused. As Table 1 indicates, this region is characteristic of a market culture, one reason why globalization is associated by many with the development of a universal market order.

We have been here before. In post-medieval Europe, for example, development moved us away from a feudal order in fiefs and towards the embryonic bureaucracies of the absolutist states of the 18th century. A gradual decentralization towards a market order then took place from the 18th century, facilitated by the spread of literacy and education. Figure 2 traces this movement in the C-space.

It has always been assumed that development elsewhere will follow this course.

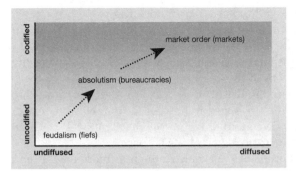

Figure 2: Cultural evolution in the C-space

Economic take-off requires a rule-based society and freedom to compete in open markets. Markets today have thus become a universal value even for countries such as China, still heavily located in the lower regions of the C-space.

An organization's corporate culture will follow a similar path in the C-space as it grows. It may start off as a highly personalized family business or entrepreneurial start-up in the fief region of the space, but as it grows it gives way to a more impersonal bureaucratic order. When the founding entrepreneur can no longer recognize the faces coming into work on Monday morning, a different way of managing is required. As the enterprise continues to grow, some form of decentralization becomes necessary, leading not only to a greater codification of rules and procedures but also to a more extensive diffusion of information within the business. In many cases, internal markets are created – for capital, people, goods and so on.

Corporate versus national cultures

As the growing business moves up the C-space and to the right, it may internationalize its operations. It is then exhorted to "think global but to act local." Yet how realistic is this? Does it not create a potential clash between a corporate culture and a national one? Global managers will find it difficult to act local across more than at most one or two cultures. Local managers, in turn, will find thinking global quite a stretch.

Is it possible to act local without thinking local to some extent? Thinking local is not done in a day. It requires a lengthy accumulation of tacit knowledge, habits, values and beliefs that do not easily diffuse outside a given culture. Think how difficult it can be to understand the humor of a new culture even when its language has been mastered. In the absence of an ability to think local, acting local easily becomes an empty ritual, a behavior associated with day-trippers rather than long-term residents.

Alternatives to convergence

In the case of both national and corporate culture, growth and development have been assumed to entail a movement up the C-space and to the right – a convergence on a single cultural order. Moving up and across the C-space achieves important efficiencies, reducing both the costs and ambiguities of communicating and increasing the numbers that can participate in cultural exchanges. It also has its problems. With the loss of a tacit context comes a depersonalization of relationships, a loss of community, and a general inability to cope with uncertainty.

Some cultures seem disinclined to move up the C-space. Sometimes there is a strong preference for keeping relationships personalized rather than impersonal. In others a lack of physical and institutional infrastructure makes it difficult to codify cultural exchanges in the upper regions of the C-space.

Consider the case of China (discussed in detail on p. 224). The Chinese leadership claims that the country is moving towards a market economy. The claim presupposes that the country is decentralizing on the back of well-codified institutional structures in the bureaucratic region of the C-space.

Yet, *pace* 50 years of a command economy, the country remains more feudal than bureaucratic. If it is decentralizing at all – and the evidence suggests that it is – it is doing so in the lower region of the C-space, from a fief-like order to a clan-like one. In clans, it is operating a kind of network capitalism, which, being based on *guanxi* (connections) and interpersonal trust, is far removed from a market order.

Is China doing so badly? The country has turned in one of the highest economic growth rates in the world since the early 1980s. Is the country modernizing? Probably. But contrary to expectations, it is doing so in the lower regions of the C-space. Western managers operating on the assumption that modernizing cultures will all sooner or later converge on their way of doing things could thus be in for a rude shock.

Interestingly, when it comes to corporate cultures, western managers who have moved their enterprises up the C-space are now trying to build their competence once more in its lower regions.

Cultures that seek to codify everything by reducing it to matters of procedures (bureaucracies) or price (markets) by degrees lose their capacity to deal with novelty and uncertainty. In large western businesses this translates into a loss of entrepreneurship. Many large companies, following the example of 3M and ABB, are now seeking to restore an entrepreneurial culture by creating small businesses within large ones.

The impact of IT

Here, recent development in information technology could help. The information revolution is taken by many to favor the culture of the broker. To some extent it does. By vastly increasing the data-processing and transmission capacities of organizations, whatever the level of codification, IT effectively pushes the diffusion curve to the right in the C-space (*see* Figure 3). The broker can thus extend his reach, as indicated by the horizontal arrow in the diagram, to a greater number of people.

Yet it turns out that IT also has something to offer the Zen master. As the vertical arrow in Figure 3 suggests, a given population can now be reached at a lower level of codification than before: the fax replaces the telex, and video-conferencing allows face-to-face meetings at a distance. Whether or not Zen masters avail themselves of these new technologies, they offer practicing managers the prospect of building up highly personalized cultures independently of geographical distance.

The advent of high-bandwidth communication could thus restore an element of community to what is currently perceived as an increasingly impersonal market order. If cultural convergence is to come about, therefore, it might well occur around the clan-like networks characteristic of Asian cultures rather than the impersonal

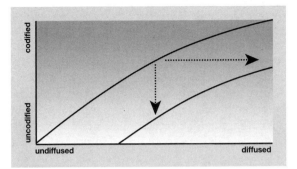

Figure 3: The impact of IT on the diffusion curve

market order that many western observers take to be universal.

We have been moving in a small-is-beautiful direction for some time. Today companies are shrinking in size, more is being outsourced to a small network of partners and, in spite of those custodians of the market order, the Securities and Exchange Commission and the Monopolies Commission, collaboration between companies receives as much attention as competition.

It may be global in its reach, but it is the culture of the village that we should be attending to. The problem is that contrary to what Marshall McLuhan supposed when he coined the term, it is not a single global village that is being created by IT but literally tens of thousands of them. Operating within one village requires one kind of skill; operating across several requires another. If the right skill is lacking, conflict could result. There are therefore dangers as well as opportunities in a culture of global villages.

Dangers because by bringing people closer together we lose the impersonality in relationships that often protects individuals from exposure to differences in values and norms. The great virtue of the market order is that it functions with only a minimum amount of adaptation to and alignment with local cultural requirements. *Opportunities* because if the personalization of global relationships is skillfully managed it will teach managers to think locally but at a distance, thus effectively increasing the range of cultural environments that their enterprises are capable of adapting to.

To the extent that managers can chew gum and walk at the same time, they must now learn to simultaneously think globally and locally. Acting locally is no longer enough.

Cultural adaptation versus cultural conformity

An effective corporate culture is a source of competitive advantage for a company if it achieves the right degree of fit with the range of environments in which it finds itself operating.

The assumption that cultures converge on a market order is one that eliminates cultural variety in favor of consumer variety. It provides a greater choice of products – *sushi* bars in Manhattan, French restaurants in the Ginza – but a declining heterogeneity of the cultural environments in which to consume them. Managers then only have to adapt to a single universal culture – that of the market. How nice if it also happens to be one in which they grew up. The need for hard learning is thereby obviated.

Companies that believe in convergence on a universal market order may be less inclined to create a corporate culture capable of adapting to a range of different national cultures. Where an organization's products have a high technical content, this has not mattered much. Nuclear power stations and long-range airliners have until recently been perceived as "culture-free" technical objects. No longer. Building power stations or aircraft tails in China has a nasty way of converting technical problems into cultural ones. On the other hand, organizations that believe that cultural differences will persist, that what distinguishes the French and the Italians is not about to disappear, may find it difficult to create a unified corporate culture that transcends national differences.

Such businesses need to bear in mind that to adapt is not to conform. An enterprise needs to maintain its cultural identity if it is to profit from it. Adapting a corporate culture to the multiple, divergent demands of multiple global villages may be the biggest challenge that international corporations face as they enter the new century.

The dragon breathes enterprising fire

Pedro Nueno looks at the changing economic face of China and how the reforms there can and will provide potential for the entrepreneur.

If the question is "are there entrepreneurs in China?" the answer is yes. If the question is "are there foreign entrepreneurs in China?" the answer is also yes. And plenty of them in both cases. Entrepreneurship is so rooted in human nature that unless it is strictly forbidden it emerges with strength. This is what is happening in China today.

Scholars have long debated whether some ethnic groups are more entrepreneurial than others. As the article on p. 200 of Part 5 described, the fact that ethnic Chinese entrepreneurs control large portions of the economies of south-east Asia shows that some Chinese can be superb entrepreneurs. About 1 percent of the population of the Philippines is ethnic Chinese, yet they control 40 percent of the economy. In Indonesia and Thailand, with 4 percent and 10 percent ethnic Chinese respectively, they control half of the domestic business activity. In Malaysia, about one-third of the population is ethnic Chinese but they control two-thirds of the economy. Hong Kong, Taiwan and Singapore have a majority of ethnic Chinese and they control practically the whole domestic wealth.

Entrepreneurs, as Harvard Business School's Howard Stevenson has said, are opportunity driven. They find out the resources they need once they have identified the opportunity (*see* Part 1). A network of contacts and trust is essential. Networking and trust are well-known characteristics of the Chinese culture. Many of the Chinese who left the People's Republic of China (PRC) and became famous entrepreneurs in south-east Asia kept their links with their communities on the mainland. Many have made their fortunes in activities related to the PRC in areas such as trade, finance and real estate.

Super-entrepreneurs such as Stanley Ho (with a net worth estimated at more than $2 billion), who has, among many businesses around the world, the exclusive franchise for the operation of the lucrative casinos of Macau, seem to be in good standing with the senior levels of the Chinese authorities. The Hong Kong tycoons associated in the Better Hong Kong Foundation to promote confidence in Hong Kong after the Chinese takeover in July 1997 combine their businesses in China with generous donations to charities on the mainland to establish good political relations through a demonstration of social responsibility.

These personalities are well known in China. Media networks carry information about them and they are idolized as role models. The Chinese authorities appear to let them play this function, using them as catalysts for the abundant entrepreneurial initiative in the PRC.

It is hardly surprising, therefore, that in December 1996 the first post-colonial chief executive of Hong Kong was announced as shipping magnate Tung Chee-hwa, appointed with the obvious blessing of Beijing.

Entrepreneurs in China: who are they?

Since the start of economic reform in 1978, the output of state-owned enterprises (SOEs) has gone down to less than half and the trend continues. Collectively owned enterprises have doubled their industrial output, and individually owned enterprises have taken more than 10 percent of industrial output, growing at more than 25 percent a year. It needs eight or more people to form a collectively owned enterprise and therefore this group ranges from co-operative-type enterprises to entities where in fact one member controls the company and the others are relatives or sleeping partners.

The bulk of foreign investment in China comes from Hong Kong, Taiwan and Singapore. Part of this investment is made by Chinese entrepreneurs who manage to establish companies abroad and invest back in the PRC.

Most Chinese entrepreneurs are former executives of SOEs who identify an opportunity while working for the state and have the contacts to transform that opportunity into a venture. In Japan, leaving a large company to start your own small business is not well received and you would not expect a lot of support from previous contacts (former employer, customers, suppliers, the financial community). In China, this is not the case; entrepreneurship seems to be highly valued in Chinese society.

Entrepreneurs starting their own companies in China might have problems attracting employees, however. This is because SOEs normally supply housing, healthcare and pensions. Or at least, that was the case until recently.

1996 was the first year the SOE sector as a whole lost money. In the two or three years previously, roughly one-third of SOEs made money, one-third lost money, and one-third broke even, managing an overall positive balance. In the seven years up to 1996, state sector losses multiplied by seven. These enormous shells – some partially empty – carry tremendous social obligations and this is one of the question marks over the reform of the Chinese economy.

As in western countries, there is an important portion of marginal entrepreneurship made up of very small individual enterprises, sometimes run by senior citizens and most of them part of the parallel economy, engaged in elementary forms of trading in food, textiles, household and other consumer products. This sector is particularly difficult to quantify.

Some private Chinese companies are true success stories. Vanward Enterprises is a privately held, fast-growing manufacturer of home appliances. The company produces 500,000 gas water heaters each year, employs 1,500 people (of whom 10 percent are engineers), operates 200 service centers in China, and has overseas offices in Hong Kong and Singapore. Vanward, owned by three brothers, carries out its own research and development and is expanding its product range to include microwave ovens, electric water heaters, electric rice cookers, electric heaters, and so on. The company has ISO 9001 certification and has begun to export. Companies such as Vanward are the hidden champions of the Chinese economy.

Foreign entrepreneurs in China

Foreign entrepreneurs in China are mainly found in the service sector and their clientele is also primarily foreign. They are established in most cases as representative offices of "mail box"-type companies based in Hong Kong. They provide advice on trade, finance, head-hunting, training, real estate, marketing, public relations, auditing, strategy, and so on, and some employ more than 100 people in China. In general, these enterprises must bill a foreign entity.

One can find highly qualified professionals who are fluent in Mandarin, knowledgeable about doing business in China, and who benefit from the strong flows of foreign direct investments. While "blue chip" companies tend to use the well-known global "brands" for their service needs – and all the brands have a presence in China these days – there is room for entrepreneurs with industry or business connections abroad who can offer lower prices and a personalized treatment to smaller companies with smaller projects.

Access to capital

As in the West, most Chinese entrepreneurs start their ventures from their personal savings and those of members of their network of relatives and friends. In some instances the networks might include people in key positions in government or SOEs. If this is the case, a somewhat privileged access to funding might take place through longer-term financing of suppliers, shorter-term payment of receivables, or even direct borrowing possibilities.

Other advantages of the network might also be used. Insider information or influence in land classification, for example, might be the contribution to a project of a well-connected entrepreneur who may then also find partners in Hong Kong or Taiwan willing to provide funding.

Well-run companies can make enough profits to finance their needs for working capital and investment. Banks are also sources of financing, and a successful manufacturer such as Vanward would not have the problems with a bank that its western counterparts might have.

There is no doubt that there is a level of corruption in China. This is recognized by the authorities, publicly criticized, and there are efforts to control it. While the situation in China is far from what can be found in Russia or some Latin American states, there is no doubt that some Chinese entrepreneurs benefit from access to easy government or SOE money.

Venture capital has recently been introduced in China with the creation of the Minsheng Bank. Related to the All China Federation of Industry and Commerce, this agency's aim is to provide financial support to entrepreneurs, particularly those with high-tech projects.

The future of entrepreneurship in China

As China continues to reform its economy and more Chinese managers improve their management skills, as the weakening of the SOEs offers less protection to Chinese workers, and as banks become more sensitive to the financing of healthy projects, the rapid growth of the private sector will open more and more opportunities for entrepreneurs.

Along the coastal provinces clusters of privately owned companies are emerging as suppliers or subcontractors to successful, larger privately owned companies, joint ventures or dynamic SOEs. But as economic reform makes progress and the market economy advances, unemployment in China will undoubtedly grow.

Entrepreneurs might benefit from this flexible labor market while at the same time providing a solution – probably the only possible solution – for millions of Chinese workers.

Tackling adversity with diversity

Enterprise exists in every culture, not least in the so-called "developing" countries, though it may be very different from the classic western model. **Michael Scott**, **Akin Fadahunsi** and **Sarath Kodithuwakku** look at two examples from Sri Lanka and Nigeria.

There is a myth that entrepreneurship is largely a phenomenon of developed, industrialized countries and that if only it could be transferred, together with western management practices, problems of so-called "underdevelopment" would be solved.

Yet the evidence is that entrepreneurship is a generalized social role found in all societies, merely varying as the context changes. If entrepreneurship is seen as the "creative extraction of value from environments," then the elements we have been discussing in *Mastering Entrepreneurship* – such as vision, opportunity spotting, risk and profit taking, resource mobilization, and network development – may take a different (and sometimes invisible) form in different environments but are always present.

While international agencies seek to disseminate developed country models of best practice, there are equally interesting lessons to be learned from indigenous wealth-extracting methods.

The rich diversity of entrepreneurship is illustrated by the following two studies. These are part of a program of research into indigenous entrepreneurship in Africa and South Africa developed by Dr Peter Rosa at the University of Stirling. The first, in Sri Lanka, shows how, in an apparently uniform and scarce environment, being entrepreneurial is a survivalist strategy through which "winners" arise. The second, in Nigeria, demonstrates how wealth can be created by entrepreneurs through a parallel economic system.

Creating success in the Sri Lankan countryside

An intriguing question for students of enterprise is "can we pick winners?" All the evidence is that we cannot and one reason is the large number of possible influences on success.

The Sri Lankan study set out to understand why, in a rural area, some people are more successful than others and what contribution entrepreneurial activity makes.

Studying wealthy farmers is not the same as studying entrepreneurs. Wealth might have come from previous generations through cultural and political effects or through access to better resources. Isolating the effects of enterprise from all the other political, resource and cultural factors is usually the major problem researchers face. Fortunately a kind of natural experiment was discovered in the shape of a land scheme.

During the 1980s the Sri Lankan government provided cleared land to new settlers, all similarly without wealth. With scarcely enough land to meet subsistence, few outside resources and little education, we might expect to find villagers in abject poverty. With a monoculture (rice paddy) and set ways of producing it, one might expect uniformity – and indeed to the westerner all villagers look poor.

Yet there is an underlying diversity of activities that over a decade led to large inequalities of wealth. Economic activities include not only cultivation – rice paddy, cash crops – but also rice milling, hiring out of tractors and animals, village shopkeeping and money lending.

The agricultural cycle gives rise to shifting demands for labor and equipment. Middlemen are active at harvest, buying from farmers, who then engage in highly impulsive consumption – to the benefit of shopkeepers. This is followed by a demand for credit as farmers again need cash for fertilizers to start the next year. The task of the entrepreneur is to spot opportunities in this agricultural cycle of activities and match them with available or mobilized resources, resulting in capital accumulation and wealth creation.

How these processes operate in all their diversity can be illustrated in the following case study of a family with three adults and three school-age children. They cultivate nine acres and have a two-wheel tractor, a permanent building for storing paddy, four draught animals and a cow. They start their cultivation early and they do as much of it using their own labor as possible to conserve cash. The tractor is hired out for plowing, winnowing and transport and they have a stand-by driver. They choose a planting method that is more risky in terms of yield but which needs less labor and is more effective in weed control. Savings are used to buy the fertilizer necessary for high-yield varieties.

By being early in the cycle, the family can subcontract its own labor to farmers who are falling behind. They do not sell all their produce at harvest but can store some until prices are higher. They also act as local collectors of rice for outside middlemen, with whom they have long-term trusting relationships.

The wife initiated the leasing of extra land, the profits of which help pay for the tractor, as well as providing cash for her money-lending activities. She appears to have earned about Rs 100,000 during the past eight years from an initial Rs 2,500 and has accumulated savings of about Rs 20,000 in her bank account.

Apart from paddy the family also grow vegetables for their own use, and sell any surplus. Their cow has been leased to a fellow villager who feeds it and receives the milk, while every other calf is given back to the family. Bulls are used to plow their paddy lands and also for transportation purposes. The bullock cart is leased to transport paddy and fire wood for the villagers involved in rice processing.

Entrepreneurial lessons

What can be derived from this case study? First, there is "pluriactivity," that is the family are involved in many things, from farming, to trading, to leasing, to money lending. Just like a juggler with many balls in the air, entrepreneurs typically have more than one activity current at any one time.

Second, they combine various resources and it is the skill in accumulating and combining that enables them, thirdly, to activate new opportunities as they spot them.

Of course, pluriactivity itself leads to more chances of new opportunities being perceived. The capital accumulation process is itself a ratchet: profits reinvested (for example in a tractor) create more wealth for the next cycle.

All this implies rational thought (exactly when to plant, what varieties, at what rate to lend and so on) and hard work, accompanied by deferred gratification. (The family had the choice of building a new barn or a new house – they chose a barn in the expectation of building a larger house later.) The development of key relationships is crucial and especially the reliance on interpersonal trust. Finally, the family makes use of information sources not to do what everybody else does but to seek more profitable windows in the market.

Building wealth through the Nigerian cross-border trade

The previous case shows how entrepreneurship can be a survivalist strategy in constrained circumstances and the ways it can differentiate successful from less successful farmers. The following study shows how entrepreneurship can thrive even where it officially does not exist.

According to official statistics in Nigeria, most trade is carried out by governments or multinational companies. There appears to be little contribution from indigenous entrepreneurs, reinforcing a commonly held belief that Africa does not have enough entrepreneurs with the capability to move beyond survival into significant wealth accumulation.

This is linked to the difficulties indigenous entrepreneurs face in acquiring management and entrepreneurship skills appropriate for success in the formal sector, coupled with a tendency for bribery and corruption to cream off any added value.

The study indeed confirms the two major constraints on cross-border trade to be foreign exchange-related problems (the non-exchangeability of the Naira through official channels) and harassment of traders.

Yet these very problems have been turned into entrepreneurial opportunities, and there exists a huge informal, or parallel, economy, transporting large volumes of goods and allowing considerable wealth to be accumulated by successful traders. There is, for example, an "alternative" financial system based not on government sales of restricted foreign currency but on the activities of several thousand currency traders who are the real determinants of the Naira's exchange rate.

For most traders, the constant harassment is a way of life. For example, at border crossings there may be a dozen checkpoints (one army, one customs, the rest police), each of which imposes searches. There are several strategies for evading harassment. Traders can simply pay up to lubricate the speed of transfer; they can use bush paths (but this risks robbery); goods can be concealed, mainly to avoid extortion rather than smuggling to avoid duties. But the most common method is to use specialist intermediaries, independent carriers called *kelebes* who operate from "stations" a short distance from the border posts.

The *kelebes* carry the trader's bags or other containers while the trader casually walks across the border. Once over, a fee is paid to the *kelebe* (and any helpers he has subcontracted). A high level of trust is needed for these transactions to be completed since the *kelebe* could easily make away with the goods, especially if the trader were detained. The reliance on trust is even more pronounced in the case of large-scale goods transported by lorry. Here the specialist intermediaries are drivers who undertake to get the goods across the border, using bribery to join armed convoys for example.

These are complicated procedures: the detailed mechanics of cross-border trade take years to learn and there is a system of apprenticeship as effective as any in the formal sector. The rewards can be substantial and successful traders have moved into a wide range of activities, from car and computer imports to cotton processing on farms bought from trading profits and conglomerate businesses with assets of millions of Naira.

Entrepreneurial lessons

While there are many petty traders who simply establish well-tried routines and never innovate, the study identified others who were constantly looking for new profitable products – and "pluriactivity" is again a feature.

The most successful entrepreneurs tend not to operate themselves but to subcontract the risk to others. This "brokerage" role is a crucial aspect of entrepreneurship. Trust in relationships is paramount to the informal system. Just because there is a disregard of written rules (the official system) does not mean that well-observed rules do not exist.

Profit is extracted by several intermediaries at "boundary exchanges" and the complexities of the trade require much learning-by-doing. Infrastructure chaos is paradoxically beneficial to traders because it keeps the multinationals out.

The official view may pessimistically be that harassment of traders adds costs to products, inevitably passed on to already poor consumers. Loss of revenue to government leads to higher taxes and more external borrowing from neo-colonial institutions. Bribery and corruption impoverish the traders, decreasing both motivation and wealth accumulation possibilities.

There is a different picture. The system would appear to produce entrepreneurial opportunities for far more people than would otherwise benefit from "official" trading. Traders benefit by being able to reduce competition from less knowledgeable competitors because it takes so long to learn the system. An army of intermediaries also makes a living out of the system who would otherwise not have any utility under a more regulated system.

Conclusion

Entrepreneurship appears to thrive wherever one looks for it. It may not take familiar western forms but the essentials of value extraction are always present, limited only by the ingenuity of the informal entrepreneurs themselves.

Three styles of Asian capitalism

Gordon Redding compares and contrasts the entrepreneurial and organizational styles of Japan, Korea and the ethnic Chinese.

Not only are ways of doing business in Asia subtly different from those in the West but they are also different within the region itself in important ways. It is a region of immense variety, far more so than is Europe, and runs the gamut from an advanced democracy such as Japan to some of the world's worst totalitarian regimes, from the depths of poverty in Cambodia or the far west of China to the immensely wealthy Japan and the conspicuously spending rich of Hong Kong.

The 30 miraculously golden years just passed have seen the emergence of three powerful systems of business, each represented by a particular kind of organization: in Japan the large, complex networked business, known as the *kaisha* or, in its extended form, the *keiretsu*; in South Korea the now internationalizing *chaebol*; elsewhere, in areas where business needs strong local knowledge and connections, the Chinese family business, that most unobtrusive and little-understood instrument of wealth creation and progress.

Each of these instruments for putting together the components of economic behavior has emerged as a distinct response to its surrounding circumstances. They are embedded in the cultures and development histories of their societies. They are not copies of western forms and their behavior may not follow western rules or ideals. In simple terms, they exist for different reasons.

Where the prime reason for existence and driving logic for the large US corporation is return to shareholders, that of the *kaisha* is to employ people. The *chaebol* has derived much of its dynamism from its contribution to the national development goals of Korea. The Chinese family business exists primarily to create and sustain family fortunes.

The outcome of these varying routes to modern capitalism is that the Japanese form is a large, professionally managed and very complex enterprise with wide ownership; the Korean is a huge family business run like a regiment; and the Chinese is a small family business networking to escape the limitations of its scale and doing so successfully.

These different kinds of organization compete on equal terms in world markets. In Asia today are some of the world's most competitive forms of enterprise, able to hammer each other in world markets on equal terms. In doing so, however, there is no logic which says they have to all have the same book of rules.

Three questions remain especially hard to answer in observing this scene. Why are the Japanese and Koreans masters of the co-ordination of complexity on a huge scale in their organizations when the Chinese normally stay efficient with small-scale companies run on a personal basis? Will the ethnic Chinese in the region now creating large organizations take them through the same managerial revolution which brought professional management and public ownership in the western case, or will their large companies remain dependent for strategy on a presiding genius and be thus unstable and vulnerable to the chances of succession, like China itself? Will China find in its vast laboratory a new hybrid form of economy which takes from the success of the so-called Overseas Chinese and applies network and family capitalism to the task of finally modernizing an ancient and essentially imperial polity?

A subtext of this latter question is whether Hong Kong will be permitted to continue its demonstration of how to run a modern state of Chinese people under something other than autocracy. Was Machiavelli right in saying that the only sure way to take over a state used to governing itself is to ruin it, otherwise it will carp for ever about its lost freedoms and eventually undermine its new master?

Masters of large, masters of small

When a society develops a form of organization that is so common it becomes typical, it usually means there is a shared heritage of influences which has shaped its modern organizations. These influences are historical and the more recent ones are those connected with the way a country modernizes itself, in particular the way it organizes access to capital and to human skill. Whether you get your capital from a market, from the government, from banks or from your friends will make a big difference to how you go about using it and accounting for its use.

Capital from the market drives the frenzy of Anglo-Saxon companies to meet the quarterly expectations of a ravenous investing public, also incidentally directing investment rationally to fields of maximum return in the short run. For the Japanese, capital from the market is of less account than is capital from companies in the same group or from banks, and their interests are less in short-term gain than in the accumulation of long-term strength. Korean *chaebol* have a history of dependence for capital on government and of a consequent need to accommodate government guidance on strategy. Although Korea is now changing rapidly, such habits of mind are embedded and die hard. The end result in both cases is that it has been possible for each of these systems of capitalism to take the long perspectives needed to foster major corporations handling very complex industries.

Other features, older and deeper than modern policies, have helped to make it possible for large Japanese and Korean organizations to co-ordinate human skill, capital, technology, and market know-how to produce world-beating products such as the Lexus or to take a huge chunk of the world market in semiconductors. These extra features include societal norms supporting acceptance of authority and discipline, a sense of the importance of the organization in one's life and a consequent wish to belong to it, an association of individuals with the collective good of the group, and intense competitiveness on behalf of the nation via the company.

Attention has been drawn by Francis Fukuyama to another societal feature critical to economic efficiency. The notion of trust, what he calls the "social virtues" or what others call social capital, has an important part to play in explaining why the Japanese and Koreans can handle very large-scale organizations efficiently and the Chinese cannot.

Trust has developed to a high level in a society when you can do business with strangers. In the West this happens when the society has built a fabric of commercial law and bodies such as free-standing professions like accountancy, and so on, which serve to underwrite much risk and encourage exchange to grow more dense. In turn this raises the intensity with which resources are used and the resulting gains in productivity account for the transition from the pre-modern condition to the modern.

Although civil society in Japan is not a copy of that in the West, it nevertheless works similarly and the level of trust between strangers is both high and in constant use. The Korean case is different from the Japanese. The Korean economy is organized into great vertically structured units with roots deep into the small-business sector via subcontracting that serve to produce high levels of efficient linkage and modern levels of efficiency in the use of resources.

The Chinese family business specializes in small-scale efficiency, which at first glance is a contradiction. In Taiwan, Hong Kong (and increasingly South China) and throughout Asean the 50 million or so ethnic Chinese have perfected a formula for business which has turned them into formidable world players. Their domains are OEM (original equipment manufacture) production, property, services, retailing, trading and, in the region itself, capturing lucrative franchises in such fields as power, terminals, tunnels and gambling.

OEM's strength provides entry to the world business system. Here products go through faster and faster cycles and IT encourages smaller production runs and tighter delivery times to the world's boutiques, or to the assemblers and packagers of the latest bells and whistles on the latest toys, executive and otherwise.

It is in these circumstances that there are little businesses specializing in shirt collars and employing 30 people but linked to seven other little outfits specializing in buttons, fabric wholesaling, fabric dyeing or shirt-sewing. They receive an order involving a shipment of thousands of shirts to Los Angeles by next Tuesday and are able to say "no problem."

By letting others worry about brand-naming, distribution and market risk, as well as design, single companies can grow to manufacture the world market in GI Joe toys, 40 percent of the US market in hairdryers, huge proportions of the markets in cheap cameras, torches, photo albums, underwear, tennis racquets, as well as innumerable small components lying out of sight inside your average computer, washing machine or waffle iron.

This network capitalism of the ethnic Chinese in the region is designed to respond to markets which companies from advanced economies would say are disorderly, volatile and very difficult to cope with. Information is not openly available in the region about the right price to pay, whom to trust, what to expect of anyone, which official rules need navigating and how, who is creditworthy and for how much, how you get paid and where are the necessary skills. This information is the province of the ethnic Chinese throughout many of the region's service and manufacturing industries.

The accumulating and holding of such knowledge are seen as strategic and the use of it is largely to pursue opportunity in the holes in such unlevel playing fields. This is often done by collaboration with other members of the net with whom capital, risk and more information come to be shared. This works as a response to uncertainty for the Chinese, for whom the meaning of danger includes opportunity.

The ethnic Chinese's secret has been the release of entrepreneurial talent and the building of systems of stable co-ordination of economic behavior to allow such talent to be fed with capital and efficiently controlled while at the same time escaping from the scale limitations which normally go with entrepreneurs. To connect these small businesses into world markets is no mean feat when it is done without bureaucracy. This is the achievement of Chinese capitalism so far in the past 30 years. But what happens next? And will China be radically transformed in consequence?

Doing business in the "Wild East"

The experience of entrepreneurial growth differs considerably across central and eastern Europe. But **Bert Twaalfhoven** and **Daniel Muzyka** offer some broad guidance to the region and advice to indigenous and foreign entrepreneurs.

There is no easy way to describe the development of entrepreneurship in a whole region of the world, nor is it easy to characterize the transition in central and eastern Europe; it is unprecedented in recorded human economic history. It is apparent, however, that this region of the world is experiencing both the best of times and the worst of times as the economic transition unfolds. The recent downturn in the region, which has had differential impacts by country, only emphasizes the point. The good news for entrepreneurs in the region is that opportunities still abound in many areas.

The assumption at the time of the *Wende*, or fall of the Berlin Wall, was that the emergence of entrepreneurs and entrepreneurial business would represent one of the primary pillars in the economic reconstruction of central and eastern Europe. The other pillar was to be the remobilization and redesign of the vertically integrated state enterprises that existed under communism.

The informal economy, particularly in Russia, is very large and no one has exact figures. Early projections by the European Foundation for Entrepreneurship Research (EFER – a non-profit organization whose goals are to develop and support growth-oriented entrepreneurship in Europe and which has participated in many initiatives in eastern Europe, including the identification and training of key academics who would help develop a new generation of entrepreneurs) in preparation for a 1990 conference on entrepreneurial business in the region predicted an increase from one million to two million entrepreneurial businesses in 1989 to about four to five million by 2000. The OECD estimates that by 1995 there were at least 12 million entrepreneurial enterprises in the East. These businesses have become the primary engine for economic redevelopment in the former communist republics.

Why has entrepreneurial business taken such a center stage role? The answer is both positive and negative.

Almost everyone expected the large state combines to provide at least one of the pillars for reconstruction. These businesses accounted for most of the economic activity. To give you some comparisons, it is reported that significantly more than half the people in the US are employed in companies with fewer than 50 people; in the former East Germany, 11 percent of the population was involved in such enterprises.

It proved very difficult to reconstruct these behemoths. "Corporate culture," if we can use the term, as well as the asset base and the very nature of the products were all obstacles to effective economic performance. As we witnessed at an aerospace show in Moscow, one enterprise moved from manufacturing rockets to the construction of lawnmowers. Without requisite marketing skills, most of these activities were unsuccessful and the asset base proved to have little value. Finally, as operating entities they often proved too costly to operate, providing very low productivity and even lower quality. In the end, the economic value generated from the revitalization of the state-owned combines was less than expected.

While entrepreneurial activity in central and eastern Europe is adding value, there are a few cautionary notes. The entrepreneurial business that has emerged still represents only about a third of the number of small and medium enterprises in China. Furthermore, the 12 million businesses in the area are a volatile lot. Central and eastern European entrepreneurs often witness very fast growth (for example 100–200 percent a year) but also experience very high death and restart rates.

Small and medium enterprises, created by a new generation of entrepreneurs, have not rescued the economy in its entirety. For example, unemployment in Poland, which was an artificial 1 percent under the communist regime, is 17 percent today. This represents the price of restructuring, which even very active entrepreneurial activity cannot erase.

Development

The nature of entrepreneurial activity in central and eastern Europe has gone through some distinctive phases. The first entrepreneurs were often operating arbitrage imbalances in existing resources and were finding opportunities at the borders, bringing cheaper goods from Russia to relatively richer countries in central Europe.

Furthermore, the transport and movement of commodities such as aluminum and petroleum gave some individuals and companies the ability to make significant amounts of quick cash, especially when coupled with massive fluctuations in currency. It is reported that by buying Russian commodities destined for trans-shipment in rapidly deflating roubles, Estonian entrepreneurs were able to realize massive gains selling these commodities on world markets in US dollars.

The evolution of entrepreneurial business next moved heavily to the importation of relatively higher-quality durable consumer goods from the West. This was coupled with increasing numbers of joint ventures with western and Asian businesses to build on local assets, including cheap but knowledgeable labor, and growing consumer and industrial markets.

The evolution has continued with increasing numbers of "home-grown" local businesses – some growing very rapidly – producing locally developed products and services, sometimes for export to world markets.

Is the state of entrepreneurship the same throughout central and eastern Europe? Have entrepreneurs and entrepreneurial business developed in parallel ways through the former communist republics? The answer is no. The reason is that it depends upon where you started.

We would summarize the primary conditions for the growth of entrepreneurial business in three factors:

- infrastructure
- resources
- product-markets.

The first, the infrastructure, includes legal systems, telecommunications, transportation and so on that all serve to support business. In some countries these were more developed than in others.

The second involves the availability of resources, especially from the financial sector. Throughout central and eastern Europe, the financial system has not responded fast enough to the needs of entrepreneurs and entrepreneurial business. While it was hoped that the system would play a key role in supporting growth business, the financial sector was not able to get off the ground rapidly enough to provide the kind of support required. Entrepreneurs were often left to their own sources of capital. In fact, the financial sector did not really understand how to deal with individual entrepreneurs. It was used to asset-base financing and the concept of depreciation hardly existed. Assets were kept on the books at the purchase value.

The third is the existence and nature of product-markets. In some countries, a consumerist tradition existed with the distribution channels and spending capacity to back it. In others, individuals could barely afford staples and were less than excited about products they did not perceive as necessary.

Given the differences among countries in the area on these factors, it is no mystery that entrepreneurial activity is different in both level and type. Other factors that seem to have had an impact on the ability of the various countries to support and develop entrepreneurial business include such conditions as the length of time under communism, the evolution of the post-communist political economy, the long-standing cultural attitudes toward business, and the prior existence of business relationships and networks.

Some countries were under communism only from 1945 while others, such as Russia, initiated it in 1917. The size and affluence of the cultural diaspora (for example the large Polish population in the US and Canada) was also a factor in the rapid development of new entrepreneurial business.

The following are some examples of the difference in development of entrepreneurial business.

Poland has been very successful and well served by the growth and development of new entrepreneurial businesses. Poles from outside the country were willing to further accelerate efforts started under the communist regime to liberalize business.

The Czech Republic has been very successful in throwing off the weight of repressive state-owned enterprise in favor of a new small and medium-sized business sector and significant numbers of growth businesses. Drawing on good education and historic parallels with German enterprise, German capital has found its way strongly into the Czech Republic, making it a successful country that is building some new world-class industrial companies.

Slovenia has also done very well in supporting new enterprise and permitting the development of entrepreneurial business. Entrepreneurship has a long tradition in the area, though it was previously limited by law. Strong traditional links with northern Italy, Austria and Germany that go back many years have also helped.

These countries, along with Hungary, represent the more entrepreneurially progressive countries in central and eastern Europe. Two other groups of countries are shown in Figure 1. Those in Group 3 are still struggling with the early stages of the development of entrepreneurial business. Even with these, however, the signs are clearly positive. Group 2 countries are exhibiting signs of improvement in the infrastructure, resource systems and product-markets required to support higher levels of entrepreneurial activity.

What all of this experience has shown is that there are multiple assets and liabilities in the economic landscape of central and eastern Europe after the *Wende*. There are significant natural resources, large numbers of well-trained technical people (including engineers and scientists – there are 12 million engineers in Russia alone, for example) and in many cases, a significant desire for change. On the

Group 1: Progressive	Group 2: Developing	Group 3: Embryonic
Czech Republic	Bulgaria	Albania
Hungary	Croatia	Armenia
Poland	Estonia	Belarus
Slovenia	Latvia	Georgia
	Lithuania	Kazakhstan
	Romania	Russia
	Slovakia	Serbia
		Ukraine
		Uzbekistan

Figure 1

liability side, cultural attitudes and expectations, a poor infrastructure and a poorly organized and oriented financial system have all served to slow down the successful development of growth-oriented entrepreneurial business.

Nature of entrepreneurial activity

Entrepreneurs in central and eastern Europe have found many opportunities and many paths to entrepreneurship. Some have joint ventured with western companies. Some have split off from large state-owned enterprises. Others have found opportunity in services that have not existed before in local markets. But there are two characteristics of the development of entrepreneurial activity on the part of local entrepreneurs that are different.

First, entrepreneurs often develop a set of "horizontal" activities. For example, one entrepreneur we know made money in currency dealing. With this money, he was able to set up a series of loan companies that evolved into giving loans primarily for real estate development. From this set of activities, he later evolved into the real estate investment and trading business. Having not found a good set of building contractors, he then moved into the real estate construction business.

Many entrepreneurs have moved horizontally across fields in this manner. For many this was unfortunate as they reached beyond fields where they had been competent as well as lucky into areas where serious personal weaknesses in their management skills led to disaster. For a few who possessed the right skills and orientation, this was a way towards developing serious wealth. Interestingly, this type of horizontal entrepreneurship is a phenomenon that exists today in Korea, Japan and the financial holding companies of Italy and Belgium. However, the modern world is increasingly demanding global specialization.

The second characteristic is related to the first. Entrepreneurs were usually managing a portfolio of activities at any one time. Along with the management responsibilities they accumulated from the horizontal expansion of activities, entrepreneurs also acquired what they instinctively saw as a portfolio of businesses with a varying risk profile. The wiser ones were willing to close down activities they found no longer profitable as local markets and opportunity evolved.

In some economies in central and eastern Europe, the nature of entrepreneurial activity has evolved to resemble the nature of entrepreneurial activity in western Europe. Enabling this transition is the presence of "western-styled" venture capitalists, appropriate business systems, and corporate and contract law.

Recommendations to local entrepreneurs

Given the varying nature of the environment in which they develop, entrepreneurs in this region face many different challenges. However, there are some common patterns we can discern from discussions with some successful growth entrepreneurs from around central and eastern Europe.

At an informal conference, entrepreneurs from the region cited several consistent operating weaknesses. The most profound involved the inherent lack of marketing and sales management skills. This weakness only served to emphasize the impact of 40 years of a communist system that found no value in such activities.

A second area of weakness was employees and management. They found their managers were often not willing to take real responsibility for business activities. They wanted the rewards from new activities but were unwilling to show significant initiative in pursuing these activities. This is particularly true of Russian-dominated countries where decision making is hierarchical. They also found their employees less than totally reliable, having retained many bad habits from the old regime such as late arrival and early weekend departure. While these attitudes are changing rapidly in some countries, entrepreneurs still found that they needed to manage the turnover of their employees because some were simply not able or willing to grow with them.

A third weakness they cited involved their business partners, suppliers and distributors. Due to a desire to make short-term gains in new deals and currency speculation, entrepreneurs have often found business partners to be less than totally trusting and trustworthy.

They also stated that two areas where they needed to develop skills, based on their own experiences, were in the nature and role of working capital and business finance in general. Financial planning – the setting and management of regular budgets – was an area of general weakness.

The weaknesses in resource allocation and gathering became even more important in the face of the lack of trust found in the banking sector. The scramble for money and the appropriate allocation of resources was a pressing problem that was exacerbated by a need to find resources from among family and friends.

One successful entrepreneur at the conference, who was a former, privileged factory head in a state combine under the old regime, said that while there was success, there was also significantly increased stress. He reported that his family did not understand why he could not, as company president, leave for the *dacha* on Friday morning and not engage in work all weekend. He noted that not only was business practice from the West becoming a reality but so were all of the side effects.

Beyond dealing with these problems, we have a few suggestions for local entrepreneurs. First, focus your business activities. Expanding into new, if related, enterprises may seem a reasonable idea and may be your best way to create new businesses. On the other hand, building a strong set of competencies and a business network is probably the surest way to succeed.

Second, be prepared to build barriers to further competitors coming into the business, especially in the face of extensive "copycat" competition. As one Hungarian entrepreneur noted: "Success attracts success; when someone finds a successful niche, they instantly have competition."

Third, evolve with the customer – business is getting more sophisticated and so are the markets, distributors and customers. Underestimating the consuming public in the East on the basis of prevailing standards will limit long-term success.

Fourth, continuously develop the skills and abilities of your people. Investment in people does take time and resources, but it is a necessary element for long-term success. This requires that you also develop your own skills along with those of your staff. This investment should be made regardless of that fact that a number of the trained individuals will become impatient and receive better offers due to their skills. The reputation as a firm that believes in its people is something of long-term value.

In line with the last two points, we would make a fifth recommendation: do not measure yourself solely against local competition but use the broad standard. New competitors lurk outside the borders of the countries of central and eastern Europe. One very successful software company from the area went so far as to set up an office in the most competitive environment for its business – Silicon Valley – as early as possible.

Recommendations to western entrepreneurs

Many entrepreneurs we have met, as well as larger western enterprises, have either moved into central and eastern Europe or are thinking of doing so. We have a few recommendations, based on the experience of others and the development of the market, to make to those who would like to enter the "Wild East." Our recommendations start with the need to heed the lessons we have just reviewed.

The first would be to not underestimate consumers. Some entrepreneurs have led the way into this region with substandard-quality products and services. They might find a temporary market but they soon find that, via imports, joint ventures or locally developed products, they have been displaced. Never underestimate your customer.

The second point is to move with understanding into your markets. Take a local partner. No matter how educated or perceptive you are, a local partner is always going to have a better perspective. Further, pay special attention to how other entrepreneurs, who may have parallel or similar ideas, have moved into the market. Learn from their successes and failures. Since there are few hard and fast rules in this situation, recent experience is a good teacher.

Third, we would suggest that you plan to over-invest in training. While management experience and employee attitudes and training are continually improving, significant levels of training are still in order. Training can be realized through the normal formal means but also through rotation into operations in the West. Some western enterprises suggest that without regular visits to western operations, people "slip back" into bad habits.

Training itself must impact business skills, employee orientation and, in some cases, technical skills. As noted earlier, the reality of training, however, is that in some countries, increased training only fuels a higher turnover rate. Trained employees, with experience from a well-established and successful international enterprise, will find welcome homes in other developing enterprises.

Fourth, set realistic time frames for returns. This is not such a problem for western managers but it does appear to be a problem in some entrepreneurial initiatives due to prevalent growth rates in the East as well as the unrealistic expectations of local management. Some western entrepreneurs have found that their local management teams have fallen apart when ventures did not become ultimately successful in a year or two. Make sure everyone knows and shares how long it will take to "make it."

In the end, two practical messages from many western entrepreneurs and companies establishing entrepreneurial enterprises in this region are "do not attempt everything yourself" and "get western-styled auditors and accountants to ensure proper budgeting and control."

You cannot afford to over-extend yourself by engaging in too many activities. Move one step at a time with the assurance that the results you are seeking are correct, reasonably planned and realized.

MANAGING GROWTH

7

Contributors

Neil C. Churchill is Professor Emeritus at INSEAD, and formerly Paul T. Babson Professor of Entrepreneurship and director of the Center for Entrepreneurial Studies at Babson College, Massachusetts.

Sandra Vandermerwe is Professor of Marketing and International Services and Chair of Management at Imperial College Management School.

Patricia P. McDougall is Senior Fellow in the Johnson Center for Entrepreneurship and Innovation at Indiana University's Kelley School of Business, USA.

John W. Mullins is Associate Professor of Marketing at the University of Denver's Daniels College. His research interests include marketing strategy, risk, and the factors that facilitate the growth of new products and new companies.

Rodney C. Shrader is Assistant Professor of entrepreneurial studies at the University of Illinois at Chicago, USA.

Bernard Taylor is Executive Director of the Centre for Board Effectiveness at Henley Management College, UK.

Benjamin M. Oviatt is Director of the Herman J. Russell Senior, International Center for Entrepreneurship at Georgia State University in Atlanta, Georgia, USA.

Fernando Bartolomé is Professor of Management at the Instituto de Empresa in Madrid and Visiting Professor of Organizational Behavior at INSEAD. His research interests include individual and interpersonal behavior.

Jonathan Levie is a member of the Strathclyde Entrepreneurship Initiative at the University of Strathclyde, Scotland.

Hans A. Breuninger is a Senior Consultant at Management Partner in Stuttgart.

Michael Hay is Associate Professor of Strategic and International Management at London Business School and Director of the Foundation for Entrepreneurial Management.

Contents

Introduction

Part 7 explores the issue of growth. We begin by asking the important question: "Why grow?" It is important because the vast majority of new ventures clearly do not grow to any great extent – and part of this must be by choice. We then examine the various stages that an enterprise may go through as the company develops. In particular, we look at two key elements for success – appropriate marketing strategies for a growing venture, and the balance that the entrepreneur must strike between "home and work." We conclude by looking at the factors that define successful entrepreneurship.

To grow or not to grow

Sue Birley considers issues involved in the decision whether or not to grow a business.

Throughout this series, there is an implicit assumption that anyone who starts a business will also want to grow it. Yet we know that there are countless people who deliberately start what we choose to call lifestyle ventures – those where self-employment or low employment is the primary aim. Despite this, we constantly hear politicians across the world using the immortal phrase "if every small business would employ just one more person, our unemployment problems would be solved." Suffice to say, this is a little naive. Certainly, these same politicians do not appear to hear the silent response of "why should I?" This is a powerful question and one that is important to pose – and to understand – especially as we consider Parts 7 and 8 of *Mastering Entrepreneurship*, which are dedicated to growing the entrepreneurial venture.

I will attempt to explain by referring to a study that I have just completed for the accountancy firm Grant Thornton, *The Family and the Business* [2000, Grant Thornton, Melton Street, London]. The study was conducted by academics in 16 countries across the world including the US, Japan, Poland, Germany and the UK. In this, we asked one simple question: What are your nightmares?

We used this terminology because we believe that most of the issues that concern the owner-manager can elicit very emotional responses. Overall, the issues that generated the most concern were, in rank order:

- All my wealth is in the business; what happens if it gets into trouble?
- What happens if my partner and I have a serious disagreement?
- Would outside shareholders change the way I run the business?
- If I introduce outside shareholders, how greedy will they be?
- Could the business do better for me?

Moreover, more than half were asking themselves: "Do I really need to grow the business?" and "How much would life change if I did grow the business?"

This was not, however, a universal pattern. Responses varied by country. For example, issues of growth and the maintenance of control were serious nightmares for the Japanese. In the US, more than a third of respondents admitted to nightmares over the introduction of outside shareholders, and a further third agreed that this was of concern.

What is behind this? It is quite simple. A large number of owner-managers in all countries are, in effect, saying: "The business is the source of my income, my wealth and my pension and I am worried that if I lose control it may unravel, leaving me with nothing ... and, in any case, I started the business to be independent and in control of my own future, not to hand it over to others."

How do we answer this? In two ways:

- We know that the majority of companies that fail are small and young. In other words, the larger, and thus more credible, the business, the greater the chances of survival. This makes intuitive sense.

- A significant minority of those who responded to the study were, in fact, relatively relaxed about these issues – and they were the ones who had taken the plunge, diluted, and grown their business.

Clearly, therefore, whatever their final decision, growth is an issue that exercises all owner-managers. Since we had earlier conducted the pilot for the above study in the UK, we explored this particular issue further in the annual *European Business Survey* (Grant Thornton International and Business Strategies Ltd, ISBN 1 874378 09 6) of entrepreneurs in 17 countries across Europe by asking respondents: "What personal goals matter to you when making business decisions?" The results are consistent with the above study. The relationship between growth and control is key.

However, this is still a simple view. We know that the sector is heterogeneous, that all owner-managers do not have the same set of goals, and that goals may change as both they and the business age. Therefore, we looked for patterns and found four consistent themes. We called them:

- **the protectionists** who wanted to maintain their business at its current size, thus protecting their investment
- **the business oriented** who combined growth and control goals with a need both to protect their income and their investment
- **the dynasts** who wanted to grow their business, protect their investment and pass it on to the next generation
- **the family businesses** who wanted to keep the business at the current size and pass it on to the next generation.

They exist in all countries – but not in the same proportions.

International entrepreneurs: risk takers or risk managers?

Patricia P. McDougall, **Rodney C. Shrader** and **Benjamin M. Oviatt** discuss the particular issue faced by those entrepreneurs moving into international markets.

Ask almost anyone what an entrepreneur is and they will tell you that an entrepreneur is a "risk taker." Thus, our research showing that entrepreneurs who expand their young ventures into international markets should more appropriately be termed "risk managers" may be surprising to many.

In the past decade, entrepreneurial ventures have begun to internationalize at an earlier age and with a smaller size than usually expected. In fact, a small number of cutting-edge firms, which we refer to as "global start-ups," are competing in the international marketplace from inception. With all the inherent risks of relatively small size and newness, we have been interested in understanding how the entrepreneurs of such businesses handle the additional strategic risks of entering foreign markets so early in their existence.

Given the high failure rates of new firms, entrepreneurs who start companies may be among the highest risk takers in society. Yet it must also be recognized that entrepreneurs can significantly influence some aspects of risk. Our research indicates that entrepreneurs entering international markets do indeed attempt to "manage" risks. That is, they make calculated risk trade-offs between three factors – the political/economic riskiness of the country entered, the level of resource commitment to the country, and the proportion of firm revenue being derived from a specific foreign location.

As part of our ten-year and nine-country research on the internationalization of new and young firms, we studied 214 US firms that went public (i.e. made initial public offerings) within six years of founding. Since it takes a venture at least eight years to begin to resemble and act like an established firm, these young firms are essentially new ventures. Firms with new IPOs nearly always have a strong focus on growth, and many of them sought growth by competing in the international marketplace. Of the 214 firms studied, 41 percent were selling their products or services in international markets by the time of their public offering. Most ventures earned between 10 and 40 percent of sales from foreign markets; however, some ventures reported 90 percent or more in international sales.

Competing internationally

Conducting international business is inherently risky. The risk involves the potential loss of profits and assets as a result of changes in political, legal, or economic factors in foreign markets in which the firm participates. The firm is venturing into unknown territory, where lack of market expertise may result in wasted resources or even failure.

While stories abound of entrepreneurs who stumble into the international marketplace with no apparent plan, the ventures we studied pursued international expansion with a clear, strategic approach of risk trade-offs. Contrary to popular perception, these "risk managers" do not haphazardly enter foreign countries through any means possible and then just sell whatever they can sell. Instead, we found a pattern of trading off one type of international risk against another.

To understand international risk trade-offs, let's consider three foreign market decisions that have a direct impact on the risks confronting a venture.

- **Country entered** – countries vary significantly in the political and economic risks of doing business there. For example, a firm entering Belgium is subject to far less risk than a firm entering Russia. Entering a higher risk country increases the likelihood of loss due to increased political and economic volatility. Firms have significant discretion over the specific markets they choose to enter, and their country choices may be more or less risky.
- **Method of entry** – there are many avenues of entry into foreign markets. For example, firms may elect to serve a foreign market through exporting, licensing, franchising, joint ventures, or fully-owned production subsidiaries. An entry method such as exporting represents much less of a commitment of resources than if the firm built a production facility or established a subsidiary in the

country. If conditions sour, the exporter can much more easily redeploy their resources than can a firm competing in a country through a joint venture agreement or one that has built facilities in the country.

■ **Level of sales for a foreign location** – the more a firm relies on a particular foreign market for its sales, the greater its potential loss if that market becomes less attractive due to such factors as foreign government action, economic downturns, exchange rate fluctuations, logistical complexities, communication difficulties, and other problems.

How risk trade-offs work

Conner Peripherals started business in 1986 to design, manufacture and market 3½in Winchester disk drives. By Conner's sixth year of full operations, the company had attained an astounding sales level of $2.238 billion, with 61 percent of those sales to foreign customers. The large majority of Conner's foreign sales were to relatively low-risk markets in Europe and Japan. (At that point in time, Japan had a strong and stable economy and was rated as one of the world's least risky foreign markets.)

The company made high commitment equity investments in two low-risk countries. Conner built manufacturing facilities in Scotland and invested in a majority-owned joint venture in Italy. Connor also earned sales in several high-risk countries; however, sales in high-risk countries were so small that the company did not even report exact dollar values of these. In high-risk countries, Connor did not invest in opening sales offices or establishing manufacturing operations, but relied on the low-risk entry method of using third-party distributors.

We observed this pattern of managing international risks over and over in the firms we studied. Another company that closely followed this pattern was Cisco Systems, Inc. which was founded at the end of 1984 by Stanford University computer scientists. During the first two years of the firm's existence its founders worked without pay to design and develop its computer internet working products. The company began to sell in volume in 1987 and by 1988 16 percent of the firm's sales were in foreign markets. By its sixth full year of operations, Cisco's sales were nearly $70 million, with almost 30 percent of sales coming from foreign markets. Cisco's foreign sales were concentrated in Canada and France, both low-risk countries. Cisco made a strong commitment to these two markets by opening foreign sales offices. In contrast, when Cisco entered higher-risk countries such as Greece, Korea and Taiwan, they used relatively low-risk exporting through third-party distributors and relied on each of those countries for a very small percentage of sales. While they don't identify specific countries in the Middle East and Africa, company executives reported low levels of sales through exporting in these markets.

During the 1990s when the internet became a vital international communication medium, Cisco's technology was in strong demand, and what had been a struggling start-up quickly became one of the largest, most successful, and most widely recognized technology companies around the world.

How do early internationalizers perform?

"How will the firm perform?" is a key question any entrepreneur seeking growth through international expansion must ask. But for new and young ventures, it is not even clear how performance should be measured. Established firms typically seek profitability and steady growth. Profitability may or may not be the key concern of the new venture that is trying to get a foothold in a market, as can be seen from the high stock market valuations achieved in the late 1990s by profit-less but rapidly growing "dot.com" companies.

For high-potential ventures such as firms with recent IPOs, growth is nearly always the key dimension on which performance is assessed. We compared our international new ventures with their domestic counterparts on several traditional performance measures. The internationalizers outperformed the domestic firms in sales growth and earnings per share. In terms of profitability, there was no significant difference. Thus, we found no profitability penalty for young ventures wishing to enter international markets, and much to be gained in growth.

Should ventures internationalize early or wait?

Prior to about 1990, ventures were advised against international expansion until after they had become firmly established within their domestic markets. Academics encouraged a "stages theory of internationalization," whereby a firm first establishes itself in its home market. The firm then gradually progresses to exporting, and if successful, moves to establish distribution channels abroad. Only after the firm gains knowledge of foreign markets, languages, and cultures should the firm make more advanced investments such as joint ventures or foreign direct investment. The majority of firms in today's market still internationalize incrementally, albeit at an accelerated pace.

But as we sit at the threshold of the new millennium, it is clear that times have changed. Increasing numbers of new and small firms in many countries conduct business internationally. An 18-country study by the Organisation for Economic Cooperation and Development reveals that 1–2 percent of small manufacturing firms are estimated to be international at inception. Although that percentage may seem small now, it represents at least 30,000–40,000 firms worldwide, and the number is increasing. Furthermore, OECD predicts that within seven years a third of all small and medium-sized enterprises will derive a major portion of their revenues from international sources.

Why are some entrepreneurs pushing their ventures into international markets earlier and with greater involvement? The answer is two-fold: enabling factors, and necessity.

Technological change in the past 15 years has been the primary enabler of accelerated internationalization. Dramatic increases in the speed, quality, and efficiency of international communications and transportation mean that today's entrepreneurial venture may not be severely disadvantaged when competing with large, established firms in the international arena. Today, even a firm as small as one employee can become international through a web site with its international communications being inexpensive and almost instantaneous. In sharp contrast, consider the "dialer" job position in the 1950s in a New York City bank. The dialer's job was to dial the phone for an executive to get a South American connection. It wasn't that the executive was simply lazy; the reality was that it sometimes took as much as four hours to successfully place the call. The internet, faxes, electronic data interchange, satellite hook-ups, and a host of other telecommunication advances have broken the once natural barriers that distance and geography were to international markets.

International telephone and airfare prices have become more competitive. We recently observed a four-person venture less than a year old traveling to Bangalore, India to seek inexpensive software code writers as well as sales contracts. In short, international business is no longer the nearly exclusive preserve of large, mature, multinational corporations. Competitive advantage has shifted away from firms with large size and long experience toward firms with unique knowledge and swift response capabilities.

Other enablers globalizing the marketplace are falling government trade and investment barriers, innovations in process technologies that permit small-scale firms to compete effectively with large-scale firms, and the worldwide availability of investment capital. When Cambridge-based software company IXI Ltd sought capital, it didn't rely solely on its English investors. As IXI's founder Ray Anderson related to us in a 1992 interview, IXI's investments from Germany, Austria, and Japan helped the venture to be an early internationalizer.

In some high-technology industries, internationalization appears to be a requirement for participation for even the smallest and newest firms. There are no geographically protected niches and competing internationally is a necessity. For the product to be competitive it must be world class, not just good enough for the home market. It becomes a requirement to have a market presence in certain locations in order to be aware of technology trends and changes in customer requirements. While the international IPOs we studied were in industries as diverse as sporting goods and entertainment, the vast majority – 89 percent – competed in high-tech industries.

In closing, our interviews with international entrepreneurs and investors lead us to the conclusion that a compelling reason to internationalize early is to combat the domestic inertia that invariably creeps in on ventures that defer internationalization. Ironically, the more successful the organization, the greater the inertial drag effect typically. Organizational processes and structures become deeply embedded and employees quite simply get used to doing things a certain way, such that internationalization is disruptive to the firm.

Firms that internationalize immediately have a world vision. As a top manager of Technomed International, S.A., a French producer of medical equipment, stressed to us, the advantage of starting internationally is that an international spirit is established from the beginning. Technomed sees itself and competes as a world company, not as a French company. If a firm internationalizes early it is more likely, and will find it easier, to embrace an international identity. Just as children learn to ski more easily than adults, young ventures are likely to adapt more quickly to the international marketplace than will established domestic firms. International entrepreneurs seem to realize that ventures will not develop international competencies except by practicing international business.

The six key phases of company growth

Neil Churchill describes the six phases of growth – and sometimes extinction – common to almost every company.

Entrepreneurship is widely recognized as an activity that creates value. This, in turn, is usually seen as starting a new venture – recognizing an opportunity, fashioning it to suit the entrepreneur, acquiring the resources to pursue it and then capturing the opportunity by creating a company.

However without discounting the importance of starting a business – for nothing occurs without the start – the value is really created as the enterprise grows, creates jobs, satisfies the needs of more and more customers and, in the process, makes money for the stockholders. All of which creates value for society. A growing company continues to create value if it spawns more and more new products or services, creates more jobs, pays more taxes and so on – that is, renews itself after each product cycle.

This article describes the different periods, phases or stages of growth most successful companies experience and the nature of the changes that occur. A second article, on p. 275, examines the problems most often encountered in these stages and some solutions that have been successfully used. Finally, a third article, divided into two parts on pp. 271 and 298, deals with one of these major problems – cash – and why it is so important and how to manage it on a company and product-market basis.

Each stage of growth has its own challenges and these challenges can be approached in a number of ways.

One such framework was developed in the early 1980s and has been used ever since by entrepreneurs and consultants. It was re-examined in 1994, updated (five stages, one with two sub-stages, became six stages) and deemed by several hundred owner/managers to be applicable in helping them assess what skills and resources were needed both for the present and the future. Owners who can assess the stage at which their companies are operating can use the framework to understand better existing problems and anticipate further challenges.

The framework covers six stages of development (*see* Figure 1). Each stage is characterized by an index of increasing size, complexity and/or dispersion and described by five management factors: managerial style; organizational structure; extent of formal systems; major strategic goals; and the owner's involvement in the business.

Stage 1: Conception/existence

In this stage the company has not really come into existence. This is because (a) it is still somewhat conceptual, or (b) it has not solved the problem of obtaining customers, or (c) it cannot deliver the product or service contracted for in the necessary quantity or with the necessary quality. Some key questions are:

- Can we get enough customers, deliver our products and provide services well enough to become a viable business?

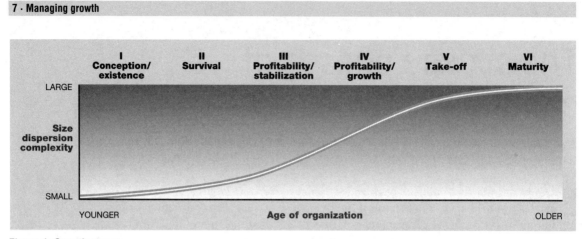

Figure 1: Growth stages

- Can we expand from that one key customer to a much broader sales base?
- Can we develop the product from a pilot production process to a production basis?
- Do we have enough money to cover the considerable cash demands of this start-up phase?

The organization is a simple one; the owner does everything and directly supervises subordinates, who in the main are of average competence. Systems and formal planning are minimal to non-existent. The company's strategy is simply to remain alive. The owner is the business, performs all the important tasks and is the major supplier of energy, direction and, with relatives and friends, capital.

Companies in the conception/existence stage range from newly started restaurants and retail stores to high-technology manufacturers that have yet to stabilize either production or product quality.

Many such companies or products never gain sufficient customer acceptance to become viable. In these cases the owners close the business when the start-up capital runs out and, if they are lucky, sell the business for some of its asset value. In other cases the owners cannot accept the demands the business places on their time, finance and energy and they quit. The companies that remain in business become Stage II enterprises.

Stage II: Survival

In reaching this stage the business has demonstrated that it is a workable business entity. It has enough customers and satisfies them sufficiently with its products or services to keep them. The key problem thus shifts from mere existence to the relationship between revenues and expenses. The main issues are as follows:

- *In the short run, can we generate enough cash to break even and to cover the repair or replacement of our capital assets as they wear out?*
- *Can we, at a minimum, generate enough cash flow to stay in business and to finance growth to a size that is sufficiently large, given our industry and market niche, to earn an economic return on our assets and labor?*

The organization is still simple. The company may have a limited number of employees supervised by a sales manager or a general foreman. Neither of them makes major decisions independently but instead carries out the rather well-defined orders of the owner.

Systems development is minimal. Formal planning is usually limited to cash forecasts and project plans. The major goal is still survival and the owner is still synonymous with the business.

In the survival stage the enterprise may grow in size and profitability and move on to Stage III. Or it may, as many companies do, remain at the survival stage for a long time.

These companies are often "hobby"-type businesses where the owner enjoys, for example, skiing and so runs a ski shop and the non-economic aspects of the enterprise are positive. Also, these can be family businesses, such as small restaurants employing a number of extended family members.

In many cases these businesses become profitable and move to the next stage. In others the founders have chosen non-viable enterprises in an overcrowded industry (often the case), badly located or faulty in conception and they cannot, or refuse to, do what is needed to make them profitable. They operate these businesses until they die or retire and while some are sold or passed on to children who wish to change them, most just cease operating and drop out of sight.

Stage III: Profitability and stabilization

In this stage the company has attained true economic health, has sufficient size and product-market penetration to ensure economic success, and earns average or above-average profits. The company can stay at this stage indefinitely provided environmental change does not destroy its market niche or ineffective management reduce its competitive abilities.

Organizationally, the company has, in many cases, grown large enough to require functional managers to take over certain duties performed by the owner. The managers should be competent but need not be of the highest caliber since their upward potential is limited by corporate goals.

Cash is plentiful and the main concern is to avoid a cash drain in prosperous periods to the detriment of the company's ability to withstand the inevitable rough times.

In addition, the first professional staff members come on board, usually a controller in the office and perhaps a production scheduler in the plant. Basic financial, marketing and production systems are in place. Planning in the form of operational budgets supports functional delegation.

The owner and, to a lesser extent, the company's managers should be monitoring a strategy essentially to maintain the status quo. As the business matures, it and the owner increasingly move apart, to some extent because of the presence of other managers.

Many companies continue for long periods in the stability stage. The product-market niche of some does not permit growth – this is the case for many service businesses in small or medium-sized slowly growing communities and for franchise holders with limited territories.

Other owners actually choose this route. If the company can continue to adapt to environmental changes, it can continue as is, be sold or merged at a profit or subsequently be stimulated into growth. For franchise holders this last option would necessitate the purchase of other franchises.

If the company cannot adapt to changing circumstances, as was the case with many automobile dealers in the late 1970s and early 1980s, it will either fold or drop back to a marginally surviving company.

Stage IV: Profitability and growth

In this stage the owner-manager consolidates the company and marshals resources for growth. He takes the cash and the established borrowing power of the company and puts it to risk to finance growth.

The important tasks include making sure that the business stays profitable so that it will not outrun its basic source of cash, to hire – a bit in advance – and develop managers of a higher quality than those needed to run a stable company. They will have to address the tasks of attaining a higher level of activity and managing it successfully once there.

Better systems are needed and attention should be given to forthcoming needs. Operational planning is delegated and strategic planning is shared with the key managers. The owner continues as the owner-manager and is active in all phases of the company's affairs.

If it is successful, the growth company may make a commitment to a higher growth rate and transition to Stage V – the take-off stage. Indeed, Stage IV is often a first attempt at growing, say regionally, before making a total commitment to growth. If a Stage IV company is unsuccessful, the cause may be detected in time for the company to shift to Stage III. If not, Stage II may be possible prior to bankruptcy or a distress sale.

Stage V: Take-off

In this stage the key problem is determining means to achieve rapid growth and how to finance it when it occurs. The most important problems that then follow are delegation, cash management and cost control.

Delegation

Can the owner delegate responsibility to others to improve the managerial effectiveness of a fast-growing and increasingly complex enterprise? Further, will there be true delegation, with controls on performance and a willingness to see mistakes made, or will it be abdication, as is so often the case?

Cash

Will there be enough cash from operations and savings to satisfy the great demands growth brings? If not, where and how can additional financing be obtained? Will the owner tolerate a high debt–equity ratio or a dilution of owner's equity?

Cost control

Rapid growth can bring such demands on managers and at such a frantic pace that things begin to "slip though the cracks" as time is spent hiring and training new people, and dealing with new and larger problems. Further, as growth can cover normal signals, there may be inadequate warnings to alert the overworked management to what is going wrong.

The organization is decentralized and, at least in part, divisionalized – usually either in sales or production. The key managers must be sufficiently competent to handle a growing and complex business environment. Systems, strained by growth, are becoming more refined and extensive. A considerable amount of planning is being done that deeply involves all key managers. While the managerial staff has grown considerably, the company is still dominated by both the owner-manager's presence and ownership control.

This is a pivotal period in a company's life. If the owner rises to the challenge of a growing company, both financially and managerially, it can become a big business. If not, it can usually be sold – at a profit – provided the owner recognizes his or her limitations soon enough.

Too often, those who bring the business through the previous stages are unsuccessful in Stage V, either because they try to grow too fast and run out of cash (the owner falls victim to the omnipotence syndrome) or are unable to delegate effectively (the omniscience syndrome).

It is, of course, possible for the company to traverse this high-growth stage without the original management. It is not uncommon for the entrepreneur who founded the company and brought it to success to be replaced either voluntarily or involuntarily by the company's investors or creditors.

If the company fails to make the big time, it may be able to retrench and continue as a successful and substantial company in a state of equilibrium. It may drop back to Stage IV or, if the problems are too extensive, it may drop all the way back to the survival stage or even fail.

Stage VI: Maturity

The greatest concerns of a company entering this stage are, first, to consolidate and control the financial gains brought on by rapid growth and, second, to retain the advantages of small size including flexibility of response and the entrepreneurial spirit.

The corporation must expand the management force fast enough to eliminate the inefficiencies that growth can produce and professionalize the company by use of such tools as budgets, management by objectives, and standard cost systems – and do this without stifling its entrepreneurial qualities.

A company in Stage VI has the staff and financial resources to engage in detailed operational and strategic planning. The management is decentralized, adequately staffed and experienced. And systems are extensive and well developed. The owner and the business are quite separate, both financially and operationally.

The company has now arrived. It has the advantages of size, financial resources and managerial talent. If it can preserve its entrepreneurial spirit, it will be a formidable force in the market. If not, it may enter a seventh stage of sorts: ossification.

Ossification is characterized by a lack of innovative decision making and the avoidance of risks. It seems most common in large corporations whose sizeable market share, buying power and financial resources keep them viable until there is a major change in the environment.

Unfortunately for these businesses, it is usually their rapidly growing competitors that notice the environmental change first.

Conclusion

The findings of the various studies involved in the development of the six-stage model strongly suggest that the levels of chief executive leadership/management skills, management team functioning and organizational culture are related to the

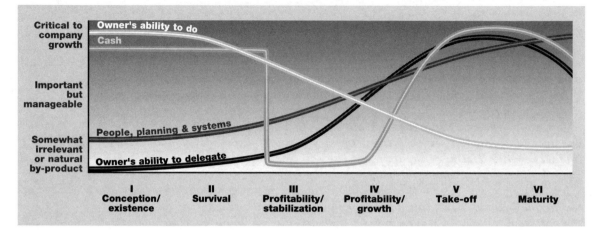

Figure 2: Management factors and stages

financial performance of organizations.

Specific skills such as vision, communications, leadership, delegating and performance facilitation are positively related to company performance. Chief executives and management teams who rate low in these skills have lower company financial performance than those who rated higher in the same areas.

Further, maintaining these skills as the organization grows can be challenging. In many companies, the higher the rate of sales growth, the lower the level of the organizational culture factors mentioned above that relate to profitability. To maintain or improve profit margins, management must focus on those elements that apparently become more difficult to execute often or well as the company grows.

The changing nature of managerial challenge becomes apparent when one examines Figure 2. In the early stages the owner's ability to delegate is on the bottom of the scale since there are few if any employees to delegate to, but it becomes critical later as the company grows. In contrast, the owner's ability to do the job in these early stages gives life to the business. Small businesses are built on the owner's talents: the ability to sell, produce, invent or whatever. This factor is thus of the highest importance.

As the company grows, other people enter sales, production or engineering and they first support and then even supplant the owner's skills, thus reducing the importance of this factor. At the same time the owner must spend less time doing and more time managing. He or she must increase the amount of work done through other people, which means delegating. The inability of many founders to let go of doing and to begin managing and delegating explains the demise of many businesses in Stage IV.

The owner contemplating a growth strategy must understand the change in personal activities such a decision entails and examine the managerial needs depicted in Figure 2. Similarly, an entrepreneur contemplating starting a business should recognize the need to do all the selling, manufacturing or engineering from the beginning, along with managing cash and planning the business's course – requirements that take much energy and commitment.

The importance of cash changes as the business changes. It is an extremely important resource at the start, becomes easily manageable at the success stage, and is a main concern again if the organization begins to grow. As growth slows at the end of Stage V or in Stage VI, cash becomes a manageable factor again. Companies in Stage IV need to recognize the financial needs and risks entailed in a move to Stage V.

The issues of people, planning and systems gradually increase in importance as the company progresses from slow initial growth to rapid growth. These resources must be acquired somewhat in advance of the growth stage so that they are in place when needed.

A company's development stage determines the managerial factors that must be dealt with. Its plans help determine which factors will eventually have to be faced. Knowing its development stage and future plans enables managers, consultants and investors to make more informed choices and to prepare themselves and their companies for later challenges.

While each enterprise is unique in many ways, all face similar problems and all are subject to great changes. That may well be why being an owner is so much fun and such a challenge.

Life beyond the "kitchen" culture

Jonathan Levie and **Michael Hay** explain why so few young companies enjoy significant growth, and offer some solutions.

Every year, literally millions of new enterprises are founded around the world. Very few of these grow significantly; yet those that do contribute disproportionately to exports, employment and growth of their nations' economies. Why do so few young companies grow in a meaningful way, and what can be done about it? This article addresses these questions.

The dilemmas of growth

Entrepreneurs are regularly faced with dilemmas of growth. For example, consider the case of a young business with one successful though increasingly uncompetitive product. New product development costs money and since young companies usually have little in the way of retained earnings, outside equity is often the only option. The requirement to generate a return for the new shareholders almost certainly means that the company must grow in size and scope. Should the entrepreneur accept a dilution of ownership in return for the funds?

Let's assume our company successfully develops its second major product. Some time later, it gets a large order from a multinational. The order represents 50 percent of its present annual capacity, which is already 80 percent filled. Should the entrepreneur accept the order?

This may not be an easy decision. Further outside finance may be needed to fund the necessary expansion in fixed and current assets (in this case, debt may be an option). In addition, the increase in size of the organization may require the entrepreneur to change the way the business is run, effectively reducing his or her direct control of day-to-day operations.

The issues that created dilemmas of growth for our hypothetical entrepreneur were intense competition and static markets, increased organizational complexity, and greater reliance on external resource providers. According to survey research conducted at London Business School,[1] most owner/managers resolve these issues by treating them as barriers to growth rather than as agents for change.

We compared the results of three UK-wide surveys of small and medium-sized private companies conducted in 1992, 1994 and 1995 and found that perceptions of barriers to growth changed little with the economic cycle.

The most commonly cited major *external* barrier to growth was a market characterized by intense competition and lack of growth. Relatively few respondents included lack of access to finance, labor or equipment as major barriers. Two main *internal* barriers to growth recurred in all three surveys: management capability to handle growth, and owner/managers' reluctance to cede perceived control in return for growth finance (either equity or debt).

A common strategy for living with these perceived barriers is to identify and hold some small protected market niche and practice financial and managerial self-sufficiency. However, low barriers to entry to the industry (in printing, for example) or market or technological instability (in software, for example) reduce the feasibility of such a strategy.

If management is unable or unwilling to grow out of its present strategic position of weakness, competition will intensify over time as more capable (or simply more resource-rich) competitors enter its domain.

Respondents in the survey may not have fully appreciated this link between internal and external barriers. Those who recognized internal barriers as very important tended to come from low-growth businesses. Yet when asked to weight the relative importance of internal versus external barriers to growth, respondents tended to give greater weight to the external barriers.

The control barrier

In our view, the first barrier to be overcome is the control barrier. This is the perception that to gain the resources needed for the organization to grow and thereby survive, the entrepreneur must surrender control of the company – to new shareholders, to bankers, and to others in the organization.

Many owner/managers refuse to grow their companies because they associate growth with loss of control. We argue that this association is based on an inappropriate model of management and that, if this is recognized, focus can then shift to the more real barrier of management capability for growth.

Our main point is that by thinking in terms of control – rather than use – of assets, the entrepreneur is using old models of capitalism that equate ownership with control and old models of administrative thinking that see control as the only form of management. Research in the US has shown that high-growth companies make greater use of external resources than low-growth companies. In other words, the agenda of management in high-growth businesses is not control or ownership but use of assets. This conceptual difference is not just about renting rather than owning. It is fundamentally about how to manage assets.

Research in the US reveals that chief executives of higher-growth companies put greater emphasis on developing an organizational culture that motivates employees and on creating and communicating a vision for the organization's future. This motivation and communication are transmitted both within the business and to the owners of external resources. Successful motivation and communication by chief executives (as measured by their staff) were associated with higher sales and higher returns on investment.

The research found, however, that during rapid growth, these important behaviors often came under intense pressure and profitability declined. A major reason may well be that chief executives were just too busy fire fighting at operational level or immersed in the new challenges that growth brings (such as communicating with new stakeholders) to fulfill the crucial role of motivator and communicator to the organization and its other resource providers.

Inside the organization

Let us describe what growth is like for unprepared organizations. A frequent complaint of both entrepreneurs and of their staff is that the culture of the company becomes colder as the organization grows.

As one Danish entrepreneur put it, the culture of the very young company is like that of the family kitchen – warm, intimate, where problems are shared and solutions sought informally, and where there is a clear sense of togetherness. Then, as more and more strangers enter and the kitchen expands to accommodate them, it becomes more of an impersonal institution. The entrepreneur complains that he or she doesn't know everyone's name any more. Staff who were there from the early days complain that relations with the entrepreneur are not what they were.

This estrangement results in misunderstandings, resentment and jealousy of the "9-to-5" newcomers and of the staff appointees who have privileged access to the entrepreneur. Employee comments on the entrepreneur such as "he's changed," "she is more remote," "he only cares about making more money now" are typical.

As relationships become more distant, performance measurement becomes more formal. Long-serving employees get passed over for promotion and personnel problems fester. Staff turnover increases, or the threat of unionization looms. The entrepreneur cannot understand the change in atmosphere in the organization and looks back wistfully on the kitchen culture of yesterday.

These problems stem from a failure to communicate the changes that are taking place in the organization – and in the role of the entrepreneur. Frequently, rapid growth means that the entrepreneur will be devoting more time to managing external resources, such as major foreign customers, merchant banks, corporate shareholders, the media, and the stock market. This tends to take up much more of entrepreneurs' time – away from the company – than they expected. All their staff see of this is that they are not available the way they used to be.

To make matters worse, the entrepreneur's former colleagues are now supposed to report to new functional managers, often recruited from larger organizations. These new managers tend to change the information flows inside the organization from a web to multiple vertical funnels because this is how they were trained. Large-company systems and structures, however, may actually impede growth in a smaller organization, whose strength comes from the rapid and focussed combination of cross-functional skills.

Faced with this scenario of the future, it is no wonder that so many owner/managers of young businesses are reluctant to grow. Is there an alternative to this unhappy path of corporate evolution? The answer is yes.

Turning barriers to growth into agents for change

First, the entrepreneur has to be conscious of his or her critical role as principal communicator of the changes that are and will be taking place, both in the company and in the role of the entrepreneur within it. Organizations undergoing change need a strong figurehead. Research shows that the chief executive's efforts on this dimension are critical.

Second, one structural solution, used by many successful entrepreneurial organizations, is to replicate, rather than replace, the old kitchen culture. This can be done by superimposing on the emerging functional structure a mosaic of project-focussed, interfunctional teams. Canny entrepreneurs bring in advisers, customers and suppliers as team members where appropriate. These teams are formed in response to specific needs and disbanded when the project is complete.

Third, the entrepreneur has to match the financial growth targets with appropriate individual and organizational growth targets. In young, growth-oriented firms, investment in people tends to run a poor second to investment in sales.[2] Yet the best actual growth is found in companies whose CEOs have a balanced mix of goals: customer satisfaction, financial strength, and organizational strength.

Leader of teams

The entrepreneur's role in team management, as with the original team he or she brought together in the kitchen, garage or rented premises, is to recruit, motivate, envision, resource, and reward the teams.

Conceptually, the multiple teams can be managed in the same way as the first team. (For example, reward systems still need to be based on collective results. In many start-ups, the entrepreneur will share some equity with the initial team. Significantly, our 1995 survey results suggested that businesses with employee share ownership schemes tended to have faster growth over the previous five-year period than companies with other incentives such as performance or profit-related pay.) There is one important difference, however, between then and now. This time, the entrepreneur will not be able to lead the team because there is not one team but many.

The transition from team leader to leader of teams can be extremely difficult for an entrepreneur, who became successful by doing, not by getting things done through others. Some entrepreneurs eventually realize that they are just not enjoying the new role and sell out or bring in outside management.

Research suggests, however, that bringing in new management is not necessarily the answer. The solution is to match the form of management to the phase of evolution of the organization. A young company undergoing rapid growth still needs entrepreneurial management. The role of the entrepreneur in a rapidly growing young business, however, is subtly different from that of the entrepreneur at start-up, as we have attempted to show.

External resource providers

The fear of loss of control to people inside the organization is an innate fear of entrepreneurs. Much more explicit is the fear of loss of control to outsiders, particularly financial resource providers such as bankers, venture capitalists and private equity investors (business angels).

This fear is valid, but only if the relationship with these resource providers is poorly developed. Failure to build and maintain close relationships of trust and mutual benefit with these resource providers can result in loaded legal agreements, persistent demands for time-consuming but trivial data, and unexpected withdrawal of resources just when they are most needed.

As with relationships inside the company, this is a communication issue. We have seen examples where a history of good communications maintained share prices during profit downturns, kept a bank manager calm as the company teetered on the brink of insolvency, and maintained the loyalty of customers during a product quality crisis.

Of course, some resource providers may not respond to the need of the young organization for long-term relationships of trust and mutual benefit. The path of growth is not smooth, and the entrepreneur will, at some stage, need to rely on those external resource providers to keep their nerve. If a relationship does not look like it will withstand difficult times, it is best to seek out a new partner. After all, resource providers should be agents for change, not barriers to growth.

Balanced excellence

The leaders of young, growth-oriented companies tend to have a strong external focus. They concentrate on growing markets and cultivating potential partners. They tend to have a blind spot when it comes to investing in people and processes, and as a result, organizational capability becomes outpaced by ambition. A key growth management skill, therefore, is to balance financial ambition with organizational ambition: to have everyone in the entrepreneurial organization develop and implement their own demanding set of personal development targets which will help deliver the entrepreneur's growth vision. That way, employees buy into the vision because it is ensuring their own development. And they, too, become agents for change, not barriers to growth.

1 Hay, M. and Khamshad, K. (1994) "Small firm growth: intentions, implementation and impediments," *Business Strategy Review* 5(3):49–68; *The Quest for Growth: a survey of UK private companies* (1994) London Business School/Binder Hamlyn; *The 1996 Pulse Survey: survival of the fittest* (1996) London Business School/Arthur Andersen/Binder Hamlyn.

2 *Linking Goals to Performance: the third pulse survey of private business* (1999) London Business School/Arthur Andersen.

Abilene Caterpillar

This case was written by **Neil C. Churchill**, Professor Emeritus at INSEAD. It is intended to be used as a basis for discussion rather than to illustrate either effective or ineffective handling of an administrative situation.

Stan Treanor took over the family's Caterpillar dealership in 1976 when sales were $23 million and equity was $3 million. During the following six years, business was very good, with sales increasing to $119 million and equity to $20 million – due strictly to earnings. Then in 1982, the market for oil collapsed and, since the company's main source of revenue was engines for drilling rigs, sales plummeted to $23 million. As Stan put it: "That didn't take any six years, so I had to learn very quickly to manage on the downside."

In the fall of 1981, Boone Pickens, the oil speculator, gave a talk at Abilene Christian University and mentioned that he could buy oil companies for their reserves cheaper than he could drill for them. At present day prices, Pickens said that if he drilled, he could get back only eighty cents on the dollar. This impressed Stan for, if everyone believed that, they wouldn't be doing any more drilling.

As Stan recalled: "This waved a red flag. And I started making some changes in the credit department. Also since I didn't know what was going to happen – neither how far down things would go nor how fast they would fall – I thought I should begin to trim the sails so I wouldn't capsize when the storm came. I didn't want to stop ordering inventory because if I was wrong, I would lose sales and incur opportunity costs. I just wanted to trim the sails and survive whatever storm would arise."

Stan began with receivables and almost immediately told his accounts receivable manager to tighten up on credit and collect all the account balances that were either getting large or were slow in collection. This was difficult for her because, as Stan said: "She was really nice and could handle customers wonderfully in an upside market because the customers loved her, but on the downside market she just couldn't get tough enough. I worked with her but she just couldn't do it. It got to where I would tell her that, 'If you don't get such and such a day's receivables down by such and such a date you're terminated.' But she just couldn't do it.

"I had to replace her and I did so with a guy who loved playing in that environment. He was probably the greatest credit manager I could have had and he did a great job. He rescued the company, but he became the victim since I later had to terminate him. I don't know what else I could have done; he had made so many customers mad at him and the sales department hated him although they understood why it was necessary that he did what he did after we'd got everything collected. But when we began to build relationships, we just couldn't do with him. It wouldn't work, so I had to get someone else. You go through a constructive destruction process; after we finished that we had to rebuild. It's sad but I don't know of any other way we could have done it."

Since Abilene had a practice of "carrying the paper" itself on customer sales rather than financing customers' purchases with the banks, the second thing Stan did was to sell them off to a finance company.

He sold all $15 million of these notes to CIT on a "non-recourse" basis at a price calculated on a 16 percent interest rate. Abilene had charged 21 percent or 22 percent interest when the notes were issued, as it had been a period of very high interest rates, so Abilene made a profit on the transaction. As Stan put it: "What I want to do is get rid of all those notes because if I had to start repossessing those tractors, then I'd have a bunch of used inventory in a downmarket and I didn't want that exposure. Making a profit was just a delightful bonus."

At the time of Pickens's speech, Abilene had 500 drilling engines in inventory and in non-cancellable orders that totaled about $30 million. Stan felt that these were too many and started to sell the engines and the rights to the orders to fellow dealers. They all thought he was crazy, as did Caterpillar, but he sold most of them for what they cost him and the rest at a variety of discounts. All during this period, Stan was still ordering items that were needed since the company kept selling and servicing equipment throughout the decline.

Stan's philosophy was: "If an item isn't creating enough value, liquidate it and do it quickly because the loss is already there whether you want to recognize it on the books or not." He closed down facilities, laid off people, and sold telephones, disks, fork-lift trucks, everything that he felt couldn't create value. He did it quickly and before others realized what was happening, stating: "I think it really saved us, because the people that waited really got little if anything for their assets."

Since Stan had no idea as to either how fast or how far the business would contract, he was concerned as to how he would deal with the employees. He considered putting everyone on half-hours or on four-day weeks; whether he should cut wages or whether he should lay off 25 percent or so at the start and more if things kept going down. He also realized that when he got down to the bottom, it would be very competitive and the companies that survived would be those which were the most efficient with the most productive people.

Stan had productivity rates that Caterpillar sent out to every one of its dealers. These contained information on the performance of each department for each Caterpillar dealer in the United States. This information included overall average productivity rates as well as the productivity rates of the best 25 percent of the dealers and the worst 25 percent of the dealers for each department. As an example, the average number of dollars each person would sell in the parts department was $400,000 per person per year, in the sales department, $1.5 million per person per year, and so on.

What fascinated Stan, and got him thinking, was the difference between the performance of the top and bottom 25 percent of the dealers in almost every department. He saw it this way: "What I saw was that the difference between the departmental performance of the best 25 percent of the dealers and the bottom 25 percent was three to one. For example, in the parts department, if the average was $400,000, for everyone, the 24 dealers in the top 25 percent category would average about $600,000 per person per year and the lower end $200,000. This three to one average difference from top to bottom, or 50 percent from the average to either extreme, was present in almost every department. It was almost unbelievable."

Stan decided that he would use the productivity rates to downsize his company. For each one of his departments, he set them slightly below those of the top 25 percent dealers. In parts, for example, instead of $600,000 he used $550,000. He then projected a three-month moving average of sales, annualized it, and divided it by the productivity figures. This produced the number of people that he should have in that department. He made the same calculation for each department, gave the managers the calculations, and instructed them to lay off the least productive people as they contracted towards the targets. The result was, in Stan's words: "As we contracted, the managers followed these calculations. As sales went down and down, we shrunk the company through three major layoffs."

The result in the service department was a 30 percent profit after allocated expenses but before interest and taxes where the average Caterpillar dealer's was typically 15 percent, and in the parts department, Abilene was at 12 percent and the average of the other dealers was 9 percent. As Stan put it: "We actually ended making more profit, after the contraction, in the parts and service departments than we did before, when things were good. It was just phenomenal." But he continued: "Terminating all those people was very difficult. But if you are going to survive, you are going to have to be the most effective producer in a buyer's market. In a seller's market you don't have to worry about efficiency, you're worrying about opportunity profits, but when the market goes down you've got to be worrying about efficiencies, costs and profits.

"It was hard to lay off people we had worked with for years, but when the house is on fire, you jump, you really have to move quickly. I tried to communicate with the people and with few exceptions, they understood and were not hostile. I had many employees who came up to me later on the street and said, 'Look, Stan, you don't remember but I used to work for you and I know you're going through a hard time and if things get turned around I'd like to come back and work for you, and we understand why you had to do it.' It's more how you lay off people. If you just send them a pink slip through the mail, that's pretty bad, but if you sit down and talk to them about the situation and why we have to deal and communicate, they understand."

The financial statements before and after the contraction showed a reduction in assets, equities and sales of 75 percent. Stan took the $56 million that he received from the collection of receivable and the sale of inventory and assets and paid $22 million to the banks, $15 million to his vendors, and retired $19 million in stock. As Stan stated: "Since our sales were down 75 percent, we were not utilizing our invested capital very well so we decreased the capitalization. There was no need for all that capital in the business any more."

During this period of decline, Abilene Caterpillar took a number of write-offs but continued to make profits on operations. Overall it had negative profits of 0.3 percent on sales the first year, in the second year a profit of 2.3 percent after tax, and in the third year, with the recession continuing, the company was out of the woods with a profit of 3.5 percent of sales.

Stan explained: "The hardest thing for me was to recognize emotionally and intellectually that our growth just couldn't go on. How many times do you hear all the big companies saying things like, 'Our purpose in Caterpillar is to grow in the future as much as we have in the past.' And while they were saying that, they lost $3 billion! I think the biggest problem that has to be dealt with is management's view of the organization's purpose. Intellectually you may know that you can't grow any more, there is nothing to grow on, but a lot of managers still keep adding and building and they go bust when their creditors come in on them. You have got to recognize that growth cannot be the purpose of an organization. The purpose is to serve society's needs. Thus, if society's needs contract in the area that you're managing, you need to contract the resources."

The above case is an abridged version. Copies of the complete case may be obtained from the European Case Clearing House, telephone (+44) 01234 750903; fax (+44) 01234 751125; e-mail ECCH@cranfield.ac.uk

The customer-focussed mission

Sandra Vandermerwe explains the power of customer focus to achieve entrepreneurial success.

Be they new, old, large or small, modern businesses can succeed only by being entrepreneurial. Yet being entrepreneurial without focussing efforts, energy and resources on customers does not lead to sustainable growth or success.

Driving and sustaining growth means getting bigger by getting better at identifying and articulating customer opportunities and turning these into commercial success stories that others cannot easily copy. It means going beyond just putting more innovative products and services on the market – quicker, faster, cheaper – to developing deep and lifelong relationships with customers in chosen markets by giving them exactly what they want when, where and how they want it.

The true marketing mindset is proactive

The true customer-focussed mindset is entrepreneurial because it involves having the imagination to perceive a world that doesn't yet exist and others do not immediately see. As all the classic entrepreneurs – such as the oft-quoted Bill Gates, Richard Branson and Jeff Bezos – have shown, being proactive means having the courage to anticipate rather than just respond to customers and thereby actually creating and becoming the future.

Being proactive also means recognizing that customers do not really know what they want, as the marketing textbooks would have had us believe in the past, and that therefore customers must often be led and educated to raise their expectations. The whole idea for entrepreneur Sherry Coutu, founder and Chairman of iii (Interactive Investor International), was to get ordinary people to self-identify as investors, rather than just savers (as most did), and to take control over their financial destinies. Thus she has succeeded in creating new wealth and opportunities rather than just stealing share from the traditionalists. Nearly half a million investors visit the iii site from which they get information, make their investment decisions, transact, and regularly monitor decisions.

However, being entrepreneurial means more than just "seeing" things differently or seeing different things. It involves knowing how to articulate imaginative ideas into language and concepts that others can and want to understand and make actionable. The customer-focussed mindset becomes a way of thinking, an organizing logic around which all decisions throughout the new or existing business can be made: what to do (and what not to do), who does what, how, when, where, how well and, increasingly, how best to invest e-business dollars.

Getting customer lock-on

The customer-focussed mindset seeks consciously to achieve customer "lock-on." Customers become part of an "installed base," or group of people who want the firm or institution as their dominant or sole choice on an on-going basis because they have good and sufficient reason. They then not only do business with the company or institution in ways different from the past, but they do so over time, even over a lifetime. This differs from the days where a customer would flit from supplier to supplier seeking the best deal, which typically meant the lowest price (though not the best long-term result).

Here it is not the product that keeps competitors out, nor is it the technical standard or the technology that protects an organization from rivals, but rather customers who by locking on to a company or institution become the barrier to competitive entry. And this lock-on becomes self-reinforcing: the more business the company does with an individual, the greater the intimacy, sharing of knowledge, ideas and information, the lower the costs and the greater the potential for *longevity of customer spend* (even over a lifetime), *depth of customer spend* (a greater share of wallet), *breadth of spend* (opportunities to sell value-added products and services), and *diversity of spend* (brand stretch into new areas).

The lifelong value of customers is central to this customer-focussed strategy, not margins on products, as is building a critical mass of these customers rather than making and moving more and more "core items," and acknowledging that the value of products, no matter how innovative, diminishes over time while the value of customers increases over time. "Lock-on" is different from "lock-in" where customers may be disenchanted by an industry but have no option because all players operate in the same way or the switching costs of changing are too high, or there is only one real supplier for as long as that technology wave lasts. In all cases companies lose out to newcomers.

Defining new "market spaces"

Businesses take off or renew themselves because they grow market and business instead of fighting for a larger share of a shrinking or profit-diminishing pie. They do this because entrepreneurs, be they newcomers or corporate, move from static definitions of market share in product or service categories to "market spaces."

Market share as a success indicator is dangerous – not only does it say nothing about markets, particularly future markets, but it hides them and disguises the real competitors. For example, while Lego, the legendary Danish toy maker, had a huge market share both in Europe (90 percent) and the world (72 percent), it was actually losing out on "families with kids spare time," the real issue, to videos, computers and other entertainment and learning innovations. To capture revenues in this total family edutainment market space, Lego has stretched its brand into theme parks, with plans that by the year 2050 most of the planet's population will be within half a day's drive of a LegoWorld.

The customer-focussed mindset deliberately looks for opportunities to add value in new "market spaces," explicitly expressing market space as a descriptor of what customers do/should do/could do to get the desired outcome or result, and taking a fully integrated view of the customer which cuts across traditional product and industry boundaries in which traditionalists get stuck.

For instance, while financial institutions kept themselves in their rigid silos, customers were looking for financial services that spanned events over their lives and broke through conventional boundaries, giving entrepreneurs such as iii's Sherry Coutu the gap she was looking for, or enabling Virgin to lock customers on by ensuring them liquidity, security and prosperity over a lifetime. Instead of being badgered to "pay back or else," customers who need extended credit to deal with various activities and events – both predictable and unpredictable – now deal with one company. They pay for all their cash transactions, including their mortgage scheme, insurance, loans and savings, in such a way that they have enough cash available until retirement, at which point they will have paid off what they owe and be able to get a fixed amount on their savings on which to live.

Market spaces focus energy and fix resources. This is important for both the newcomer or the enterprise struggling to recast itself entrepreneurially. IBM truly began to transform, pulling together the disparate products and services within and outside the company, only when global electronic networking capability was articulated as the "market space." The fact that Jeff Bezos did not look at books as his target but customer lock-on in the knowledge and information management and discovery market space programmed his initial strategy and had a lot to do with the way he differentiated Amazon and got the critical mass of customers which has set him apart and ahead.

Operating in the "customer's activity cycle"

Recognizing that value can be created only in the customer's space, the customer-focussed mindset understands and articulates activities in the "customer activity cycle" (CAC); *"pre"* the experience when they are deciding what to do, *"during"* the experience when they are doing it, and *"post"* the experience when they are keeping it going, updating and reviewing. The entrepreneur pushes to provide a total customer experience in chosen market spaces rather than providing just bits and pieces. He also recognizes that if value gaps or discontinuities happen in the customer activity cycle, companies (and even industries) become vulnerable, which is how newcomers become killer entrants. Looking beyond merely products, opportunities are "seen" because the critical value-adding activities customers go through are identified. The entrepreneur then works backward to ask:

- What are the opportunities for adding value?
- Who does what?
- What do we have to be good at in order to get the desired outcome for customers – now and in the future?

Entrepreneurs take advantage of the discontinuities or value gaps caused by complacent organizations and industries which are boxed into their own so-called "core offering." Together with partners they become best at doing whatever is needed to provide customers with a total experience in these "market spaces" and it is by getting continuously involved in these activities that they grow.

While IBM was thinking products instead of customer activities (*see* Figure 1), it gave others – which have subsequently grown as big as IBM – the gap they needed. By the time a consulting company such as Andersen Consulting had been with a corporate client for months, or a software house such as Microsoft had been working on a customer's systems and then training the staff, the best IBM could hope for was to win on price and specification. Maintenance and repair had become routine, reactive and slow at the old IBM, enabling "lean, keen and mean" third-party operators to fill the gap. Without a relationship base to review and update decisions, staying in the customer activity for the next cycle and creating lock-on became increasingly impossible.

Today we see a very different IBM, intent on delivering "global networking capabilities" where the core item (the PC) is becoming more and more incidental,

Figure 1: 'Value gaps' in the customer activity cycle: IBM customer (simplified)

mirroring what is going on in many industries. Growth is coming from entrepreneurial entities which create, provide and support value-added services through the CAC (such as in Figure 2).

Bezos did not just provide cheap books. Amazon got its lead because it found a way to add value to customers by taking the hassle out of buying books, i.e. getting to the store; looking for a book; waiting to be served; standing in queues to pay; lack of follow-up when books were not in stock; and when they were, having to go through the whole procedure again. And Gates has done the same in travel: though making quantities of difficult information easy for customers to get and use for

Figure 2: 'Value adds' in the CAC: new IBM (simplified)

travel decisions, "pre," "during" and "post" traveling activities, was always the prime role for travel agents (anyone can sell tickets), the traditional players simply didn't come up with a customer-focussed mission. So they lost their lead. Microsoft launched Expedia in the US, UK, Germany and France to provide all the value-added products and services needed to enable people to travel for business or pleasure, 24 hours a day, with data updated every half hour.

Virgin started challenging the capacity-managing commodity algorithm of taking people from A to B by offering limousine services to and from airports, which quickly mushroomed into several other value-added services to integrate both the customer's transcontinental business and their personal travel experience at each critical point in the activity cycle. But Richard Branson goes beyond filling gaps: he deliberately creates gaps to provide breakthrough value – for example his latest idea to convert an aircraft into a flying hotel and restaurant. By reducing the personal space allotted to business-class passengers during the take-off ("pre") and landing ("post") part of their travel experience, the extra space and part of the cargo will be converted into sleeping, leisure, eating and exercise areas "during" the long-haul experience where the real value is needed by customers.

Personalizing offerings

Being proactive means being able to anticipate what the customer wants because the enterprise has an intimate, integrated and long-term view of the customer. It means being precise, able, through the management of knowledge and use of new electronic technology, to know exactly what customers want, and having the capability and flexibility to deliver that to them – instead of only what the company makes, has in stock, or is promoting at that moment in time.

Customers are seen as individuals. The worst that could happen is to lose and have to replace these individuals because it presents not only a huge expense but also an opportunity cost in terms of longevity, breadth, depth, and diversity of spend. Innovations revolve around creatively using resources, information and technology to cater to the unique needs of these individuals. Amazon made it a priority to know who was buying its books. In this way, it took advantage of the fact that no one – neither publisher nor bookstore – in the traditional linear chain knew anything about end users and it made it its business to know the needs of individuals better than anyone else and to cater to them. Bezos said: "We know 2 percent today of what we will know ten years from now, and most of that learning is going to revolve around personalization – the notion of making a (cyber) store ideal for a particular customer, not for a mythic average customer."

Personalization is also about proactively adapting offerings to get desired outcomes. At iii the underlying philosophy of the technology interface is to get the maximum outcome to suit each unique investor's habits and profile as they gather assets. One example is looking into a customer's portfolio to determine which assets might be underweighted or overweighted: if a customer was underweighted in pensions, the system would alert the individual and would not only offer a set of analytic tools to assess the pros and cons of different pension plans, but also provide a link to these different offerings.

Mastering the art of connectivity

The reason that entrepreneurs reshape industries is because they redefine boundaries and amass partners with whom they network and align to produce on-going value around the customers' activity cycle. Knowing full well that customers respond holistically and want integrated experiences, and that they couldn't care less how companies are organized, who reports to whom or who owns what, they bring the correct people and entities together to form one value-creating delivery system, either from within or from without. The point is that they know they can't win alone and that they don't have to own or do everything themselves.

Skandia AFS, the Swedish-based financial company, has a constellation of alliances made up of local agents, financial advisers, brokers and bankers across the globe to build superior offerings for customers. With a growth rate of nearly 50 percent per annum, the company employs only around 2,200 people, but it uses the resources and collective learning of the 80,000-strong giant "federation network" which it converts into on-going customer value. Yet what are "seen" and "felt" by the customer are the flair and force of the Skandia employees linking and bonding with customers throughout their activity cycle.

Setting rigorous service quality standards is particularly important when working with partners who interface with customers. Direct Line (the first enterprise to sell insurance over the phone in the UK) wanted to be indispensable to customers when and where those customers needed it, not just sell them cheap motor insurance. So the company moved around the customer activity cycle into accident repair in the market space known as personal mobility. Its repair center consists of 140 shops, a set of independent players integrated under the Direct Line brand. The customer calls Direct Line when they have a problem, the car is picked up, fixed, returned, and automatically charged through their bank or card. Standards such as provision of a 24-hour recovery service, 24-hour collection and delivery to and from the customer's home, contacting the customer within 30 minutes of a call for help, and recovering the stranded vehicle within an hour are set and monitored by Direct Line.

Using the economics differently

The customer-focussed mindset adjusts its economic algorithm. Rather than try to make as much money up front as possible, it invests to get the customer lock-on. Rather than chase margin of single products/services/countries, it is interested in leveraging high-quality cash flow from the long-term value of the customer by getting longevity, depth, breadth, and diversity of spend. And it lowers its cost of acquisition and marginal costs of transaction the longer and stronger the customer relationship. It asks:

- What will customer lock-on take?
- What will it cost?
- What will we lose if we don't do it?
- What will that cost?

Being an entrepreneur, whether starting out or recasting an established corporation or unit, is not enough to get sustainable success. For that a customer-focussed mindset is needed. Conscious effort must go into understanding, articulating and communicating this logic to guide behavior and resources. They then can realize the real goal: to grow and sustain new business and wealth, taking the enterprise into a future yet to be defined which they themselves will help create.

Cash flows and the operating cash cycle

In this first of a two-part case study, **Neil Churchill** and **John Mullins** provide a model for determining the rate of growth a company can sustain from its own cash resources.

Doing business takes cash. Doing business, profitably, produces cash. The problem is that the cash usually goes out before it comes in.

When the business is growing, even more cash goes out before it comes in. Often when you are growing fast, the cash going out continues to exceed the cash coming in and you are forced to raise additional capital through loans and equity offerings.

We have all heard stories about a company that was growing at a rate of 20 percent or 25 percent a year and develops a new product or method of distribution. It suddenly finds itself growing at 50 percent or 100 percent a year. The owners are euphoric over their success, delighted with their profits, but dumbfounded when they find themselves out of cash and stopped dead in their tracks. Why does this happen?

Their cash required for growth in the next period exceeded the cash produced by the current period's sales. As this two-part article will demonstrate, when you exceed the rate of growth your past sales and normal credit terms can finance – your maximum internally financiable rate of growth, or MIFROG – you need additional capital, a need you must plan for in advance.

This article shows entrepreneurs how to examine cash inflows and outflows and use them to determine cash needs for growth. It provides the tools required to answer two critical questions for growing companies: how fast can we grow without the need for external financing beyond normal working capital sources, and how can we use asset management and operations management to increase the internally financiable rate of growth?

This rate of self-financiable growth, or MIFROG, is applicable to a company, to a product or product line, to a market segment (such as Germany or the US), or to distribution channels such as direct sales to consumers or through distributors. We now examine the key components of MIFROG: the operating cash cycle (OCC) and the amounts and duration of the cash flows within it.

The operating cash cycle

Every business has an operating cash cycle (*see* Figure 1). Companies invest cash in materials or merchandise, engage in various marketing and operating activities and then deliver and invoice for their product or service. Unfortunately, they must then wait until some time later to collect the accounts receivable and put the cash to use once more.

The length of the operating cycle determines the rapidity with which cash is used. The shorter the cycle, everything else being equal, the faster you can redeploy your cash and the faster you can grow from internal sources.

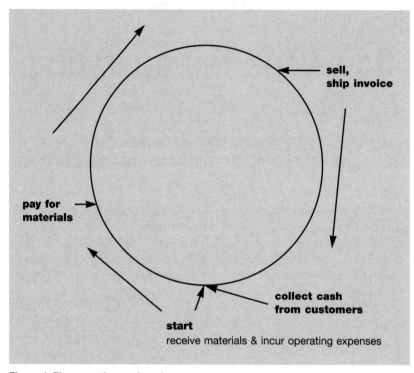

Figure 1: The operating cash cycle

Let's look at the operating cash cycle for a hypothetical retailing or distribution company, the M&C Company as described in Figure 2. This company holds its inventory for 80 days before it sells it. Its customers then wait 90 days before they pay their invoices. Thus M&C has a total cash-to-cash operating cycle of 170 days.

But not all the cash it puts out is tied up for the whole OCC, as we will see in the following section. Within the OCC, cash is tied up for longer or shorter durations depending on the timing of the outflows. Working back from the end of the cycle (bottom of Figure 2), M&C ties up cash in accounts receivable for 90 days, as described above. Prior to that it ties up cash in inventories for 80 days. However, its suppliers provide it with 30 days' trade credit, so its inventory cash is outstanding for only 50 days. Thus, M&C's total investment in working capital totals 140 days – the 90 days of accounts receivable plus the 80 days of inventory offset by the 30 days of trade credit – shown by the first shaded area in Figure 2.

Besides inventory and trade accounts receivable, M&C uses cash for everyday operating expenses. In the absence of accrued expenses or other credit, these expenses, such as weekly payroll, selling expenses, weekly utility bills and the like, occur all through the 170 days of the operating cash cycle. This is shown as an even flow in the shaded portion of the chart at the bottom of Figure 2.

We can calculate the amount of cash employed in the operating cycle by looking at M&C's cash flows in Figure 3. Thus to produce a dollar of sales we need $0.60 of cash for inventory (which becomes cost of goods sold) and $0.35 for operating expenses. Since the inventory/accounts receivable is not tied up for the whole OCC but only for 140 days, the cash employed for cost of goods sold is $0.60 × 140/170 days or $0.494. For a dollar of sales we also need $0.35 of cash for administrative

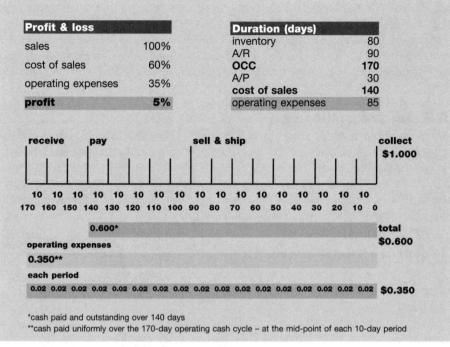

Figure 2: M&C Company: cash flows in and operating cash cycle

and operating expenses. Since this cash is spent evenly over the period, the total of each expenditure multiplied by its days outstanding is $29.75.

When this is divided by the days in the OCC, the "average" operating cash outstanding is $0.175 – the same amount you get by taking a simple average over

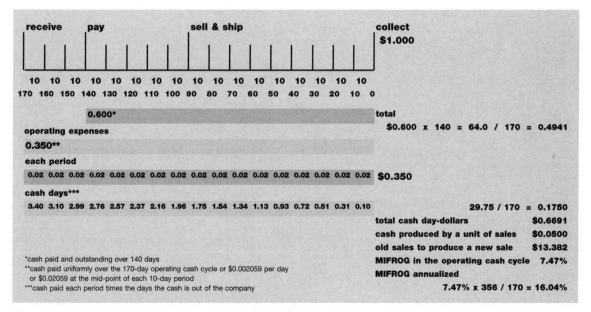

Figure 3: M&C Company: cash flows in and operating cash cycle

the period, $0.35 \times 85/170$ or \$0.175. The sum of the two gives us the cash employed per dollar of sales in the OCC – \$0.494 + \$0.175 or \$0.669.

Fortunately, M&C operates profitably, so for every dollar of sales it produces, it generates five cents of cash (*see* top of Figure 2), which it can reinvest to produce additional sales. This is the last number we need to calculate the MIFROG over the OCC.

MIFROG over an operating cycle

As shown in Figure 3, M&C needs to invest \$0.6691 over the operating cash cycle in order to generate \$1 of sales in that cycle. Part of this amount comes from current operations as \$0.05 per dollar of sales. Thus M&C needs \$0.6691/\$0.05 or \$13.38 of sales in a past cycle to fund \$1 of sales in a new cycle. This gives the company a rate of growth of "new divided by old" of \$1 divided by \$13.38. This is a MIFROG of 7.47 percent over M&C's 170-day operating cash cycle.

This article concludes on p. 298.

Breaking down the wall, scaling the ladder

Neil Churchill looks at some of the potential problems – and their solutions – that companies face as they enter long-term growth.

As stated in *The six key phases of company growth* (Part 7, Section 1), value is created when businesses start but much more value is created when enterprises grow. A growing company creates jobs, develops and disseminates innovative products that satisfy the needs of more and more customers and, in the process, makes money for the stockholders and creates value for society. However, growth brings challenges that are often new to the founding entrepreneurs, who are not always prepared to handle them well.

This article examines the dynamics of growth, the demands it makes, the challenges and changes it brings, and suggests some ways of dealing with these demands and capturing the opportunities growth can bring. It does so under seven headings: the wall; the flow; the force; the links; the ladder; the reality; and the harvest.

The wall: delegation

As a company grows it becomes larger and more complex. Additional people must be hired, often possessing an increasing variety of skills that, collectively, go considerably beyond those possessed by the entrepreneur.

To do their jobs effectively, these people need both information and "intellectual space." The owner-manager must change from a personal, hands-on style of managing people to one of coaching and managing managers. Delegation of authority is particularly difficult for founding entrepreneurs for two reasons.

First, these entrepreneurs have closely managed their companies through lean times and find it extremely hard not to interfere when they see a worker doing something wrong and wasting resources. They want to jump in and fix the problem rather than holding back and dealing with the problem through the worker's manager.

Second, they have a tendency to believe that all the managers they hire have the same information, motivation and drive that they themselves possess. Thus they have a tendency to turn a whole task over to a manager without having a meeting of the minds as to what is to be accomplished and what milestones are to be attained and when. In essence they abdicate authority rather then delegate it.

This "wall" of delegation seems universal. I was once talking to the director of a Scottish economic development agency and commented that when American companies get to around 40 to 50 employees they "hit the wall," in the sense that marathon runners do, and either learn to delegate or drop back and fail to grow. He commented that this occurred in Scotland, too, but at around 25 employees. He posited that the difference was due to the fact that his market was smaller and that Scottish companies had to export earlier than in the US. This increased the complexity of their business and they had to start delegating earlier.

The basic keys to delegation are four: delegate responsibility; agree upon the objectives to be attained; grant others the authority to take the actions needed to achieve the objectives; and collect and monitor information on how things are progressing.

There is a fifth key in an entrepreneurial company that lives upon innovation. This is, first to measure progress towards the agreed-upon goals – not the methods – utilized to get there and, second, evaluate this progress not just to see if the goal has been reached but to see what has been learned that may cause a re-examination of the objectives in the light of enhanced knowledge.

These and other steps (which will be covered later in articles on the entrepreneurial corporation) must be taken if you want the company to continue to innovate by growing without bureaucratization, a process that is likely to "blow out the entrepreneurial flame" that formed the base of the company's success.

The flow: cash

Everyone knows that starting a business requires cash, but not everyone realizes that growing a business also takes cash. The two-part article on cash flow that began in Part 7, Section 1, p. 271 and concludes on p. 298 explains how profitable operations produce a cash flow that can be used for growing the business. It also shows how rapid rates of growth can outrun this cash flow and require additional capital if growth is to be maintained. It further looks at the role of operations management and asset management in improving this cash flow and a company's MIFROG.

Beyond growth, cash must be managed strategically. Entrepreneurship involves innovation, and innovation entails a certain amount of uncertainty. An unresolved problem such as Problem A in Figure 1 can block any awareness of even larger problems down the road. Thus entrepreneurial managers follow the strategy of venture capitalists and disburse cash incrementally in order to gain additional understanding of the situation before committing all the finance required.

They spend a modest amount of money to acquire knowledge of a venture situation and then use this knowledge to re-examine the situation and then either stop the project and "cut their losses" or go ahead and spend more to gain additional insight into the potential of the project. This is called an "options approach" to capital allocation. To the extent that time and competition permit, this slow approach to a new opportunity husbands scarce resources.

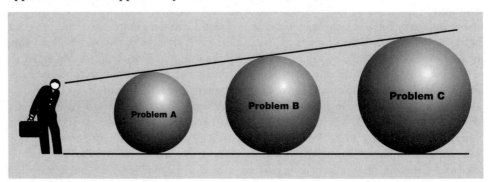

Figure 1: Venturing into the unknown

The force: leadership

The entrepreneurial company moves by focussing on innovation. The spark-plug for this at the outset is the entrepreneur. As the company grows, other people join in, a hierarchy develops, and face-to-face contact is supplemented, if not supplanted, by more formal means of communication.

Without constant reinforcement of the company's goals, sub-goals develop and people begin to work towards different ends. The entrepreneur must recognize the need to communicate his or her passion, commitment and vision to everyone in the company – to get them to "sign up" and achieve personal satisfaction in furthering the organization's goals.

A 1994 study[1] found that the chief executives of high-growth companies ranked forming and communicating vision the third most important skill after financial management and motivating others, whereas their counterparts in low-growth companies ranked it number seven.

The links: networks instead of staff

Start-ups and growing businesses are usually both undercapitalized and chronically short of cash. Instead of having all the resources they need to bring people and skills inside the business, entrepreneurs use "networks" of people who can help them out on an as-needed basis.

Some of these people are paid for their part-time services, such as lawyers, accountants, consulting specialists and the like. Others in the network are not paid but share information on technical problems, market trends, suppliers, customers, and which specialists to use for what and when.

Networks even involve competitors. Entrepreneurs who compete with each other for customers, technical breakthroughs and market share co-operate when faced by a common "enemy" such as a big company or an industry-wide technical or market problem. One watering-hole in Silicon Valley was known for this networking where entrepreneurs, faced with technical problems, would get solutions from competitors – albeit with information six months behind where the competitor was at the time.

A particularly important use of networks is to obtain a mentor or adviser or even an advisory board for the owner-manager. The problems facing entrepreneurs in a growing business may be new to them but they are not unique in the world. Having a mentor or an adviser who "has been where you are going" is an invaluable asset for an entrepreneur. Such an adviser, or board of advisers, can warn about problems on the horizon, help craft solutions to problems and, since the job at the top is a lonely one, be someone an entrepreneur can confide in and "bounce ideas off." Further, like all the nodes in the network, they come quite inexpensively.

The ladder of opportunity

The focus of growth for entrepreneurial companies is recognizing opportunities and crafting them to fit the business in order to be able to seize and exploit them. A truly entrepreneurial company is always on the lookout for new opportunities, particularly if they are a little bigger than what can currently be handled. The true entrepreneur finds the opportunity first and then marshals the resources to be able to exploit it.

This is represented in Figure 2 by the shaded and unshaded portions of "opportunity" boxes. The business currently has a resource-capability represented

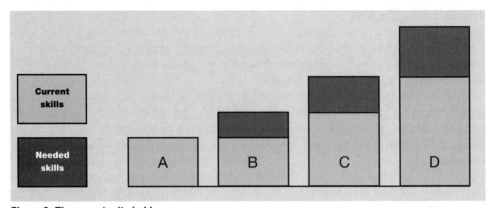

Figure 2: The opportunity ladder

by unshaded Box A. The entrepreneur sees an opportunity that requires the resources of Box B, which exceed its current capability by the shaded area. If the company is successful in capturing this opportunity, it then has the skills represented by the unshaded area of Box C. If it finds and captures an opportunity the size of this whole box, it then develops more resources and can again look for bigger opportunities and so on.

What is important is that the successful capture and exploitation of a new opportunity can help the organization climb the opportunity ladder. An opportunity the size of Box D would probably never be available to a business the size of A but, by seizing and exploiting bigger and bigger opportunities, the organization is able to "play in a new athletic field" and grow and prosper.

The important thing for the entrepreneur to realize is that an opportunity should not just be evaluated on its financial return to the company but on where, if successfully captured, it will lead the business by increasing its financial resources, its capabilities, its credibility and its reputation. The important question is: "How does this opportunity help me climb the opportunity ladder?"

The reality: the biological imperative

Companies may last for many decades but entrepreneurs do not. As owner-managers grow older, their personal goals change. While they might risk all they had at age 28 on a good opportunity, since they possessed little and had both time and energy to make it back again, at age 60 they are much less inclined to take such a risk and be forced to live those 80-hour work weeks all over again.

As the goals of the owner-manager change, so do those of the business. And with this change in goals so must there be a change in strategy. This strategy change is one of the reasons family succession is so difficult. The goals of those entering into management are often quite different from those who are phasing out, and conflict, often unresolvable, ensues. When successful succession occurs, it is wonderful, but it must be carefully planned for. When it does not work, someone else has an acquisition opportunity.

The organizational imperative

As organizations grow larger, their methods of operation change. One such change is the process of dynamically developing the strategies needed to achieve the company's vision and attain the company's goals.

At the start the company goals are simple and clear: first survive, then make a profit, and finally grow. Initially, the strategy is set by the founding entrepreneurs where it flowers in their minds at unpredictable times – when they awaken at 3am, while they are driving, or looking in the bathroom mirror. It is also communicated to others in the company in a quite informal and personal manner.

As the company grows in size and complexity, so does its strategy; and the process of developing and modifying it needs to become more formal. With increased complexity and with delegation, this formulation and reformulation becomes a joint process with other members of the management team since they now possess knowledge that the owner-manager does not have which is critical to the company's strategy.

These more formal and complex organizational processes, structure and controls that emerge with growth produce a middle management to facilitate operations. Unfortunately, this middle management can easily begin to "march to their own drummer" and a bureaucracy results. This bureaucracy has been termed the "enemy of entrepreneurship" by a past chief executive of one of the most entrepreneurial large companies in the US. Only the leadership and constant attention of the owner-manager can provide the "force" necessary to prevent the rise of bureaucracy.

The harvest: exiting the organization

The final stage of the owner-manager in the company is when he or she chooses to exit or to reduce the level of their activities in the company. The obvious choices are family succession, sale to others, or going public through an initial placement offering. (These issues will be covered in depth in Part 10.)

A sale of the company can occur in a number of ways. First, and most commonly, to one or more members of the family through management succession. If this is not desirable, the second most common way is to management via a management buy-out or a management buy-in or sale to an outside organization (to be covered in Part 8). Thousands of businesses in Europe, founded after the Second World War, are involved in one of the above processes.

Two other harvest strategies also exist. One, often overlooked, is for the owner-manager to shrink the company into a more manageable size and to focus it on the activities that are at the core of the business's profitability. This can make the business more valuable and easier to manage, giving the owner-manager time to make a choice of selling it at higher value or putting it on "auto-pilot" and withdrawing totally or in part pending a final disposal of the business. This strategy is far more desirable to the other alternative of liquidating the business by disposing of its assets.

In closing

As Sue Birley pointed out earlier in this part (p. 245), not every owner-manager wants to grow. One owner-manager said to me at the end of the first three-week unit of a nine-week owner-presidents program at Harvard Business School: "Neil, I am not coming back to Unit II. I like this program and have learned a lot, but everyone here wants to grow. I own two ski lodges, one at Aspen, Colorado, and one at Snowbird, Utah, and I like to ski. I don't want to grow." While we know the exhilaration of growth, we have seen its problems and the demands it makes. Who can fault him for choosing as he did?

Copyright © Neil C. Churchill 1997

1 "Stages of small business growth revisited, insights into growth path and leadership/management skills in low- and high-growth companies," (1994) Eggers, J. H., Leahy, K. T. and Churchill, N. C., *Frontiers of Entrepreneurship Research*, Babson College, Wellesley, Massachusetts, USA.

Secrets of the "supergrowth" league

Bernard Taylor describes the lessons learned from a 15-year study of "middle-sized" companies in the UK, Germany and the US.

This article summarizes the conclusions of a 15-year study of 200 high-growth, medium-size companies over the period 1979–80 to 1994–95. This involved 15 researchers in the UK and two in Germany interviewing chief executives and writing around 100 case studies. The research was supported by grants from Price Waterhouse and the Anglo-German Foundation. The German research study was carried out by Professor Dietger Hahn and Dr Ulrich Grüb of the University of Giessen Institut für Unternehmensplanung. The resulting book (*Supergrowth Companies: entrepreneurs in action* (1996) John Harrison and Bernard Taylor, Butterworth-Heinemann, Oxford) is the first longitudinal study of UK high-growth, medium-size companies.

We defined "medium size" in 1980 as companies with a turnover of £10–£100 million and in 1990 we raised the benchmark to £20–£200 million. To justify the label "high growth," we required that companies should have grown by at least 20 percent per year over a five-year period.

We included all kinds of independent companies, whether privately or publicly owned, on the London Stock Exchange or one of the mini-markets, but excluded two sectors – property and financial services, where some of the profits are made by deals rather than by regular trading, as well as companies in turnaround and recovery and those that had grown mainly by acquisition.

We had 176 companies in the original sample and found that on average they had grown by around 40 percent a year over five years from, say, £10–£100 million to £50–£500 million in sales and from £1–£10 million to £5–£50 million in profits.

Why study high-growth, medium-size companies?

These "supergrowth" companies are the vanguard of UK business. They succeed because they innovate. They break new ground, open up new markets, launch new types of products and services, introduce new forms of organization and more cost-effective ways of operating.

They create wealth and jobs. The 200 companies that we analyzed probably generated 50,000–100,000 jobs and £3–£4 billion of capital over a ten-year period. The supergrowth companies are the unsung heroes of industry. The impact they have on the national economy and on local communities is quite out of proportion to their numbers. While large companies, banks and government departments are closing operations and shedding thousands of jobs, these companies are setting up new businesses and taking on new people.

The importance of this mid-size, high-growth sector was recognized in the US in the early 1980s by the establishment of the American Business Conference (ABC), which brought together the leaders of mid-size companies that had grown at least 15 percent annually for the past five years.

Mid-size is a relative term that varies with the size of the market. The Americans define mid-size as $25 million–$1 billion turnover – about 15,000 companies in the US, less than 1 percent of all businesses. McKinsey researchers found that in a five-year period, from 1978–83, these mid-size companies had increased their workforce on average by 10 percent a year while over the same period the Fortune 500 had lost three million jobs.

Researchers in Germany, too, have discovered the importance of *Mittelstand* companies. They found that the more successful companies had kept their businesses simple and uncomplicated with narrow product ranges, target customer groups and a few preferred suppliers.

The lessons

A major benefit to be gained from studying high-growth, mid-size companies is that they can provide examples of best practice for other entrepreneurs who wish to grow their companies.

Lesson No. 1: Find a market niche you can defend

Successful medium-size businesses do not confront established brands in their key markets. Instead they invent new products and services and open up new market segments. They also create barriers to entry in the form of patents, distribution licenses or supply agreements with large customers.

Alan J. Brazier of Vax International invented Vax, a vacuum cleaner that would not just clean but also wash and dry carpets and floors. After years of frustration he established his own factory, put together the funds for a television advertising campaign, and in two years, from 1985–87, established Vax as the number one cleaner in its segment with a market share of 67 percent. When Hoover launched a similar product, Brazier took it to court for infringing his patents and won a seven-figure settlement.

Lesson No. 2: Compete in areas that require speed, flexibility and customer service

In our study, the leaders of UK supergrowth companies cited "flexibility to adapt to changing customer needs" as the most important factor in their success.

Also, when asked to compare their companies' performance with their competitors, they thought their companies' main competitive advantages were in "customer service" and "management organization" – this usually referring to a "star-shaped" organization composed of a small central team and an array of business unit teams that could communicate easily and take decisions quickly.

Lesson No. 3: Diversify into related products and adjacent markets

After establishing a position in a niche market, the supergrowth company's second priority is to diversify quickly into related market niches in order not to become over-dependent on one product, one customer, or the economy of a small region.

Peter J. Wood, an "intrapreneur" who operates within the Royal Bank of Scotland, pioneered the telephone selling of motor insurance policies in the UK, and his company, Direct Line Insurance, quickly became the market leader, selling more than two million motor policies a year. By 1994 the business was making £110 million profit on gross premiums of £685 million. In ten years his staff had grown from a nucleus of 30 people to 3,000 in 1994. But competitors were not idle. Wood knew they would attack his core business and he moved quickly to offer the same target customer group a range of related financial services in household insurance, mortgages and home banking.

As Lord Weinstock is reported to have said: "A niche becomes a grave." Having established a new product in a market niche, the entrepreneur is quickly surrounded by competitors offering similar products, often at a cheaper price. The only answer is to keep innovating.

Lesson No. 4: Leave the industry before the window of opportunity closes

Supergrowth companies thrive as new industries merge and grow. At the embryo stage, they succeed by introducing new products and services, opening up new channels of distribution, pioneering novel production methods, and experimenting with innovative management approaches. During the growth phase they expand geographically from regional to national and later to international coverage. They offer a wider product range and serve different customer groups.

The embryo and growth phases may take five to ten years. For the medium-size company, these times are exciting and highly profitable. But, in due course, industries mature, innovations are copied, large international competitors arrive and, in the UK and the US where there is an active market in companies, medium-size companies are quickly acquired, merged and consolidated into major groups.

When the industry begins to consolidate, the leader of an emerging business has to decide whether he or she wants the company to become a major player – which usually means losing control of the business – or to sell the company and possibly start a different business.

Charles M. Fisher, the Chairman and Chief Executive of Sharpe & Fisher, is a UK family businessman who saw that his industry was consolidating and moved out just in time. Founded in 1912, Sharpe & Fisher was a builder's merchant based in Cheltenham, but by the 1980s its star business was its DIY store operation Sandfords, which accounted for almost half of the group's profits. Charles Fisher and his management team examined the prospects for Sandfords and decided that as a family business they would not be able to compete with the buying power and the marketing strengths of fast-growing national multiples such as B&Q and Texas. They sold Sandfords at its peak for £40 million to Ladbroke's Texas chain.

Since then, from 1991–95, the company under Charles Fisher used the money to expand its original chain of builder's merchants from six to 23 by acquiring private companies at recession-reduced prices. The chain is concentrated in a band between Sussex and Wales. Despite the severe recession in the construction industry, profits more than doubled, and earnings per share increased five-fold.[1]

The international dimension

Comparisons with supergrowth companies outside the UK are very revealing. Most UK supergrowth companies are publicly owned and professionally managed – most of their founders are "professional entrepreneurs," managers trained in large companies such as Ford, IBM and ICI. They are mostly selling services, which means that some find it difficult to trade overseas. When they do, they like to acquire a company in the same niche or, like Body Shop and Kwik Fit, they sell through franchises.

The companies usually have a limited life because they are acquired by large companies. They are not often supported by government loans though some have used bank loans, often to their cost. They usually, sensibly, rely on retained earnings and equity capital. With rare exceptions they do not expect technological support from universities, and they find that large UK companies, except for some retail multiples such as Marks & Spencer, do not yet understand the Japanese idea of customer–supplier partnerships.

German mid-size companies are more often family owned and family managed. They are well integrated into their communities, funded by the regional banks, and are sponsors of local activities such as football teams. They frequently work closely with universities and research institutes. A large proportion of them are in manufacturing and have long-term relationships with major customers such as Siemens Nixdorf, BMW, and Daimler-Benz. Many of these companies are big exporters and they normally sell through agents around the world.

US supergrowth companies grow much bigger than their UK counterparts and they stay independent longer. They also have more funds available. Their home market is bigger than the European Union and they can tap into huge technological resources in the major universities and the defense industries. There are also many more supergrowth companies in the US, partly because "entrepreneurship and small business" is a favorite course in most US business schools.

However, in each country these mid-size, high-growth companies are a powerful force for innovation and growth, attracting investment, introducing new technologies, opening up new markets, and creating wealth and employment. They succeed by identifying, and often creating, a new market niche, responding imaginatively to customers' requirements, expanding quickly into related product-markets, and innovating continually.

1 "Small quoted companies," *The Director*, April 1996.

Corporate Clothing Consultants (CCC)

This case is extracted and edited from a fuller version written by **Sandra Vandermerwe** and **Sue Birley**, both of Imperial College Management School.

Greta Abrahamson, Chris Levine and Archie Leggatt were entrepreneurs in South Africa. Greta and Chris were leading couturiers, dressing wealthy, sophisticated women and, as such, were keen rivals. Archie owned and ran the premier fashion design school in the country, supplying designers to major fashion houses across the world. Yet in mid-1988, their lives changed completely when they were approached individually by South African Airways (SAA) and asked to design company uniforms to match the new SAA corporate identity.

The proposition was deceptively simple – the reality was very different. They had to clothe pilots, air hostesses, technicians and ground staff all over the world, a total of 12,500 employees. But that was not all. In the changing political climate, they were told that the corporate identity program was considered vitally important to the country. They would be paid a minimum fee and given free international travel. In short, they were being asked to work for "god and country." How could they refuse? Suffice to say, they could not and so Corporate Clothing Consultants (CCC) was born as a part-time activity.

By the end of 1996, the company had more than 100 employees, 52 subcontract manufacturers and had clothed many of the major companies in South Africa, including SA Telcom, Nedbank, Fedex, Boland Bank and ESCOM, the South African electricity company. CCC had also expanded into the global market in 1996 by winning a competitive tender to clothe the employees of TNT, a major international courier. So what was the secret of this success story?

> **"None of us could afford to refuse and we all knew it. To be left out would have been infinitely worse than whatever had to be done."**

The opportunity

Like all successful entrepreneurs, they recognized the moment and seized the opportunity. Moreover, they used their first contract to learn about the business, to develop a clear understanding of customer needs, and to develop creative ways of capturing customer interest. They believed that they should be projecting an image of quality and service while at the same time making people feel good about themselves. This was not easy.

Getting the clothes to individuals, each of whom was a different size and shape and had different tastes and needs depending upon climate and job, was complex and had to be managed with precision.

The partners

CCC was an unlikely combination. Three successful, energetic, creative people, all with very different personalities, their own clear view of the fashion business and their own ways of working – and yet it worked. The reasons are simple:

- In fashion terms they found they were on the same wavelength. For example, in preparation for the SAA deal, they had each designed clothes of similar style and quality. As a result, trust was added to professional respect.
- They were all perfectionists, believed in attention to detail, and were constantly innovating, using every new job as an opportunity to hone and enhance their service.
- Having begun, they were hungry for success – growth was the only option.

"In fact, we designed for each other, not SAA."

The service

Most of the competition had a range of 40 standard trousers and blazers from which the client chose and to which the suppliers added a corporate logo. CCC was very different. It produced a new design, including the cloth, for each client. Indeed, by 1996, the concept had evolved well beyond the original design service requested by SAA to providing the client with not only design but also buying, manufacturing, warehousing, pest control, delivery, and insurance.

This meant looking carefully at the users of the product and adding value for them. CCC designed styles that gave the staff maximum choice. They gave the client a quality image in the marketplace and employees individual service, offering a telephone hot line and consultants to help them get results out of the clothes in the most effective way.

Managing growth

Clearly, they had a good feel for the market and for customer needs – but so do many aspiring entrepreneurs. However, not all manage to deliver their promises, particularly at such a rate. What are the managerial lessons for this case?

Like most entrepreneurial teams, the members of CCC have evolved a way of making decisions that has no written rules – except that they talk all the time. They use their networks and are constantly on the look-out for new leads. They also understand their limitations. For example, they do not have the level of technical ability to control the details of stock movements and costs. So they hired a professional.

"We set about learning what the employees need and want, and then we translate it into clothes which management also likes."

They go to great lengths to give customers what they want, even if it means going outside the traditional business. To do this, they constantly talk to their clients, and also, perhaps more importantly, they constantly involve employees – who have to wear their clothes – at all stages of the process.

"People often find the three of us quite intimidating. They assume that we are judging them by what they are wearing but then the funny combination amuses them, they relax, get to know us and find we are really quite nice."

Any successful new venture is based upon the skills, passions and credibility of the founders. Employees rarely have these to the same degree and the trick for any entrepreneur in growing a venture is to know which activities to delegate and which to hold close. Greta, Chris and Archie built the credibility of CCC on their reputations and abilities as designers. This was the one activity they were not ready to delegate – and it paid off. Potential clients were always surprised, and pleased, to see at least one, and often all three, turning up to do presentations and to talk to employees.

They have built critical mass through careful development of a large network of suppliers and are equally careful about relations with them. They know that they are attractive to these suppliers because their orders are not seasonal, as with retailers, but they do not trade on this. Indeed, they are considerate of suppliers' cash needs and always pay on time. Last, but not least, they enjoy themselves. And their challenge? To maintain all this in the future.

"We don't want a quick fix. We know it will take time and investment."

Home and work – a volatile mixture

The pressures that private and professional life exert are great and their interaction often stressful – most of all for the entrepreneur. **Fernando Bartolomé** examines the issues.

Most people would like to succeed at work and in their private lives. We have a relatively standard way of thinking about what that means: to have a good job and advance in one's professional career while having a good marriage and a good relationship with one's children.

Some may define success – in particlar, success in private life – differently. Some men and women today may say that success doesn't necessarily mean marriage or having children. However, these are the exceptions among the people I work with: mostly successful executives in large multinational corporations.

The model of professional and private life success for these people fits the conventional model. The only change that I perceive is that while only a few years ago the conventional model of private life success for male executives was to have a traditional family with a stay-at-home wife, the proportion of people for whom the ideal is a dual-career family is increasing slowly. But this increase is mostly among women, not men. Indeed, if one listens carefully to men who also say that their ideal is a dual-career family, one discovers that they are "closet traditionalists" and would be much happier if they found a traditional wife.

How difficult is it?

Is it easy to have it all? No. It is extremely difficult and it is becoming increasingly so. There are several reasons for this:

- Work demands are increasing. Organizations are trying to do more with less. Personnel reductions, particularly among middle management, are pervasive.
- Work stress is increasing. The main source of stress is not only work demands but uncertainty and insecurity. In the past, excellent performance was almost a guarantee of a secure job. Today outsourcing and globalization put even the job of the excellent performer in jeopardy. This stress is multiplied by the frequent lack of transparency from the top of organizations about their strategic personnel decisions. When people feel highly stressed at work, it is very difficult for them to pay attention to their private lives.
- The relationship between the genders is changing. We live in a brave new world where men and women expect more out of their relationship and are struggling to get new definitions of what a good relationship is. Our parents' model has become obsolete. We have to reinvent what a good relationship between a man and a woman means today. These experiments are risky and stressful.
- Our standards of what it means to have a good relationship with our children have been raised. The definition of what being a good mother means has remained quite stable. But the definition of what being a good father means has changed substantially.
- Both men and women would like to have it all. Many women today are unwilling to "sacrifice it all" for their families.

Women feel the problem most intensely

After a period when they tried to be "superwomen" and have it all, many women reached the conclusion that this was impossible and gave up some aspect of their lives. Some chose not to marry. Many decided not to have children or have fewer. Many postponed having children until later in their lives.

Furthermore, research shows that even in dual-career families, women are still doing about 70–80 percent of domestic "jobs" in private life. Even very "liberated" women tend to feel more responsible for the quality of private life and particularly for the well-being of their children than men do.

In my research on these issues I have found that when I ask executives how men and women in an ideal world should divide the job of taking care of their children until they reach the age of five, the average response is that the ideal division should be 70 percent for the mother and 30 percent for the father. Many women share that view. When I ask them how much each parent actually did, the average man did about 20 percent of the job.

What can be done?

The problem is difficult but not impossible to deal with. There are no perfect solutions, but there are some ideas that may help.

First, we should put things in perspective and avoid clichés and easy answers. Let's debunk a few clichés.

"The main problem is time." Not true. In my research I find consistently that executives devote only 50 percent of their waking hours to work. And this is true even if they work long hours.

For example:

1 week =	168	hours	
Average weekly sleep	49	hours	
Total waking hours	119	hours	
Daily average commute	1	hour	
Daily average time at work	10	hours × 5 =	55 hours
Average work hours during the weekend	4	hours	4
Total working hours			59

59/119 = approx. 50%

Executives are often startled when they make this calculation. They can't believe the numbers. But they are accurate. Note that the percentage of waking hours devoted to work would decrease substantially if we included holidays and vacation time in our calculations. Time is indeed an issue. But not *the* main issue.

"*The main problem is my boss.*" That may be true in some cases but it is often an excuse. Many executives who say this have never discussed with their bosses how to protect their private lives. Women are better than men at doing this. However, even women may find difficulty negotiating these issues with their bosses and therefore avoid doing it.

What the individual can do

- Stop blaming others. Stop blaming the organization, the boss, incompetent subordinates, demanding clients, etc.
- Start analyzing what one could do without asking for anybody's permission to improve the situation. Learn to manage one's time better. Learn to prioritize. Learn to delegate. Learn to cut unnecessary activities such as meetings.

Some of these things one may do alone. Some may need co-operation from others. A lot of time and energy can be saved this way.

In my work with executives I often ask them the following question: "How many hours would you save a week without your results deteriorating?" Average response = six hours.

My next question should be obvious: "Why aren't you saving those hours?" The typical response is to blame stress, the boss, clients, etc. But I am convinced that the problem lies elsewhere, and it is called lack of passion.

Develop private life passion

For many men and some women, taking care of their private lives is more *duty* than passion. "I ought to attend the PTA meeting" or "I have to pick up the children from school" or "I have to take them to the doctor." There is indeed a lot of duty that needs to be taken care of. Some of it can be delegated to others: day-care centers, babysitters, school, vacation camps. A lot cannot be delegated. And there is much that *should not* be delegated.

For example, we may be tempted to delegate the more painful or uncomfortable activities, but this may be totally wrong. This is often a problem for men. A child cries in the middle of the night, and a man may tell his wife: "Why don't you take care of him? You are much better at it." In some cases the woman may volunteer. It is very easy to feel grateful and go back to sleep. Easy, yes. But also stupid perhaps.

Learn to recognize opportunities

Taking care of a sick child is both a pain and an opportunity. An opportunity to discover more deeply your love for your child, to communicate your love to your children through your actions, and to learn maybe to become a better partner.

Avoid the mañana syndrome: seize the day

I work with people of different ages. When we discuss this topic, the older they are, the sadder they feel – because they can't go back.

A few weeks ago, I was conducting a session on this topic. A young executive was paying a lot of attention and looked very sad. During the coffee break I asked him what was going on. He answered: "You got me a bit late. One of my children is already eight years old. But the other is three. With that one there is still a lot I can do."

His sadness was right and natural. There are a few essential things he has missed and can't recover. There are only a few years when you can hold a baby in your arms. And they happen only once. "Carpe diem!"

Develop a sense of priorities

I often ask executives to prioritize three areas of their lives – children, couple, self. When I ask them what is the right order, many say children, couple, self. But the right order is the opposite: self, couple, children. Some women find that idea troubling. But, if you think about it, it is logical and evident. You can't take care of anybody if you don't take care of yourself. You can't have a healthy relationship with anybody if you have a lousy relationship with yourself. The best way of taking care of your children is to take care of your marriage. If you destroy your marriage, you will hurt your children. The best way to take care of your children is to take care of your spouse and give them a great example of what it means to love and respect another human being.

Prioritizing doesn't mean that one thing is more important or has more value than the other. All may be equally important. But it does mean that one has a sense of how each aspect of one's life relates to the others and what is the best way of achieving a positive synergy.

Beyond the individual

The responsibility starts with the individual but doesn't end there. To protect the quality and stability of private life and particularly to protect families, society as a whole has an important role to play. I will suggest here briefly some of the elements of this societal contribution:

- **The crucial role of a healthy economy**. Unemployment, underemployment, job insecurity, poorly paid jobs are the most serious threats to the well-being and stability of families.
- **The importance of social justice**. A better distribution of income, a more just society, and a better distribution of work, if the economy doesn't produce enough employment, are important contributing factors to creating the economic and social conditions where families can thrive.
- **A decline of materialism and consumerism**. At the deepest level, materialism conflicts with something that I would call "relationism." When we hectically seek material wealth and possessions, when we try to achieve

happiness by buying the best car, the latest record, the ideal Caribbean vacation etc., we may pay too much attention to things and too little to people and relationships. Things do not bring us together. Corny as it may sound, love does. And it requires valuing people more than things.

Cultural changes in our conception of male and female roles

The quality of private life and particularly the quality of family life will improve when men and women feel equally responsible for the quality of their private life and when they have an equal degree of passion for it. A woman still suffers more when she has to leave her children in a day-care center than a man does under similar circumstances.

Women would like to have a more fulfilling professional life but without risking the quality of their private lives. The first wave of feminism fought under the banner of "women's liberation" and often interpreted that liberation as jettisoning female roles and functions that they believed themselves to have been brainwashed to assume. The second wave of feminism is ready to assume the existence of deeply rooted feminine impulses, such as nurturing, to value them and to integrate them into a richer ideal of what being a woman means.

Unfortunately, men have not yet achieved an equal transformation. Very few wanted to be liberated from their traditional roles. It was actually the feminists that suggested to men that they should desire to be liberated of their traditional roles as money earners and sole providers of economic security. There were few men fighting women to defend their right to feed a baby or get up in the middle of the night to nurse a sick child.

But today, forced in part by their wives, some men are slowly but surely starting to discover the value of these aspects of their lives and are proposing for the first time in history a new, much richer definition of the "fathering" role.

Structural changes

The term "family-friendly policies" is now widely used at state and company level. The more advanced a society, the more varied are the tools that it offers people to help take care of both work and family. But laws and policies are often ahead of practice. Laws are easier to change than people. When a society, for example, offers family-friendly solutions to men and women, women use them much more often than men. A 1994 report illustrates this very well.

In the Netherlands in 1994, 36.4 percent of the labor force had part-time jobs. However, while 65 percent of the women had chosen this option, only 16 percent of men did. There are many reasons for this, including the differential pay between men and women. But, certainly, the willingness of women to sacrifice professional success in favor of paying attention to family needs plays an important role – as does the unwillingness of many men to accept similar kinds of sacrifice.

Some worrying facts

The fertility decline in most European countries is a deeply worrying trend. Whether this trend is due to increasing selfishness and materialism or to economic insecurity, and whether it may be reversible, are fascinating questions. But the trend itself is extremely dangerous.

Special problems for the entrepreneur

Some characteristic facts about entrepreneurs are:

- they are never 9–5 people
- the working day is never long enough for them
- they tend to dominate their companies and impose their personality on others
- they impose their rules and demand that others work as hard and as many hours as they do
- the somewhat artificial separation between professional and private life does not really exist for them from a psychological point of view.

The clichés – "he is married to his company," "the company is his baby," or, in some cultures, "the company is his mistress" – are psychologically extremely accurate. I have met executives in large corporations who are passionate about their jobs. But entrepreneurs' passion is different. In their case, their company is an extension of themselves. One could assume that so are their children. But they are not.

Why may this be so? I'd like to propose several psychological hypotheses that make sense to me. First, children are the result of a brief act of conception. A company, on the other hand, represents the fruition of a complex, prolonged, and extremely involving act of creation. There is a second hypothesis that intrigues me. Most entrepreneurs are men. Their children are the result of a joint act of creation, and in that venture it is the mother who plays the most crucial, involved, creative role. A child "belongs" much more to the mother than to the father. (As the saying goes, one can be sure of who his mother is. As to his father, there is never any certainty.) In creating a firm, on the other hand, the entrepreneur is both father and mother – he is even the midwife. The company is his baby in a way that his children are not and it provides him with the most unique opportunity to project himself. This leads to an extremely strong narcissistic involvement. Thus, when things go well, the gratification is huge. When they go wrong, the entrepreneur cannot think about anything else.

An interesting research question would be to ask if women entrepreneurs are as deeply interested in their firms as men are. Obviously a woman's involvement in creating a child is much more complex and profound. Certainly our society expects her to become more involved in the nurturing of her children. A Freudian psychologist would hypothesize that this investment of emotional energy in her children would diminish the energy available for investment in work. This makes sense, but is it so? What do women entrepreneurs feel more passionate about: their companies or their children? Anecdotal evidence seems to indicate that women entrepreneurs are also more emotionally invested in their companies than in their children.

Another factor that may contribute to entrepreneurs' extraordinary degree of involvement in their organizations is the fact that most of them are self-taught. Most do not start with the tools of the educated MBA. Or, if they have them, they quickly learn that many of those tools do not work very well in the quirky world of the entrepreneurial concern. Additionally, many entrepreneurs discover that the tools and approaches that experts propose to them – especially about how to handle people – are useless because they are "designed" for managers and do not fit the entrepreneurial personality.

At the core of the entrepreneur's motivation there is the desire to express himself and control his destiny, to be himself, to be his own boss, to create his own child. That impulse runs against following the advice of others. As a consequence, the self-taught entrepreneur often finds himself with his hands, heart and mind full of the simultaneous jobs of learning, nurturing and growing his firm. This leaves him with very little time, and almost no energy, to nurture his family.

Some hopeful signs

Hopeful signs exist, however. There are, for example, indications that in Scandinavian countries the fertility rate is again climbing.

When one visits families or watches them in their homes or in the streets, we discover with pleasure that men are much more involved in raising their children today than they were only a few years ago.

Companies which have introduced family-friendly policies report excellent results in reducing employee turnover and increasing productivity.

Special problems for the family business

Family firms are not easy places in which to work. They are difficult for family members but also for non-family employees. Creating a family firm means accepting one of the highest risks a person may take in life because it involves mixing at the deepest level professional and private life and, consequently, risking failure in both.

Many family firms are Greek tragedies in progress or just waiting to happen. The main victims are the family members, but everybody, including non-family employees, is profoundly affected when things go wrong. Even under normal circumstances the life of the non-family employee can be particularly stressful. He or she has to deal not only with functional business problems but also with all the complex psychological problems involved in working in a family firm.

In his article "Real work" (*Harvard Business Review*, January–February 1989) Abraham Zaleznik established a distinction between "real work" and "psychopolitics" in organizations. And he argued for the need to focus on real work and to avoid the dysfunctional distractions of psychopolitics. In the family firm, psychopolitical problems are magnified to an extraordinary degree, and the organization may die or suffer enormous damage unless its members are able to recognize these problems and deal with them effectively.

Conclusion

Entrepreneurs are rarely highly introspective people fascinated by psychological problems. This does not mean that they may not be psychologically intuitive and skillful under normal circumstances. But when important emotional or relational problems develop in their firms they rarely have the analytical tools or the necessary skills to handle them.

Those who are healthy or wise enough may realize that they need help and be willing to ask for it. If they are lucky, they may find a competent expert to help them, but, unfortunately, these wiser entrepreneurs are rare.

Being oriented towards action and control, top executives in general, and entrepreneurs in particular, are highly reluctant to depend on others and ask for help. Some are reluctantly willing to ask for technical help with finance or production problems. Asking for psychological help is much more difficult for them. They are, understandably, afraid of opening that Pandora's box.

And yet these men and women who decide to create their own firms or to get involved in the complex adventure of building a family firm should be warned from the start that one day they are likely to need help in dealing with the specially difficult human problems that are typical of these firms. They also need to be aware that failure to ask for help may lead to massive failure in both their professional and private lives.

The future

The road is long. There are forces that will help and others that will hinder progress. But the effort to help men and women in our society to fulfill themselves at work and to excel in their private lives is worth continuing.

It would be wrong, however, to expect others – the state, the company I work for, my boss – to take care of this issue for me. In the end it is each individual who has to assume the main responsibility to achieve his/her goals as a human being and to be consistent with the values he/she professes to have.

Re-inventing Germany's *Mittelstand*

Daniel Muzyka and **Hans Breuninger** report how some of Germany's famed *Mittelstand* companies are rediscovering the spirit of entrepreneurialism.

West Germany's economic landscape is populated by *Mittelstand* companies, businesses that belong in the small and medium-sized sector. Three-quarters are family owned and a large percentage are manufacturing-based. Many *Mittelstand* companies started around the turn of the 19th century while others were founded after the Second World War. There can be no doubt that since the war, *Mittelstand* companies have been a major engine for German industrial growth and played a substantial part in the economic boom of the 1950s and 1960s.

They have succeeded in capturing opportunities on a regular basis, not only within Germany but also in the European Union and on a wider global scale. The label "Made in West Germany" came to stand for first-class technology and high-quality craftsmanship and was recognized worldwide. In the 1990s, the *Mittelstand* share of world markets was between 70 and 90 percent. It was often enough to guarantee a good share of export markets without a great marketing and sales effort and contributed largely to the famous German trade surplus.

Although in Germany *Mittelstand* companies still represent DM50 billion in exports, many of these companies have begun to show signs of "age:" outdated organizational structures; outdated management models; slow and costly product development processes; lack of innovation; little creation of value-added. Another difficulty is that the new generation no longer appears to care for the family heirloom and even wants to divest itself of it.

We believe that the key question for these companies is how to become entrepreneurial again in their business processes – how to regain and maintain their capacity to identify and capture opportunity in a flexible and continuous way.

The first phase of our study involved the selection of a series of companies that appeared to have been successful in changing, at least to a degree, to a more entrepreneurial, successful, value-creating organization. What we observed was that many of the changes that had seemingly taken place within the organizations over the past five to ten years had come about by way of a major entrepreneurial transformation.

We wanted to understand the nature of this transformation and the models to which they have been transforming. We were interested in researching two major questions:

- What is the nature of the opportunity-driven, self-sustaining management model evolving within German *Mittelstand* companies?
- What is the nature of the transformation that was required from traditional *Mittelstand* management practices so that this new management model could be implemented?

Our intention was to get as large a cross-section of the German industrial sample as possible while including the service sector. We finally decided on the following companies: MHZ (Mechanischer Hachtelzug) (windows and furnishings); Kolb & Schüle AG (textiles); Binder Vacuum Technic (vacuum cleaners); Golding GmbH (costume and fine jewelry); Trinkaus & Burkhardt (private bank). All are typical *Mittelstand* companies that are also active in the international markets, exporting their goods or services.

With the support of these companies, we developed research cases to understand and chart the development and transformation processes they had undergone. In interviews with executives and management, our questions tried to explore the state of the companies before the changes occurred and what happened afterwards; what triggered those changes, and who and what was the major force driving them.

Our research resulted in 12 basic findings, which will be discussed below under four main themes:

- **performance focus:** performance/operational goals
- **strategic orientation:** opportunity orientation, growth and renewal imperative, value innovation
- **organizational system:** networking systems, transformational approach, pan-technical orientation, information architecture
- **operational system:** rationalized value chain, extended supply chain, balanced growth and profit measurement.

In attempting to become more entrepreneurial and innovative, the companies had to make adjustments in objectives, structure, processes and behavior. Creating self-sustaining organizations required re-engineering and re-orienting multiple elements in the business systems, including issues across all functions.

The performance focus

A first observation about these companies was the pervasive understanding of the need for an overall strong performance. This was accomplished, in part, by improving the perspective and the goals of the organization. Performance at an organizational, team and individual level became the name of the game in these companies. All three were fairly evident and shared. A further accomplishment was a more open communication of the actual company performance. These organizations have opened accountability for, and increased the profile and awareness of, overall organizational performance. Performance information is more obvious than it has been historically.

The second point involved the question of who knows about the goals in the organization and what they are. In these innovative organizations virtually everyone had understood not only the goals for their own organizational unit but also the goals for the whole of the company. Management had recognized that if people do not know where they are going they will choose any road.

Strategic orientation

The strategic orientation of these companies proved slightly different from the traditional enterprise in the following aspects.

Traditional companies worry about resources, assets, the balance sheet, and the organizational funds. The strategic orientation in the companies in our sample was directed largely toward identifying and capturing opportunity. The selection of opportunity was clearly based on the skills and abilities of the organizations as well as on the realization that opportunity would lead the organization in required new directions.

This more active search for opportunities was combined with a growth imperative – growth became a central strategic theme. However, this did not have to mean growth for the sake of growth. In the case of the researched organizations, there was a focus on growth with the primary intent to ensure a major renewal of product lines and business.

One of the most striking observations from the study was the focus on value innovation within the organizations. Traditionally, many of the companies had produced and sold products based on their expertise and technology (that is, "if we believe it is better, then the market should accept it as better because it incorporates our improved technology").

The companies all appeared to have an iterative model of creating and introducing new products and services that involved the search for a combination of real customer need and the skills and abilities the company could bring to bear in order to create value for both parties. Innovation became ultimately a value-based, not technologically-based, process.

One of the consequences was that this drove the development of products through successive contacts with the customer before product introduction. This also prompted the companies to seek out market niches and to grow through the exploitation of successive niche opportunities. The companies were re-oriented to the pursuit of market-based opportunities. They acquired a more pervasive understanding of a need to capture opportunity for both renewal and growth and a more public awareness (within the companies) of the need to focus on opportunity at all levels.

The organizational system

Another finding was that communication and knowledge transfer appear to be much more networked in recent years in these companies, creating a "networked" architecture and its processes in the organization. One of the great enemies of innovation in European companies today is the existence of the so-called "silo problem" where information and decisions must go up the organization, go over, and hopefully come back down again so that a problem can be solved. The companies researched seemed to have found a partial solution. They work in teams and in project groups, and new problems or challenges are worked on horizontally across the company.

While networking, systems of networks and so on are fashionable concepts, the question remains whether they are an efficient way to communicate and operate in organizations. We found that while they may not be 100 percent efficient, in each of these organizations it could be seen that teams consisting of people from different functions were able to work together and to process innovations.

The leadership in these organizations worked aggressively to improve communication and knowledge transfer. In some cases, developers or product managers, who rarely, if ever, saw a customer, were sent out to conduct market research with end users. The main improvement, though, was in creating new business products and services through a co-operative, pan-technical approach. No longer could individuals be simply secure in, or proud of, their technical knowledge; they had to apply it with others to create value.

The notion of change was also embedded in these organizations: change as the status quo. Most of these organizations had gone through a recent transformation, trying to move the organization from one style of management to another. Typically, at the outset of a transformation the present model is defined and a future one is portrayed. Between the two there is often an amorphous mass, defined as transformation or a corporate change process.

The companies in our sample proceeded differently. They took the mass in the middle, where everything was still unsolved, and taught people how every one of them could play a part in the change process. Therefore, it never became a question of "earlier/later" or "before/after" but of companies that continued to innovate, that continuously renewed themselves, and that constantly profitted from this mass.

Based on their competence and expertise gained, they pursued the change process, which was often driven around the opportunity being pursued at a particular time. In the end, transformation on a fluid (as required but unplanned) basis became a way of life. Any impact on personnel seemed to have been minimized by circumventing job cuts and focussing on re-orienting and retraining people.

In several cases, the organizations in our research displayed an approach to developing opportunity and innovating products that was significantly more "cross-technology" and cross-functional (or cross-skills) than can be found in other companies of their size. They exercised a "pan-technological" approach and found opportunities in mapping several skills and technologies together with customer needs. A lot of the products and product ideas that these companies have developed have come from the sharing of technical knowledge – not from better solutions for a technology.

A fundamental support of the performance of these organizations came, however, from an increased knowledge and a better management information architecture within the organization. (It should be said that the information architecture included not only hardware-based solutions but also better organizational processes to collect, analyze and disseminate knowledge.)

Information in these organizations is widely available. There is an open information architecture that permits the companies to collect, disseminate and leverage information in a competitive fashion. This also had an impact on the nature of control. The broad availability of information on performance and reaction to market situations made operational control more subtle. Because of greater visibility and transparency, individuals were prone to control their own actions.

Information literally created power for these organizations. In some cases, it made them the equal of much larger competing organizations. In most cases, the availability of "facts" rather than of opinions or beliefs helped them to improve decision making, to act more quickly, and to enhance cross-technical/cross-functional co-operation.

The operational system

The organizations had taken broad steps to rationalize their value chain in focussing on those activities that were the key to growth potential and return. They had retreated from a need to supervise all value-added steps. Instead they exercised only a nominal control over quality or technology.

This did not require downsizing but meant a review of their value chains and a greater refocussing on activities that would provide them with growth potential and, for the most part, maximum return. In many cases, they abandoned the concept of producing everything in-house. This led to higher economic returns. They actively addressed the question "where do we add value?" and focussed operations on the areas that were identified.

In order to open up the value chain, even in terms of medium-sized players, the companies established strong supplier relationships, especially across borders. They sought out cost- and value-effective partners outside Germany while retaining either major value-added processes nationally or the possibility and capacity to undertake them in Germany if necessary.

Despite their size, the companies tried to achieve lower levels of cost by moving at least some of the production out of high-cost areas, that is Germany, and found similar production quality elsewhere if they provided appropriate controls. In many cases, this followed actively sought information and contacts with suppliers throughout the world.

The organizations measured their operational performance with a more balanced view of success. They tended to measure both the efficiency of operations (the traditional measure) and the effectiveness of operations (can they achieve challenging goals?).

Even if they were worried about "enjoying profits at the expense of growth," it was interesting to see that these organizations seemingly measured their operational performance by actively balancing growth and profitability. It left them with asking themselves whether they were sacrificing growth or renewal possibilities for the sake of short-term profit.

Conclusion

The conclusions to be drawn are that German *Mittelstand* companies must be smarter and more adaptive to capture the opportunities. "More of the same" – better or improved technology, harder work within the same organizational structures and so on – will not suffice.

Part of the adaptation may be a recognition that significant parts of production cannot be economically undertaken within Germany. Lower cost of transportation, differential national development of skills, and significantly lower labor costs have had their impact. For many middle companies to be active players tomorrow, they may have to decide whether "Made in Germany" is still economically viable.

However, these companies have also made the point that active co-ordination, key development and utilization of core technologies, and active discovery of opportunities, can add up to creating a significant value-added role for German companies.

A full version of this article, "The secret of new growth in old German *Mittelstand* companies," by Daniel F. Muzyka, Hans A. Breuninger and Gerda Rossell was published in the *European Journal of Management* in April 1997. Telephone 01865 201529. Fax 01865 251960.

CASE STUDY

Unlocking the door to self-finance

In the second part of a two-part case study **Neil Churchill** and **John Mullins** explain how the MIFROG model can be used to compare performance and forecast cash needs.

The first part of this article, which appeared on p. 271, dealt with cash inflows and outflows over the operating cash cycle. But while the growth rate in an operating cycle is important, most managers think in terms of growth per year. Annualizing the MIFROG (the maximum internally financiable rate of growth) for different products or markets, or comparing MIFROGs for different companies, requires a common time period for the analysis.

It is apparent that if M&C, the fictitious company being used as an example, can grow at 7.47 percent in 170 days, it should grow more in 365 days. Thus we multiply the MIFROG in a single cycle by the length of the year divided by 170 days. This gives us an annual MIFROG of 16.04 percent. This means that if M&C grows at a rate slower than 16.04 percent, the company will produce more cash from sales than its growth requires. On the other hand, if M&C grows faster than its MIFROG, it will need to raise cash from external sources. Thus the MIFROG rate provides a tool for forecasting cash needs.

The levers that control the cash for growth

We can see from the M&C example that the factors that influence the MIFROG are, first, the amount of cash it takes to produce a unit of sales, second, the duration of each of these cash flows and, third, the amount of cash the resulting unit of sales brings to the company.

If management can decrease the amount of cash needed, decrease the duration that the cash remains out, or increase the cash produced by a unit of sales, the MIFROG increases. These actions are illustrated in Figure 1 along with the original situation, an annualized MIFROG of 16.04 percent.

Lever 1: Decrease the amount of cash required

Let us assume that management can decrease the cost of goods sold by one percentage point and the cost of operations by half a percentage point as shown in Figure 1. The cash required to finance a sale decreases from $0.669 to $0.658, a saving of $0.011 in each operating cash cycle. If the cash generated by the sale had remained the same – $0.05 – due to an equal price decrease, *old sales needed to produce a new sale* would have been $13.16, the OCC self-financed MIFROG rate would have risen to 7.60 percent, and the annual MIFROG to 16.32 percent. Not a large increase. Fortunately for the company this did not happen. It left its prices the same and cash increased to $0.065 per dollar of sales.

Profit & loss:	Present situation	With profit improvement	With shortened durations	Duration & profit impr.
sales	100.0%	100.0%	100.0%	100.0%
cost of sales	60.0%	59.0%	60.0%	59.0%
operating expenses	35.0%	34.5%	35.0%	34.5%
profit	**5.0%**	**6.5%**	**5.0%**	**6.5%**

Duration (days):				
inventory	80	80	76	76
A/R	90	90	84	84
OCC	170	170	160	160
A/P	30	30	30	30
OCC	140	140	130	130
operating expenses	85	85	80	80

Operating cash cycle for self-financiable growth				
cost of sales	$0.600 x 140/170 = $0.494	$0.590 x 140/170 = $0.486	$0.600 x 130/160 = $0.488	$0.590 x 130/160 = $0.479
operations	$0.350 x 85/170 = $0.175	$0.345 x 85/170 = $0.173	$0.350 x 80/160 = $0.175	$0.345 x 80/160 = $0.173
cash-days consumed	**$0.669**	**$0.658**	**$0.663**	**$0.652**
cash produced	$0.050	$0.065	$0.050	$0.065
old sales needed to produce a new sale	$13.382	$10.129	$13.250	$10.029
OCC SFG	7.47%	9.87%	7.55%	9.97%
Annualized SFG	7.47% x 365/170 = **16.04%**	9.87% x 365/170 = **21.20%**	7.55% x 365/160 = **17.22%**	9.97% x 365/160 = **22.75%**

Figure 1: M&C Company: levers to control cash available for growth

Lever 2: Increase the amount of cash produced

With sales producing $0.065 cash per dollar, the company needs only $10.129 of *old sales* to produce a dollar of *new sales* (Figure 1), the OCC self-financed MIFROG rate rises to 9.87 percent, and the annual MIFROG to 21.2 percent. While the $0.015 increase in *cash produced* amounts to 30 percent, the *cash required* is only $0.011 or only 1.64 percent. Note the power of the profit margin. This is why software companies, once their products are developed, can grow so fast. They charge $150 to $300 for a product whose cost of sales is less than $20. If the company had just raised its prices by $0.015 and left the cash requirements alone, it would have had an OCC SFG rate of 9.72 percent and an annualized SFG of 20.86 percent – an almost identical result.

Lever 3: Decrease the duration of the cash flows

The third lever is shown in the last two tables in Figure 1 and is applied to both the initial and the improved cash consumed scenarios. Four days (5 percent) are taken off the inventory holding period and six days (6.67 percent) taken off the accounts receivable collection period.

The result is an OCC of 160 days instead of 170 days, which produces increased OCC and annualized MIFROG rates of 7.55 percent and 17.22 percent respectively for the "present profit" situation and 9.97 percent and 22.75 percent for the "improved profit" situation, since there is nothing to prevent management from pulling all three levers at the same time. This is an increase of more than 40 percent in the company's growth rate without external capital.

Profit & loss		Duration (days)	
sales	100%	inventory	80
material cost of goods sold	40%	A/R	90
labor cost of goods sold	20%	**OCC**	**170**
operating expenses	35%	A/P	30
cash operating expenses	95%	**cost of sales**	**140**
profit excluding depreciation	**5%**	operating expenses	85

Capital equipment	
present capital equipment per $100,000 of sales	$60,000
present capital equipment per $1 of sales	$0.60
depreciable (and expected) life	10 years
depreciation per sales dollar per year	$0.060
depreciation per sales dollar per OCC	$0.0279

Operating cash cycle for self-financiable growth	
material cost of sales	$0.400 x 140/170 = $0.3294
labor cost of sales	$0.200 x @ = $0.1529
operations	$0.350 x 85/170 = $0.1750
cash replacement of fixed assets	$0.06 x 85/170 = $0.0279
cash required in an operating cycle	**$0.6853**
cash produced	$0.0500
old sales needed to produce a new sale	$0.685 / $0.050 = $13.706
OCC SFG	7.30%
Annualized SFG	**7.30% x 365/170 = 15.67%**

@ Labor costs are incurred equally over the first 80 days of work. If each 10-day period's costs are multiplied by the days remaining to cash collection, in the same manner as operating expense was calculated in Figure 3 in the first part of this article (p. 273), and the total then divided by 170 days, the resulting average cash flow out for manufacturing labor is $0.15294.

Figure 2: M&C manufacturing

MIFROG and multi-period cash flows

We have, until now, considered only a simplified situation in which the OCC encompasses all the cash flows necessary to finance a dollar of sales. However, most companies have to add physical capacity from time to time, spend money on R&D due to market or technological trends, or react to competition that may require increased marketing programs that span multiple periods. Cash needed for such investments, whether for plant and equipment, R&D or other multi-period purposes, must be planned for.

Where multi-period cash flows exist, two changes must be made. The first involves the cash produced by a sale. The second involves apportioning the cash required to buy the capital equipment, to finance the marketing programs, or support R&D over the OCCs benefitting from these expenditures.

Let's change the M&C Company into a manufacturing company by adding some machinery and equipment in the amount of $60,000 per $100,000 dollars of sales and separating cost of sales into materials and labor (*see* Figure 2). If this equipment has a ten-year life, its cash component must be included in the required cash calculation. This is $0.06 per year or $.0279 in the OCC of 170 days. Adding this to the cash consumed by operations we get a total of $0.6853 that must be produced by sales in an OCC and a MIFROG of 7.30 percent which annualizes to a MIFROG of 15.67 percent.

Calculations, comments and caveats

The formula
The calculation of the MIFROG can be put into a formula as shown in Figure 3.

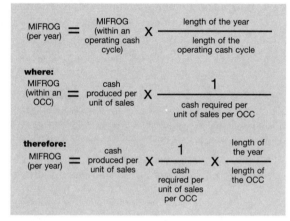

Figure 3

The cash components and their lengths
The length of the OCC is that of the longest cash component required to produce a unit of sales. In the examples above we have talked only of two such flows within the OCC: cost of goods sold and operating expenses.

There can be others extending over different periods such as prepayment of television advertising "spots," letters of credit in advance of inventory delivery, and the like. The OCC is the longest of all the cycles.

Consider the example where there are four cash component flows as follows:

- letter of credit for materials to be shipped to company   45 days
- inventory after receipt   50 days
- account receivable   60 days
- prepaid TV advertising   90 days

In this example, the longest cash-to-cash flow is that of cost of sales. It is the sum of the letter of credit, the inventory, and the accounts receivable − 45 + 50 + 60, or 155 days since the TV advertising was paid 90 days before the show that produced the accounts receivable and the letter of credit went out 95 days before the sales were made.

If, however, the advertising expense had to be paid 120 days in advance, the OCC would be the sum of the 120 days of advertising and the accounts receivable of 60 days producing a 180-day OCC.

Given the 90-day prepayment of advertising, the days outstanding of each cash flow are as follows:

- letter of credit cash   155 days
- inventory cash over the letter of credit payment   110 days
- prepaid advertising   150 days
- administrative expenses   155/2 days

Comments

The MIFROG rate is a powerful tool for bringing together operating management considerations that usually focus on the profit and loss statement and financial management considerations, which in turn focus on the balance sheet. MIFROG can be calculated for subsidiaries, product lines and product/market segments. It can be based on past averages or on planned, future performance. Thus it can provide unique insights into the consequences of management decisions.

Caveats

MIFROG is, however, based upon aggregated cash flows grouped together over different periods of time. It is close, but not always the same, as the steady-state growth based upon a set of complex interacting factors. For situations where an exact number is needed, a spreadsheet approach is usually more accurate. MIFROG provides understanding for managing; the spreadsheet provides the accuracy needed to show a cash plan to a financial source. Both should be well-worn tools in your planning kit.

BUYING A COMPANY

8

Contributors

Mike Wright is Professor of Financial Studies and Director of the Centre for Management Buy-out Research (CMBOR) at the University of Nottingham, and Director of Zeton Ltd. His research interests include management buy-outs, venture capital, privatization and entrepreneurship.

Robert M. Johnson is a successful entrepreneur in both the US and UK. Previously he was lecturer in entrepreneurship at London Business School.

Ken Robbie is Senior Research Fellow at CMBOR, University of Nottingham. His research interests include management buy-ins, venture capital and entrepreneurship.

Patrick Dunne is responsible for 3i's MBI and Independent Director Programs. In the past five years he has probably been best known for pioneering the BIMBO concept in the UK. He is the author of *Running Board Meetings*, Kogan Page (1997).

Robert Smith is Group Chief Executive of Deutsche Asset Management Group Ltd.

Conor Boden is responsible for 3i's Management buy-in program.

Michael Hay is Associate Professor of Strategic and International Management at London Business School and Director of the Foundation for Entrepreneurial Management.

Michael Ullman is an entrepreneur, businessman and Visiting Lecturer in Entrepreneurship at INSEAD.

Contents

Introduction

Part 8 examines a different route to ownership for either an individual or a management team – that of buying a company, often using leveraged finance. Individuals, management teams, investors and corporations buy other firms for a variety of reasons. They buy them for competitive reasons, in order to acquire additional skills and competencies, to secure source of supply or distribution, or simply to acquire important technologies. Entrepreneurs and entrepreneurial firms acquire companies for all of these reasons. In addition, buying a business is a natural way in which many entrepreneurs and entrepreneurial teams begin to realize their opportunity. Acquiring a company can sometimes be a way to speed market entry, to get assets cheaply (production capacity, established distribution, brand name, etc.) and/or to acquire an opportunity in the form of an enterprise which is not fully realizing its potential.

Entrepreneurs around the world purchase businesses. The terminology to describe these purchases is, however, somewhat different depending upon where you sit. In North America, the purchase of a business by its existing management team is usually described as a "leveraged buy-out (LBO)." In Europe and Asia, such a purchase is often described as a "management buy-out (MBO)." For purposes of this text we will use the terminology which is commonly used in Europe and internationally – we will call the purchase of a business by its existing management team, a management team that sees entrepreneurial potential that is not being realized in the business, an MBO. Other terms – for instance, management buy-in (MBI) – will be introduced as part of this section.

In this part, we look at the growing phenomena of the management buy-out and the management buy-in. We explore the costs, rewards and risks from the perspective of both management and other investors. We ask what is especially attractive about this form of investment from the perspective of the investor and what are the criteria that they apply when deciding to invest. We look at the issues that face the new owners as they attempt to grow the company and to harvest their investment.

Entrepreneurial spirit propels buy-outs

Mike Wright and **Ken Robbie** provide an introduction to the worlds of MBOs, MBIs and BIMBOs.

Since 1980, buy-outs have developed into an extremely important facet of industrial organization. There are 1,200 buy-outs a year in western Europe, with almost 700 of those in the UK where they account for more than half the number of take-over transactions (*see* Figure 1). In value terms, in the US $41 billion of buy-out deals were recorded in 1998, with the 1999 figure hitting the $50 billion mark. (*See* Figure 2.) Buy-out deal numbers in the US were back to the levels last seen in the late 1980s – in 1998 there were 306 completions.

Considerable differences exist between the size of buy-out markets in individual countries (*see* Figures 3 and 4) with the US and the UK the most important. Highly developed financial, mergers and acquisitions, and private equity markets have been key drivers of their growth. In contrast countries such as Italy, Germany and France, despite their economic size, have lagged behind. Elsewhere buy-outs have been recorded in smaller numbers, although they have been used in the transformation of central and eastern Europe, and African countries such as Zambia, towards market economies. Restructuring opportunities led to several major private equity houses setting up buy-out activities in Japan at the end of the 1990s.

Buy-out opportunities come in several forms. The majority are management buy-outs (MBOs) and involve the acquisition by incumbent management of the business where they are employed. Typically the purchase price is met by a small amount of their own funds (3.3 percent on average for buy-outs of greater than £10 million in the UK in 1998) and the rest from a mix of private equity and bank debt.

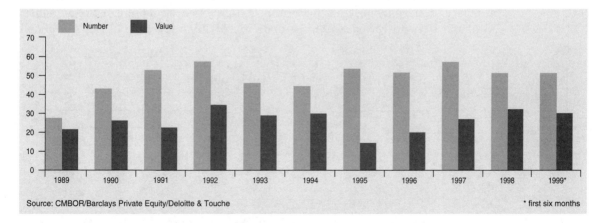

Source: CMBOR/Barclays Private Equity/Deloitte & Touche

* first six months

Figure 1: MBOs and MBIs as percentage of UK takeover activity

Source: BUY-OUTS, Securities Data Co.

* 1999 figures to Dec 6, 1999

Figure 2: US buy-out market

Management buy-ins (MBIs) are a similar form of transaction but differ in that the entrepreneurs leading the transaction come from outside the company. The BIMBO – buy-in/management buy-out – is a hybrid form involving both existing and new management.

The late 1990s also saw the development of IBOs (investor buy-outs) where private equity groups initiate and lead transactions, with management playing a marginal role. Other variants include MEBOs, where management and employees both provide equity. IBOs, in particular, and MBIs are frequently also associated with Leveraged Build-Ups (LBUs) where the initial transaction is used as a nucleus for subsequent major acquisitions. In the US, 46 percent of investments made by buy-out financiers involved corporations that were intended to serve as platforms on which to build larger groups. Such deals are typically aimed at consolidating fragmented industries, and include a need to ensure that entrepreneurs are involved who have the skills for this – as many financiers do not.

Buy-outs are commonly but erroneously portrayed as short-lived, highly leveraged transactions (LBOs) led by leveraged buy-out associations that are little more than a disguised form of asset stripping. This view typically associates the gains from buy-outs as emanating from financial engineering rather than having anything to do with entrepreneurship.

Even in the US, which is usually associated with huge LBO deals, there are large numbers of more modestly sized and less highly geared management buy-outs. Although UK and European buy-outs do involve high leverage in their financial

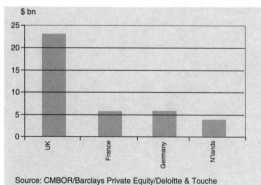

Source: CMBOR/Barclays Private Equity/Deloitte & Touche

Figure 3: Main European buy-out markets by value (1998)

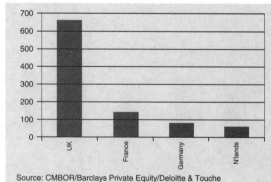

Source: CMBOR/Barclays Private Equity/Deloitte & Touche

Figure 4: Main European buy-out markets by number (1998)

structures and a high emphasis on cash flow generation, they also demonstrate significant entrepreneurial actions.

Direct equity ownership has given a significant impetus to the development of entrepreneurship, which fits in with the increasing recognition that entrepreneurship can involve the purchase of an existing company as well as the creation of a new one. Moreover, entrepreneurial actions can involve both major restructuring of existing operations as well as the development of innovations.

The leading individuals in MBOs and MBIs display similar characteristics and motivations to those of entrepreneurs generally. From our research, the incentive of having equity in the business is the single most important motivating factor for management at the time of the transaction.

Moreover, managers attribute the most important reasons for improvements in post buy-out performance to their increased control in running the business, their direct equity ownership and the opportunity to develop their own strategy. Prior to buy-out the management of Duracell were frustrated as they had a hard time convincing corporate management in the parent corporation Kraft to agree new projects, and had to deal with the bureaucracy of a large corporation that impeded the implementation of innovative actions. Following buy-out, management were able to undertake projects such as the development of rechargeable batteries and smart batteries that played a significant role in the revolution in laptop computers.

Crucially, the stimulus to entrepreneurial action by managers is bolstered by the monitoring and control devices exercised by private equity firms and banks through detailed reporting requirements, board representation and the operation of debt covenants, as well as the commitment to service outside sources of funds.

In buy-outs that arise on divestments from larger groups and from the privatization of state enterprises in particular, such mechanisms are held to reduce agency cost problems arising from the divorce between ownership and control in the former parents.

Developments in both the US and UK markets at the end of the 1990s, however, indicated that an increasing number of transactions were happening not just in mature cash generative industries where efficiencies, debt structure and limits to managerial spending (such as in the Safeway LBO) decreased downside risk as well as creating major improvements in value and performance, but also in fast growing industries including high-tech sectors where highly entrepreneurial skills and access to additional financial resources for the development of the business were critical factors.

In this evolution of the buy-out, private equity backers are increasingly being asked to behave more like traditional venture capitalists. This is most apparent in internet-related transactions with buy-outs such as Exchange Holdings in the UK and traditional buy-out associations such as TH Lee and Putnam Capital launching specialist internet funds in the US, and the Carlye Group a fund for Europe. In such circumstances the importance of an entrepreneurial "mind-set" may be key to the success of the company in independent circumstances when entrepreneurial ambitions are no longer constrained by corporate bureaucracies.

What characterizes the development of buy-outs over the past 15 years is the adaptability of the concept and the diversity of situations to which it may be applied. This is seen in the patterns of development of large and small deals, differences between buy-outs and buy-ins, and changes in the sources of transactions.

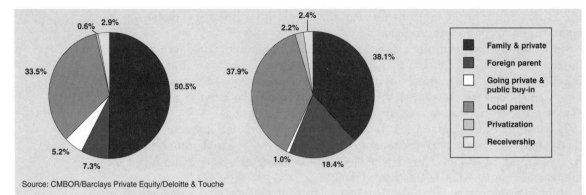

Source: CMBOR/Barclays Private Equity/Deloitte & Touche

Figure 5: Sources of buy-outs/buy-ins in UK and Continental Europe (1998)

Sources for buy-outs

Internationally, the most common sources of buy-out opportunities are divestitures, whether as divestments of parts of larger domestically or foreign-owned groups, family companies facing succession problems, or entire buy-outs, either of publicly traded companies or state-owned enterprises (*see* Figure 5).

Corporate groups may seek to sell subsidiaries as part of a planned strategic disposal program or more forced reorganization in the face of parental financial problems. Publicly quoted companies have, however, increasingly sought to dispose of subsidiaries through an auction process, partly in order to satisfy shareholder pressure for value maximization.

Though divisional management may still need to be involved in the disposal process, concerns that managers may in the past have acquired companies at highly advantageous prices mean that is it no longer common for them to be the preferred bidder, especially for larger deals.

For larger disposals, several private equity firms may be bidding against each other (as well as trade buyers) to complete an IBO. Increased competitive conditions are placing pressures on private equity players to identify investments that can generate attractive enough returns for the fund providers. In order to reduce the potential risks involved, private equity firms either retain existing management to run the company with an equity stake or, as in a buy-in, bring in experienced management to do so. Pressures to restructure large corporations in Japan are also creating corporate disposals in the form of buy-outs, the management buy-out of Sumisho Amenity Life System in 1999 being the first such disposal from the Sumitomo Corporation.

Privately held companies have become an increasingly important source of buy-outs in recent years. In 1986 only a fifth of buy-outs in the UK came from this source; by 1998, privately held family companies accounted for half of the market.

While private deals are smaller on average than divestment buy-outs, recent years have seen large transactions such as AM Paper. Driving this development has been the greater recognition by family vendors of the viability of such deals, the appeal of maintaining the independent identity of their business, tax implications, and greater attention by intermediaries and financiers to this segment of the market. Part of this, however, has reflected the growing number of private equity-backed companies which have sought an exit through a secondary buy-out transaction (*see* Figure 5). In continental Europe this source has traditionally been

Pom'Alliance – a French buy-out from private owners leading to industry restructuring

The case of Pom'Alliance, a FF137 million leveraged build-up type management buy-out completed in France in 1996, illustrates the use of buy-outs to restructure industries dominated by family businesses with limited financial resources and entrepreneurial leadership. These businesses might well not have been able to achieve the next stage, of creating wealth through economies of scale or through the creation of an organization in which perceptions of entrepreneurial opportunities could be realized.

The Pom'Alliance buy-out involved the coming together of five family-owned businesses – Durand, Tocze, Jacob, Pom'Champ and Nord'Pom – in the highly fragmented potato conditioning and distribution sector in France. Initial attempts at a management buy-in to deal with founder succession in Tocze, a major issue in France where founders are often highly reluctant to let go yet are unable or unwilling to grow the business, failed because the company was considered by the venture capital community to be too small and too financially fragile to achieve growth in a highly competitive market. Although it was one of the largest producers with 5 percent of the market, its net profit to sales ratio was only 8 percent. The result was a search to put together a group of family businesses in the sector where owner-managers would be willing to come together to achieve scale economies, national coverage (important in selling to the highly concentrated supermarket sector) and develop new products. The companies together became the largest player in French fresh potato conditioning and distribution, accounting for 20 percent of the market. Shareholders from all five companies became shareholders in the new group, accounting for a total of 60 percent of the equity, with Barclays Private Equity accounting for the balance.

Key to the success of the buy-out was the recognition by the individuals concerned that one of the younger shareholders in Durand had the leadership and entrepreneurial skills to become president of the new group. Without this buy-out arrangement, it is highly unlikely that the owners would have been willing to sell out to another company, nor that the entrepreneurial manager in Durand would have been able to realize his entrepreneurial aims.

The buy-out has changed the nature of competition in the industry from localized producers in fragmented markets to a national-level market and creates the opportunity for exclusive deals with seed producers over new genetic types of potatoes. Following the buy-out two further family-owned potato distributors in other regions of France were acquired and integrated into the new group. Between the buy-out and 1999, operating income increased by 50 percent while the amount of potatoes processed increased by more than a third to 300,000 tons. However, illustrating the problems that founders typically face in working within a large group, the former owner of Pom'Champ/Nord'Pom, who had a 5 percent stake in the buy-out, left shortly afterwards.

A new CEO with US experience in marketing/selling branded products to supermarkets was recruited to realize opportunities in this part of the business, while incumbent management were allowed to practice their skills in sorting potatoes.

very important in countries such as France and Italy, while in Germany the largest buy-out to date was of the formerly family-controlled company Friedrich Grohe in July 1999.

The growing influence of second-time and serial entrepreneurs and the need for fixed-life private equity funds to recycle investee companies will help to bolster the number of buy-outs and buy-ins involving private concerns.

Whole-firm buy-outs have been an important feature of the US market for many years, but have only recently come to prominence elsewhere. From only a few in the late 1980s, the late 1990s in the UK have seen a large number of public-to-private transactions with small to medium-sized capitalizations. These firms generally experienced difficulties with being listed on the stock market. Larger transactions are now occurring with competing bids also in evidence, notably in the case of

Hillsdown Holdings acquired by Hicks, Muse, Furst, Tate after a rival offer from Candover Investments, a British buy-out specialist. In the US, public-to-private transactions also increased again in the late 1990s, though they have yet to return to the levels of a decade earlier. In July 1999, Browning-Ferris Industries was taken private at a value of $9.2 billion.

Privatization buy-outs from state ownership may involve several methods, with buy-outs of complete firms being very important. In the UK necessary restructuring over the past twenty years has resulted in several hundred buy-outs in traditional cash generative sectors such as the bus industry, and also in highly innovative activities such as that highlighted by BTG, a company which holds patents and licenses in medical and high-tech products. In emerging economies restructuring of state sector activities expected as part of international financing packages may result in the disposal of formerly state-controlled companies through buy-outs. At the end of the 1990s increasing interest was being shown by some US buy-out firms in South Africa.

Enhance performance

In recessionary periods buy-outs can play a major part in restructuring failed or failing businesses and, in an environment of generally weakened corporate performance, often represent the only viable purchasers when parents wish to dispose of subsidiaries. But such transactions need to be viable in a market economy. Increasingly, they involve profitable subsidiaries of failed groups where managers may have been prevented from undertaking entrepreneurial acts because of the financial constraints imposed by the failing parent.

Buy-outs are one of the most common forms of privatization, offering opportunities for enhancing the performance of parts of the public sector, widening employee ownership and giving managers and employees incentives to make best use of their expertise in particular sectors. By 1999 there had been more than 300 such deals, more than four times the number of flotations of privatized companies.

Despite traditional management buy-outs coming under pressure from vendors, especially for larger divestment deals, buy-outs initiated by internal management will continue to remain attractive for smaller disposals as they are a cost-effective way for vendors to realize attractive prices for businesses where individual management may be particularly important for the stability of the business.

There are important notes of caution for any management wishing to initiate an opportunity for a buy-out. Great care is needed in the early stages to ensure that confidential information is not disclosed to outside parties (advisers and prospective financiers) without the vendor's permission. Failure to negotiate this initial hurdle is likely to lead not only to the failure of the buy-out to get off the ground but also the instant dismissal of the management. Professional advisers have an important role to play in these circumstances in placing a buffer between management and the vendor.

It is also important for management to ask themselves searching questions about their commitment and ability to complete a buy-out and subsequently make it work. Do managers genuinely want to trade the (increasingly relative) security and demands of a larger organization for the very different demands of a buy-out? Will good line managers and divisional directors make the successful transition into good owner-managers? Advisers and prospective financiers will also want to obtain positive answers to these questions.

Wellman – a privatization transaction followed by a major acquisition

At the time of the privatization buy-out in January 1998, Wellman (since renamed Newmall) comprised three divisions all operating in the engineering sector. The transport equipment division consisted of a number of UK-based businesses, active in the vehicle emissions testing and parking equipment markets, and others which manufactured magnetic recording and impact printers. Subsidiaries included: Bradbury Lifts, Crypton Engine Diagnostics, Spraybrake Spray Booths, Peters Bus Doors, Parking Technology Car Park Systems, as well as Transerve Service and Data Recording Computer Printers and Heads.

The thermal engineering division manufactured boilers, pressure vessels, and industrial furnaces, heat exchangers, condensers, chemical process equipment and submarine life support systems, mainly in the UK. Finally, there is the US-based ESP business, leader in the development, manufacture and service of car emission test systems.

Operating from a head office in Yorkshire, Wellman had sales of £128 million and after-tax profits of £6.8 million in its last financial year up to March 1997. Having fallen to a 12-month low of 23p, following warnings about problems in the UK garage equipment business, the buy-out offer of 50p per share represented a premium of 77 percent over the price of 28p which existed before bid rumors lifted the price to 39.75p. The buy-out deal valued Wellman at £76 million. Alchemy, a private equity house, invested £20 million for a majority stake, with management taking 19.6 percent of the equity for an investment of £2.8 million. A debt package comprising a £20 million revolving facility and £30 million term loan was arranged by Bank of Scotland and jointly underwritten by Dresdner Kleinwort Benson, which has also invested £2 million in return for a 5.4 percent equity stake and provided a mezzanine facility of £22.5 million with an 8.75 percent equity warrant attached.

Alchemy felt that Wellman had a history of undisciplined acquisitions followed by profit warnings, which had adversely affected its market price. It was apparent to Alchemy at the time of the deal not only that Wellman needed to be restructured but that the group contained a jewel in ESP. As a consequence a second deal was carried out in the US to buy out ESP's main competitor.

Following the buy-out there was speculation that an early IPO of one of the group's three divisions as a restructured entity could be valued at more than the price paid for the whole of Wellman. Although this reflotation has not occurred, significant restructuring has taken place. A number of disposals from within the company's transport equipment and thermal engineering divisions have recouped the purchase price.

Since the buy-out, Newmall has been restructured into two groups: Newmall, which owns the US interests, and Really Newmall, which owns Wellman's UK interests. As a result of two refinancings all of the initial acquisition debt has been repaid as well as part of the original equity investment. Funds from asset disposals from within the transport equipment and thermal engineering divisions have been used to begin expansion of the group's US division, including a $266.3 million bid for the Californian-based vehicle emission testing equipment manufacturer Envirotest Systems Corp, which has already been unanimously accepted by the Envirotest board. To do this deal, Newmall formed a wholly-owned indirect subsidiary, Stone Rivet. An $803 million funding package was put together, consisting of $80 million invested by Alchemy through ESP, together with a refinancing package of $723 million provided by Credit Suisse First Boston in the US. Pre-tax profits for the combined ESP and Envirotest entity have been forecast at $120 million. Expansion of the business into Europe is likely.

Wealth creation

Most studies of post buy-out performance changes have concerned the short period after the transaction and generally confirm substantial improvements in profitability, cash flow and productivity measures between one year prior to buy-out and two or three years subsequent to it. Improvements in working capital management, particularly credit management, and productivity are important sources of improved performance.

Important contributions may also come from the private equity investors in the buy-out. With their experience of their own portfolios which may include related businesses, they frequently get involved in sharing strategic insights and implementing improvements in operational and strategic controls. Increasingly in the UK, and reflecting experience in the US (such as the buy-out of Berg Electronics), buy-outs are followed by the acquisition of other companies in the same industry, giving opportunities for synergies and the evolution of a group which will be more attractive to public markets on an IPO. For instance, Hicks, Muse, Furst, Tate's $310 million buy-out of the Mumm and Perrier-Jouet champagne houses from Seagram is expected to be used as a platform to build global brands in the wine and spirits industry.

The authors' survey of strategy and performance in UK buy-outs showed that outsider-driven deals such as IBOs and MBIs were more likely than insider-driven deals to engage in merger and acquisition strategies, with IBOs more likely than other types of buy-outs to increase their range of products and markets. There was considerable evidence that buy-outs at the end of the 1990s were engaging in more growth-oriented strategies than in rationalization.

Although experience in the US LBO market has indicated that much of the gain in buy-out transactions may be a result of downsizing, increasingly US research, as well as our own UK research, points to the importance of innovative behavior by management teams. Significant increases in new product development are found to occur post buy-out, especially in smaller venture-backed transactions, which the entrepreneurs concerned believe would not otherwise have happened.

Our UK study showed that asset sales were generally low and were typically offset by new capital investment, particularly in plant and equipment. Our recent research shows that over years three to five after the change in ownership, buy-outs on average perform significantly better than comparable non-buy-outs.

The performance of management buy-ins has, however, been generally less strong, though they have typically involved more extensive restructuring. Coming from outside with less detailed knowledge of the business, it has often proved more difficult than expected for management and investors to achieve enhanced short-term profitability.

Often, for this reason, pure management buy-ins are replaced by hybrid BIMBOs that combine the advantages of insiders' skills and knowledge and the outsider's entrepreneurial dynamism. The new interest among private equity players for non-traditional buy-out opportunities may have a significant effect on overall buy-out wealth creation.

Exits and rates of return

There is considerable debate about whether buy-outs are a long- or short-term form of organization.

Research in both the US and Europe shows that buy-outs have a heterogeneous life-cycle – some last only a short time while others retain the buy-out form for long periods. While about half of larger buy-outs are sold or floated within four years, the majority last well in excess of seven years.

The principal factors influencing the longevity of a buy-out relate to the objectives and needs of the parties involved – owner-managers, financiers and the company itself. The extent and form of exit from buy-outs and buy-ins will always be influenced, at least to some degree, by the cyclical nature of stock and takeover

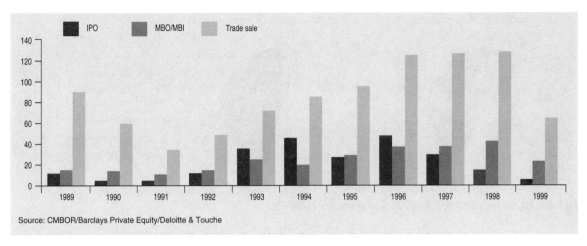

Figure 6: Exits of buy-outs and buy-ins (1989–99)

market conditions. In the UK the number of transactions exiting through the IPO route fell significantly in the late 1990s (*see* Figure 6) and in 1999 were principally of IT-related and internet companies, benefitting from the attraction of this sector to investors.

There are also clear pressures leading to exit by means of a secondary buy-out or buy-in involving either a new set of managers from outside or the secondary layer from inside the company. In some cases these may involve inter-institutional deals and be motivated by circumstances where the first buy-out was backed by a private equity company relying on a closed-end fund that needs to exit within a limited life span.

Initially this exit route tended to involve relatively small companies in very specific niche markets, which may therefore not be attractive to strategic buyers or be feasible candidates for a stock market flotation, but in the first three quarters of 1999 the three largest such transactions were greater than any conventional trade sale exit. In some markets, such as France, secondary deals involving inter-institutional sales may be important means of making an exit for the institutions where incumbent management have significant majority ownership and wish to remain independent. It is also a major influence in countries where stock and merger and acquisitions markets are less developed than in the UK and US.

Buy-out and especially buy-in entrepreneurs may not simply be "one-shot" wonders who have taken advantage of a promising opportunity that has been presented to them. As the market matures further, an increasing number of entrepreneurs who have bought out or bought into companies are exiting and seeking to become involved in further deals, adding to the growing phenomenon of serial entrepreneurs.

Financing and structuring

Among key factors in the long-term success of individual buy-outs and buy-ins have been the initial pricing of the transaction and the financing structure.

Prices are influenced both by economic conditions and by the desire by sellers to maximize the sale price and avoid accusations by shareholders that assets have been sold too cheaply to insiders. A number of mechanisms, such as auctions, earn-

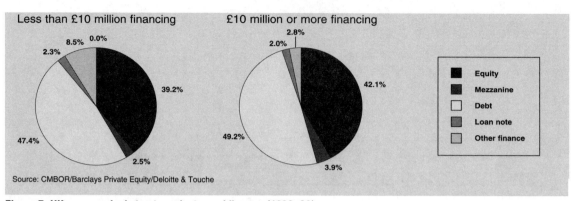

Less than £10 million financing

£10 million or more financing

0.0%
8.5%
2.3%
39.2%
47.4%
2.5%

2.8%
2.0%
42.1%
49.2%
3.9%

- Equity
- Mezzanine
- Debt
- Loan note
- Other finance

Source: CMBOR/Barclays Private Equity/Deloitte & Touche

Figure 7: UK average deal structures by type of finance (1998–99)

outs, retained equity stakes and other non-embarrassment clauses, have been developed to deal with these issues.

The result, however, is the potential danger that, for investors and management, prices may become too high. It is thus necessary for management to keep clear in their minds during the negotiation stage that it may be better to walk away from a deal that is too highly priced rather than be carried away with misplaced enthusiasm to buy, whatever the cost.

Buy-outs will typically be financed by a mixture of senior secured debt and a range of equity and quasi-equity instruments (*see* Figure 7). For larger buy-outs, especially when auctions and buoyant conditions mean that prices well in excess of the security value of assets have to be paid, subordinated (mezzanine) debt may be used. Mezzanine has found itself in competition with other types of subordinated lending. In particular, after a lull for most of the 1990s, high-yield debt ("junk bonds") has re-emerged in the US, and a European market for such financing instruments has been established. The buy-out market has also seen the development of so-called "alphabet debt," where banks provide different layers of senior debt in a deal, each with different terms (the "A" layer may have traditional repayment terms, the "B" layer may have deferred capital repayments and a longer time horizon, and the "C" layer may be repayable on exit).

European mega-deals may now have several different layers of subordinated debt and notes, a long way from traditional equity, mezzanine and senior debt structures. These financing instruments both allow more debt to be taken on, hence enabling a higher price to be paid in an auction, and to achieve a greater match between a company's cash profile and the servicing of external funding. In the US, mezzanine players have started to invest in convertible stock, taking a control position and even investing in internet companies.

Quasi-equity instruments, such as cumulative, convertible, participating, preferred, ordinary shares, are important in ensuring the private equityist obtains a regular dividend, in putting pressure on managers to perform, and/or seek to realize an investment in a timely fashion. Depending on the taxation regime, convertible unsecured loan stock may be used to perform a similar function.

Private equity backers will typically be looking for an annual IRR (internal rate of return) on their investment in the upper 20s – slightly more for MBIs but less for large transactions. Bank lenders will be putting more emphasis on cash flow aspects and less on asset backing than in most corporate finance transactions.

The Future Network – an entrepreneurial buy-out followed by rapid build-up and IPO

Future is a leading publisher of video games, home computing and other specialist magazines, and internet websites in Europe and the US. Future is also the leading publisher in the video games and specialized magazine sectors in the UK, France and Italy, and at the end of 1998 had a market share of 30 percent in these sectors in the US. Future was established as a start-up operation in 1985, and through organic expansion and acquisition group turnover had grown to £89 million in 1998.

In 1994 Future was acquired by Pearson but in April 1998 was sold to an executive team – which included the original founder – for £116 million and the repayment of inter-company indebtedness of £8.94 million. The deal was backed by Apax Partners, with Citibank providing mezzanine and senior debt.

The buy-out was followed by major organic growth and acquisition activity. In early 1999 Future acquired 15 video game and home computing titles from the Il Mio Castello group. It entered an agreement to acquire Imagine Media, a Californian-based company owned by Future's founder, and publishing titles such as *PC Gamer* and *Business 2.0*; it also established a subsidiary in Germany. These acquisitions led to further equity subscriptions by Apax and Chris Anderson, as well as mezzanine facilities from Citibank, Intermediate Capital Group and RBS Mezzanine. There was also an extension to the senior debt facility. The effect of these acquisitions was to increase the 1998 turnover by £70 million to £159.9 million.

In June 1999 the company's share capital was reorganized, and Morgan Stanley sponsored a placing of 45 million ordinary new shares with institutional investors in the US, UK and other European countries. This raised £133.3 million net for Future which was going to be used to repay almost four fifths of the indebtedness incurred by the buy-out and the Il Mio Castello acquisition. The balance of this indebtedness was to be refinanced to allow Future to continue to develop its US and German operations, and internet activities. Further growth was expected to come from: the existing video game and home computing magazine business; the exploitation of synergies between the smaller US and larger UK operations; growth in France and Italy; the development of other specialist consumer magazine market segments; development of internet activities; and growth in other geographic markets. Chris Anderson's shareholding represented 24.2 percent of the enlarged capital.

In the short period following the IPO, there was significant institutional interest in the company, sharp rises in the share price and further acquisition activity. This included the acquisition of four video games titles in Germany, the launch of Future Net (a global internet business) and the rights to publish official Manchester United and Chelsea soccer magazines. A secondary placing was arranged, with 18 million further shares placed at 620p each. This involved Apax being released from their original lock-up agreement for these shares with their shareholding in Future falling to 14.5 percent.

This range of financial instruments enables buy-outs to be financed in sectors beyond those involving the classic LBO case, that is those which are mature with stable cash flow and low investment needs, and includes those with significant investment requirements and in technological sectors. For example, in the UK, 6 percent of the buy-out market involves companies in computing-related and electronics communications systems sectors. In some countries, specific financial incentives may be put in place to encourage buy-outs. In France, the market was stimulated by tax concessions to managers buying out in order to encourage the use of buy-outs to deal with succession issues in family businesses. In Japan, public loan guarantees, and relaxations of regulations on stock options, have been introduced for companies taken over by management in order to encourage restructuring of the large *Keiretsu* groups.

Where there are differences in the valuation placed on a business by managers and institutions, the transaction may use an equity ratchet with the size of management's equity stake dependent on performance targets.

Set over a specific period of time, these instruments are a mechanism for helping ensure that financiers' target exit horizons are achieved. However, setting the precise terms of equity ratchets is difficult, with frequent disagreements between private equityists and management over the point at which they are triggered.

Monitoring and restructuring

In general, relationships established between management and private equity firms appear to be an important basis for creating the flexibility required for effective monitoring. This emphasizes the need for managers buying out to take great care in selecting their private equity partner.

While larger buy-out candidates do seem to make more use of advisers in choosing between potential financiers, this is less true at the smaller end of the market. It is necessary to remember both that there is a need to select a financier with whom management can establish a successful working relationship, and that there is something of an inherent conflict between the interests of managers and financiers, since, for example, a greater equity share for managers means a lower share for institutions. These issues need to be addressed carefully at the time of the deal, with the knowledge and skill of the managers' advisers providing the means to ensure that their interests are properly addressed.

Covenants attached to the provision of debt also involve close monitoring relationships between banks and their buy-out clients. Breaches of these covenants are typically an early warning signal of problems rather than a signal to put the company into receivership.

When problems arise, difficulties can emerge in restructuring smaller deals where management are important majority shareholders, and in buy-outs with syndicated finance. While consensus between institutions and management is important in taking rectifying action, this may be difficult. The recent trend towards smaller syndicates, with members with compatible objectives, has gone some way to addressing the problems of delay in obtaining agreement about the nature and extent of restructuring that have arisen in larger syndicates.

Increasing competition for deals and increasing entry prices at times of market buoyancy underlines the need for management and private equity partners to have clear objectives as to the direction of the buy-out or buy-in. The need for outside investors to help management to add value through strategic development assumes greater significance in such circumstances.

Particular problems arise with management buy-ins, which show a significantly higher failure rate than buy-outs. Despite considerably greater investor monitoring than is found in buy-outs, there may be major difficulties with due diligence at the time of the transaction, with consequent difficulties in effecting turnaround strategies.

The cost of due diligence in relation to transaction value in smaller buy-ins, time constraints in negotiations, as well as problems in identifying information, often mean that it is not carried out effectively. Institutions and intermediaries have become much more aware of the potential risks in MBIs and are paying great attention to the screening and matching of both entrepreneurs and target companies through dedicated programs (*see* the article by Robert M. Johnson on p. 330, *Innovative funding for first-timers*).

Rewards and risks on the MBO road

Robert Smith explains how a buy-out works and how success can result in substantial rewards.

Traditionally, most management buy-outs occur because a parent company wants to get rid of a particular subsidiary or, in the case of a private company, because an entrepreneur who has built up his or her own business has no one within the family to succeed him or her, so they turn to second-line management to buy the business.

However, this situation has started to change as the MBO market matures. Increasingly there are in effect bands of "nomadic" managers who spot a potential turnaround situation and want to go in if the parent can be persuaded to sell. These are more and more supported by small "boutiques" of two or three people – usually from an investment banking background – who find buy-out opportunities and also find the management to put in. Usually they work up the transaction so that by the time they come to an investment bank such as Morgan Grenfell they have a business plan, an agreement with the parent company, a price, and they are actually telling us on what terms we should shape our investment.

But to go back to the traditional scenario of a manager considering a buy-out. Generally he or she will have talked to an accountant who specializes in MBOS. They will then eventually come along and talk to an investment bank like us. We take up the negotiations with the parent company or the entrepreneur, though sometimes they already have the glimmerings of a deal. We then sit down and, hopefully, say "OK, we think this can work and it looks as if it would stand this much debt and this much equity." The next stages take in a study of the business plan and due diligence, processes that have been described earlier in *Mastering Entrepreneurship*.

Another new development in the MBO market is that while everyone gets an accounting report, there is a real move to getting a consultant's report, which will look at particular aspects of the company such as the likely movement of market prices or the costs of environmental issues.

In the old days buy-outs were done in a couple of weeks. One that took two or three months was the exception; now they are the exception for the opposite reason. Buy-outs have become a very long process, often six or nine months, and a lot of it is to do with banks negotiating covenants with the vendor.

Usually the managers faced with an MBO opportunity have little idea of all that is involved. They may never even have spoken to their high-street bank manager, certainly never met an investment banker. The idea of equity, ratchets and preference shares is far removed from their experience.

Incidentally, though, while they may have no idea what is going on at the beginning and they can often get the feeling that things are getting out of their control as their advisers seem to be doing all the talking, they learn very quickly. Within two weeks they usually know everything.

Given incentive

They are also worried about putting up money. However, generally speaking, the actual sum that managers put up is not important. Let's say we are dealing with a £100 million buy-out. In effect we say to the management team: "You can have 10 percent virtually for nothing." That 10 percent is itself almost an arbitrary figure; 5 percent may seem too small; 20 percent too big. Yet if the deal goes through and we exit at a good price, there will be large sums of money available for everyone. If there is a performance ratchet in place, the managers can end up with a 20 percent or 30 percent share.

But to go back to the original 10 percent. This is given to managers virtually for nothing because the principle is from each according to their ability. So, for example, if we know a manager has done buy-outs before and is worth several million pounds, we might not be too keen on his just putting up £10,000.

Let's assume a typical £100 million MBO with £50 million of equity. The management team would probably be asked to put up £500,000, say £100,000 or so each. For that they will receive 10 percent of the equity. Really they should get 1 percent because the investment bank has put up 99 percent of the money. But the bank cannot do it without the management. They make the widgets and they have to be given an incentive.

The problem with this from the bank's point of view is that, if we do even moderately well, the bank gets its money back but the managers make ten times their money. Fortunately or unfortunately you cannot do anything about that because managers simply would not do a deal on the basis of 1 percent. So, unless managers are really disastrous, they are going to make some cash out of an MBO.

They can make a lot of cash. To go back to the example, if we double the equity and the company is now worth £100 million – and it should double, generally you are not doing particularly well if your portfolio doesn't more than double over three to five years – managers now have, as of right, 10 percent of the equity, worth £10 million, for the £500,000 they put up.

However, the ratchet might be operating at that level so they might actually get £15 million or £20 million. If that £50 million becomes £150 million, you would be getting hugely more than £15 million. As the bank has trebled its money, the managers would be getting £30 million or £40 million.

Where, then, is the risk, for managers? Well, an MBO is very, very hard work and sometimes things fail to work out. It's high pressure and high risk and banks can rightly be very tough when they are investing sums as large as £50 million. Generally they take a very hands-on approach to the management. For example, we almost always change the finance director. We always put in an independent non-executive chairman. One of us always goes on the board. If a year or 18 months into the process things are not happening then we have to do something about it. You can't just say "gosh, we made a mistake; we'll write off £50 million."

Managers can also get worn out during the process. You get "deal fatigue" where people will agree to almost anything just to get the deal done, and that's where you make mistakes.

A management team to lure investors

What are investors looking for in an MBO/MBI? **Daniel Muzyka**, **Michael Hay** and **Sue Birley** sum up the priorities for those wishing to buy into a business.

Management buy-outs and/or leveraged buy-outs are an important part of the entrepreneurship picture worldwide, but especially in Europe and the US. Among other things, there is a large base of existing businesses, significant amounts of corporate restructuring, and a very large inter-generational wealth transfer of businesses, many created after the Second World War.

All of this establishes a set of opportunities that may be exploited as a base for entrepreneurial ambitions by existing managers (MBOs), external entrepreneurs wishing to buy into the business (management buy-ins or MBIs) or some combination of the above.

The major question posed by many wishing to undertake a buy-out is "what are the investors looking for?" – in essence, "what do we have to look like to be an attractive and credible investment opportunity?" Two questions related to whether the business is an attractive investment are: "Would someone back me as managing director of a buy-out/buy-in?" and "Would our management team be viewed as a good bet to exploit the value in a potential buy-out/buy-in?" These questions are related to what investors are looking for in a buy-out/buy-in management team.

We undertook to address these questions in a study with the support and co-operation of BDO Stoy Hayward, the UK accountants. In the process we surveyed approximately 60 management buy-out investors. This provided us with some useful insights into what they look for in a business opportunity, the leader of a management buy-out/buy-in team, and the management team in general. The research first explored the factors they look at and, through various means, managed to capture the relative ranking of importance of each of the factors.

Overall business factors

The factors that buy-out/buy-in investors look at when evaluating opportunities are, with a few small exceptions, largely the same as those which venture capitalists consider (*see* Figure 1 and Part 3, p. 103). The findings from the study suggest that the relative importance of the various factors is also similar.

Looking for the right management team

Management team factors reign supreme on the list of opportunity evaluation factors. The relative set of competencies of the team is also very important. The relative skills and capabilities of management to continue properly to manage the business on a free-standing basis combined with their ability to build and capture new value in the business appear to be a key interest of potential investors.

In terms of strategic competitive factors that MBO/MBI investors look at in evaluating an opportunity, the one that they appear to look at most closely is the ability of the business to sustain its existing competitive position after the buy-out or buy-in.

	Figure 1	
1	Leadership capability of management team	**management team factor**
2	Track record of management team	**management team factor**
3	Sustained share competitive position	**strategic-competitive factor**
4	Track record of team leader	**management team factor**
5	Completeness and balance within management team	**management team f.**
6	Complete business data	**deal factor**
7	Leadership capability of team leader	**management team factor**
8	Ease of cash-out	**financial factor**
9	Organizational/adminstrative capabilities of team	**management competence f.**
10	Expected rate of return	**financial factor**
11	Recognized industry expertise in management team	**management team f.**
12	Degree of product-market understanding	**product-market factor**
13	Marketing-sales capabilities of team	**management competence factor**
14	Process/production capabilities of team	**management competence factor**
15	Price/earnings ratio	**financial factor**
16	Major capital expenditure	**financial factor**
17	Financial/accounting capabilities of team	**management competence factor**
18	Clarity of method of exit	**deal factor**
19	Market growth and attractiveness	**product-market factor**
20	Business meets fund constraints	**fund factor**
21	Relative experience of investors in industry	**fund factor**
22	Ability of investors to influence nature of business	**fund factor**
23	Apparent method of exit	**deal factor**
24	Nature and degrees of competition	**strategic-competitive factor**
25	Seasonality of product-market	**product-market factor**
26	Working capital	**financial factor**
27	Current market share of business	**product-market factor**
28	Sensitivity to economic cycles	**product-market factor**
29	Ability to syndicate deal	**deal factor**
30	Time to payback	**financial factor**
31	Sale of assets	**financial factor**
32	Market size	**product-market factor**
33	Business and product fit with fund portfolio	**fund factor**
34	Location of business relative to fund	**fund factor**
35	Number and nature of co-investors in deal	**deal factor**

Figure 1: Ranking of general opportunity criteria

	Figure 2	
1	Ability to inspire others to action	**people skills**
2	Ability to build and maintain an effective management team	**people skills**
3	Ability to instigate, implement and manage change	**people skills**
4	Ability to manage a business in a crisis situation	**people skills**
5	Ability to maintain an overall strategic perspective	**business skills**
6	Leadership capabilities in product-marketplace	**business skills**
7	Perseverance in pursuit of achievement	**leadership style**
8	Ability to drive important decisions past objections	**leadership style**
9	Ability to take and manage risks	**business skills**
10	Ability to articulate vision	**vision and values**
11	Ability to articulate and persuade others of views	**people skills**
12	Creativity in defining solutions to problems	**decision process**
13	Ability to resolve business conflicts	**business skills**
14	Ability to share thinking with team	**people skills**
15	Degree to which the individual is action-oriented	**leadership style**
16	Ability to frame problems	**decision process**
17	Ability to select and focus on appropriate details	**decision process**
18	Ability to manage, learn from and move on from failures	**personal skills**
19	Strong professional career	**personal skills**
20	Confidence in own abilities and mission	**vision and values**
21	Ability to manage with incomplete information	**decision process**
22	Ability to resolve interpersonal conflicts	**people skills**
23	Ability to convey a sense of values	**vision and values**
24	An open decision-making style	**leadership style**
25	Listening skills	**personal skills**
26	A deductive analytical style	**decision process**
27	Ability to stick to decision once taken	**leadership style**
28	An inductive analytical style	**decision process**
29	Financial and accounting capabilities, skills and orientation	**business skills**
30	Ability to achieve consensus with his team	**people skills**
31	Ability to be consistent in decision-making	**leadership style**
32	Degree to which leader is directly involved in teamwork	**leadership style**
33	Technical leadership capabilities in area of interest	**business skills**
34	Orientation toward direct control of tasks	**leadership style**
35	Adminstrative capabilities	**business skills**

Figure 2: Ranking of leadership criteria

Financial and product-market related factors are only moderately important. This may seem surprising but the logic appears sound: if the business does not have a good management team, what good are the projected returns?

The ability to implement is prized over the ability to analyze and conceptualize what could be done. Of the financial factors that are seen as relatively most important, on average the ease of cashing out and the expected rate of return are the most highly regarded.

Fund and deal factors (the potential investment's relationship to the fund and factors related to the specific deal and deal structure) are of limited relative importance. This is not to suggest that they are totally unimportant but that when they are compared to other factors they take on relatively less importance. What it does say, though, is that buy-out/buy-in investors who see a deal with a good management team, even if it is not physically next door or among their most desired industries for investment, are likely to take notice and invest.

Stronger expectations of a business track record

The one factor related to the specific deal that does stand out, however, is the completeness of business data. MBO/MBI investors, unlike their venture capital counterparts, do have the luxury in these circumstances of looking at the track record of the business.

A business deal that is presented to them with a complete record is more likely to be prized than one without. This tends to reduce the basic uncertainty surrounding the possibility of returns and gives the investors the ability to focus on the magnitude and nature of the hidden value in the business. The message to the business team is obvious: put together as clear and concise a story regarding the business as possible.

Expectation of a short investment horizon

As you might expect, investors in management buy-outs are not looking at the same long-run sorts of investments as venture capitalists. They see value in existing operations and seek to invest in realizing the value, be it through repositioning the business, restructuring the operations and/or the leveraging of new product opportunities. However, they wish this repositioning to take place in a two to three year time frame.

The very long-run value creation is left to the management team with the hope that several years of investment and partnership will sufficiently help to create and communicate the value in such a way that they may realize a good return on their investment.

This shorter time horizon is also partially reflected in the increased sensitivity of MBO/MBI investors to the relative seasonality of a business. If one measures exit times in a few years rather than the five to seven year horizon of a venture capitalist, then seasonality can have an impact on exiting.

Furthermore, the time horizon may also be affecting the moderate importance attached to the clarity around the method of investor exit when looking at an opportunity. This is not something a long-term venture capitalist would be concerned about.

One of the issues we explored that is related to the nature of the returns was the relative role of asset sales. Was a business more desirable if, in the process of exposing the basic value of the business, there were assets that could be sold off? The answer to this question is fairly straightforward: there is little general interest in the sale of assets. This particular factor ended up 31 out of 35.

Leadership criteria

With regard to the criteria that they look for in the leader of a management buy-out/buy-in team, the answer from investors is both clear and consistent with their investment horizon and interests. The factors they look for and evaluate in a leader are more related to their basic motivational skills than the nature of their decision-making process (*see* Figure 2).

Investors are looking for someone who can build and maintain a highly motivated management team dedicated to realizing economic value through action and change. In essence they are looking for someone who will quickly articulate and drive the necessary changes past objections as well as mobilize people to undertake the necessary actions in order to induce required change.

They are also realistic in looking for someone who can manage the changes they undertake. With change comes some form of crisis and investors prize crisis management skills very highly.

It is suspected that due to their horizons they are less interested in the leader's abilities to manage long-term values or to build long-run consensus. Furthermore, they are not looking for leaders who build their portfolio of skills strongly upon their

1 Effectiveness of group decision-making	team decision-making
2 Ability of team to lead the organization	team and the firm
3 Previous profitable track record	team effectiveness
4 Sucess in managing business-related conflicts	team effectiveness
5 Trust within team	intra-team relations
6 Commitment to group goals	intra-team relations
7 Ability to manage interpersonal conflicts	team effectiveness
8 Balance in team skills	demography
9 Level of collective motivation	team effectiveness
10 Team understanding of/commitment to investor's needs	team and the investor
11 Respect for team by lower management levels	team and the firm
12 Personal financial commitment	team and the investor
13 Group creativity in decision-making	team decision-making
14 Attainment of cross-functional solutions	team decision-making
15 Collective sense of ownership	intra-team relations
16 Team's trust of lower managment levels	team and the firm
17 Consistency in analytical approach	team decision-making
18 Fit between team and investors	team and the investor
19 Team spirit	intra-team relations
20 Personal interaction/communication	intra-team relations
21 Commonality of/desire for group goals	intra-team relations
22 Need to augment team size/change team composition	demography
23 Consistency in team (group) behavior	intra-team relations
24 Career improvement motivation	team and the firm
25 Size of team equity	team and the investor
26 Team size	demography
27 Age of team members	demography
28 Commonality in age of team	demography

Figure 3: Ranking of team criteria

administrative abilities. Also tied to this is the little relative value they attach to specific management styles. In fact, comparatively little attention appears to be paid to the nature of the leadership style exhibited.

What the experience of the buy-out/buy-in investors suggests is that would-be MBO/MBI entrepreneurs may wish to take an inventory of their management style and to reconceptualize their role as a business leader. The leadership style they may have as managing director of a business within a holding company or larger corporation may not be appropriate. The leadership abilities that can bring success in a corporate context (for example, building a management team in a corporate division, building a consensus around the direction of the business, and satisfying the informational and political needs within the corporate hierarchy) may not be suitable in the buy-out/buy-in context.

Nature of the management team

We also explored the characteristics MBO/MBI investors look at in evaluating management teams. These characteristics were then ranked by these investors through our research (*see* Figure 3).

The picture that emerges is a concern on the part of investors that the potential management team has the ability to manage their business-related conflicts and reach decisions in an expeditious manner. Trust within the team is something that is relatively highly regarded by potential investors, as is a previous track record as a team. Other characteristics that are important are overall commitment to a single set of goals, balance and motivation within the team, and a general understanding and appreciation of investor needs. The ability to manage inter-personal conflict is also prized.

How they achieve these elements is something that is of less concern to potential investors. Again, the shorter-run horizon may be making itself clear in the relatively moderate weight attached to such factors as team spirit, trust of lower levels of management, collective sense of ownership, group creativity, and the like.

From this research with potential investors there appears to be no consensus on, or relative importance attached to, the demographics of the team (team size, age and so on). While balance is prized, the need to augment or change the team is not something of ultimate importance to investors. Nor, for that matter, is the relative long-run consistency, fit and underlying motivation of team members. As long as they are committed to the buy-out/buy-in for the initial period, the long-run motivations are set aside.

Reflecting the logic of venture capitalists, MBO/MBI investors made it clear both through their comments and the surveys we conducted that personal financial commitment was important but that the absolute amount of such commitment was less important. The investors have the required money, they just want to know that depending on their means the team has enough commitment and therefore motivation in the deal to lead them to maximize their performance.

In summary, the ultimate team is one that is able to articulate and act on what needs to be done. The ability to deliver in the shorter run is a matter of major concern for investors.

The bottom line

If you have a business you believe has relatively clear potential for value creation, given the right team and a change of ownership, do not hesitate to contact a buy-out/buy-in investor. Money is clearly available and they are interested. The business need not be in any particular sector or necessarily geographically close to potential investors. No particular industry or other business characteristics are important beyond the competence of the proposed management team and a basically sound business. The bottom line is that a good bottom line will yield investors.

CASE STUDY

The React Group

Written by University of British Columbia Professor **Daniel Muzyka**, and Entrepreneur-in-Residence at INSEAD **Michael Ullman**, this edited case was developed to describe a particular business situation rather than to illustrate either effective or ineffective handling of a particular situation. The development of this case was funded through the generosity of the International Alumni Fund of INSEAD. This case is disguised.

Robert Andrews, President of the React Group, a conglomerate of 15 companies in the clothes manufacturing business, is meeting with his Vice President of Finance, Jim Woodward. They are reviewing the cash position of the group as of September 1, 1989 and are faced with some difficult decisions.

A cash shortage they had predicted nine months before was now scheduled to occur earlier than expected. Given the rigorous covenants and aggressive repayment schedule associated with the debt from the leveraged buy-out, combined with certain unexpected operating problems, the React Group would be unable to meet its next scheduled payment on its senior debt obligations due on November 15, 1989. Management would have to begin to make some difficult choices, including "rationing" cash to meet payments to suppliers.

Andrews decides that a meeting of the banking syndicate must be called and that negotiations to reschedule the company's debt must be undertaken in earnest to avoid default. By the end of the day, Andrews has contacted and scheduled meetings for the next week with the lead bank in the syndicate (Norton Simon), the React Group's lead venture capitalist (Roper Capital), the company's solicitors (Nelson Walters) and the corporate accountants (Raymond Jones) regarding the impending cash problems.

The React Group, one of a growing number of management buy-outs in the UK, was formed from the clothing division of Gartner Ltd, a company which had recently been taken over by an aggressive, successful and well-publicised conglomerate, Multicorp. Multicorp, having acquired Gartner for its home furnishings business, had been willing to consider the sale of the clothing business.

The React Group was a diversified clothing business which both manufactured and imported the whole spectrum of clothing from children's to adult wear. Customers for various companies in the conglomerate included Marks and Spencer, the large British clothing retailer. In addition, several of the divisions of the React Group made various well-known branded lines, including athletic clothing such as swimwear. There were many seasonal businesses, but various of the businesses peaked during different seasons.

Many of the businesses were relatively small, located throughout the UK and Ireland. Clothes were also imported from the Far East through a successful importing operation. The businesses all shared a common focus on the design and marketing of clothing.

The early days of the new management's reign were busy. The businesses had deteriorated markedly due to a softness in the UK economy and a lack of sufficient management attention. As a result, the agreement to take over the company, signed on July 28, 1989, preceded two disastrous operating months for the business.

A new financial director and management accountants were added, who brought in control systems that provided management with a significant capacity to monitor the financial status of each of the group's 15 companies. Central cash control and reporting were instituted.

In line with Robert Andrews' beliefs about the clothing trade, the new entity proved much more responsive in its reincarnation. A new image was forged and the "React Group" – a group of companies that would react more quickly to market and customer needs – was formed. A corporate communications organization was chosen to build and communicate this new image.

The new management also replaced many of the top managers of the company. Seven of the 15 major heads of businesses were replaced. In addition, weak parts of the overall enterprise were cut and several companies were sold almost immediately.

After the financial director came on-board in November, several issues became apparent. First, certain contingent liabilities in the range of £6 million were uncovered, primarily in the import business. Most budgets proved to be quite near to the business plan of eight months before, but the larger contingent liabilities relating to the foreign exchange cover and to letters of credit of the import business were eating up 60 percent (as opposed to 20 percent) of the agreed overdraft. It also became clear that there would be a lack of required cash in the first quarter of 1990 unless trading improved.

Discussions with Norton Simon indicated that it felt no need to tell the rest of the syndicate about the likely cash shortfall in 1990. Norton Simon indicated that this cash shortfall was only projected, outside of the published budget time scale and all debt payments were current.

Andrews realized that he had yet another daunting task ahead of him. Cash flow projections would simply not cover the debt repayments and the operating needs of the business. Projections suggested that by mid-November, the business would have a cash shortfall of at least £10 million.

Discussions with individuals at Norton Simon and other professionals suggested that they appreciated management coming to them so early and that something probably could be worked out. Having only been able to run the business for six months, and at the point when he was just feeling comfortable, Robert Andrews did not want to "foul the deal."

Another, more pressing issue was confronting him, however. New bankruptcy laws, for which there was little precedent, had an ominous tone which appeared to imply the management at React. Management was personally responsible for amounts owed to unsecured creditors after it was known by management that sufficient cash was not available to meet them. This was referred to as "wrongful trading." The liability could run into the millions of pounds since suppliers to the React Group were paid on the order of £1 million per week.

The November 15 deadline passed relatively uneventfully.

Andrews recalls: "As we expected, we just didn't have the cash. We went into technical default. And we began a new round of negotiations. Of course we got the formal letters from the lead bank for the syndicate noting that we were in technical default. However, none of the banks, including the lead bank, wanted to call the loan. The negotiations continued. We had the feeling that all of this could be worked out and that people would act reasonably – there was enough interest around to continue to make this deal work. We were, however, operating with very little cash."

At this point, the search for additional capital began in earnest. To make the business viable and protect the interest of the unsecured creditors, it was quite necessary to seek additional funds and/or to reschedule the existing debt. Two significant funds, Zeon and European Ventures Unlimited (EVU), appeared to be interested.

Management also attempted to become more creative. Andrews and his team began looking at alternative deals, including bringing in a trade buyer to provide an equity infusion. As part of this analysis, it considered selling off bits of the business. With the assistance of strategy consultants (London Strategy Consultants), they ran scores of economic models.

During this period the banks discussed various options but were fundamentally unwilling to make any new commitments. There was a real reluctance on the part of any of the existing players to inject "new money." Combined with the fact that Roper was being unhelpful and Norton Simon was sending various signals but was unable to actually achieve a solution to the problem, the negotiations dragged on until December.

Finally, in December, some options were beginning to emerge. However, the options were conditional upon the agreement of various parties in order to execute them. Zeon was very excited about the possibility of providing an equity infusion based upon an increase in the scale of the React Group around the strategic core businesses. It was unwilling to put in the cash required at that time for a simple downsizing and preferred that EVU come into the deal with it.

Norton Simon suggested that management should work more closely with EVU. However, EVU made strong suggestions that management should sell off several of the core businesses, including those supplying Marks & Spencer (an account management felt was important and profitable), while reducing the business to strictly branded businesses. In addition, EVU noted that if Norton Simon and React Group management wanted their continued advice, they would have to commit themselves to paying £200,000 in fees to EVU if the deal did not go through and would have to pay an additional £300,000, under any circumstances, for a full audit of the business by an auditor specified by EVU.

Management did not agree with the approach of EVU. However, they determined that for purposes of their fiduciary responsibility to the unsecured creditors, it would be necessary to allow EVU to continue to work with all parties, even to the point of having themselves removed as part of the deal. EVU'S accountants were employed to undertake another long form audit of the React Group businesses – an audit which took into January of 1990 to complete. The audit indicated that the businesses were generally valuable and viable with proper financing.

By this time, management had decided that even if their percentage of the business was cut in half, it was still better to take the deal. In these circumstances management cannot legally refuse any deal that keeps the company alive. Management also identified an option by which certain "non-strategic" businesses could be sold for approximately £12 million, providing much of the cash needed in the short term. The banks, however, would still have to "roll up" some interest and reschedule some of the debt in order to make the business viable. This would "clean up" the balance sheet, a requirement in these increasingly conservative times. So, by the end of the year, negotiations with the banks were at a critical stage.

All of the negotiations continued but a critical juncture had been reached. On January 2, Robert Andrews and his associates had met with their legal counsel who made it clear that they were at the point of having to act – the unsecured creditors were now clearly at risk with negotiations deadlocked and no written offers on the table and no apparent resolution in sight.

The attorneys also pointed out to Andrews and his associates that despite the goodwill of the venture capitalists in evaluating the businesses, no written commitments had been forthcoming. As a result of the statements and the position of the venture capitalists, the syndicate banks all went into further heavy discussions.

During the first week in January, all of the parties who had been put on to the field kept jockeying for position. Unbeknown to the management of the React Group, various parties to the deal were meeting separately to plot independent courses of action not involving management. Roper had put together a new management team. Norton Simon phoned the management of React and said that Merchants (an investment banking group brought in to advise management) and Roper were going to present the new management team to the syndicate. This was to occur on Friday January 14.

However, the new management team did not even make it past the first screen and was rejected by the syndicate. Robert Andrews and his associates went back to a meeting of the syndicate banks with their position. There could be disposal of peripheral businesses but they felt that the unsecured creditors would be best served by the on-going operation of the company and the maintenance of the key strategic businesses. Management of the team would have to be provided with cash to run the strategic core businesses while selling off about £12 million in "non-essential" businesses (including concessions from the debt providers) and the debt providers would have to "share the pain" by providing concessions that would attract new equity into the business.

At this point, Norton Simon asked EVU to make a final presentation and made representations to the syndicate that EVU was willing to "do the deal" if only they could wait a few days. EVU, after first agreeing to make a bid for the business and then deciding not to bid, finally decided to present a deal on January 27. The bank syndicate members met along with management and the existing venture capitalists to hear EVU's presentation, which turned out in Andrew's words to be "truly unrealistic." Norton Simon and the banks were quite "upset" at the presentation. After EVU had completed its presentation, they were asked to leave along with management.

The decision was finally in the hands of the banks – management had no other options and no time to structure any. Their conclusion was simple. Robert Andrews says: "After hearing that EVU had no reasonable deal to offer, the bankers simply said 'enough is enough.' They indicated they would provide no further financing and that management should reach its own conclusions."

On the evening of January 26, Andrews called in the receivers who had been waiting in the wings for the past few weeks. Discussion of what should be done and what were management's rights and responsibilities ensued. At that moment, Robert Andrews and his management team ceased to have effective control of the React Group.

Robert Andrews offers many reasons for the failure of the React Group: the buy-in nature of the deal; the amount paid for the company; the position of the banks; the nature of the venture capital industry; and the role and nature of advisers.

He notes that subsequent to the failure of the React Group, many deals in the City have fallen, leaving banks with an image problem. He believes that there is a different psychology among the banks today – they are more likely to attempt to make a deal to keep the business together: "They can get more if they put them in administration rather than into receivership. The motivation is economic as well as creating an image of responsibility."

In the end the React Group was parceled up and sold off. Though the final report of the receivers has not been filed, early indications are that the banking group did not realize the 80 pence on the pound that it expected from the sale of assets.

Robert Andrews received several offers of executive positions despite the well-publicised failure of his business. He accepted a senior executive position with a Paris-based textile enterprise.

Innovative funding for first-timers

Robert Johnson explains "funded search" – a way in which young entrepreneurs can find others to pay to set them up in business.

Kirk Dodson is a very talented young entrepreneurial individual with a few years' work experience and nearing completion of his MBA. He tells you that his aim is to run his own business and asks you for advice on how best to reach that goal. What do you tell him?

Most people would strongly advise Kirk to get more industry experience, including managerial experience, preferably in charge of a small company or a division of a larger company. Then, say the wise counselors, he will be in a position to run his own business. Certainly that is appropriate advice for many people but for some (like Kirk) there is another alternative – buying their own business right away.

Rubbish, you say. How can anyone with little industry experience, no real managerial experience and little capital (indeed still in debt from financing an MBA) be serious about buying and running a business?

It is not as far-fetched as it sounds. An increasing number of graduating or recent MBAs have found that there is a quicker and more rewarding path for getting into business for themselves – using a "funded search" to find and buy a business to run. In a funded search an entrepreneur raises a search fund (say £100,000) from a group of individual investors (say ten individuals investing £10,000 each) to pay the expenses of the search and a nominal salary during the search period (say 18–24 months). Working full time, the entrepreneur researches target industries and searches for a company to acquire.

Once a company has been identified and a deal negotiated with the seller, the search fund investors have the option – but not the obligation – to invest *pro rata* in the acquisition. If an investor chooses not to invest, his original investment rolls over into the acquisition on the same basis as the new investment funds. As part of the deal, the entrepreneur (now the CEO) receives equity in the company – usually a combination of shares at completion of the acquisition and additional shares based on performance.

There are a number of key factors necessary to make a funded search work.

First and foremost, the young entrepreneur must have the commitment and the talent to run a business. From the investors' point of view this is the real risk in the deal – can this person actually run a company? The criteria for a target acquisition must take this into account, which means that the searcher must find a stable business that does not have a lot of inherent risk in it. This may mean a "boring" business but sometimes boring businesses turn out to be fun businesses and even highly profitable when properly managed.

Has the concept worked? I am aware of 18 people in the US and two in the UK who have raised search funds; all are either now running their own companies or are searching. Two of the US entrepreneurs have sold their companies, producing generous returns for their investors.

What must the young entrepreneur bring to the table? Enthusiasm, commitment, persistence and the ability to run a business – now. What does the investor buy in the search fund? Essentially, an option; then, the opportunity to be involved with a bright young entrepreneur in what may be his or her first big winner.

The changing face of buy-ins

Patrick Dunne and **Conor Boden** assess the growth and potential of management buy-ins in Europe and describe what it takes to make a successful deal.

The management buy-in market is changing fast. In the UK, for instance, MBIs now consistently attract substantially more funding than their longer established counterpart, the management buy-out. The average MBI deal value in the UK has also increased dramatically, doubling in 1999 to more than £70 million.

In continental Europe the MBI is still at a relatively early stage of development, largely because awareness of what an MBI entails is low among owners of companies and managers. However, the characteristics and particularly the motivations of these owners and managers suggest significant growth ahead.

The views we will be expressing here are based on 640 UK and 60 continental

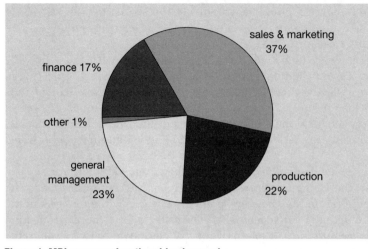

Figure 1: MBI manager functional background

European MBIs that 3i backed up to the end of 1999.

An MBI involves a manager or team of managers from outside a particular company, together with their financial backers, purchasing equity control of it. In the process, the manager becomes executive chairman, chief executive, managing director, Geschäftsführer or président directeur général – in other words the boss – and gains a significant equity stake.

The past few years have also seen the emergence of two powerful variants of the MBI – the BIMBO and the BINGO. In a BIMBO the MBI team joins forces with managers within the business, enabling them to obtain equity through a partial MBO. Hence the hybrid name. BIMBOs possess several advantages over a conventional MBI and these are described later. In a BINGO a sizeable (more than 25 percent of the total funding) amount of growth capital is raised in addition to that used to buy the business. This cash is then used for a major growth project such as a new factory or other significant capital expenditure.

Who carries out management buy-ins?

Contrary to popular belief, buy-in managers are not super-hero financial wizards swooping in on ailing companies, rapidly transforming them and then selling them on. The people who do these buy-ins in the UK, France, Germany and Italy seem to be remarkably similar in profile and all want to grow the company. There are essentially two main types: the break-out manager and the second-time entrepreneur.

The break-out manager

An early to mid-40s frustrated divisional chief executive within a larger corporation with five or more years' experience as a chief executive. They have no particularly dominant functional background before they became CEO, though more have been in sales and marketing than any other single function before becoming CEO.

Break-out managers typically invest a minimum of £100,000 in the UK and £200,000-plus in France and Germany. This will be the greater part of their net worth. Their motivations may be one but usually several of the following:

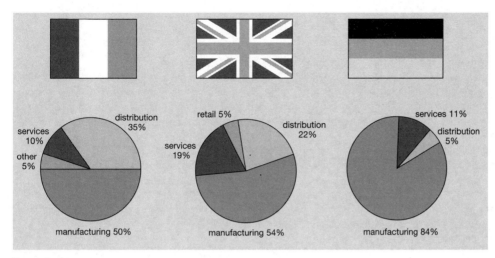

Figure 2: Sector

- to gain independence and control over their destiny
- to make significant capital, thereby gaining financial independence
- to escape frustration with their current position – career progression may be blocked or perhaps more senior roles appear unfulfilling or bureaucratic
- an MBO is not possible because the business they run is not for sale at a feasible price
- they may have a former colleague or friend who has done an MBO and consider themselves at least as able
- they consider a start-up too risky and are more comfortable building on a business that already has critical mass
- they could be a corporate victim, having been taken over, delayered or downsized.

Break-out managers face a number of common dangers. They may not be a suitable manager for the companies typically available. Many of the most successful larger corporations are run along functional lines and do not prepare people well for running independent companies. Trying to look for a target while still being in employment in these demanding times can be another difficulty. For many the real trigger is a takeover of the company they run.

In France and in Germany the fear of failure is a very important deterrent. As there have been fewer MBOs, the envy motivation is lower. Status in the local community is more important than in the UK and therefore a senior position with a larger group might be more attractive despite lower wealth. One fascinating trend across Europe that has emerged in recent years is what I call the "Boss Chop Factor." This is encapsulated in the domestic scene outlined in the box on the next page, which could just as easily be taking place in Paris, Düsseldorf, Barcelona or Turin.

Second-time entrepreneur
This type of buy-in manager has the following characteristics:

- slightly older than the break-out manager, late 40s or early 50s

Boss Chop Factor

Highly successful 45-year-old Joe Starr is managing director of a company within a large group. He arrives home with some excellent news for his wife Ann.

"Hi, got some great news."

"Oh no, we're not moving again are we; we've only just settled here."

"No, no this time we stay but I get to run the whole division. They have decided to retire Stan (his current boss) early and have given his job to me. Twenty percent more cash, a sweet option deal and a new Mercedes S Class."

"That's great, well done. Let's celebrate and go out."

Later that evening, over a meal and champagne,

Ann turns to Joe and says:

"Why did they retire Stan?"

"Well, I guess they thought he had run out of steam and decided he should make way for a younger man, give me a chance to really prove myself."

"How old is Stan?"

"Fifty."

"Aha. So I guess that gives you five years max."

Joe is suddenly quiet. He's never really had to think about this before. It's a somewhat terrifying prospect – perhaps he should do something to get control over his own future?

- already successful through an earlier buy-out, start-up or even buy-in
- has sold out and has no intention of giving up business or indeed working for anyone else
- tends to invest the same as a break-out manager despite having considerably greater wealth
- may want to take a chairman's role and not be as totally consumed as in previous ventures.

The relatively high numbers of MBOs in the UK over the past ten years have provided a growing pool of second-timers. Lower numbers of MBOs across the continent, combined with the fact that owners of companies tend to hang on longer, mean that the pool of second-time CEOs is likely to be smaller. However, the tradition of the wealthy local worthy backing a friend or former employee is much stronger, which ought to mean that there is a good supply of investing chairmen.

Figure 3: Reason sold

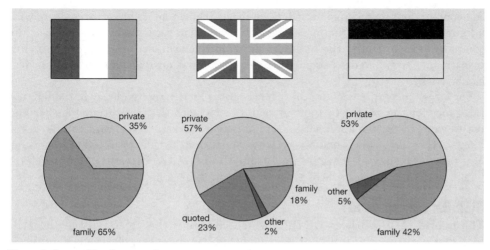

Figure 4: Ownership of companies

What else motivates them? They may be bored or frustrated or lack any real purpose if business has always been their life. Some may have a strong desire to prove it wasn't luck the first time.

Potential dangers for this group are that, of course, they may have been lucky the first time – the industry or general economic cycle may have been kind. More commonly, they may have burned themselves out or lost some of their sharpness through becoming wealthy. Despite the dangers, second-time entrepreneurs are often the most attractive from an investor's perspective.

How do buy-in managers make money?

The entrepreneurs' aim is fundamentally to make the business they buy worth more than the price they paid for it. Their equity is also geared up. Every pound, franc or lira they put in will normally buy more of the equity than their financial backers who put in their money, as in an MBO, in the form of base equity, redeemable stock and debt. If successful, the investors get some of their money back along the way and the rest on eventual sale. It is sensible to have lower levels of debt in an MBI because of the higher risks involved in a new team who despite their no doubt excellent record may not fit when they get there.

What sort of businesses are bought by buy-in managers?

The heartland of MBIs, as shown in the figures, are the private and family companies, the European *Mittelstand* of £10–£100 million-turnover businesses. Ironically, most MBI managers spend most of their time hunting among the non-core subsidiaries of the large groups.

That there are succession issues in thousands of German *Mittelstand* companies is well documented and evident (*see* p. 293). However, despite these companies making theoretically wonderful MBI targets, they are not so easy to achieve. Vendors tend to leave selling until they are in their seventies.

In terms of a preferred buyer for their life's work, the order seems to go something like this: a friend, a friend of their banker, another client of their banker, then someone in their own image but a bit younger, all of whom will have to come up with a figure which matches the most optimistic valuation received by the owner at the company's peak. Sadly, the business may have languished and need significant investment capital, hence causing further pricing pressure. So doing a sensible deal can be tricky.

For larger corporate vendors there has been an increasing tendency in the UK and in France for the vendor to want to deal directly with the institutional backer and not to want to receive approaches from managers directly. "We want to talk to the money," they say. This is one reason why the UK market has returned to something of a feeding frenzy as mergers and acquisitions (M&A) directors and merchant banks send their truck loads of prospectuses out to backers.

BIMBOs: why so good?

The hybrid MBI/MBO, or BIMBO, which combines the objectivity of the MBI manager with the continuity of people within the business, often has significant advantages over a pure MBI:

- **More reliable information** Managers within the business will usually respond to the MBI managers' invitation to join in the equity and be more open than they would perhaps otherwise be. They will also be involved in preparing the business plan for moving forward.
- **Less acquisitional drift** It is normal for any company going through a sale process to lose momentum. The good managers are out looking for jobs just in case. The vendors are dreaming of the cash that's about to arrive. An inordinate amount of time is spent showing people around, assisting due diligence, and in adviser meetings. In MBOs, this is known to occur to a much lesser degree because the people within have a strong incentive to make sure it is in the best shape possible when they take over. A BIMBO goes a long way to achieving this.
- **Better motivation** Incumbent management's equity provides greater motivation. Discussions over who gets what slice of the cake may also result in a more tightly knit team from the start and less fractious behavior during a critical time.
- **Competitive edge** A BIMBO sends a clear signal to the vendor about the MBI managers' approach. Vendors particularly concerned about what happens to their employees when the company is sold will regard this favorably.

Of course there is a danger in BIMBOs and that is that the manager involves the wrong people in the equity and thus removing them later may be more cumbersome. Our view is that the benefits of the approach far outweigh this risk.

Conclusion

Managers embarking upon the MBI route are making a clear statement in their belief in their own abilities as a managing director. There is no doubt that the MBI has become an established way for managers to gain independence in the UK and it is becoming more prevalent in continental Europe.

Risks can be mitigated and opportunities created through the BIMBO route. The individuals that lead these MBIs are exceptional managers and growing numbers of MBO and MBI realizations have produced a pool of potential second-time entrepreneurs.

MBIs are fundamentally about growth. The only real way to fulfill the MBI manager's dream and to make money for investors is through genuine growth in the business. Many are also raising significant growth capital in addition to acquisition funding at the time of their MBI.

Routes to a successful turnaround

Michael Ullman provides advice for those who want to transform a failed company.

Taking over a company that has failed may not be every entrepreneur's ideal but the opportunities for successful turnaround are significant, the potential profits large, and the process not as difficult as many assume; and potentially, it is at least as exciting as beginning a start-up business from scratch.

Just how many companies are revitalized in this way is hard to ascertain since turnarounds like this are not always very visible. However, estimates suggest that in the UK alone many thousands of companies that go into receivership do not disappear at all but are reincarnated. In some sectors, notably the small retail sector, the amount of this "churning" is considerable.

Why companies get into trouble

Companies that get into trouble usually do not have very good financial accounting and financial reporting. Trouble sneaks up on them and, as it does so, management starts thinking that the problem is the top line – their sales; they very rarely start thinking how they can cut costs or increase margins – the keys to a successful turnaround. In trying to increase sales they invariably drop their margins, further compounding the problem.

Another truth about failing companies is that the failure is almost always the fault of the current management. That is why businesses have to go into receivership – so that the management can be changed. If you take over a company and fail to root out the current management, the chances are that you will end up losing a great deal of money.

Because of this management failure, the external environment in which a company is operating usually has very little to do with the causes of failure. This is why a turnaround can be relatively simple to achieve. In normal circumstances you can take over a failing business and have it breaking even in a month – give it penicillin and the patient responds. This applies mainly to the manufacturing sector. Service companies are slightly more difficult. Margins there are much more affected by the market, and the external environment does have an impact – but the general concepts outlined below are still of use.

How to bring about a turnaround

The keys to a successful turnaround are raising prices and reducing turnover. When companies set prices they tend to be either cost-plus or competition-based; but how many businesses go bust because they overprice their product compared with those that have underpriced it?

One of the universal lessons about turning companies round, apart from the rather obvious thing of putting in appropriate financial reporting and controls, is that when you get there, if you fire the management and reduce the sales, you will be astonished at the results.

This is because the former management was probably running round like headless chickens chasing sales at the expense of margin. Furthermore, they tend to mess up the manufacturing process by making it more complicated and less economic. The management takes on production runs that the factory manager, if he had any control, would never allow. The knock-on effects in terms of product proliferation and distribution costs just go on and on compounding the losses.

Successful turnarounds generally involve very little change other than a refocussing of the business. A lot of manufacturing businesses, even though they are run by people with a marketing background, are very unfocussed. In one business we took over we dropped 25 percent of the turnover. We concentrated on existing core customers, just going back to basics, making sure the product quality was where it ought to be so that customers would repeat-buy the product. You can't fool customers all the time, though there is a naïve assumption that you can, and, if you do actually give them the right quality, the results can be amazing. In that business, sales were up 30 percent on the core lines.

The main aspect to improving margins is taking out costs. That does not mean firing half the workforce – though it will probably mean losing the directors and any redundant staff. It is much more a case of sensible trading. For example, companies in trouble tend to spread their supplier base – they take on more suppliers – because they are not paying them, which leads to even more inefficiencies.

If you do get into trouble, and if you have the financial systems in place, then you'll know you are in trouble. What you need to do is go to your core suppliers and admit that you are not going to be able to pay them quite as promptly as you agreed. But you also say that you will pay them the difference it costs them not to collect the money from you. In other words, you get extended credit and pay them interest costs.

The alternative, spreading the supplier base, means you get poor service and poor prices – which increases costs. When we took over one business we had a meeting of major customers. On an annual turnover of £5 million, we reckoned we had identified cost savings of 10 percent in the first five days. A lot of that came from suppliers being reassured that they were going to be paid and having proper trading terms.

The importance of management

New management is a vital ingredient in a turnaround and it is important to work with people you know. You should not recruit strangers for this sort of operation. You need to know how people react and whether you can work with them – but be aware that this can be a limiting factor in looking at businesses.

There are criteria for choosing the managers you put in, but if you are taking over failing businesses, you tend to be buying them from receivers so you have a very short time-frame to originate a plan. You have to be able to get together the resources in terms of replacement managers quickly. But it still holds true that no-one should take over a failing business without having a management team ready to go in.

Remember, too, that the existing second-tier managers, who are normally quite competent people, have usually been extremely fed up with the way the business has been run so that giving them the opportunity to set things right is normally a very liberating experience and you get lots of co-operation. In other words you can just take the top layer off and bring up the rest – a ploy successfully carried out by Hanson for years.

Rewarding the new management appropriately is very important but, contrary to a lot of current thinking, many managers are not very equity minded. Handing over equity can be a two-edged sword for the entrepreneur. For example, in one company I reorganized in the 1980s, the managers were, with some difficulty, persuaded to buy a stake. At the first opportunity they wanted to sell out, gaining about £500,000 each. Although I was the majority shareholder I was obliged to sell the company, which was a shame because we sold it too early.

Rewards should be much more geared to profit-sharing and the like. Most people work for fairly instant rewards – money, status and cars. One has to be aware of what it is that motivates people and not just assume it is equity. I know of one sales director who made the owner of his company immensely rich; his undying loyalty was "bought" when he doubled sales one year and the owner gave him a gold Rolex watch. That rather trivial incident taught me more than any theory of executive remuneration.

Finding and assessing companies worthy of turnaround

Finding companies suitable for turnaround is, on the surface, very easy. After all, the major business press such as the *Financial Times* devote sections to advertising companies for sale every week.

You can also approach those likely to be in the know such as accountants, venture capitalists and bankers. However, you can get unstuck this way and waste a lot of time. The best thing to do is to concentrate on an industry that you know, and use your network. After the first successful turnaround you will find that they come to you.

There are enormous opportunities in what we might call "dumb" industries – ones that are not fashionable or high-profile and where management talent is not greatly evident. One example is the packaging industry. People say no-one can make money in packaging but, of course, you can; it's often just a question of putting in the most up-to-date equipment. As a rule of thumb, failing companies most suitable for turnaround have a minimum turnover of about £5 million, are involved in manufacturing and employ between 50 to 300 people.

Assessing the viability of turning round a business usually involves touring the factory with the management team you hope to install to see what improvements can be made in terms of cost reduction. This does not apply to buying a well-run business, where you have to pay a premium. In many ways, the more badly run a business is the more attractive it is. You can see all sorts of ways of improving things as you go around the factory and usually they are fairly obvious and can be done quickly.

However, there are some caveats. One of the many things that companies in difficulty cut back on is maintenance and investment. You should be very careful with a highly mechanized business because it may look fine superficially. But if the insides are falling apart it could cost you a fortune. You can make an offer to take over a business that is conditional on getting things working but this can be difficult if you are buying from a receiver.

Indeed, dealing with receivers is generally very difficult, certainly in the UK. There are few – if any – ground rules because receivers are unusually free of any form of control or restriction. They can do exactly what they like. It has been known, for example, for receivers not to accept the highest bid they are offered and if you have made one higher than the one they accept there is nothing you can do about it.

A lot of the time you are also playing blind man's bluff on price so you need to have quite a margin of safety. You take on a lot of liability and the receiver will give you no assurances on assets. You don't know who's going to start claiming goods. You don't know who the other bidders are or even if there are any other bidders.

It is possible to buy just the assets of a business but if you do so without the liabilities that make it an on-going concern, then that is almost like a start-up. You may have got a lot of equipment cheaply but it's very hard work. You really do need both assets and liabilities. Even if suppliers have lost money with the previous owners you can usually negotiate terms.

However, to do that, you need working capital and that is something people can underestimate. That's why it is always a good idea to involve active partners, including venture capitalists and banks, in a turnaround deal, sharing the risks and rewards equally with them. Venture capitalists in particular can also be a useful source of financial and management discipline.

When the turnaround is complete and the once failing company is back on a healthy path, what happens then? In general, most entrepreneurs involved in turnarounds are looking for an exit. Few are prepared to devote their time exclusively to running the business. In the great majority of cases, turnarounds take place so that the company can be sold on.

CASE STUDY

Harley-Davidson

This is an edited version of a longer case study written by **Richard Schoenberg**, Imperial College Management School.

arley-Davidson had been owned by the industrial and leisure conglomerate AMF between 1969 and 1981. AMF's early strategy had been to expand production substantially, although the resulting rise in sales had been accompanied by a marked deterioration in product quality.

Since 1973, however, conditions in Harley-Davidson's market had become far more competitive as overall motorcycle sales declined and Japanese manufacturers entered the heavyweight segment of the market where Harley-Davidson had previously been dominant. Although Harley-Davidson had remained profitable, its share of the US heavyweight motorcycle market fell from 99 percent in 1972 to 30 percent in 1981.

Uncomfortable with AMF, 13 members of Harley-Davidson's then management purchased the company from AMF in spring 1981 for approximately $80 million. The majority of the new owners were keen motorcyclists and celebrated the independence of the company by organizing a mass "Freedom Ride" to proclaim their vision of "providing motorcycles by the people for the people."

Early actions

The early 1980s were not easy for the newly independent Harley-Davidson. The world economic situation was worsening and motorcycle markets continued to decline. Harley-Davidson responded aggressively to bring its capacity into line with demand and to reduce its costs. In autumn 1981 the York assembly plant was cut back to one shift from two and 200 clerical jobs were cut. The following spring 1,600 of the remaining 3,800 employees were laid off. The company reported operating losses of $15 million for 1982 on a turnover of $210 million. Annual production of motorcycles fell 25 percent to 30,000. Reports began to appear in the press that America's oldest motorcycle manufacturer was close to bankruptcy.

In November 1982 Harley-Davidson filed a petition with the US International Trade Commission (ITC) requesting protection from alleged unfair foreign competition – in essence alleged "dumping" by Japanese manufacturers. It further argued that protection would give it breathing space to improve production efficiency and develop more competitive products. The ITC upheld the case and imposed additional import tariffs on Japanese-manufactured machines over 700cc for a five-year period.

Production improvements

Even before the ITC hearings the buy-out team had begun implementing production changes. A major step was the introduction of a "materials as needed" (MAN) inventory system where parts were delivered to the assembly line "just in time." Action was also taken to reduce machine tool set-up times. In addition, Harley-Davidson began to view suppliers as "partners in profit," awarding long-term contracts to those that consistently met stringent quality and delivery requirements. The assembly line was reorganized into a series of "work cells" and employee involvement was further encouraged through a new pay scheme. The combined benefits of these changes were significant. The company's 1987 annual report boasted that since 1981 manufacturing had achieved a 50 percent improvement in productivity, a 68 percent reduction in scrap, and major improvements in product quality.

Research and product development

The buy-out team also moved quickly to enhance research and development capability, raising expenditure to 5 percent of sales. A major pay-off was the introduction in 1984 of a new engine, for which much of the early design work is said to have been undertaken during AMF's ownership.

The new "Evolution" engine was soon fitted to all but the Sportster models and showed marked improvements in reliability, performance and maintenance. Product development has continued but in incremental rather than radical steps.

Customers

Harley-Davidson's product has to be viewed in context. The main attraction of the motorcycles is not as a means of transport but rather one of "image, charisma and style." In the mid-1980s Harley-Davidson began actively marketing this style to young professionals while being careful not to alienate its traditional customer base of blue-collar workers.

The company made great efforts to involve purchasers with the culture associated with its products. Each motorcycle purchased came with a year's automatic membership of the Harley Owners Group (HOG), renewable thereafter for a small fee. Members received regular publications informing them of both club and product news as well as invitations to local HOG "chapter" events such as bike runs, dealer open evenings and pub meetings. Each chapter was sponsored by the local Harley-Davidson dealer.

In addition to local chapter events there were larger national HOG rallies. The presence and active participation of top company executives was always a feature of these gatherings. HOG was first established in 1983 and membership grew by about 30 percent annually. By 1994 there were 250,000 HOG members in 800 chapters worldwide.

Parts and accessories

Riders of Harley-Davidsons had long been in the habit of customizing their machines and in 1986 the company responded to this by considerably expanding its parts and accessories range in three separate brands, each marketed via its own lavish brochure.

Licensing

The mid-1980s also saw moves into the licensing of the Harley-Davidson brand names and trademarks. A "MotorClothes" line was introduced featuring tough but stylish motorcycle leathers through to children's socks, all manufactured under license. MotorClothes were sold exclusively through dealers, thereby both increasing dealer revenue and attracting new customers into the showrooms. In other cases the name alone was licensed: Harley-Davidson hi-fis, a Harley-Davidson café in New York City and even a range of men's toiletries. Not only did the licensing bring in additional revenue, it also further promoted the brand name and image.

Dealerships

Harley-Davidson also made considerable efforts to build strong relationships with its direct customers, motorcycle dealers, and to assist them in improving their own performance.

In 1987 a "Designer Store" program was launched under which dealers were encouraged to redesign their showrooms to provide an improved shopping environment with near equal emphasis on displays of accessories and MotorClothes as on the bikes themselves.

Financial performance

The initial turnaround was largely complete by 1986. Not only had profitability been restored but turnover, profits and market share were all beginning to show steady increases. The opportunity was taken to float the company in June 1986 with a public offering of 2 million shares at $11 a share together with $70 million of 12.5 percent unsecured subordinate loan notes.

The year 1986 also saw the company diversify away from its reliance on motorcycles. Holiday Ramblers Corp, a manufacturer of premium motor homes and travel trailers, was acquired for $157 million. Holiday Ramblers was run as an autonomous operation post-acquisition with separate management to the motorcycle business.

In a further demonstration of the company's growing strength the buy-out team went to the US government in March 1987 to request that tariff protection against imported Japanese motorcycles be lifted one year before it was due to expire. It was the first company in US history to take such action.

The company's share of the US heavyweight motorcycle market continued to rise steadily from 31 percent in 1986 to 55 percent by 1989 despite the fact that the overall motorcycle market was declining by almost 10 percent a year over the same period.

The early 1990s saw a revival of growth worldwide in motorcycle registrations and Harley-Davidson maintained its share comfortably in all major markets. At the end of 1993 it held 58 percent of the US, 10 percent of the European and 21 percent of the Japanese/Australian heavyweight motorcycle markets.

This success was reflected in the tremendous loyalty of Harley-Davidson customers. A staggering 96 percent of Harley owners claimed they intended to buy another – a figure thought to be one of the highest loyalty levels of any industry. This loyalty was also illustrated by the attendance of 100,000 people at a "reunion party" in Milwaukee organized by Harley-Davidson to mark its 90th anniversary. Harley riders spent more than $10 million on food, goods and services in Milwaukee during the reunion and raised over $1 million in sponsorship for the muscular dystrophy association – a charity heavily supported by Harley-Davidson.

ENTREPRENEURSHIP
IN THE ORGANIZATION

9

Contributors

 Neil C. Churchill is Professor Emeritus at INSEAD and formerly Paul T. Babson Professor of Entrepreneurship and Director of the Center for Entrepreneurial Studies at Babson College, Massachusetts.

 Zenas Block is Clinical Professor of Management at the Stern School of Business, New York University, and adjunct professor at Rensselaer Polytechnic Institute.

 Ian MacMillan is the George W. Taylor Professor of Entrepreneurial Studies at the Wharton School of the University of Pennsylvania and Executive Director of the Wharton School's Entrepreneurial Center.

 Sandra Vandermerwe is Professor of Marketing and International Services at Imperial College Management School, London.

Contents

Introduction

Part 9 looks at the ways in which large organizations in both the public and private sectors have attempted to introduce entrepreneurship. Two types of strategy are examined. The first is concerned with changing the whole style of the organization from bureaucratic to entrepreneurial; and the second is concerned with developing new business through some form of corporate venturing. To illustrate these perspectives, we present two case studies of successful venturing.

The evolution of entrepreneurship in large organizations

Daniel Muzyka and **Neil Churchill** look at how large organizations can be more effective at capturing opportunity.

There is significant evidence that corporations do not last as long as they used to, no matter how successful they once were. In addition, there are many examples of start-up entrepreneurs effectively "taking on" seemingly powerful large corporations and winning. Corporations in general are trying to move faster and create and capture more opportunity.

As a result, large organizations have strived over the last decade to promote additional entrepreneurial activity and to capture more opportunities than their normal product development systems seem to permit. This has provided entrepreneurship experts with plenty of food for thought. However, the evidence is strong that nothing leads to failure like success. Even many of the most successful companies have been unable to identify and capture as many opportunities as quickly as could entrepreneurs "in the wild." This would seem to be good news for scholars and researchers as additional work is obviously in order.

Under the ubiquitous Taylor model of industrial organization, formulated nearly a century ago, the logic was to capture and systematize business activity in the form of clear, well-defined processes. Research and development were responsible for discovery, marketing was responsible for bringing discovery to the customer, production had its strictly defined role, and so on. Functional control was key. And as for new business development, it was to be centralized, systematic and efficient, and therefore less risky. Significant research has been dedicated to improving both the efficiency and effectiveness of internal product development processes.

Executives in larger organizations and successful entrepreneurs have begun to realize that it is not always possible to rely solely on a process for future business evolution. The door must be left open to innovation and opportunities that come from other sources and along other paths. Successive generations of ideas have emerged as to how best to do this. Some companies placed certain activities in separate organizational units – called "skunk works" after Lockheed's famous unit (which originated aircraft from the U-2 to the Stealth fighter). Their purpose was to take responsibility for developing and testing ideas that might otherwise be missed and to boost the set of ideas and product/service options available to take to market.

During the 1970s, a new generation of organizationally separate units with innovation and opportunity development responsibilities evolved. Some companies (Exxon, for example) set up separate new venture or corporate venturing subsidiaries and business units. These units were responsible for developing opportunities which were usually, but not exclusively, outside the product or technology range offered by the company. Some of these corporate ventures (IBM's PC division, for example) created significant economic value. Many were not so successful.

During the 1980s, the idea of developing and supporting entrepreneurs within the main organization ("intrapreneurship") became more in vogue. Many companies now had a basic strategy and organizational system incorporating innovation processes. However, they held a door open to the efforts of individuals and teams working on innovations that spun off from the company's main product portfolio. In the end, capturing these opportunities led to additional growth and renewal of the organization.

Each of these elements – the normal product development process, corporate venturing, and individual entrepreneurial activity – became part of the puzzle. Each appears to lead to improved opportunity capture by larger organizations. If you add concepts like "empowerment" and new ideas in management theory related to adaptation, you have captured some of the main contributions from the 1990s to the question of how you make organizations more entrepreneurial. The questions that persist today are: (1) how can we make these elements integrate better? and (2) how can we improve our models of management to permit organizations to be even more effective at capturing opportunity? With shorter and increasingly irregular product life cycles, these questions need to be addressed.

Today, managers and management researchers are turning back to the basics. We are all looking for a more self-renewing model, organizations that can update their portfolio of activities more fluidly. And while this is going on, entrepreneurs operating within the economy are continuing to find significant support and access to resources, even for large projects.

Corporations that wish to have a significant future can no longer depend upon the failure of entrepreneurs to initiate their own businesses. Successful entrepreneurial organizations have come to realize that there is a central role for the very type of entrepreneurial activity that was present at the early formation of their businesses. They themselves must deliver by becoming entrepreneurial corporations.

Stimuli and stumbling blocks in a new venture

Ian MacMillan and **Zenas Block** outline ways of identifying, evaluating and selecting opportunities for corporate venturing.

Not all ideas are opportunities and many opportunities are not right for all companies. When a company provides overall direction and focus designed to improve the fit between its vision, strategy and goals and the ideas generated, it increases both the number of acceptable ideas and the efficiency of the selection process.

Sources of opportunity

Opportunities can be found within a business itself, in the industries and markets it serves, and in the external environment. Most viable opportunities spring from problems, needs and change – for example a tamper-proof lock developed in response to a rise in the crime rate or new cancer treatment drugs developed from monoclonal antibodies as an outcome of major changes in biotechnology.

Internal sources

Internal sources of opportunity may be found in every aspect of a business. Examples include the need for, or the possibility of, reducing rejects in a manufacturing process, improving overall quality, supplying better service or replacing a raw material.

Identifying an organization's special competencies can also become the basis for creating a new business or improving its competitive position. What skills does the organization have that are outstanding and unequivocally excellent? Here are two examples:

■ Japanese carmakers had to manufacture more reliable cars to penetrate foreign markets where their service network was inadequate. They elected to build cars that required less servicing rather than try to improve the service network. Their outstanding competence was the ability to manufacture high-quality products at low cost. As this strategy hinged on the reliability of components, they taught their suppliers how to manufacture extremely dependable components. The success of this approach immediately became evident in the reliability of their cars.

■ General Electric in the US, unable to obtain suitable materials from the plastics industry, created its own special plastics for use in its electrical products. After developing this special competence, GE decided to aggressively enter the engineered plastics market. This is now one of GE's major businesses, producing an operating profit of $1 billion in 1991.

The great advantage of basing new ventures on internal sources of opportunity is familiarity with the identified resource. The great disadvantage is that there may not be any worthwhile opportunity to which that resource can be applied.

Although the odds of achieving success with technological innovations are small, such innovations have produced the really big hits, creating whole new industries. This was the case with semiconductors and biotechnology and will surely be the case with superconductivity. Businesses created this way tend to continue for many years, an example being DuPont and nylon.

Industry and market changes

Changes in a given industry or market are a major source of new opportunities, as Peter Drucker, the management theorist, has pointed out, and are probably the best source of opportunities with a high probability of success.

There are many examples of ventures generated by industry or market change. As pension fund administrators became a larger factor in the stock market, the need for solid research increased. The highly successful US firm Donaldson, Lufkin, & Jenrette was formed in response to this opportunity. The growth of department stores was accompanied by a trend toward stocking only the better-moving items and reducing the inventory of speciality items, such as blue jeans and other product lines. As speciality items became unavailable, speciality retail stores, the fastest-growing business sector of the 1980s, were born. Examples include toy chains, athletic shoe chains and the Gap stores, which originally specialized in jeans and then, in response to the changing demographics of the 1990s, adjusted their product line to achieve renewed growth.

Wal-Mart is arguably the most successful business formed in response to industry and market developments. When Wal-Mart started, discount stores were mainly in larger cities and high-quality national brands were sold at high prices in smaller cities. Clerks in department stores often responded to product requests: "We're out of it but we'll order it for you." Sam Walton saw this gap and filled it with the fastest-growing retail chain in history, which kept prices low, provided better service, maintained high inventories of stock and used leading-edge information systems.

The needs and wants of the existing market are the most reliable sources of good opportunities in the short run. But the ability to foresee and meet future needs is the source of long-term opportunity and competitive advantage.

The external environment

Threats and opportunities produced by the external environment can be excellent sources of venturable ideas. Changing demographics, lifestyles, perceptions and values, government regulations and tax laws, as well as social problems such as crime and drug abuse, all create problems and the need for solutions.

Opportunities that buck environmental forces will face a difficult obstacle while opportunities linked to environmental forces will rise, like ships with a rising tide. Consider the explosive growth of fitness centers, low-calorie, low-fat, low-cholesterol foods; and the flood of services and products related to lifestyle changes and perceptions on health and exercise.

Paradoxically, though, this trend has been paralleled by the success of, for example, Lady Godiva chocolates and premium ice creams, which runs directly counter to environmental factors. One explanation offered is that the calories consumed are a reward for all the exercise and dieting. Another is that, for some, indulgence is and always will be present.

Drucker argues that the process of opportunity identification can be systemized and that opportunities can be found by monitoring seven basic sources: demographic changes, new knowledge, incongruities (gaps between reality and expectations), industry or market structure, unexpected successes or failures, process needs and changes in perception.

There is an incongruity in the success of the steel industry's minimills, which defied the principles of economy of scale and led to significant changes in the steel industry. Another incongruity involved the practice of building increasingly large vessels for trans-oceanic shipping to reduce costs. In fact, capital costs were actually higher and both pilferage and idle time in port were greater. This incongruity led to containerized ships, drastically reducing loading time and labor costs and providing increased security.

An example of an unexpected failure was Ford's Edsel automobile. Prior to that failure, automotive marketing segments had been conceived in terms of income demographics. Its experience with the Edsel led Ford to re-examine its marketing approach and move to the concept of lifestyle marketing segments, a key factor in the great success of the Mustang.

Federal Express unexpectedly saw an increase in shipments of high-priced, low-weight computer components. Upon investigation, FedEx learned that this unexpected success was attributable to companies using its service to keep their inventory levels down, which opened up new and previously overlooked market possibilities.

Process needs refer to interruptions or bottlenecks in a process. The Polaroid Land Camera filled a process need – eliminating the delay between capturing a moment and finding out whether the moment had, in fact, been captured. According to legend, it was Edwin Land's daughter who asked him: "Why do we have to wait?" The question led Land to invent the Land Camera and Polaroid film.

Many factors can trigger a flow of ideas, with change and problems being the best sources. Information and a resulting awareness of developments both within a company and industry and in the world at large are essential to the process. Training, education, exposure to information available at trade shows and conventions, publications such as trade and professional journals, and information sharing – all these are powerful stimulants.

Evaluating and selecting opportunities

Deciding to pursue a new business opportunity should be done only after it is determined that the opportunity itself is both valid and right for the company and that the company has a business strategy and plan to which it is prepared to commit itself.

A number of questions must be answered and then a preliminary judgement made as to whether the proposal merits proceeding to the next step – concept testing or feasibility study.

Is the opportunity consistent with the organization's strategy?

It is not always possible to make a decision regarding strategic fit at an early stage of evaluation if size and profit potential are part of the strategic objectives. But if, at face value, an opportunity is inconsistent with a company's strategy, then it should be passed up. We are not suggesting that the venture must fit current capabilities but rather strategic objectives. In order to succeed, many companies must diversify to some extent – penetrate new industries, gain new knowledge and enter new markets – and if strategic fit meant perfect fit with today's competency and knowledge, such companies would be doomed to inevitable decline.

But what about opportunities that seem too good to pass up? What about a business proposition that looks attractive but involves entering a new industry that the company has rejected as a strategic objective?

In this case, a spin-off may be desirable. The venture may begin with full funding and majority ownership by the parent but, as the spin-off succeeds, the parent's ownership may be greatly reduced. This is not uncommon in Japan, where the parent organization may end up a minority investor. In fact, 17.5 percent of the largest Japanese companies are spin-offs. Examples include Toyota Motor Corporation (spun off from Toyota Auto Loom Works) and Yamaha Motors (spun off from Yamaha Musical Instruments.)

To determine strategic consistency, the business concept must be scrutinized. The initial concept should indicate the product/service to be provided, the market segment targets, customers to be targeted, a guesstimate of market size, and the venture's potential value to the organization.

Aside from economic benefits, a venture can offer less tangible benefits, such as serving a defensive function, enhancing a company's reputation or providing a learning opportunity. In some cases, a company may start a new venture simply to study a business to determine whether and how to enter on a larger scale.

The following questions should be asked about any new-business concept.

What factors produce the opportunity?

By answering this question, a company can estimate how long those factors are likely to last. For example, a drop in interest rates might provide an opportunity for a new venture related to the building industry. How long rates are expected to stay low will affect the decision as to whether to enter the new venture, as well as how quickly to enter and exit. In contrast, environmental legislation is here to stay and as a source of opportunity can be regarded as fairly durable.

What are the character, size and nature of the market?

At what stage of its life-cycle is the market: not yet in existence, just emerging, static, growing, exploding or declining? Who are the players? What is known about present and potential competitors? What is the current and potential size of the market? What about pricing practices? Quality levels? Margins? What will this venture contribute in terms of value to the customer and with what competitive insulation?

The venture capital industry is a useful source of information about opportunity evaluation. Academic researchers have identified the following characteristics associated with successful ventures:

- Rather than identifying a market in general terms, successful ventures identify the true market in very specific terms, including a well-defined notion of the actual customer population to whom the value added by the proposed new product or service is clear.
- A market size between $10 million and $100 million is more likely to yield success than a very small or very large market. (This finding may not apply to corporate ventures by large organizations although it is quite appropriate for smaller businesses with limited available capital. For some corporations, even markets having a potential size of $100 million may hold little attraction.)
- Market growth rates between 30 percent and 60 percent are most favorable.
- Competitive insulation through patent protection or unique technologies involving products or services that cannot be provided by others to the same standard is a major success factor.
- Successful ventures tend to achieve a market share of at least 20 percent.

To identify the factors necessary for a proposed new venture's success, a company has to ask: how must this function differ in the new business from our present businesses in order for the venture to succeed? Here are some obvious examples:

- A manufacturer of consumer goods moving into industrial markets. Direct selling must be done by people who understand their customers' business and can develop strong relationships with them.
- A manufacturer moving into retailing. The company must understand such issues as managing inventories; providing security to protect against theft; recruiting and training salespeople who are congenial, knowledgeable and helpful to customers; and selecting business locations.
- A manufacturer, retailer or distributor entering a new industry. The organization must develop knowledge of customer needs and wants, major competitors, supplier sources, technology, usage patterns and problems.

When analyzing required success factors, a company must also understand the relative importance of the various functions involved (such as marketing, manufacturing, finance, human resources and R&D).

For example, in the retail business, merchandising (what to buy, how to price, how to promote) and information systems are critical; in commodity businesses, buying and trading reign. If a company is considering, say, a venture in which the marketing function is primary, it can be disastrous to initiate the venture under a manager whose skills lie mainly in technology management.

An organization seeking clues to the factors required for the success of a proposed new business should study leading companies in the target industry and identify what accounts for their outstanding track record.

Is the opportunity worth the effort?

To determine feasibility and potential value, an organization must analyze each opportunity's economic potential, asking itself what the upside gain and downside loss could be. For guidelines, we turn once again to the venture capital industry, in which the economic characteristics of successful ventures reportedly include the following:

- a break-even time of less than 36 months
- stable gross margins of 20 percent to 50 percent
- after-tax profit potential of 10 percent to 15 percent
- multiple rather than one-shot investments
- low asset intensity
- differentiation on the basis of product rather than price.

A few of these attributes are obviously inapplicable to many corporate ventures. A required break-even time of 36 months is not feasible in the case of ventures that are based on new technology, that have a high potential or that involve new or emerging markets.

Low asset intensity is undesirable if the corporation's economic power is to be used to erect entry barriers to competition. New industries are not created with low asset intensity (for example, semiconductors, biotechnology) nor can new entrants to a field, such as the automotive industry, be competitive without heavy investment in manufacturing facilities.

Some additional factors that venturing corporations should consider include:

- impact on overall corporate performance during the venture's early period – profits, ROI, cash flow
- impact on existing customers and business
- potential impact on total sales, profit, positioning and the value of company stock
- impact on the company's overall competitive advantage.

Is the opportunity feasible?

The ideal opportunity is one for which an organization already possesses precisely the mix of special competencies needed to provide the success factors and where the strategic fit is clear. But if the company lacks the means to provide the required success factors, it can also assemble the necessary competencies through alliances, joint ventures and so forth.

One universally required success factor is knowledge and experience in the proposed industry (except for cases in which the industry itself is entirely new).

Unless an organization has or can employ knowledgeable people or can acquire a foothold firm enough to provide that knowledge and experience, the opportunity should be dropped or delayed until the company can learn something about the business through a small-scale entry or an acquisition.

This article was adapted from a chapter in *Corporate Venturing: Creating New Businesses Within the Firm* (Harvard Business School Press, 1995).

The boss as a force for change

Wherever we work we are all entrepreneurs now. **Sandra Vandermerwe** and **Sue Birley** report on their research into how corporate executives act like enterprising leaders.

Once upon a time, the world was clearly divided between entrepreneurs and corporate executives, between the public and the private sectors. No longer. Now we expect civil servants to behave in a "business-like" fashion, entrepreneurs to create large organizations and bureaucratic managers to behave entrepreneurially. They all must compete for customers. Clearly, we believe that "nurture" can transcend "nature," that we can change behavior to fit changing circumstances, that the entrepreneurial bug can be caught at any age. Witness, for example, the civil servants and corporate executives who have abandoned the apparent safety of employment to become owners through the mechanism of a management buy-out.

But they are the tip of a very large iceberg. Corporations and governments throughout the world are seeking a new type of corporate leader – not the manager of stability or the professional bureaucrat, but one who approaches problems creatively and entrepreneurially and who thrives on the management of change.

What is it like for those chosen to make these transformations happen? What are the issues they have to deal with, and what are the factors they think necessary for success? To find out we asked executives from major organizations such as Baxter, BT, Ciba Geigy, Citibank, IBM, ICI, Jiffy Packaging, NatWest Bank, PricewaterhouseCoopers, Singapore Airlines and Zurich Insurance who had been (or are) involved in radical "customer transformations" to tell us about their experiences.

Selection of leaders

Our respondents were very clear why they had been selected for such projects. Some felt they had been chosen for their selling and influencing skills, some for their networking and co-ordination skills and some for attributes such as enthusiasm, energy, courage or patience – all of which contribute to the entrepreneurial character. The conspicuous absence of traditional skills, such as planning or cost-consciousness, is interesting.

Team selection

They were also clear on the selection of the team. They wanted people who were focussed and self-drivers, self-starters, self-motivated, self-confident and with a strong sense of urgency – in short, corporate entrepreneurs. (While they did require technical skills, functional background was rarely mentioned.) It seems that these change agents can come from anywhere in the organization provided they are prepared to take the risks associated with making new things happen.

> *"I have made it work if I have changed minds, not because I have increased sales by x percent."*

Success factors

All reported that their projects had been wholly or partially successful, and they measured this by the level of acceptance of both the project and the process, by both their colleagues and by their customers. They accept that they have to deliver bottom-line results but are also concerned about capabilities for growing the organization. They claim the two can only happen simultaneously by making the transformational process work.

The breakthrough

We asked about breakthrough events. When did they first feel that it was working? The biggest impact came from the "buy-in," or acceptance, of senior management. This was demonstrated through clearer direction, more effective support, demands to do more on the project or to extend it. All were process-based, reflecting a growing acceptance of change. Involvement and buy-in from customers was mentioned by 30 percent of respondents, and a special event, a meeting or forum in which a radical shift in thinking took place, by some 25 percent as a catalyst for change.

The blockers

More than half our respondents were plagued by things such as corporate politics, the wrong people in certain roles, suspicion, cynicism and members of the team hiding problems. Some top managers were reluctant to get involved "until they began to see results." There was also a tendency to short-termism, incrementalism and conflicting priorities. Trouble arose from poor communication and arrogance.

Reflections

We also asked if they would do anything differently a second time round. Again, the responses were concerned with the process. They would have involved more people earlier from various parts of the organization and would have "engaged" top management more visibly. It is clear from this that the role of senior management is critical to the success of customer transformation – at least in the eyes of those asked to take on the task. This is not surprising. We find the same result when we examine corporate venturing strategies. Therefore, we asked about the role their boss played in the process.

> *"I am the boss!"*
> *"He gave us space to change ourselves."*

The boss

As expected, the focus of responses was on active involvement. Bosses were used to remove organizational road blocks, to "get the rest of the organization off our backs" and "to sell the idea up the line." They managed political and cultural tensions, insisted that the project was high priority, and created an environment of trust. Some were more passive, simply "allowing it to happen," while a few felt that their boss had been a negative influence who "bowed too much to internal politics" or was an arbitrator in conflict situations rather than a leader of change.

On a personal level, the "good" bosses were seen as sounding-boards and coaches, always there to give moral support.

Critical attributes for the future

All of our respondents had been involved in major customer transformation within their organization and so we asked them to sit back and reflect, to tell us what they felt had been the most important challenges in achieving a customer focus, and how they felt this would change over the next decade. The answers, shown in Figure 1, speak for themselves.

It all points to a need to be proactive, not reactive, and to have imagination – a word that appeared frequently as critical in driving customer-based trans-

Up to now	For the future
The marketplace	
Adapt to market needs;	Evolve and develop needs with customers;
Understand customer needs;	Anticipate customer needs;
Superior products;	Specific customer offerings;
Instigate innovations (quality);	Manage innovations faster (innovate);
Build relationship with customer;	Make customers partners;
Know competitors' products;	Know how competitors tick;
Good market data.	Dialog with the market.
Organizational style	
Reduce bureaucracy/politics;	People working in teams, mutually trusting and respecting one another;
Manage enterprise-wide for cohesive offering;	Manage trans-enterprise with partners;
Get things done.	Manage complex projects.
Systems	
Good budgeting;	Good feedback mechanism;
Ensure information technology works.	Understand impact of and harness emerging technology.
People	
Get people to work well;	Mobilize people's energy and drive;
Train and control staff;	Develop leaders, renew human capital;
Compensate staff;	Reward and involve staff in success;
Stop internal strife;	Fight the correct competition as one united front;
Select the right people.	Get the correct skill mix.

Figure 1

formations. This was combined with creativity and an ability to recognize, interpret and evaluate new market opportunities and turn them into actionable projects. To do this, these entrepreneurs – for that is what is being described – need good communication skills, vision (the ability to encapsulate customer needs conceptually) and the ability to persuade their colleagues "to get out of their boxes," see the big picture and act accordingly.

"True progress involves tenacity and patience."

People are being asked to both "think and do" – to operate on two levels – strategically and operationally. They need to be able to disseminate and sell their ideas internally – up, sideways and down – as well as into the market. This requires a certain type of personality. In their eyes, they must be flexible – listening and learning from what they hear – trustworthy, open, resilient, tough, enthusiastic and extrovert, with integrity, honesty and honor – plus a sense of humor. Furthermore, they must be patient. Consistency in pursuit of their goals is essential.

"I so admired Colin Marshall from British Airways who never lost sight of the vision and never got dismayed by the gap between what he wanted the company to be and where it really was."

Where have we heard all this before? In the entrepreneurship literature. No longer do we see these people as impatient, determined misfits. Now they are seen as integral to making change happen within organizations.

The new entrepreneurial organization

Leaders of successful customer transformations have told us that to make them work, organizations must:

- develop new, proactive and process skills – this may entail pulling in more creative people from outside. It definitely means letting people go with their instincts and feelings
- encourage experimentation and reward success as defined by how customer-competitive it makes (or is likely to make) the corporation. This also involves managing failures successfully
- learn how to work on twin tracks – do what needs doing better now and, simultaneously, new things that may take longer
- unlock the enterprise within, defining risk differently and having "venturesome" people make key resource decisions
- develop new leadership skills with a new set of language and tools to reflect not the entrepreneurial or management world of yesterday, but what is needed today and in the future.

Most of all we need coaches at the top of modern organizations who will let corporate entrepreneurs "own their ventures" and get on and make them work. The corporation's responsibility is to support and reward this in new and innovative ways.

Question: Can existing top management take on this new role? Or will the new role require new top management?

The full paper on which this article is based is published in *Long Range Planning* in June 1997, Vol. 30, No. 3, 345–352 under the title "The Corporate Entrepreneur: leading organisational transformation."

KAO Corporation

This edited case was originally prepared by Professor **Shuichi Matsuda** of Waseda University's Entrepreneurship Research Unit (WERU), Tokyo.

KAO was founded in June 1887 by Tomiro Nagase, as Nagase Shoten, an imported fancy goods wholesaler. The company operated under the slogan "A clean nation is a prosperous nation." In the 20th century, KAO caught up with and in many areas surpassed the major domestic competitors, Shiseido and Lion, to gain the leading position in the Japanese toiletry industry.

The company has continued to grow by expanding into personal care and household products, with aggressive entry into foreign markets as well as overcoming declining growth in the mature domestic toiletries market.

Management style of KAO

The group's management is based on three fundamental principles:

- maintain a consumer-oriented spirit
- all individuals have equal value
- combine abilities and goals to maximize effectiveness.

These principles drive KAO's three main managerial practices: total system management, group management, and R&D career focus.

Total system management enables every function of the corporation to work together effectively. KAO's total system management practice makes its venturing system unique. All functions, such as R&D, operations, marketing and sales activities, are put under the charge of a single manager in a single venture framework. This manager is completely responsible for the direction of R&D and how the product should be introduced into the consumer market.

KAO also uses total creative revolution (TCR) to raise quality. The TCR program is designed to encourage creativity and combine personal objectives with commitment to the organization.

Group management combines all employees into a single, large group for each major product area. This system allows more effective management practices and more timely information-sharing. This single group concept creates an environment in which employees are encouraged to find and apply their own particular abilities toward better job performance.

Group management depends significantly upon making frequent personnel transfers, based upon individuals' requests. This practice constantly expands an individual's personal expertise and at the same time brings these new ideas to bear in different areas. The strategy also increases the number of employees with multi-functional abilities who understand the functions of many areas of the organization. This practice is particularly important for continued growth.

R&D career focus

KAO focusses primarily on identifying seeds, such as new technologies, rather than on consumer needs, and over 60 percent of the marketing staff have worked in R&D. The basic R&D or technological research perspective is reflected in the career paths of senior managers. As of 1993, four out of five senior managers had career experience in R&D. This means that researchers and engineers must develop their ideas in great detail before presenting them to senior managers. This seeds-oriented approach, with its R&D career focus, also gives true scientific innovators a more satisfying work environment.

Systems and practices to promote successful corporate venturing

KAO's basic strategy is to create simple and flexible organization structures that allow for the efficient development of new products, and that at the same time give greater autonomy to individual activities.

Full internal vertical integration

With a seeds-oriented R&D approach, KAO develops about 70 to 80 prospective substances every year, of which four or five are selected for the next stage of chemical analysis. In this stage, key properties of the new substances are identified and developed to maximize their effectiveness. The various derivatives are then developed into key materials which will be further developed and marketed in several areas.

By vertically integrating the entire process, from creating and evaluating new materials and producing raw materials, to designing final products as well as undertaking marketing and sales, KAO can develop more creative products with greater efficiency. This vertically integrated R&D approach is one of KAO's most crucial practices.

Twice a year, all KAO's top managers gather to discuss key R&D strategies. During the conference, approved ideas receive the authorization necessary to push them into the product development stage. In addition, long-term strategies for creating products which will be worth the challenge are identified.

At a quarterly convention, attended by top management and the heads of areas such as sales and operation, ideas under development in R&D divisions are introduced to others in the organization. Furthermore, each week, top managers meet to decide whether or not certain new business or product ideas are worth further development. If approved, an idea is presented to the management committee, which reaches a final decision within two weeks.

When a new project gains approval, its proposer becomes project leader and all necessary specialists are selected. Yet all project team members hold other responsibilities concurrently. KAO managers believe that the success of any project depends heavily upon selecting the most qualified individuals, and top managers therefore supervise the project leader's staff selections. Reports on the project's progress are made every two months to the idea evaluation committee. If a project is decreed non-viable at any stage during the venturing process, the committee immediately halts its development and redeploys the staff.

Exploiting existing corporate resources to start the floppy disk business

Until 1981, KAO had produced and sold only surfactant, a raw material used to produce floppy disks, but had no intention of developing the actual disks. Since no-one thought that a leader in the toiletry industry like KAO would consider developing floppy disk products, Tetsuga Imamura – a researcher at KAO's Tochigi Laboratories charged with considering the feasibility of manufacturing floppy disks – had a great advantage: his customers in the floppy disk industry were generous in sharing key information. Imamura also sent a researcher with the highest experience of R&D in this field for further study at leading universities. KAO's R&D teams learned that surface activity control, a fundamental technology used for producing quality soap, was highly useful in the development of floppy disks. KAO's main product lines were already based upon this technology and its highly competitive surfactant technology gave it an additional advantage.

After much discussion, in 1984 KAO executives made the final decision to manufacture floppy disks. They knew that one must have sufficient resources available when entering into a risky new business. At the time when KAO made this decision, its core business had been continually achieving a double-digit growth rate both in sales and earnings.

Global strategies to expand the floppy disk business

A commercial floppy disk manufacturing facility was constructed in 1985 at the Tochigi plant, and a floppy disk division was created with Imamura as manager. In 1986, KAO became the thirteenth manufacturer to introduce floppy disks into the Japanese market.

Imamura responded to this saturation by changing the focus from the domestic market to the North American market, where users would evaluate quality and price without preconceived notions. KAO constructed its first plant in Canada, and this market shift soon proved to be extremely lucrative. In 1986 demand for the floppy disk products reached 500 million units in the US, 100 million in Europe and 45 million in Japan.

KAO continued to market its floppy disk products to computer manufacturers and computer software firms as OEM supplier in Japan, while focussing its efforts on targeting the North American market. KAO's strategies for international growth were:

- to concentrate floppy disk production and sales in the North American market
- to ship floppy disk products to south-east Asia from Japan
- to acquire corporations in order to increase production capacity
- to focus on the OEM market and supply products to most international computer manufacturers and software firms
- to boost production of the 3.5-inch floppy disk before demand dictated it, with the forecast that demand for high-density, smaller floppy disks would soon increase rapidly
- to begin an international business for duplicating information recorded on 5-inch floppy disks
- to increase the familiarity of the KAO brand worldwide
- to have centralized R&D in Japan.

Soon after production in foreign markets began, the US and Europe drastically curtailed floppy disk imports. However, KAO remained almost wholly unaffected. By channeling production through corporations it had acquired in North America, KAO could act as a domestic manufacturer. In 1986, KAO acquired Didac of Canada and in 1987 it merged two existing companies in Spain and began to manufacture there. KAO acquired the plant and head office of Centennial Technology in 1988.

KAO's successful execution of these international growth strategies put it in the top league. KAO products gained credibility through competitive pricing and quality, and KAO is now the world's largest supplier of floppy disk products in terms of OEM. The company also holds the position of third largest supplier in the international floppy disk market.

Financing the project proved more challenging than KAO had expected. The most serious problem was the sudden, sharp reduction of market prices. In 1984 a 3.5-inch flexible disk cost ¥1000. But by 1986, when KAO began floppy disk production, the cost was ¥250, and just over ¥100 by 1992. KAO had forecast that the market price would be lowered by 20 percent each year, yet the actual price dropped by 50 percent. If, at the beginning of the venture, KAO market economists had estimated such a reduced price level, management may well have turned the project down. In 1989, because of these financial concerns, top management met to reconsider whether or not to continue the venture. Imamura was asked to submit a feasibility study of the business to determine ultimate cost and whether or not KAO could afford it.

After reviewing the initial business plan, he took the following measures to reduce total cost and increase sales volume:

- greatly increase production at the Canadian Didac plant, since its manufacturing costs were calculated to be about half those at Tochigi
- update the plant with highly productive, labor-saving equipment to produce high-quality floppy disks at lowered cost
- manufacture ten major raw materials and parts within the firm – a policy based on KAO's vertical integration concept. This improvement in productivity reduced variable cost.

An international floppy disk business headquarters was established in Massachusetts. In order to speed up the decision-making process by integrating top management with innovators, Vice-President Sumiaki Sasaki was temporarily transferred to the new headquarters.

KAO was fortunate to have become one of the world's leading floppy disk suppliers using only 10 percent of its cash flow. Had the funds required to make it a leader been much greater, KAO would have had insufficient resources to collect key information or to select the best direction for developing new products.

Contribution of floppy disk business to further venturing efforts

The technologies and knowledge which KAO gained from the floppy disk venture have contributed greatly toward R&D for the production of new materials and products. In 1990, KAO launched magnetic tapes for DAT (digital audio tape), including back-up tapes, as DAT manufacturers started marketing their products under unified specifications and standards. KAO views the production of back-up tapes as a promising undertaking since DAT would be used for storing computer data.

The total international demand for floppy disks was estimated to reach 3.3 billion units in 1993, and projected trends vary for each type of floppy disk. But KAO researchers believed that floppy disk products had a limited storage capacity and therefore pursued R&D in the area of optical storage discs such as CD-ROM.

Contribution of the floppy disk business to existing business

In the long run, the floppy disk business was expected to benefit KAO's core activities in the following ways:

■ since KAO's floppy disk products increased international market familiarity with the KAO brand name, the company could more easily introduce its toiletry products to foreign markets

■ the floppy disk business experience enabled KAO to train well-qualified staff with international business experience within a short period

■ the development process of the floppy disk business stimulated further R&D as well as engineering and technological innovation within the organization.

What KAO learned from its experience in the floppy disk business was applied to the development of strategies for further globalization and diversification as it planned for the twenty-first century.

When top management decided to enter the floppy disk business, it drew up a business plan. Ten years later, when Vice-President Sasaki reviewed it, he discovered that only one of the original objectives – sales performance – had been achieved as intended. It was KAO's policy of frequently evaluating the progress of various ventures, and making necessary changes to increase efficiency and quality, that led to its success.

Most of the information for this study has been compiled from interviews with several managers, in particular: Executive Vice-President Sumiaki Sasaki, who has maintained total charge of this project from the beginning; Executive General Manager of R&D, Tetsuga Imamura; General Manager of Floppy Disk Business Center Izumi Miyazawa; and General Manager of Personnel, Masatoshi Kitahara. In addition, the company's historical records, speeches by Chairman Yoshio Maruta, and various related materials such as that from periodicals, papers, financial reports and Nikkei's financial data, were used to complete this study. The author would like to acknowledge the editorial assistance of Shelley Rossell.

Fostering the entrepreneurial spirit

Daniel Muzyka and **Neil Churchill** advise on how to maintain the process of innovation in a growing business.

One of the perennial questions posed by executives in companies of all sizes is: "How do I grow?" In larger organizations the question may be: "How do I get more growth out of my organization?" or "How do we regain our earlier spirit for growth?" while executives in entrepreneurial activities ask: "How do I preserve entrepreneurial activity as I grow?" These questions are all concerned with maintaining or increasing entrepreneurial activity within an organization. They have always been pressing but are even more so today. The reasons are clear. Many companies have been downsizing for more than five years, getting "inefficiencies" and "slack" out of the system, and focussing their operations. As a result, many have failed to retain an adequate capacity to innovate and capture new opportunity.

So what is entrepreneurial activity? In the first article in *Mastering Entrepreneurship*, we defined entrepreneurship as a process that can take place in many different types of organizations, even government.

The process comprises building a vision of an opportunity, fashioning it to fit the company and the market, marshaling resources to capture it, and then capturing the value in the opportunity by building the business. The essence of entrepreneurship is the identification and economic capture of market value, based on matching an innovation with a need. In this context, the questions above can be distilled into one: how do I build and preserve room for individuals and teams to engage in the entrepreneurial process within my organization?

We are not saying that corporations, as they grow, fail to put into place systematic processes for developing innovations and new products and businesses. We are suggesting, however, that this is not enough: they also need to provide the continued capacity and option for individuals and teams throughout the organization to identify and develop opportunities. These people need to find a hearing for their ideas and have the support required to at least try to develop them. Merging ability, motivation and means for identifying new opportunities make a company truly entrepreneurial.

An entrepreneurial corporation must support entrepreneurial behavior and have a certain orientation, competitive logic, drivers, processes and tools that contribute to building and reinforcing entrepreneurial behavior and an entrepreneurial attitude. Over the past 15 years, we have researched entrepreneurial corporations in many industries and of many sizes – corporations that appear to maintain high levels of value-creating business development, innovation and entrepreneurship over the long term. This article outlines some of the common elements.

Orientation

One basic orientation in organizations that have remained entrepreneurial over a long period is the pursuit of new business opportunities that produce value for their customers and, in the process, for themselves. One of the elements in organizations that have remained entrepreneurial over the long term is a basic orientation. Individuals throughout the organizations know there is a continuous search for opportunity. While the business may not grow every year, constant orientation toward growth and renewing the business produces a steady stream of new opportunities. This also recognizes the fact that corporations are unlikely to get entrepreneurial activity if they do not ask for it.

Such organizations are very demanding in terms of performance. In fact, performance is frequently evaluated in terms of the level of opportunity pursuit and innovation achieved. There is significantly less emphasis on making individuals with large budgets and head counts seem important. What you contribute or build is of significantly more importance in the corporation rather than apparent importance of your job description as measured by resources you control. Several organizations we have studied demand that x percent of their total turnover should come from products introduced within the last y years. This may not drive absolute

Figure 1: Competitive logic

growth but it is the sort of measure that ensures continuous new product and business development.

Competitive logic

Combined with this orientation toward growth and renewal is a basic competitive logic which we saw in medium-to-large entrepreneurial companies. The company's overriding competitive strategy is to create profit by continuously developing and introducing high value-added products (*see* Figure 1). Innovation is continuous and directed at creating value.

These companies are rarely low-cost, low-margin competitors. They introduce products that create value for customers, capture the value through value pricing, and benefit from high gross margins in the process. These comparatively high gross margins are then sunk back into further innovation and entrepreneurial activity aimed at generating an even larger set of value-added products.

Drivers

Two distinctive forces drive them to pursue opportunities. The first is useful tension in the organization (we call it organizational traction because it ensures continuous movement) and the second is an active "action-learning" cycle.

Organizational traction (*see* Figure 2) consists of a number of countervailing forces that operate in all the long-term entrepreneurial organizations we have studied. On one side are the consolidating forces – the recognition of what has been done well,

consolidation	dimension	progression
gratification	organizational commitment	challenge
reinforcement	continuous innovation	search
attribution	performance allocation	collectivity
termination	resource deployment	accessibility

Figure 2: Organizational traction
Countervailing forces

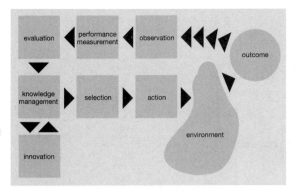

Figure 3: Management decision process

clarification and sharing of knowledge, and focussing on successful activities. On the other side are forces of progression – a continuous challenge for higher levels of performance, the search for new types of innovation and opportunity, accessibility of resources needed for innovation, and a focus on building and sharing for the greater good.

With constructive management of these countervailing forces, an organization can build a culture that incorporates a sense of satisfaction and continuous commitment to new opportunity.

The action-learning process that characterizes many entrepreneurial corporations is a regular assessment of options, actions, and evaluation, combined with the active development and maintenance of knowledge (*see* Figure 3).

It can be difficult initially to distinguish significant differences in management style between entrepreneurial organizations and more classic organizations. One of the differences that becomes more apparent is that managers find ways to communicate, test and reflect on their activities more frequently. In addition to communication, the knowledge embodied in the organization is easily accessible by would-be entrepreneurs.

In entrepreneurial corporations there is significant and active analysis and retention of lessons learned. This knowledge base is augmented through active innovation and experimentation. An important part of the constant emphasis on knowledge acquisition is the identification of distinctive skills and competencies and the search for new ways to leverage and evolve these competencies in pursuit of new economic opportunity.

Managers in these organizations may not always adopt the "normal" solution to a problem if they believe that, with a little change, the problem may be avoided in future or made less significant through a little investment in the time and effort required to experiment with new problem-solving techniques. The same applies to their approach to underlying product technology.

Architecture

The search for new "value innovations" is a very open process requiring a very open organizational architecture. What does this mean? The answer lies in the opportunity matrix shown in Figure 4. Corporations tend to focus innovation on certain types of opportunity (nature of opportunity) that arise from certain sources and associated processes (source of innovation).

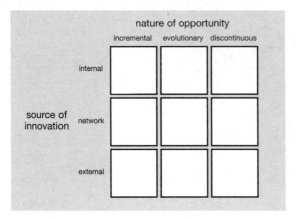

Figure 4: Sources and nature of opportunity *The opportunity matrix*

The first dimension of the matrix shows that opportunity comes in several "flavors." The least dramatic are incremental opportunities. These represent small adjustments to existing products and services. On the next level up are evolutionary product line improvements – the next generation of products. The final and most dramatic type of opportunity is the discontinuous – referred to as "blockbusters" in the drug business.

The other dimension of the matrix is the "source of opportunity." This may be in the internal product development process. At the other end of the spectrum, an opportunity may originate from a customer or from entirely outside the organization.

The interim possibility is that an idea originates through the business network of individuals outside the direct line of those involved with new product or business opportunity development or from a supplier, distributor or alliance partner.

Most successful organizations focus on different combinations in the matrix; never neglecting incremental and evolutionary developments on successful existing products but searching for the high-value discontinuous ones. For example, some big drug companies are focussed on opportunities that arise mostly through their own internal development process and that will prove to be significant products in the marketplace. Other companies interview their customers extensively about what they would like in the next edition of their product – the next evolution.

What differentiates the entrepreneurial corporations we have seen is that they can cite products or businesses developed through all of the combinations. There are processes and paths through the organization for opportunities of any magnitude that originate from any source. This architectural openness is vitally linked to the pursuit of opportunity and entrepreneurial behavior in the organization.

Processes

Several processes generally support a company's entrepreneurial and innovative activities. Each of the entrepreneurial corporations we have observed has had a high level of communication and networking activity. The corporate cultures within these organizations were almost academic in nature, with individuals competing to share and build ideas. One managing director noted that his organization "communicated perhaps very inefficiently, but obsessively and effectively." In another successful, middle-sized company, top management had gone so far as to actively train people how to ask questions in order to further refine communications.

Extensive networking, combined with dynamic teaming was a common trait in all the organizations we observed. No matter what the organizational structure, the organizations worked formally and informally to ensure active networking.

Internal clubs, interest groups and *ad hoc* cross-functional teams all contributed to networking and knowledge development. No matter what the organizational form, individuals would work persistently throughout their careers to develop personal networks.

As for resource allocation, these entrepreneurial organizations worked persistently to ensure spare resources were distributed throughout the organization and were available to support new initiatives. These resources take many forms – individuals who are not being used 110 percent, venture funds within the organization and spare funds. These organizations were also skilled in the art of incremental investment and evaluation. They "bet" on initiatives, watched patiently, but would re-evaluate performance, always asking the question: "Should we terminate now?" The point is not that these companies are awash with money, but that they carefully manage their funding to make sure it is applied properly.

Beliefs

A few key beliefs and behavioral norms permeate the entrepreneurial organizations we have seen. First, the recognition that to venture is sometimes to fail and individuals are allowed to fail without compromising their membership in the organization. One company manager noted: "If you are not failing you are not trying, and without trying, you won't get new opportunity." The second, which is closely related, is the management of risk. Calculated risk is supported and encouraged. Personal and organizational mechanisms are in place to limit risk. They do not prevent risk-taking, but limit overall losses from risky opportunities. The organizations actively help individuals to manage failure and ensure that small failures are learned from before they become large problems. All of this is supported by a strong culture of incremental review that is biased toward evaluating whether there is achievement rather than whether there is expenditure of time and resources.

The other pervasive beliefs include:

- organization structure is flexible and designed to serve opportunity and strategy
- corporate strategy and direction are emergent and created through the choice and pursuit of opportunities
- individuals seek value through membership in organizations which can be realized by recognition and creation of a sense of community.

All of these are underpinned by a fundamental belief in decentralized decision making; letting those with the best perspective on a particular opportunity attempt to develop it.

How to (re)create entrepreneurship

Building and maintaining more extensive opportunity-focussed entrepreneurial activity is not a simple proposition. There is no magic pill that will provide a solution. Nor will re-engineering, restructuring, or regularly turning over the management do the job. All of these tend to destroy an organization's delicate knowledge and network fabric.

Why do so many initially entrepreneurial organizations lose the capacity to fully identify and pursue available opportunities? First, many successful growth companies fall victim to a focus on the resources they have created. Second, they tend to focus too much on the businesses that made them successful, at the cost of sustaining the organizational processes that played an equally important part. Thirdly, they try in vain to preserve what they have by establishing excessive numbers of rules, systems and controls. Eventually, the organization turns to meeting budgets and acquiring control of internal units rather than pursuing new opportunity.

To maximize the amount of entrepreneurial activity or to rebuild that initial entrepreneurial activity:

■ focus people on opportunity, growth and renewal. Demand performance, even on both profit and turnover

■ open the information infrastructure; ensure that withholding information is not a source of individual managerial power. Encourage individuals to share knowledge, technology and skills in pursuing and exploiting opportunity

■ distribute some resources throughout the organization. Make them accessible to individuals who wish to develop opportunities

■ make sure individuals and teams have the training and coaching needed to support them in their activities

■ let go of some of the central control of decision making.

Often, successful entrepreneurs are their own worst enemies because they feel they have to be at the center of every new process to develop new opportunities. The most successful long-term entrepreneurs are those who are able to maintain the entrepreneurial flair of their original firm while installing minimum co-ordination and control mechanisms. Let individuals be entrepreneurial, and let them promote entrepreneurship throughout the organization! Don't lose your initial feelings.

CASE STUDY

Siemens Nixdorf's new dynamism

Mark Maletz describes how Siemens Nixdorf accepted the challenge of becoming a more entrepreneurial company.

The challenge of change – managing it, enacting it and leveraging it – has become one of the most important topics on today's corporate agenda. Twice each year, top executives from many of Germany's most important companies meet, under the sponsorship of BMW, Deutsche Bank and Siemens Nixdorf, to discuss the challenges that they face in building more competitive skills and organizations.

Specific change challenges discussed at these workshops are highly varied – ranging from new organizational structures to the role of leadership. Issues associated with new behaviors and with the emerging role of behavior as a competitive advantage have surfaced at every meeting.

One clear conclusion is that flexibility, responsiveness, innovativeness and openness are the characteristics that today's corporations require and that they should replace control, rigidity, predictability and caution. This entails a transformation for many companies from bureaucracy to entrepreneurship. Through such transformation, companies can better leverage their people, at all levels, to help to design the change itself and then to become on-going leaders of innovation. The more turbulent the industry and change, the more urgent the need for this transformation becomes.

Discussion in the workshops frequently refers to US cases to describe the ways in which highly entrepreneurial companies deal with change. Initially, participants responded with some skepticism, explaining that it is easy to be entrepreneurial when one is situated in the heart of Silicon Valley.

There, companies are surrounded by some of the world's most entrepreneurial organizations with easy access to talent, capital and technology. A more rigorous test, they decided, was whether the transformation towards entrepreneurship could succeed in Germany.

Siemens Nixdorf, one of the sponsors of the change workshops, accepted this challenge. It operates in the high-tech arena and competes directly with its Silicon Valley counterparts and therefore faces the challenge in any case. The remainder of this article will address the key elements of the transformation to entrepreneurship using Siemens Nixdorf as a case study.

Siemens Nixdorf is the product of the merger between Siemens' computer unit, Siemens Dateninformationssysteme, and Nixdorf Computer in 1990. There were significant expectations at the time of the merger concerning the new company's ability to be both disciplined and innovative, but these expectations weren't realized. Between the time of the merger and the summer of 1994, the company lost hundreds of millions of deutschmarks every year.

In response to these mounting losses and a "loser image" in the marketplace and within the Siemens parent, the company retreated into precisely those behaviors that made it difficult for it to compete – bureaucracy, command and control, parochialism and inward focus.

Finally, in the summer of 1994, top management at Siemens hired a new CEO for Siemens Nixdorf, Gerhard Schulmeyer, and asked him to restore the company to competitiveness. Schulmeyer had been responsible for the American operations at ABB where he had established a highly effective matrix organization. He had previously been a key executive at Motorola where he was instrumental in the creation of Motorola University and in Motorola's cultural shift towards quality and process improvement. The combination of this experience in cultural and structural change put Schulmeyer in a strong position to lead Siemens Nixdorf's transformation.

The change agenda was clear – create a highly profitable, entrepreneurial business capable of operating in the global, high-tech marketplace. To accomplish this, broad-based cultural and structural changes were required based on four key dimensions:

- a shift in the organizational culture to first nurture and later demand entrepreneurial behavior from all employees
- a new organizational architecture that would facilitate entrepreneurial behavior
- an investment in developmental activities (focussing on both behaviors and skills) that would prepare individuals at all levels of the organization to operate in the new culture and structure
- new systems (management and information) to support the transformed organization.

Pursuing this required committed and visible leadership from the top. Schulmeyer reshaped the company's top team, recruiting executives capable of role-modeling the behaviors required for the new company culture and of using and mentoring others in the use of the tools and techniques of entrepreneurship. The new top team consisted of more than a dozen executives from some of the most entrepreneurial and successful companies in Europe.

However, a dozen executives, no matter how talented, cannot lead transformational change alone. They require the pro-active support of senior managers from across the company. The new top team therefore convened a group of more than 100 senior managers from every part of the company and asked them to lead the transformation in partnership with the top team. This group became the company's executive management team.

They met regularly (roughly quarterly) to monitor the company's progress and held themselves accountable for progress from meeting to meeting. This represented an important role-modeling of performance orientation that world-class entrepreneurs invariably learn and demonstrate.

Culture change

Siemens Nixdorf's culture change program mobilized thousands of employees as co-producers of the company's new culture in partnership with executive management. The program was punctuated with four meetings in Hanover between December 1994 and October 1996. Each meeting was attended by 300 to 400 employees interested in helping to shape and catalyze the culture change. The meetings were organized around distinct, but related, themes.

Meeting 1: the voice of the employees

It provided employees with an opportunity to reflect on the new values and behaviors that were needed by Siemens Nixdorf and then to establish action teams (59 in total) that would move the company towards these values.

Meeting 2: the voice of the customers

Fifty-four key customers joined the 350 employees, ensuring that they would have a voice in the company's transformation. The customers also participated in the follow-up work of the 20 action teams formed at the meeting.

Meeting 3: the voice of the partners

Forty key business partners also attended the event, ensuring they had a voice in the transformation process. This was important in the light of the company's commitment to dramatically increase its partner-driven revenue. The partners were fully fledged members of the action teams.

Meeting 4: instilling the capability to change

This meeting focussed on preparing the employees to put into practice the change skills and tools that the first three Hanover meetings had brought up.

Each of these meetings had prepared employees to behave in a highly entrepreneurial manner and to accept the responsibilities and accountabilities inherent in entrepreneurship. For example, each action team was committed to achieving some results within 90 days of the meeting and substantial business impact within 180 days.

The company also launched an initiative to discover, assess and fund innovative business ideas. This included the formation of an internal venture capital fund for use by internal entrepreneurs with business plans for new products, services and solutions. A key element was the development of a network of internal resources that could support entrepreneurial business development. For example, an employee with a business idea but no financial background could be linked with an entrepreneurial financial analyst.

A key characteristic of successful entrepreneurs is the ability and courage to reflect, learn and adapt. To encourage this behavior, Siemens Nixdorf launched a "Friday forum" in which workgroups across the company would meet once a month to discuss matters of mutual interest. These forums provided the opportunity to learn from successes and failures and to make modifications to on-going business and change activities. They also taught employees to support one another more effectively and to draw on the resources and knowledge of the workgroup.

Because successful entrepreneurs have keen insight to the business environments they operate in, Siemens Nixdorf also launched benchmarking activities focussed on the best companies in the market. This included numerous visits to companies around the world, including regular trips to Silicon Valley.

The meetings and their culture change initiatives introduced new behaviors that Siemens Nixdorf required for its transformation to entrepreneurship. They also mobilized the employees into driving the transformation itself.

New organizational architecture

The new organizational architecture at Siemens Nixdorf was based on a high degree of decentralization and followed six principles:

- One face to the customer. He wants a direct answer to a simple question: "Who is my representative at Siemens Nixdorf?" He should never be confused by the company's internal organization.
- Smooth service that begins and ends with the customer. Any salesman the customer sees has to be part of a single process from design to delivery.
- Delegation of authority and responsibility to the lowest level. The real decision makers must be the business unit entrepreneurs in the field. The regional managers and world-wide business leaders are primarily coaches, mentors and enablers.
- Bet the future on businesses that have a defendable core competence. To prosper, a business unit must hold a clear leadership position in Germany, be one of the market leaders in Europe, and a player elsewhere in the world.
- Customers of equal importance have equal access to the company's resources. This does not mean that all customers, regardless of size or needs, have an equal claim on the company. But one of the characteristics of the company's former

orientation was that strategic foreign customers did not always enjoy the same access to the company as German ones.

■ Different business units require different structures. The company consists of service, solution and product businesses; the structures for these different businesses should be designed on their individual requirements (consistent with the other five principles).

Adhering to these principles resulted in a network structure of approximately 250 business units – each with a geographic customer focus and a line-of-business focus (for example, a unit might target the Spanish PC market). This two-dimensional structure was intended to be a first step towards a dynamically reconfigurable network model. The organization would first learn how to operate in a two-dimensional matrix and then the static matrix structure would be relaxed and business units would be reconfigured in response to customer demands.

Unlike many matrix organizations in which those in the middle feel caught between two managers with relatively little real authority, the unit manager for each business unit was given full profit and loss responsibility for his or her unit. The regional manager and line-of-business manager served almost as a board of directors, coaching the unit manager while letting him get on with managing his business unit.

An interesting lesson was learned from all this. The original plan was to call each manager responsible for a business unit an entrepreneur. Testing of this idea showed that those called entrepreneurs would keep the name for themselves – resulting in no more than 250 entrepreneurs in the whole company. The plan was therefore changed so that any employee could be called an entrepreneur. A key sign of an effective unit manager would be the ability to develop new entrepreneurs within his business unit.

Developmental activities

"Do we really have 250 middle managers capable of acting like entrepreneurs and experienced enough to manage their own business unit?" That was a key question. Part of the answer came from the culture change program, which demonstrated that a broad cross-section of employees were capable of behaving entrepreneurially when given the chance.

The other part of the answer came through the introduction of an "entrepreneurship development program," attended by every prospective unit manager and led by Babson College, INSEAD and IMD. Participants carried out self-assessments throughout the program and during the final week decided whether they were ready to assume unit management responsibilities.

Another important activity was the management development program, lasting a week, open to any key manager, and designed to prepare him to operate in the entrepreneurial company that Siemens Nixdorf was becoming.

New systems

Entrepreneurial management often requires better information than other forms of management. Moreover, moving from a two-dimensional matrix to a dynamic network model also requires sophisticated information systems. At Siemens Nixdorf there were four key system improvements that accompanied the transformation to entrepreneurship:

- introduction of an integrated financial management package to provide business unit profit and loss information
- development of a business assessment methodology to be used throughout the company for purposes of portfolio management (across business units) and business model optimization (within a business unit)
- introduction of balanced scorecards of performance and new incentive systems across the company. These scorecards emphasized both business performance and behavioral competencies
- development of new channels to maximize communication and make information available across the company in order to encourage networking among business units and support the dynamic nature of the organizational model. This included placing new media (including electronic discussion forums) on the intranet.

At the end of 1996 Siemens Nixdorf's transformation towards entrepreneurship had been underway for about two and a half years. During this time, the company achieved a break-even financial position, dramatically improved its customer orientation and image in the marketplace and conceived and developed many new business opportunities.

An important example of the pursuit of new business opportunities is the creation of an array of internet-enabled lines of business. Several groups of entrepreneurial employees launched new lines of business through this. One group provides customers with internet-related services, leveraging the competencies that the company developed to meet its own needs. Customers are given the opportunity to benefit from the internet learning curve that Siemens Nixdorf mastered.

In Siemens Nixdorf's mainframe business, a team of entrepreneurs launched a new product, code-named "Sunrise," that would transfer the BS2000 operating system to a client server platform – a vital issue in the diminishing mainframe market. Soon after launch the product had already attracted substantial customer interest.

Such successful entrepreneurial developments provide evidence of change within the company. While at the time of writing the journey may not be complete, it is clear that Siemens Nixdorf has substantially met the challenge of entrepreneurial transformation put in motion at the change workshops.

Case postscript
By Daniel Muzyka

A couple of years later, Siemens Corporation decided to reintegrate various operations of Siemens Nixdorf into other Siemens divisions and to spin off the retail and banking business in Siemens Nixdorf Retail and Bank. A number of the changes initiated by the transformation effort had an impact on other Siemens divisions. Siemens Nixdorf Retail and Bank was acquired by a group of financial investors (including KKR and GS Capital Partners) and began operating under the name Wincor Nixdorf in 2000. Gerhard Schulmeyer is President and Chief Executive Officer for Siemens Corporation. He has been given responsibility for Siemens' interests in the US.

HARVESTING

10

Contributors

 Rod Selkirk is director of venture and development capital group NatWest Equity Partners.

 Chris Harrison is a partner in Ernst & Young and national head of its UK entrepreneurial services practice.

 Elizabeth Tashjian is Associate Professor of Finance at the Eccles School of Business, University of Utah.

 Benoît F. Leleux is S. Schmidheiny Chair in Entrepreneurship and Finance, IMD.

 Lawrence A. Weiss is Associate Professor of Accounting and Control at INSEAD and Visiting Professor of Accounting at MIT Sloan.

Contents

Introduction

Part 10 brings us to the end of our story and to the exit route. We ask what are the various ways in which entrepreneurs can "harvest" their investment by taking some or all of the value out of the business. We ask: when should this happen? Is there a right time? Of course, not all can make this choice and we explore the problems of bankruptcy and failure. For the rest, we look at the two main voluntary exit routes of trade sale and initial public offering.

Harvesting at the right price

Sue Birley looks at the complex question of when – and if – an entrepreneur should sell out of the business he or she has created.

Harvesting enterprise: what does it mean and when should it be done? For farmers, it is easy – when the grapes are ready or the corn is ripe. Or is it? Even the farmer must judge exactly when to harvest. Too soon and the crop will fail to reach expectations; too late and the weather could ruin it. So it is with business. Too soon and the value will not have reached the optimum; too late and competition may have destroyed profits.

So what do we mean by harvesting? Quite simply, it is the sale of some or all of the equity of a company. This can be through a number of possible "exit routes:"

- a trade sale to another company (*see* p. 390)
- the sale of the investment to another corporate investor such as a venture capitalist (*see* Part 3, p. 105)
- the sale of equity to another individual – such as a "business angel" or a fellow shareholder – or through a management buy-out or buy-in (*see* Part 3 – buy-outs and buy-ins are covered in Part 8)
- the sale of equity to "the public" through an IPO (initial public offering) on a stock exchange (*see* p. 394).

For the investor or venture capitalist, this would seem to be a relatively straightforward decision – just a matter of finding the right time to sell, deciding the exit route and agreeing a price with the purchaser. Not quite. In a private company, there may be restrictions on the ability to sell – the owner-manager may be required to offer to the existing shareholders, who cannot or will not buy. He or she may be a minority shareholder and so have no power to make a decision to sell the entire company. Many venture capitalists call these the "living dead" investments.

Even assuming the entrepreneur is free to seek buyers for his or her shares, the value of minority holdings can be considered as worthless to prospective buyers, though there may be an agreed, and binding, exit mechanism, which includes a pricing formula. This is analogous to agreeing the divorce settlement prior to the wedding – always difficult but sometimes well worth it.

For many entrepreneurs, all this is even more complicated by the fact that they may be both owner and manager and so have two possible "exit" decisions. The first, that of delegating managerial responsibility to others, we have dealt with elsewhere. The latter, that of realizing your financial investment, is what we are concerned with in this part of *Mastering Entrepreneurship*. However, it may be that both arise at the same time – for example, the entrepreneur may have no obvious family successor and so may wish to retire by selling the company. Whatever the situation it will not be easy, either technically or emotionally.

The decision to sell, always assuming that it is a voluntary decision, is almost certainly related to the price that you expect to receive for your equity – and that is a lifestyle decision. You will be juggling two interlinked questions in your mind:

- What is the company worth?
- Will this give me sufficient capital to enjoy the rest of my life in the manner to which I wish to become accustomed? Of course, this will be related, in part, to whether you already have a company pension plan and how you intend to invest the proceeds of the sale.

That in turn relates to two more factors:

- the size and profitability track record of the company
- the state of the market.

Either way, it is not a decision that you can usually make overnight, nor without advice. Valuation, as we have seen earlier in *Mastering Entrepreneurship*, is much more an art than a science. Certainly, human nature being as it is, an owner is probably likely to be more optimistic than others about the value of the company.

What does this mean? Well, that the value to you of the income stream generated by your company may be greater than to a purchaser. It can be hard for someone who has spent many years of their life building a business to be told that while they think it is worth, say, $20 million, a buyer may only value it at $15 million. Of course, it does not always work that way. Sometimes the value is significantly higher than expected – getting to that point is the trick. But that is just the start. Unfortunately, sellers are not necessarily in control of the timing of the sale. For example, preparing the documentation for flotation can take six months and bulls can transform into bears overnight.

A trade sale may be ideal but no-one is interested in small fast-food franchise chains – at the moment. But even before that, companies need to be prepared for a sale – the house put in order, a respectable track record in place. But *caveat emptor* is important here. Sometimes they can be over-prepared, with the balance sheet and profit and loss account presented in the very best light and the "entrepreneurial toys" of houses, private planes and boats well hidden!

Potential buyers who are skilled in this field know this and will be looking to strip out the "toys" and "organizational patching" that may clutter the balance sheet so that they can understand the underlying strengths of the company. Think of it as buying a house. How easy it can be to miss the crack in the wall, the poor electrical wiring, the sagging roof, particularly when it has been recently decorated (perhaps in anticipation of the sale) unless you are a professional or have professional help.

So the questions to be answered are:

- Do I wish to realize all or only part of my investment?
- Do I wish to continue to be associated with the company after the sale?
- What form of payment do I want from the sale – equity in another company, cash on deferred terms, a pension, a consultancy retainer?
- Which exit route will give the greatest return?
- If I decide to float, what will it cost and who will help me?
- If I decide to seek a trade sale or sale to a third party, how do I find a buyer?

These are not easy questions and most people only do this once. Think long and hard about why you are doing it, what you want afterwards, what is a reasonable price – and seek advice.

The two main routes to a company sale

Rod Selkirk looks at the choices open to a business owner when he or she decides to make an exit.

The poet T. S. Eliot was thinking about something very different from the world of venture capital when he wrote that "the end is where we start from." But his observation holds true for our business: investors and managers who participate in buy-outs and other venture capital deals have to start thinking about exits before they even make their entry.

Those who provide most of the equity finance for a buy-out – including venture capital companies and pension funds and other financial institutions whose money the venture capitalists invest – need to know how and when they are likely to realize their investments before they commit any funds. That is because we invest not for eternity but on average for three to seven years, after which we expect to make a profit that reflects the scale of the risk we have taken on in making our investment. This puts us on the same side as management, whose financial stake in a deal is unlikely to be as large as ours in absolute terms but invariably represents a big personal risk, with a corresponding opportunity to make substantial rewards.

Management and venture capitalists thus have a common interest in growing the capital value of the business and working out ways of crystallizing that value within a medium-term time frame. So when management, advisers and financial backers such as ourselves come together to hammer out the terms of an investment, drawing up an exit strategy is an integral part of the business plan.

Two roads

There are two principal types of exit route – the sale to a trade buyer or a flotation on the stock market. (These are covered in detail on pp. 390 and 394.) There are other exit strategies, and I will return to these later, but the principal choice for management and backers is whether to float or to sell.

Take public offerings first. There is a great deal of razzmatazz associated with going public and we counsel that management takes a sober, unemotional look at the pros and cons of such a big step.

On the positive side, an IPO gives a company the opportunity to raise further capital via the equity market, often the cheapest source of finance available. It allows it to finance acquisitions by issuing shares, thus allowing it to grow more quickly than if it relied solely on organic growth and bank borrowings. Furthermore, it enables management to remain on board as directors and shareholders, thereby ensuring that they participate in the company's future growth.

From a more negative perspective, IPOs can be expensive in terms of advisers' fees, and directors of publicly quoted companies have to busy themselves with ongoing obligations that may distract from the day-to-day running of the business, for example maintaining relationships with institutional investors.

Many managers like the idea of being directors of public companies but often perfectly sound businesses do not lend themselves well to an IPO. One reason is size: shares in smaller quoted companies often lack liquidity, making it more difficult to raise capital and for shareholders to realize their investment, thereby negating the main reasons for having a stock market listing in the first place.

Market volatility

Another consideration is the volatility of the stock market. Factors well beyond the control of management teams can have an impact on the valuation a company can achieve by way of flotation or even whether the market has any interest in supporting the flotation of a medium-sized company. These include general market conditions – a rise in US interest rates could dampen institutional investors' appetite for new issues of any description. Valuations in specific stock market sectors more often reflect fashion than fundamentals.

Our decision to postpone the planned IPO of the Principal Hotel Group, a Leeds-based hotel chain into which we bought three years earlier, is a case in point. We had originally hoped to offer the company in the first half of 1996 but, together with the management team we backed, we took the decision to delay the market debut. The reason was that, in our judgement, institutional investors had had their fill of hotel issues in the previous couple of years – there had been half a dozen of them in that time – meaning that we would not necessarily have been able to achieve the best price for a company we believed to be markedly more attractive than most other quoted hotel groups.

We are confident that the company's value will continue to rise and have continued to support it with the capital resources required to finance its growth.

There have been very few IPOs on the UK stock market in the last two years since institutional investors have tended to focus on larger companies. It is probably not feasible to consider an offering as an exit route unless the valuation of the company upon offering is in excess of £200 million or perhaps even £300 million. The exception to this is the offering of companies which are, or are perceived by the market to be, very high growth. Obvious examples include high technology and in particular internet-related companies.

Increasingly, therefore, the most likely exit route for venture capital-backed companies is a trade sale.

Clean exit

There are many companies for which a trade sale may provide a more appropriate exit route. Trade sales attract less pronounced headlines than IPOs but can be the best way for management and venture capital backers to realize the value of their investments.

A trade sale represents a "clean" exit, for venture capitalists and management alike, in a way that an offering does not. It involves the sale of all of the company's equity, whereas management and backers will tend to retain a significant stake when a company is floated. Whether a company achieves a better price by way of a trade sale rather than a IPO depends on a number of factors. One is the unpredictable question of stock market valuations or market receptiveness to medium-sized companies as we have seen recently.

Furthermore, there may be special synergies that mean that a trade buyer will put a higher value on the business than stock market investors. Or the company may present an opportunity for strategic diversification, as in the near-£20 million sale of LivingWell Health and Leisure, one of the leading health club operators in the UK, to the Stakis hotel and casino group. Stagecoach's purchase of GM Buses South, the south Manchester bus company we backed in an employee buy-out in 1994, shows how a business may have a special strategic appeal to a company already active in the sector.

In practice, however meticulous the planning process, it pays to be opportunistic about how and when to achieve the exit. Indeed, the way in which the exit is achieved can be completely at variance with what was planned at the outset of the investment, as the GM Buses South case shows. Back in 1994, had you asked the fitter in the bus depot or the driver on the 192 route to Hazel Grove who would end up buying the company, the answer would not have been Stagecoach.

The original deal created an unlikely alliance of bus drivers and venture capitalists. After lengthy haggling, we at NatWest Equity Partners and the bus company's 2,000 employees won the £25 million bid for the company in March 1994. The deal was structured to give employees majority control and no-one imagined selling the business less than two years later – especially not to Stagecoach.

During the protracted negotiations to buy the company on the employees' behalf, the chief opposition to our bid came from Stagecoach. We had always assumed that the employees would end up buying us out but before too long Stagecoach came back with a bid. It proved irresistible for the bus company's employees, who turned their initial £1,000 investment into £10,000 in little more time than it took to negotiate the transaction in the first place.

The Cara computerized payroll business that we bought from Aer Lingus also shows the importance of being flexible in achieving an exit route. When we first took the stake, we were interested primarily in the potential of a small high-tech subsidiary in Germany, which we thought one day could well be a candidate for public offering. By the time we came to sell Cara, to Bull Information Systems, it was the payroll processing business that was booming and the principal attraction to Bull.

Other exits

I have covered IPOs and trade sales, the two main types of exits, but there are others. It may be, for example, that owner-managers of businesses want to realize part of their investment while retaining an active role in the management of the company they have helped to build.

There is a growing number of secondary buy-outs, transactions that enable one set of institutional investors to realize their investments while management stays on, or new management is brought in, with the backing of new investors. Such deals are coming about chiefly because many venture capital funds set up in the last ten years are approaching their termination dates – when they have to be wound up – obliging the original investors to sell out. They are replaced by fresh investors prepared to make a new medium-term commitment to the company. An example from our portfolio is the 1995 £70 million Sheffield Forgemasters deal. We took a 29 percent stake in this engineering and specialist metals group when one of the original venture capital funds reached its termination date and needed to exit.

Although most exits will come through a trade sale, secondary buy-outs are becoming an increasingly common phenomenon. No management team can enter a deal without giving plenty of thought to which of these it prefers, though it is essential to be flexible about the way in which the exit is finally completed. In practice, the choice of exit route will reflect market conditions and the preferences of management and investors. There are no hard and fast rules but it is true to say that the better the company, the fewer problems management and venture capitalists will have finding an exit route.

Navigating a course off the rocks

Elizabeth Tashjian and **Lawrence Weiss** discuss the complex details of business failure and bankruptcy laws.

In our favorite Bible story, Pharaoh has strange dreams of cattle and corn, which Joseph, the hero of the tale, interprets for him. Seven fat, or good, years will be followed by seven lean, or bad, years. The lesson of the tale, still true today, is to save in good times to survive the bad times. Unfortunately, many managers either lack the opportunity or foresight to save for the lean years.

This article explores how modern society deals with companies that are unable to repay their debts. We will first discuss why bankruptcy rules exist in their current form and then describe what the management of a failed business is likely to experience.

What is bankruptcy?

Corporate bankruptcy occurs after an enterprise defaults on its financial obligations. When a company fails to repay its debt according to schedule, the debt-holders have certain legal rights to obtain payment, including seizing the company's assets. In effect, once an organization is unable to meet its debt obligations, the debt-holders become the owners of the concern.

Without debt there can be no bankruptcy. Why, then, do companies issue debt? First, as we have already seen in *Mastering Entrepreneurship*, debt is less costly than equity because interest payments for debt are tax-deductible and because debt is supposed to be repaid before equity in the event of financial distress. Second, debt requires less costly monitoring than equity. Since equity holders are entitled to whatever value remains in the business after creditors are paid, equity holders bear the entire cost of any corporate waste in a healthy company. Equity holders can reduce the amount of waste by closely monitoring managerial actions.

The fixed-payment schedule associated with debt also restricts the ability of management to act inefficiently, by providing an early warning: failure to make a scheduled debt payment is a clear warning signal. Thus, to avoid bankruptcy and safeguard their jobs, managers must avoid violating the terms of debt contracts.

Why have bankruptcy laws?

Most jurisdictions grant creditors the right to seize the assets of a debtor who fails to adhere to the terms of a loan agreement. Outside of bankruptcy, claims against a debtor's assets are processed in the order they are filed by creditors with the local judiciary. Thus, the first creditor to file may receive full payment while the last to file may receive nothing. Just as in a bank run, the first depositor in line may receive full payment and the last nothing.

This "first in time, first in line" rule means each creditor will expend excessive resources to position itself to win any race for an insolvent organization's assets. Collectively, the creditors should forgo the expense of this monitoring and agree instead to share all assets equitably with other creditors of the same priority. Such an arrangement increases the total value of the creditors' investment by the amount of expenses of the avoided race. Unfortunately, such mutually beneficial agreements are difficult at best because it is of no advantage to the creditor who is first in line to co-operate once financial distress occurs.

Another problem, outside of bankruptcy, is the possible dismembering of a viable company when creditors fail to co-operate and race to grab a distressed business's assets. The creditors collectively lose the difference between the value of the company as a going concern and its piecemeal liquidation value.

Bankruptcy law also reduces the amount of asymmetric information between managers and the company's creditors. Supposing a company is trying to renegotiate the terms of its debt outside of bankruptcy. Bondholders are aware that managers are likely to be better informed than they are regarding the future prospects of the enterprise and are understandably suspicious of any offer. For example, if management knows the prospects for the business are strong they are unlikely to offer a debt-for-equity swap since the swap would result in excessive dilution for existing equity holders. Therefore, when management offers equity, bondholders believe the company's prospects are poor and anticipate that the equity offered by management is over-valued, thereby resulting in an unfavorable transaction for existing debt holders.

When the level of asymmetric information is high, management and creditors may be unable to agree on the terms of a restructuring out of court. However, in a court-supervised bankruptcy, information is usually shared among management and all investors in the organization, thereby mitigating the asymmetric information problem and increasing the odds that a suitable division of the assets can be agreed by all parties.

Finally, bankruptcy law can mitigate the problem of creditors holding out for better terms. Individual creditors have the incentive to free-ride on concessions offered by other creditors. Because there is no easy way to compel participation in a restructuring out of court, creditors may refuse to participate. Bankruptcy can solve this problem by compelling all claim holders to participate on an equal footing.

Modern bankruptcy law

Bankruptcy law is meant to save viable businesses that are experiencing temporary cash flow problems by providing some breathing room and a process to help reorganize the claims on the company.

It seeks to create an efficient debt-repayment system by determining the amounts owed to various creditors, classifying creditors into groups based on repayment priority and then treating everyone in a particular group equally. This equal treatment by class eliminates any benefit to an individual creditor of being first in line to file a claim and stops the race to grab assets. Monitoring costs for creditors are reduced and enterprises are provided with a chance to restructure their debt. In addition, the process brings together all the interested parties and avoids duplication of effort in tasks such as valuing the business.

Once the claims against the company and the order in which the claims will be paid have been established, the concern must dispose of its assets so as to maximize the value of the creditors' claims. The most common methods for disposing of the assets are through liquidation or reorganization.

Liquidation and reorganization

Whether a company is liquidated piecemeal or sold as a whole, the proceeds are distributed first to those claim holders with the highest priority until they have been paid in full, then to those with the next highest priority and so on until the available funds are exhausted.

Although liquidation provides for an orderly dissolution of the organization and an equitable distribution of assets to creditors, frequently the going concern value of the business is destroyed in the process. In a court-supervised reorganization, the business continues as a going concern and claim holders reach a consensual agreement on how to restructure the company's capital.

Who decides the terms?

The problem faced by bankruptcy law is how to properly allocate what economists would call "decision rights" – who decides what to do with an organization's assets. The correct answer is far from obvious.

Giving senior creditors the right to decide whether to continue operations or liquidate may be a poor choice, since they will probably elect for a quick disposition of the assets whenever this would repay them in full – regardless of whether it maximizes the value of the company.

Transferring the decision to any other group – junior creditors, managers, owners or employees – is likely to give that group the ability to transfer value from others to themselves. For example, junior creditors may delay payment or continue to operate a non-viable business unless senior creditors agree to provide them with funds beyond what they would otherwise be entitled to. Owners, who often have no more equity in the business and so have nothing more to lose, may engage in highly risky ventures in the desperate hope of a turnaround. Likewise, managers may risk all in a desperate attempt to save their jobs.

The issue becomes even more complex when, as is normally the case, there is a long delay in determining the creditors' claims and their related priorities. A common solution is to have the court appoint some outside expert, a trustee, to make the decision. This is what happens in the UK and most countries outside the US. In the US, the management of large concerns is usually allowed to continue operations and attempt to restructure.

Outcomes in bankruptcy

Despite differences in the treatment of bankrupt companies across the world, there are similarities in typical outcomes.

In the UK, the business is usually preserved while the corporate shell is not. In the US, over half of major organizations are reorganized in bankruptcy and re-emerge intact.

Under both systems, senior secured debt is usually repaid in full provided there is sufficient collateral. Employees usually receive wages and small trade creditors typically receive payment for some of their claims. Repayment to unsecured junior debt and the equity holders depends on the circumstances, the country and the individuals involved.

In the US, junior creditors typically receive cash and new securities worth less than half the value of their claims. Equity holders and the most junior creditors typically receive more proceeds from the organization's assets than they would receive under strict application of the priority of claims. Senior executives and board members are usually replaced either after or during bankruptcy.

Research in the US shows that about 70 percent of top managers are replaced by the time a company emerges from bankruptcy and that future job prospects for these managers are poor. Additionally, less than 50 percent of board members remain two years after financial distress (as compared to about 80 percent in the absence of financial distress) and those who leave have fewer appointments on average. In the UK, where a trustee takes over control of the business, board members are automatically dismissed in the event of bankruptcy and managers seldom remain.

On average, a company that restructures out of court spends less time and money and produces a higher recovery rate for creditors than businesses that liquidate. However, companies may choose to enter bankruptcy because, given the business's unique problems, an out-of-court restructuring may be prohibitively costly.

In the UK, the major clearing banks often agree to work together outside of bankruptcy to try to resolve a major organization's problems in what is called the "London Approach." Recently in the US, companies have started filing for bankruptcy and putting forward a plan of reorganization already approved by creditors. This procedure, called a pre-packaged bankruptcy (or prepak), attempts to incorporate the conventional advantages of bankruptcy while reducing some of the costs.

Is it better to restructure outside of bankruptcy?

Most firms try to avoid bankruptcy by selling assets to pay down debt, trying to negotiate an out-of-court restructuring, or both. From the company's perspective, bankruptcy can be a very expensive and disruptive option.

First, professional fees (legal, accounting, investment banking) can quickly become enormous. Second, sales may drop precipitously as customers, fearing the business will not survive, look elsewhere to assure supply and warranties. Likewise, the best employees may jump ship to ensure their long-term employment. Finally, management's time is likely to become consumed by the bankruptcy process rather than watching the competition and running the company.

Few companies choose bankruptcy without exploring other possibilities first. However, the evidence is not clear whether creditors should prefer out-of-court restructuring over bankruptcy. There is research documenting the fact that enterprises that undergo court-supervised bankruptcy reorganizations emerge with lower debt and better future prospects than concerns that reorganize out of court. Indeed, at least in the US, companies reorganizing out of court frequently end up in distress again within two years.

Furthermore, on average, creditors accept less, as a percentage of the total amount they are due, in out-of-court restructuring than in bankruptcy. Unfortunately, the evidence does not show whether this would be true in absolute terms: the lower percentage accepted outside of bankruptcy may be more than compensated for by avoiding the costs of bankruptcy noted above.

Timing and tenacity in a business sale

Selling a business is another critical test for the entrepreneur. **Chris Harrison** gives some advice on how to get the best price.

Despite the establishment in the UK of the alternative investment market (and its predecessor, the unlisted securities market) to make it easier for private companies to go public, trade sales remain the most popular exit route for business owners. This article focusses on ways in which entrepreneurs can maximize the value of their business before a sale and enhance the consideration they receive.

What is the best time to sell?
Timing can be a critical element in how easily the sale process happens and how close an entrepreneur comes to achieving his or her objectives. Above all, it is always best to sell when there is no need to, as the need to sell often weakens a negotiating position. But there are also some more specific aspects to timing.

The business stage of development
Most purchasers will be looking for a business with the ability to grow, so it is better to sell a business that is on the way up, not when it has reached its peak or the market has become too competitive. Sellers should not leave it until they suddenly realize that the tide has already started to turn.

The prime time for many entrepreneurs to sell is when the concept has been proved and substantial investment is now required to expand the business either nationally or internationally. This is an ideal situation for a large corporate buyer that can fund such expansion and gain the benefits of growth. Consequently, sale at such a time often provides the highest premium for the vendors.

Market timing
Here there are two main aspects to consider. The first is the market for the company's products or services – is it thriving and growing? The second concerns the market for similar types of businesses – does the business cycle mean that companies are buying (or wanting to) and are they paying premium prices?

Receiving approaches from companies expressing interest is obviously a favorable sign.

Time of year

With a seasonal business an entrepreneur will need to consider the time of year when the business will look most attractive. For example, it may be sensible to time a sale to take place after the season's orders have been placed so that results can be projected with greater certainty.

Preparing your business for the sale

The key to maximizing the return from a sale is understanding where the value of a business to a potential purchaser lies and, in the period before the sale, doing whatever is possible to enhance that value. Listed below are some of the steps that can be taken to maximize the value of a business to potential buyers. Many of these steps have long lead times and buyers need to consider them well before the actual sale process begins.

Clearly a business will be more attractive if profits are rising. But sellers should probably not be tempted to boost short-term profits by, for example, reducing necessary investment or expenditure on training or marketing – remember that the business may not be sold.

Sellers should also take steps to reduce the inherent risks in the business to a potential buyer. For example, responsibilities, decision making and account management can be devolved to second-tier managers who will remain with the business after it is sold. If possible, the customer base should also be increased so that sales are less dependent on a few key accounts.

There may be ways to increase flexibility for a new owner. For example, there may be assets in the business that are not needed and have little value to a prospective buyer. If the business owns and occupies property, it may make sense to sell it and rent it back. This could make it much easier for a new owner to integrate the business with other operations. It would also mean that the entrepreneur receives the full market value of the property rather than a discounted price from a reluctant buyer.

Top 10 tips for building the value of a business

- Aim to increase the business's recurring profits.
- Focus on maintaining long-term sales growth.
- Enhance the "quality" of earnings by developing relationships with key customers.
- Run the business with the same degree of governance and financial reporting as if it were a public company.
- Adopt transparent and conservative accounting policies that are appropriate to the business sector.
- Maintain flexibility by reconsidering major capital investment and through the ability to rent (rather than own) non-core assets.
- If the owner-manager is personally part of what makes the business valuable but will not be continuing to manage it, consider ways of compensating for this such as bringing in new management or transferring key business contacts to existing managers.
- Make sure that any questions over the value of business assets, tax or other compliance issues are resolved in advance of the sale – if it turns out something is awry, the seller will lose credibility and it can decimate the business's value.
- Identify and protect your intellectual property.
- Get the timing right.

Sellers should also identify and address any potential problems that could hold up the sale and reduce the consideration if they emerged during negotiations. A buyer will probably want an accountant's report, so sellers should review any problems that have arisen in recent audits and consider how they can be overcome or explained.

If the business has its own pension fund, a valuation should be carried out and any under- or over-funding addressed. Ask lawyers to identify any possible legal hurdles to the sale and to consider what warranties and indemnities might be required.

Finding potential buyers

It is usual to put together a "selling memorandum," which is a marketing document designed to attract interest in the business. While presenting the business in a good light, it should be factually accurate and objective and not make any claims the seller would be unwilling to warrant. While highlighting the business's strengths, it should also describe its weaknesses and, where possible, present them as opportunities. Professional advisers' experience will help substantially in developing the document.

Most entrepreneurs are likely to know of a few companies that may be interested in buying their business, but there may be others, not known, who could prove much more satisfactory. Professional advisers should be able to guide on this and to identify specific companies to approach. They can approach one company at a time, but it is more normal to approach several simultaneously. It is often best to set up a controlled auction process, in which a number of potential bidders are invited to make an offer for the business on the basis of the selling memorandum; a clear-cut timetable is then imposed, giving a period for negotiations and a deadline by which offers (subject to contract) must be received.

Understanding the buyer's perspective

It is important to remember that a buyer's concerns may be somewhat different from those of the seller and different buyers will have different priorities and objectives in making an offer for the business. Their interest may, for example, lie primarily in:

- the potential of offering the concept or product to a much wider market
- acquiring people, skills or intellectual property (this is particularly likely in the IT, high-tech or life science sectors)
- the business's market position
- the ability to integrate the business into their own operations
- the desire to inject new life into the business through different management, new investment or new processes.

To a large extent, what the buyer will be looking for will depend on who they are:

- A trade competitor already knows the market and understands the business but wants to increase its market share. It may be intending to integrate and rationalize the bought business with its own, achieving increased sales and reduced costs. It may believe that the company it wants to buy does things better and wants to adopt its working practices in its own operations.

- A customer is likely to feel it can expand its business and at the same time reduce costs by owning a supply company, controlling production and possibly integrating the two companies" operations.
- A supplier's main motives are likely to be to oust other suppliers, to get closer to its markets or to control distribution. It may also be able to reduce costs by rationalizing the two companies' operations.

In all these cases, it is likely that the buyer will be looking for a high degree of synergy between the business up for sale and its own.

- A financial buyer or conglomerate may not be interested in business synergy. The company's main criterion will be the potential return on the investment – both the contribution to annual earnings and the gain it makes on reselling or floating the business in the future. Such buyers will be primarily concerned that the business has the right people running it after the acquisition and are likely to take a tight hold on the business immediately after the sale.
- An overseas buyer is most likely looking for the chance to break into the local domestic market. An acquisition will give immediate critical mass and the market understanding it needs.

Negotiating a successful outcome

Try to find out how determined the buyer is to complete the deal. I have seen cases where the buyer's enthusiasm has been so obvious that the sellers have been able to negotiate from a position of real strength and obtain more than they ever hoped for.

Even if the buyers do not reveal their enthusiasm, are there pressures on them to achieve a successful deal? If it is a public company, does it have a need to be seen to acquire successfully to build its market share?

Do not get carried away with the details and the emotion of negotiations but keep strategy firmly in mind. Do not accept any more conditions than are reasonable and do not let the agreement get too complicated as it could become expensive and problematic to implement. The considerations arising from earn-outs and retentions of consideration are too complex to be considered here but should be discussed in detail with professional advisers. Also take professional advice on the tax implications of proposed conditions.

Throughout the negotiations the seller should retain control by managing the timetable and, provided that the negotiating hand is strong enough, keep the process competitive, allowing him or her to go, or threaten to go, to another party if a deadline is not met or an acceptable offer is not made.

Once a buyer has been chosen, draw up the heads of agreement and proceed to completion as soon as possible. The longer the buyer has to wait for the accountants' report and the draft sale and purchase agreement, the more likely he or she is to have second thoughts and, if the deal falls through, the more difficult it becomes to go back to other parties.

A fuller version of this article may be obtained from Ernst & Young on 020 7931 2347.

Riding on the wave of IPOs

What is the fatal attraction of an initial public offering? How to go about doing it?
Benoît F. Leleux offers some suggestions.

If 1996 is not about to be repeated as banner year for initial public offerings (IPOs), with some 680 listings on NASDAQ worth some $24.5 billion, the following years demonstrated the staying power of the current market, with 494 IPOs in 1997, 273 in 1998 and some 332 in the first three quarters of 1999. The largest ever offering, that of Deutsche Telekom in 1996, was easily surpassed in October 1999 by that of ENEL, the Italian electricity utility.

The closing years of the century also brought about a wave of new capital markets targeting growth equity, and markets catering to the newly found taste for emerging companies. Some of these were designed from inception as cross-national or pan-European in focus in an attempt to reach broader investment audiences and break the critical mass barrier.

EASDAQ, the pan-European market for smaller companies started in Brussels in September 1996, brainstormed its private institutional backers to come up with a market model that would not only permit young, high-growth companies to raise much-needed equity but would also provide the trading activity and analysts' coverage essential to liquidity. National market authorities in France, Belgium, Germany, the Netherlands and other countries also jumped on the growth bandwagon, initially targeting local clients but soon offering various forms of cross-listing arrangements.

IPOs are the definite talk of the town, but are they the ultimate indicators of good times ahead? Why the sudden interest in public markets to finance the entrepreneurial "gazelles"? Are we slowly moving towards a public form of venture capital? Are we witnessing an investor-risk culture shift and if so, what are the implications for future financings? Are issuing companies suddenly more enthused by public ownership? Why would usually discreet start-ups seek exposure to public scrutiny?

This article reviews some of the fundamental concepts behind IPOs and attempts to move beyond the roadshow magic to understand the inner workings and implications of the decision to go public and its process.

IPOs: equity for growth or insiders cashing out?

Growth generates phenomenal consumption of resources, forcing companies that espouse it as a matter of corporate strategy into chronic capital shortages. To maintain these high growth rates, regular fund injections are needed. Is an IPO the only source of money for such organizations? Far from it; and given the small percentage of businesses that actually resort to public offerings, it may not even be the most convenient or cheapest way to raise money. So, why are companies going to the public markets to raise funds?

For one thing, a publicly listed company enjoys an aura of respectability in the eyes of various stakeholders, from investors to suppliers and customers. Such respectability can translate into easier business arrangements and better trading terms. The additional exposure and visibility can also provide much needed PR.

Beyond the publicity, the benefits of which may be difficult to quantify, public markets also provide a continuously updated valuation for the company, facilitating later rounds of financing and providing an easy currency for acquisitions and estate management. The liquidity associated with publicly traded shares also provides an opportunity for early investors to diversify their portfolio holdings and provides a basis for rewarding crucial employees through various forms of stock-based reward programs.

All of this comes at a cost – and a steep one at that. For one thing, market regulators, always watchful of the public interest, allow the easy trading on the exclusive condition that information always be available to the trading parties. These on-going and extensive information disclosures usually go way beyond what most owners would feel comfortable parting with, what *CFO* magazine refers to as "indecent disclosures." In the pursuit of that same public interest, restrictions are placed on insiders' trading activities and detailed procedures are enforced for disclosure of material pieces of information. To guarantee the quality of that information, extensive auditing has to be performed by independent third parties and/or government entities.

Public equity is also far from free. If it does not carry a contractual dividend obligation, there is still the expectation by investors that returns, in the form of capital gains and dividends, will be generated to compensate for their risk-taking. Are these expectations forcing a damaging short-term performance focus by public companies?

This is really a false debate. To the extent that share prices actually aggregate the long-term prospects for the organization, short-term changes in stock prices only reflect the long-term effects of current management decisions and industry changes. In other words, a bad management decision that may not have practical implications for years will translate into a price change today. On the positive side, a public listing clearly focusses management's attention on the share price and shareholder-value creation.

Finally, going public has been shown to be a tremendously expensive endeavor. These flotation costs include not only the direct costs of underwriting the issue, performing legal and accounting due diligence, and setting up adequate reporting systems, but also the less visible though nonetheless material costs of having important personnel (management and scientific) tied up for months in the process of "roadshowing" the company to potential investors across the country and abroad.

Another significant cost is the well-documented "underpricing" of the shares, variously attributed to the underwriters' overwhelming bargaining power, the need to leave a good taste in the initial investors' mouths to entice them to later rounds of financing, or another cost of the inherent uncertainty of these situations. Whatever the explanation subscribed to, an issuer selling shares at $25 that are later priced by the market at $30 left $5 on the table.

The total costs of going public can run as high as 25 percent or more of the expected proceeds. In most circumstances, transaction costs of 25 percent would be considered outrageous; with IPOs, investment letters will often refer to such issues as wildly successful. How can we reconcile the two apparently contradictory elements?

For one thing, lock-up agreements often prevent insiders from cashing in on the public listing. Even though such arrangements are often limited in time, the only true benefactors from the early price rises are the privileged groups of investors allocated shares initially.

With allocation in the US essentially left to the discretion of the underwriting syndicate, the lucky few tend to have long-standing relationships with the underwriters, relationships that provide ample opportunities for generating additional fees.

Being public does ultimately facilitate the initial investors' harvesting process, providing both flexibility and high valuations. But could these costs also be seen as the entry ticket to the most exclusive financial club on earth? Based on its worldwide membership, the club of public companies is indeed quite selective and exclusive.

Do you need the public to grow?

For many, IPOs are almost synonymous with high-growth organizations. Is that to imply that public markets are the only or the most effective way to finance growth?

A survey by Leleux and Muzyka in 1996 of European companies that decided to tap the IPO markets in the US supports the view that financing growth and being able to capture new opportunities lies at the heart of the going-public decision. But is that a necessity? Far from it. A number of companies, such as Cargill in the US, and a score of European concerns, have been riding phenomenal growth waves without recourse to such a source of financing. The low profile afforded by private placements and bank financings can even in some instances facilitate customer relationships by not antagonizing their own PR efforts.

Keeping a low profile in effect leaves the limelight to the customer. The freedom from day-to-day scrutiny and from pressure of stock market prices can also facilitate the implementation of riskier strategies that may not have received wide acclaim by investment analysts.

The going-public decision

Assuming that public markets appear to offer the best alternative for raising the funds a company needs, would your company necessarily be attractive to the markets? In other words, what does it take to capture the public markets' fancy? A good starting point is having an excellent story to tell. Most successful IPO businesses approach investors with a simple, understandable concept or product that has the potential to generate excitement.

When Genset went public in 1999 on both NASDAQ (National Association of Securities Dealers Automated Quotation) and the Nouveau Marché in Paris, it showcased itself not as a world-class genomics research laboratory, which it was, but as a large-scale industrial production chain for DNA mapping, offering the potential genetics equivalent of the Ford model T for the automobile industry at the turn of the century. Despite intense competition from such powerhouses as Human Genome Sciences and Incyte Pharmaceuticals, Genset was able to generate the excitement indispensable for a successful IPO.

An interesting financial and operational track record can help but most IPO companies have their future in front of them – not concealed in historical statements. A significant percentage of the companies going public in the US have no revenues to show, let alone earnings or profits. Keep in mind that investors do not buy last year's results but the next decade's. Hence the importance of a great story, one that appeals to visions of enormous market potential and significant barriers to entry.

To increase the appearance of a real success story in the making, a top-notch management team is required. If you do not have such a team, no need for concern:

managers can be brought in as hired guns to take a company public. It will cost you money, usually in the form of stock options, but is well worth the expense.

How long the team will stay depends, of course, on many factors, not least of which being the way the vesting schedule for the option plan was designed. To go back to the Genset example, its roadshow featured not only the two eminent founders, Pascal Brandys and Marc Vasseur, but also Professor Daniel Cohen, a scientist of towering international repute.

To provide a form of external certification for the potential of the venture, it helps to bring along professional investors such as venture capitalists. Their experience managing the growth process in high-technology organizations is often seen as a desirable addition to the existing management team. Genset, for example, could highlight respected venture capitalists in its ownership structure, including the Sofinnova Group, affiliates from Burr, Egan, Deleage and Co., Oxford Bioscience Partners and SR One, which as a group owned more than 59 percent of the shares of the company prior to the IPO. Of the 692 IPOs in the US in 1996, 260 were venture-capital backed, raking in some $12.2 billion, 44 percent more than the previous record established in 1995. For 1998, the number was down to $3.8 billion.

With a great story, an experienced management team and a high-reputation set of initial investors, a decision is still needed on which market to seek a listing on and what method to use to float the shares. The choice of markets is getting larger by the week but for all practical purposes, the US and the UK still have a virtual duopoly on equity markets, with many promising continental European companies preferring to bypass completely their own domestic markets to float abroad.

If you decide to list in the US, the question of the flotation method has been resolved for you by the National Association of Securities Dealers since early in the 20th century: the only procedure available is a fixed-price, fixed-quantity offering. Interestingly enough, many non-US markets offer alternative procedures, including various forms of auctions. From an issuer point of view, the auction seems to offer the best prospects for selling the shares to the highest bidders/investors.

Practically speaking, though, the fixed-price approach as practiced in the US by the underwriting syndicates can very much approximate the benefits of an auction. Indeed, underwriters will usually approach potential investors in the pre-market period and elicit their informal price and quantity bids in an effort to build a book of non-legally binding commitments. The latter, though, is a pure technicality since walking out of a deal would virtually guarantee your non-participation in any of the future opportunities.

The IPO process

If taking the company public is practically a six-week affair at most, it should be clear that the actual distribution of the shares to the public is really the heart of a convoluted, four-step process. Phase 1 involves the preparation of the company for L-day (Listing day); this can best be compared to the preparation for Prom night in High School, a long-term exercise in getting the company to look its best to go to the (IPO) dance. Phase 2 is the preparation, with the IPO work group (underwriters, investment bankers, lawyers, etc.), of all IPO documentation (registration statement, prospectus, roadshow material). Phase 3 is the actual distribution exercise, through the two- to three-week roadshow. But the story does not end there. Exhausted by the process, many firms fail to provide after-sales service in the form of continued information flows to analysts and investors.

So what generic recommendations could one provide to a company contemplating an IPO? First of all, make sure you identify clearly the customer value proposition, i.e. the problem you are solving for them, and the business model, i.e. how you are going to translate the technology into a revenue stream. Second, to the extent that you are unlikely to be the only provider of that service, identify your competitive advantage and a solid rationale for why it would be sustainable. Finally, bulletproof your presentation by anticipating the casual "death wish" questions: yes, you do realize that Microsoft is in that segment too, but...

With this process perspective, it should also be clear that many exogenous factors will influence the ultimate outcome of your IPO. For example, the performance of your public competitors will affect the whole industry. To keep track of the ever-evolving factors leading to the IPO, it is a good idea to create a continually updated central repository of due diligence information including not only internal (legal, accounting, technological) but also external elements (markets, research developments, etc.).

The IPO process is strenuous for the management team. Remember that it will involve the top management echelons of the growing company for at least three months, at a time when hundreds of internal issues also need to be taken care of. For all practical purposes, the top four or five executives will be decommissioned from active duty for about that long. Many have returned from the roadshow to a disaster zone. Plan accordingly, that is to say the post-IPO Caribbean trip may not be fully warranted. Remember also that the IPO is but the first step in the public domain: this is where the company has to start to prove itself. The IPO is the beginning, not the end of the story.

Growth-oriented equity markets: is Europe finally providing credible alternatives to NASDAQ?[1]

Benoît F. Leleux compares the development of the equity markets for entrepreneurial companies in Europe and the US.

Until 1995, young growth companies looking for fresh equity injections from the public faced a very simple alternative: it was NASDAQ or nothing. Earlier attempts in Europe to create secondary markets to facilitate fund-raising by less established firms did not survive the aftermaths of the 1987 stock market crash. In 1992, the European Venture Capital Association started to wage a long-shot battle to create growth-oriented equity markets on which they could float their most promising ventures, in the hope of finally being able to generate the kind of valuations on which their investing business relies. Partly as a result of their effort, European governments also realized the importance of creating adequate mechanisms for public funds to find their way towards the most promising ventures.

These "new markets" have now been in operation for several years and have contributed significantly to the evolution of growth-oriented entrepreneurial activity in Europe. The objective of this article is to provide an overall description of the birth, development and performance of these growth-oriented markets.

Background

After the stock market crash of 1987, many of the European secondary markets for new issues collapsed or "froze," and, by the early 1990s, Europe reached a crisis in the evolution of its stock markets, which resulted in fewer opportunities for new firms to enter the markets through IPOs. The decline in IPO markets had several consequences. Most significantly, it affected the ability of entrepreneurs and venture capitalists to realize the value from successful, growing businesses and to ensure that their growth continued. A direct consequence of this dearth of opportunity was that a large number of European high-growth companies crossed the Atlantic, particularly in the early 1990s, to register on the large and liquid NASDAQ exchange, despite its more stringent disclosure requirements and higher degree of control imposed by the US securities law. By August 31, 1998, the NASDAQ "International" list contained some 135 European companies, including 52 from the UK and 18 from the Netherlands.

By 1995, though, it became quite obvious that such a situation was unhealthy for European economies, and that alternatives for raising capital had to be created in Europe. Collaboration between entrepreneurs, venture capitalists, governments, market authorities and the financial community at large resulted in the launch of new markets, such as the Alternative Investment Market (AIM) in the UK, the Société du Nouveau Marché (SNM) in France, the NMAX in the Netherlands, the Neuer Markt in Germany, the Euro.NM Belgium, the Nuovo Mercato in Italy, and supra-national entities such as Euro.NM and EASDAQ. Figure 1 illustrates the chronological development of the new markets in Europe.

There is a plethora of "new markets" in Europe, starting with the creation of AIM in the UK in June 1995. EASDAQ, an international market located in Brussels, was founded with the intention of becoming the market for aggressive entrepreneurial growth companies and was to be the pan-European equivalent of NASDAQ, which served as its model. Simultaneously, a number of European national markets saw the need to create some critical mass that would lead to a common platform for listing requirements. As a result, Euro.NM was launched in March 1996. It was to be the framework for new secondary markets across Europe, and has been joined by the SNM, NMAX, Neuer Markt, Euro.NM Belgium and Nuovo Mercato. Euro.NM (and its widely reported index, the Euro.NM All-Share) represents an association that permits the collective communication of stock offerings, but the actual mechanics of trading remain with the individual member markets.

However, this network of national markets is still evolving in terms of its role and function. All of the exchanges are automated, but utilize different types of systems

Figure 1: New equity markets in Europe

for undertaking transactions and fixing prices, and the roles of advisers and market-makers can vary from country to country. Each market is national in character, but includes companies with headquarters outside the domestic market, thus providing heightened visibility for companies. They receive visibility through constant listing, commentary from analysts, investor discussion and action on the part of market-makers that is further discussed by the financial press.

The notion of creating credibility in a marketplace is unfolding in some interesting ways. For example, some European bio-technology companies have chosen to list on NASDAQ in the belief that it gives them greater market credibility and maximizes their value. However, in the long term, those valuations have fallen victim to the fact that they are sometimes perceived to be "too exotic." This appears to relate to the fact that when the markets devalue, they treat certain stocks of companies operating outside the US more aggressively. One reason could be that US analysts do not fully understand the European markets served by those companies nor the companies' position within those markets.

Development of the European new equity markets

Figure 2 chronicles the growth of the Euro.NM member markets in terms of number of companies listed and market capitalizations.

AIM, the oldest of the markets, retains the largest number of listed companies, with over 350 in September 1999, although the rate of its IPOs slowed down during 1998 and 1999. EASDAQ, whose strategy is to attract somewhat larger companies, has been growing gradually since its launch. The Euro.NM exchanges have also shown a steady increase. Comparing the evolution of the markets in terms of the number of listings since the opening of each market, as in Figure 3, it becomes clear

Figure 2: Euro.NM member markets' growth (1/98 to 9/99)

that there are clear differences in growth rates which reflect differences in strategies. AIM developed more rapidly in terms of the numbers of companies listed compared with Euro.NM and EASDAQ. These differences in strategies are also reflected in the average market capitalization of companies listed. EASDAQ and the Neuer Markt list significantly larger firms than AIM, so that absolute numbers are misleading.

Euro.NM's and EASDAQ's relatively slower development in terms of the number of companies listed belies their actual market capitalizations. The companies on Euro.NM national markets as a whole represent the largest market in terms of value, followed by EASDAQ, showing less than half that value. The market capitalisation of the Euro.NM is largely based on the contributions from the Neuer Markt and the Nouveau Marché, collectively representing 94 percent of the total value. Market capitalizations, particularly with reference to the Euro.NM, have grown dramatically during 1998 and 1999. All these numbers pale of course in front of the 4,845 companies listed on NASDAQ proper and its $3,356 billion market capitalization at the end of October 1999, about 150 times as much as the Euro.NM All-Share!

The performance of European new equity markets

European new markets rode the mid-90s' equity bull market with ecstatic abandonment. The Euro.NM All-Share index delivered a total return of some 325 percent between January 1, 1997 and September 30, 1999, for an annualized compound rate of return of some 69.2 percent, and over 60.6 percent annualized over

Figure 3: Relative new market growth rates from inception

the period between January 1, 1998 and September 30, 1999. Over the same period (1/97 to 9/99), EASDAQ delivered an equally impressive 185 percent total index return.

Some general statistics about EASDAQ and the Euro.NM markets are presented in Tables 1 and 2.

The NASDAQ reference

The developing European new markets did not dent NASDAQ's dominance as the premier source of funding for growth-oriented companies. Some interesting statistics are presented in Table 3. Figure 4 stresses the relative importance of NASDAQ issuances compared to the New York Stock Exchange and Amex markets. On average, though, NASDAQ offerings tend to be smaller than those of the NYSE, so that the total amounts raised from year to year have been relatively comparable ($27 billion year-to-date in 1999 for NASDAQ, $25.6 billion year-to-date for the NYSE).

NASDAQ and the European new markets: fighting the same war?

The European new markets are quickly evolving to represent different companies by size and sector and, in the process, are acquiring their own unique character. This needs to be taken into account by companies wishing to proceed with an IPO and by investors and portfolio managers. It is a result of a deliberate strategy and positioning, influenced by the national location, the market-makers and investment bankers. The strategy as embodied in the listing requirements is evolving, however. Considering the evolution towards more common practices, further changes in the portfolio of companies are expected. The review of their performance in what was

Table 1: Euro.NM market statistics (September 30, 1999)

Total number of companies listed	291
Total funds raised (€ billion)	10.16
Total market capitalization (€ billion)	57.4
Total monthly trading volume (€ billion)	3.6
Total monthly share volume (million)	113.3
Average company capitalization (€ million)	197.2
Average daily trading volume (€ million)	161.6
Average daily share volume (million)	5.2
Average price change since listing (%)	91.0%
Average price change since last month (%)	−6.0%
Euro.NM All-Share index (30/09/99) (based at 1,000 points on 30/12/97)	2,290.14
Euro.NM Index Performance	
Since 30/12/98	−2.18%
Since 30/12/97	129%
Since 31/12/96	324.38%

Situation as of September 30, 1999

Table 2: EASDAQ market statistics (October 15, 1999)

No. of companies admitted to trading [1]	51	
No. of member firms	81	
Current total market capitalization (billion)	€19.6	$21.4
Average market capitalization per company at admission (million)	€180	$202
Current average market capitalization per company (million)	€385	$419
Total money raised at admission (billion)	€2.5	$2.8
Average money raised per company at admission (million)	€46	$52
Follow-on offerings (billion)	€0.9	$1.1
Current average free-float	45.9%	
Average market-makers per company	6.29	
Average daily turnover (in million, rolling year)	€12.29	$13.51
Free-float turnover rate (rolling year)[1], [2]	73.5%	
P/E-ratio (estimated EPS 1999, prices at 24 Sep 99)[3]	33.8x	
Index[1]		
EASI®™ – The EASDAQ All-Share Index	859.30	
Index change since 31/12/1996	184.55%	
Index change since 31/12/1997	85.04%	
Index change since 30/12/1998	7.35%	

Last update October 15, 1999

[1] Only includes companies current traded of EASDAQ.
[2] The free-float turnover rate is obtained by dividing the cumulative share volume on a rolling year basis by the free float.
The cumulative share volume for companies traded for less than 1 year is the total share volume traded since launch.
[3] Figure provided by First Call – Estimates.

Table 3: NASDAQ market statistics (October 15, 1999)

- The NASDAQ Composite[SM] Index closed 1998 by gaining more than 20 percent for a fourth consecutive year, up 39.6 percent.
- In 1998, NASDAQ had nine days with more than one billion shares traded.
- For the year, share volume reached 202 billion, up 23 percent from 163.9 billion in 1997.
- The market value of the 5,126 companies listed on NASDAQ stood at $2.6 trillion, up more than 44 percent from year-end 1997.
- The previous year saw 273 initial public offerings (up to October) that raised just under $14 billion.
- The market's best index performers were the NASDAQ Computer and Telecommunications, up 83.3 percent and 63.4 percent, respectively.
- The NASDAQ-100 Index was up 85.3 percent over 1997. The NASDAQ Composite at year-end stood at 2192.69, up 39.6 percent from 1570.35 in 1997.
- The dollar value of trading on NASDAQ in 1998 surpassed the previous record of $4.5 trillion in 1997 by 28 percent; 1998 trading was valued at $5.8 trillion.
- Average daily share volume on NASDAQ reached more than 802 million in 1998, up from 648 million shares in 1997.
- Twelve non-US companies listed on NASDAQ in the fourth quarter of 1998, bringing the total number of foreign companies listed to 440, more than on any other US market.

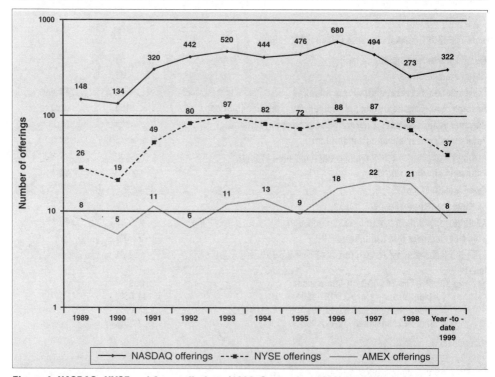

Figure 4: NASDAQ, NYSE and Amex offerings (1989–September 1999) logarithmic scale

arguably an amazingly favorable financial and economic environment is cause for optimism. These new growth-oriented stock markets, with some exceptions, have been performing well and weathered the 1998 summer storms relatively unscathed.

The recent announcement by NASDAQ that it was going to develop a direct presence in Japan and Europe is going to provide additional competition among markets for the listing of these growth-oriented companies. This can only be to the companies' benefit, as opportunities arise to access a broad range of risk-equity investors not only domestically but internationally at the best possible valuations and the lowest transaction costs. These markets, after all, are means to an end, not ends in themselves: to the extent that they contribute and will continue to contribute to the improved efficiency of the entrepreneurial process as a whole, then they are indeed fighting the same war.

1 This article is based on "European New Issue Markets: Preliminary Review," with Daniel F. Muzyka and Nathalie Guégan, *3i QED*, December 1998. I want to acknowledge here the financial support for this project obtained from the 3i VentureLab.

CASE STUDY

Unipalm

This is a summary of Unipalm Cases A and B, written by **Fergal Byrne,** Research Associate, and **John Bates**, Teaching Fellow, at London Business School.

In 1986, Peter Dawe had been working for Cambridge MicroComputers for seven years. During this time, he had become increasingly excited by the opportunities in computer networking – the specialized software that allowed computers to communicate. He was particularly keen on the TCP/IP software protocol developed in the US which, he was convinced, was the most advanced on the market. Indeed, he suspected that it would emerge as the platform networking standard. Unable to convince CMC of this, he gave up his 5 percent shareholding in the company in exchange for the rights to distribute TCP/IP software in the UK and started his own business.

Sales in the first two years were slow, but by 1988 had begun to pick up when Peter met Bob Peters, an old colleague from CMC. Bob agreed to join Peter and invested £14,000 for 50 percent of the equity in the business. Unipalm Ltd was born.

Over the next few months sales grew rapidly and by the end of the year had tripled. During this period, the company had also acquired three new directors – Arthur, a salesman, Simon, a computer programmer, and Sean to develop the training activities – who between them invested more than £50,000 for 48 percent of the equity, diluting Peter and Bob to 52 percent.

By 1990, sales had grown to £750,000 with profits before tax of approximately £140,000. Unfortunately, this success also created problems as it slowly became clear that the directors had different expectations for the company. For example, Sean and Simon were keen to start taking money out, Bob was unclear as to what he wanted, and Peter and Arthur were keen to develop the business further. Personal relations began to deteriorate.

At the same time Peter had identified a new opportunity. He was fascinated by the rapid growth in the use of the internet, the worldwide network that communicated using the TCP/IP protocol, and was convinced that Unipalm should expand in this market by becoming an internet service provider (ISP). Unfortunately, and despite the fact that his business plan showed profits in excess of £1 million after three years, his co-directors did not take him seriously and refused his request for a budget of £100,000 to develop the service.

Over the following months, matters deteriorated so rapidly that Peter decided to resign and pursue his business idea elsewhere. Whilst he was working out his notice, Bob left the company in April after a particularly acrimonious meeting described by others as a "blood bath." When Peter left the Unipalm offices for the last time at the end of May, he found Bob waiting for him in his car. Over a pint of Guinness they agreed to stick together. If the other shareholders wanted to buy either of them out, they would have to buy both.

By the end of November, the situation was becoming increasingly bizarre as no real offer was forthcoming and so Bob and Peter, who between them owned 52 percent of the equity, decided to take matters in hand. Early in December they called an extraordinary general meeting, voted themselves back on the board and fired the other three directors. There remained the question of their equity and it was only after months of acrid negotiations that a price for the purchase of their shares was finally agreed.

Meanwhile Peter had set up the Public IP Exchange Ltd (PIPEX) to develop the internet project. The partners agreed that they would become joint MDs with Bob running the Unipalm business and Peter running PIPEX, a wholly-owned subsidiary of the Unipalm Group plc. However, to move forward, they estimated that they needed a financial injection of £1 million. So they approached Rob Lucas, an investment director at 3i, the largest UK venture capital company. Rob was concerned about the disappointing financial performance in 1991 but Peter and Bob convinced him that the profits were artificially depressed due to a change in management and that the Unipalm business could generate operating profits of around £1 million in 1992. A deal was finally agreed.

There were two conditions to the investment – that Unipalm recruit both a new full-time finance director and a non-executive chairman. Chris Batterham, a seasoned finance director with considerable experience in the high-tech field, and David Thorp, an ex-3i director, joined the team. Peter was now able to develop the PIPEX business.

In order to become an internet access provider, PIPEX needed to develop an international data network, or data backbone, comprising leased domestic and international telecommunication circuits. Subscribers would connect the PIPEX network by a leased or dial-up line to a PIPEX Point of Presence (POP), a kind of telephonic switch. This network was in turn connected to the internet via a leased digital line.

Forecasting the development of PIPEX was a very inexact process. Chris says: *"It was almost impossible to build any kind of sensible business model for the internet – there was a fundamental problem of scaling and it was very difficult to predict the growth of the business . . . the required capacity per user was changing, as was the range of services that were being offered. PIPEX had, nonetheless, to build the telecommunications structure – POPs and international bandwidth – in advance. The situation was further complicated due to the difficulty of forecasting Unipalm's sales which were highly volatile from one month to another. Last but not least, shortly after I arrived I discovered that we did not actually know what our telecom costs were – we were receiving bills from British Telecom a year after usage . . . continued investment required a significant act of faith."*

Nevertheless, Peter was convinced that there was a significant opportunity just waiting to happen. Returning from a trip to the US in March 1993, he gave an impassioned presentation to the management on the future of the internet and the need for scale and growth. Although the others were not convinced, he began to consider the possibility of selling the Unipalm business to finance PIPEX and so in June he asked Regency Associates, a specialist broker, to identify possible purchasers. However, no reasonable offer emerged and management reluctantly concluded that this wasn't a viable option.

With no buyers on the horizon, they had three alternatives: to find a strategic partner, to raise interim finance, or to seek a public offering. They decided upon the latter and there followed six months of intensive preparation, led by Chris. He worked closely with the brokers, E. J. Hall, and the accountants, Arthur Andersen, to prepare the "long form report," a comprehensive analysis of the business which entailed providing information on every aspect of it.

All along, Peter was very concerned about the timing and was constantly exerting pressure on everyone to speed up the whole process. In particular, a number of high-tech IPOs in September and October had made him increasingly nervous that the "window" would soon close. As the date for the IPO grew closer, tensions mounted and relations with E. J. Hall became strained. In December, Niall Stevens, the managing director of E. J. Hall, called a meeting. He said: *"Given the relative youth of the company and the lack of earnings visibility, we believe that . . . the management structure will need to be streamlined, with one person responsible for the entire business."* When Peter declined to consider this, Stevens declined the role of sponsor in the IPO. That was it. Once again, Peter was left to reconsider his options.

Postscript

A £20 million offering of shares in Unipalm was successfully made on the London Stock Exchange in early 1994. In doing so, Unipalm became the first internet service provider to go public worldwide. The offering price of the shares was 100p.

In late 1995, UUNET Technologies, a US internet service provider, agreed to buy Unipalm in an all-share bid which valued Unipalm at £100 million. By the time the deal had closed, UUNET's shares rose in price from $39 to $75. As a result, the realized value of the deal for Unipalm shareholders was 740p per share or roughly 500 times 1995 earnings! Not surprisingly, Unipalm was the best performing share on the London Stock Exchange in 1995.

Merger and acquisition activity in the telecommunications sector accelerated in pace in 1996. In the summer, MFS Communications, a company which had established a series of local telephone networks in the US and Europe, acquired UUNET Technologies in a deal valued at $2 billion. One month later, World Com, the fourth-largest long-distance carrier in the US, acquired MFS for $10 billion.

Bob retired to Florida in May 1995, Peter left to concentrate on his investments in high technology and media in May 1996, and Chris is now managing director, Europe, for UUNET.

Copies of the cases can be obtained from The European Case Clearing House, telephone (+44) 01234 750903; fax (+44) 01234 751125; e-mail ECCH@cranfield.ac.uk

Subject index

Organization index

Name index